TELECOMMUNICATIONS AND DEVELOPMENT IN CHINA

THE HAMPTON PRESS COMMUNICATION SERIES

New Media: Policy and Social Research Issues
Ron Rice, supervisory editor

Telecommunications and Development in China
Paul S.N. Lee (ed.)

forthcoming

Contexts of Computer-Mediated Communication Revised Edition
Martin Lea (ed.)

Virtual Politicking: Playing Politics in Electronically Networked Organizations
Celia Romm

Telecommunications and Development in China

Edited by

Paul S.N. Lee
CHINESE UNIVERSITY OF HONG KONG

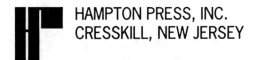

HAMPTON PRESS, INC.
CRESSKILL, NEW JERSEY

Printed in the United States of America

Library of Congress Cataloging-in-Publication Data

Telecommunications and development in China / edited by Paul S.N. Lee.
     p.   cm.
    Includes bibliographic references and index.
    ISBN 1-57273-060-9 (cloth). – ISBN 1-57273-061-7 (pbk.)
    1. Telecommunication–China. 2. Communication in economic development–China. 3. China–Economic conditions–1976-
I. Lee, Paul S.N.
HE8424.T45 1997   97-20064
384'.0951–dc21   CIP

Hampton Press, Inc.
23 Broadway
Cresskill, NJ 07626

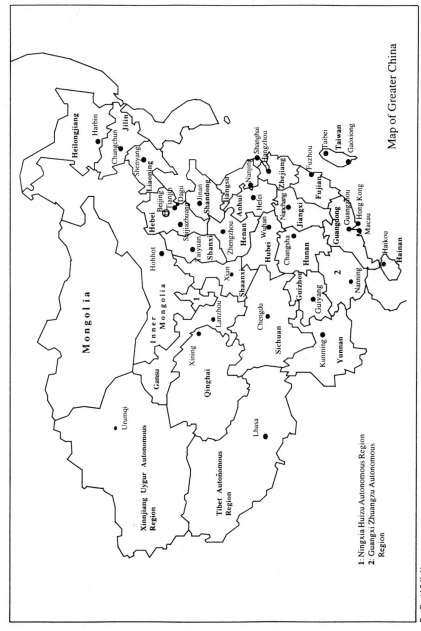

Map of Greater China

1: Ningxia Huizu Autonomous Region
2: Guangxi Zhuangzu Autonomous Region

By: David S.K. Ng

CONTENTS

ABOUT THE CONTRIBUTORS

Benjamin J. Bates received his Ph.D in Communication from the University of Michigan in 1986. He is Associate Professor at the Department of Broadcasting, College of Communications, University of Tennessee, Knoxville. His research focuses on the development and operations of media systems, and has written extensively in the area of telecommunications economics and policy.

Leonard Chu is Dean of the School of Communication, the Hong Kong Baptist University. He received his Ph.D. in Journalism from the University of Southern Illinois. His special interest is in Chinese Communication studies. His publications have appeared in *Media Development, Media Asia, Gazette, Harvard International Journal* and *Australian Journalism Review.*

Zhou He is Associate Professor at the School of Journalism and Mass Communication, San Jose State University. He earned his Ph.D. degree from Indiana University. His research interests include international communication, media and conflict, media and culture, and acculturation. His scholarly publications have appeared in *Journalism Monograph* and *Gazette.*

Junhao Hong is an Assistant Professor at the Department of Communication, State University of New York, Buffalo. He received his B.A. in China and M.A. in Communication in Canada. He was the Director of Import/Export of Shanghai Television. His research interests include satellite communication and international communication. His publications have appeared in *Gazette*, *Journalism Abstract* and *Media Asia*.

Paul Lee is Associate Professor at the Department of Journalism and Communication at the Chinese University of Hong Kong. He received his Ph.D. in Communication from the University of Michigan in 1986. His research interests are telecommunications policy, international communication and development communication. He has published in *Telecommunications Policy*, *Gazette*, *Asian Journal of Communication*, *Journal of Communication* and *Australian Journal of Chinese Affairs*.

Bryce McIntyre is Assistant Professor at the Department of Journalism & Communication of the Chinese University of Hong Kong. He received his Ph.D. in Communication from the Stanford University. He is the author of *Advanced Newsgathering*. New York: Praeger, 1991. His teaching and research interests include journalism and application of new technologies in communication.

Milton Mueller received his Ph.D. in Communication at Annenberg School of Communications at the University of Pennsylvania in 1989. He is Assistant Professor at the School of Communication, Information and Library Studies at the University of Rutgers. His research centers on contemporary issues in domestic and international regulatory policy and on the history of communications technologies and industries. His publications have appeared in *Telecommunications Policy*, *Technology and Culture*, and *Gannett Center Journal*.

Zixiang Tan is an Assistant Professor at the Department of Information Studies at Syracuse University. He obtained his Ph.D from Rutgers University in 1996 and M. Sc. in Opto-electronics and B. Sc. from the Qinghua University, PRC in 1986. He served as a Project Officer for the State Science and Technology Commission of China. The project dealt with domestic planning, financing and international cooperation in telecommunications and broadcasting. His research interests include telecommunications policy and mobile communication.

Fan-tung Tseng is Commissioner of the Research and Planning Committee at the Directorate General of Telecommunications. Before this he was deputy director of the Telecommunications Training Institute and Executive Secretary of the Cable System Task Force of the Legislative Yuan. He was the leader of a telecommunications policy study project which initiated the revision of the Telecommunications Law in Taiwan. He has presented numerous papers at conferences.

John Ure is Director of the Telecommunications Research Project at the Centre of Asian Studies, University of Hong Kong. He received his Ph.D. in Economics from the Polytechnic of East London. His extensive publications include, as co-author and editor, *Telecommunications in Asia: Policy, Planning and Development*, Telecommunications: Hong Kong and China After 1997 (in J. Cheng and S. Lo, eds., *From Colony to SAR: Hong Kong's Challenge Ahead*), and Telecommunications, with Chinese Characterists (in China Special Issue of *Telecommunications Policy*, April 1994). Dr. Ure is a member of the Hong Kong Consumer Council's Telecommunications Steering Group, and an advisor to the Hong Kong Industrial Technology Center. At the University of Hong Kong he supervises postgraduate telecommunications and information technology research and is currently running a China telecommunications research program. He is also chairperson of the Telecommunications InfoTechnology Forum, a monthly industrial roundtable in Hong Kong.

Georgette Wang is Professor at the Department of Journalism, National Chengchi University in Taiwan. She received her Ph.D. in mass communications from Southern Illinois University in 1977. She had worked as a researcher at the Communications Institute, East-West Center, Hawaii and taught in Hong Kong. She has published several books, including Information *Society: A Retrospective View*, and *Treading Different Paths - Informatization in Asia*, and *Continuity and Change in Communication Systems*. In addition to new media studies, she has widely published in culture and communication.

Zhaoxu Yan is a Ph.D. student in the Department of Telecommunications at the Indiana University. He received his M. Phi. in Communication from the Chinese University of Hong Kong, and B.A. from the Fudan University, People's Republic of China. His research interests include telecommunications technology, international communication and advertising.

Jianguo Zhu is a Ph.D. student in the Department of Communication Sciences at the University of Connecticut. He received his M. Phi. in Communication at the Chinese University of Hong Kong and B.A. in Journalism at Fudan University, PRC. His research interests include telecommunications, development communication and marketing communication.

PART I

INTRODUCTION AND BACKGROUND

Part I begins with Paul Lee's "Telecommunications and Development: An Introduction." This chapter introduces the literature about the relationship between telecommunications and development and special reference is made to the causal link between telecommunications and economic growth. After reviewing the studies on telecommunications and economic growth, he mentions four major criticisms of these studies, which also point to the current direction of research on the relationship between telecommunications and development.

In "Learning From the Evolution of Telecommunications in the Developed World," Ben Bates examines the telecommunications experience of the United States, United Kingdom, France, and Germany. He concludes that Less Developed Countries (LDCs) must realize the full potential of universal service in order to maximize long-term benefits. Benefits, he argues, arise from the use of a telecommunications system and will be maximized when all sectors of society are fully integrated into the system. His implicit advice seems to be against deregulation before basic service is accessible to all. However, he points out that state monopoly protection of earlier technologies also retards development.

China's telecommunications history has a great bearing on its present telecommunications development and policy. It is known for its strong opposition to allowing foreigners to operate telecommunications services there; even joint ventures in which China is the major shareholder are forbid-

1

den—Foreign enterprises are only allowed to provide telecommunications equipment and expertise. The emergence of alternative networks in China since early 1994 may impact this "xenophobic" policy, but the invitation of foreign partners to operate telecommunication services in China, as far as Chinese policy makers are concerned, is fraught with danger. The major reason is found in China's past telecommunications development experience with the West. Zhou He summarizes this experience and discusses its impact on policy in "A History of Telecommunications in China: Development and Policy Implications."

Leonard Chu, in "The Political Economy of Communication System in China," analyzes the control of communication and media in China's communist system. He notes four consequences brought to the communication system in China by the changing political economy in the reform era. First, the Chinese Communist Party's (CCP) grip on media and communication remains tight despite economic restructuring, but less political control and more commercialization of communication have been taking place. Second, there has been a rapid adoption of modern media in place of primitive technologies. Third, this development, along with market forces in the economy, has forced communist leaders and communication practitioners to rethink the functions of communication. Finally, the expanding communication structure has made it nearly impossible for the CCP to keep a close eye on the operation of the media, whether mass or individual. Now the CCP can only set parameters for media executives and practitioners. Chu predicts that as market forces grow, even the parameters set by the CCP will be stretched farther and farther. An increasingly loose grip on communication will affect the control and administration of telecommunications in China, although at present the operation of telecommunications is still tightly controlled by the state.

CHAPTER 1

TELECOMMUNICATIONS AND DEVELOPMENT: AN INTRODUCTION

PAUL S.N. LEE

Human activities are organized around the desire to improve life. The human desire for improvement of everyday life has never stopped, although some philosophies and religions place the best of human civilization in the remote past and urge people to look for perfection in the Other World. Since the 17th and 18th centuries, theories of progress have arisen. The impressive progress made in modern natural science raised the hope of applying its results to improve human life; meanwhile, the overseas expansion of Europe allowed the philosophically inclined to observe mankind in different "stages" of social evolution from primitive to modern cultures.

With the advancement of science, overseas expansion, and the desire to improve everyday life, the "Great Transformation" (Polanyi, 1944) finally came to Europe. Not only was agricultural production transformed and manual labor replaced by power-driven machines, but social and political institutions changed radically. The tidal wave of industrial capitalism, which defined "progress" largely as improvements in the material standard of life, soon spread outside Europe and covered the globe. By the 1880s, a few Western industrial powers had divided the world into different spheres of influence and exploited the natural resources of the colonies for the material welfare of their citizens.

European dominance, however, started to decline after the First World War. Western Europe was further weakened in the Second World War, after which the United States and the Soviet Union emerged as "superpowers." In addition, after the Second World War, a tidal wave of anticolonialism swept across the globe. Toward the end of the 1970s, over 100 independent sovereign nations had emerged, comprising a total of 2 billion people—half of the world's population (Palmer & Colton, 1978)—almost all of whom were formerly part of the old Western colonial empires. Poverty, poor health conditions, political instability, and sharp ethnic and class cleavages characterized these newly independent states. They are commonly called Less Developed Countries (LDCs).

WHAT IS DEVELOPMENT?

The LDCs have been struggling for decades to improve their standard of living. At first glance, economic growth and nation building seem to be the overriding goals in their process of development. Economic growth is the prescription for poverty and nation building is the solution to political instability. Although some LDCs in the past few decades have made remarkable progress in economic growth, such as the Four Little Dragons in Asia (South Korea, Taiwan, Singapore, and Hong Kong), many failed. Lewis (1988) observed that some LDCs can grow very fast, but this growth varies among countries and its fruits are often concentrated in a few hands. Employment growth was also slow in the LDCs, making income inequality a serious problem. Kuznets' (1955) hypothesis of wealth "trickling down" from a few hands to the masses was not supported by the reality of most of the LDCs.

Confronted with the failure of the "trickle-down" model of development, Rogers (1976) redefined development as "a widely participatory process of social change, intended to bring about both social and material advancement, including greater equality, freedom and other valued qualities, for the majority of the people through their gaining greater control over their environment" (p. 133).

In addition to uneven growth across LDCs and unequal distribution within developing nations, there is a widening gap of economic wealth between the developed and developing nations. Dependency theorists (Cardoso, 1972; Emmanuel, 1974; Evans, 1979; Frank, 1967, 1969, 1972; Sunkel, 1969; Wallerstein, 1974) believe that the conclusion of LDCs' parasitic elites with the bourgeoisie in the developed world since the 16th century and the unequal exchange between LDCs and Western industrial economies explains the current problems of LDCs.

In 1974, the participants of a seminar sponsored by the United Nations Council on Trade and Development pointed out the need to include the satisfaction of basic needs as a developmental goal. Basic needs include nutrition, health, education, and shelter. In their statement, known as the Cocoyoc Declaration, the participants remarked:

Our first concern is to redefine the whole purpose of development. This should not be to develop things but to develop man. Human beings have basic needs: food, shelter, clothing, health, education. Any process of growth that does not lead to their fulfillment—or, even worse, disrupts them—is a travesty of the idea of development. (Ghai, Khan, Lee, & Alfthan, 1977, p. 6)

Two years later, the International Labor Organization called on member states to adopt the "basic needs" approach to development. This approach stressed increased agricultural output rather than industry. It also urged investment in human as well as physical capital. Expenditures on health, education and other social services are justified on this ground.

With respect to nation building, most LDCs still remain politically unstable, despite efforts to mitigate class and ethnic cleavages and, in some cases, to establish constitutional democracies. Parker (1992) doubts whether political change in the form of wider distribution of political power is part of the definition of development. Although it may be difficult to achieve economic growth without more widely shared decision making on economic issues, he thinks that political development is a cause or consequence of development, rather than development in itself.

The concept of development at the close of the 20th century embraces at least three dimensions: economic growth, equitable distribution and the satisfaction of basic needs. In addition, some definitions also include political democracy, equitable distribution of world wealth, and environmental quality. Whichever dimension one chooses to emphasize, the central goal of development is to promote human well-being. The minimum target in development is the satisfaction of basic needs, whereas the control of one's own environment, both physical and human, is the highest goal.

Control of the physical environment involves efficient mobilization of natural resources and environmental protection and control of the human environment implies control of one's social and political life and freedom from foreign domination. Different societies have different priorities in their development process. The Western industrial states may place less stress on the satisfaction of basic needs, whereas, for LDCs, providing foodstuffs and clean water may be urgent tasks.

Development, thus conceived, consists of a hierarchy of goals and various emphases at different times. In reality, many states do not satisfy basic needs first and then move up the hierarchy of goals. There are numerous examples of states first seeking to squelch political opposition, such as Ethiopia; building up their national security establishment, such as the former U.S.S.R., or pursuing economic policies in favor of urban ruling elites or a junta.

CAUSES FOR UNDERDEVELOPMENT

Different theories are put forth to explain the rampant poverty and low productivity of LDCs. These theories can be classified into three broad categories: the individual deficiency model, the social-institutional deficiency
model, and the international deficiency model.

The individual deficiency model stipulates that traditional attitudes
and personality are the main barriers to development. Traditional values
have to be replaced by modern ones and a modern personality needs to be
introduced from the outside (Inkeles & Smith, 1974; Lerner, 1958;
McClelland, 1961; Schramm, 1964). The premise of this model is that the
root of underdevelopment lies in the "outdated" traditions of people. For a
country to develop, the people must first modernize. New ideas, products,
and practices have to be brought in from the outside. Underdevelopment,
therefore, is an internal problem solved by external means. This model lays
the blame on individual deficiencies.

The second model seeks explanations for underdevelopment from
social and institutional deficiencies. Instead of placing blame on individuals,
this model points to the structural constraints placed on individuals.
Insufficient infrastructure, inefficient markets, corrupt bureaucracies, a land
tenure system, repressive power structures, lack of management skills,
poor organization, etc. are held to be responsible for underdevelopment
(Contreras, 1980; Lipton, 1977; McAnany, 1980; Mouzelis, 1972-73;
Streeten, 1984). For a country to develop, the structural constraints on
peasants and the urban poor must be lifted either through reforms or revolution. Underdevelopment is caused by internal and social institutional structures; therefore, they must be changed for a country to develop.

The international deficiency model views underdevelopment primarily as an international problem. The main cause for the LDCs' poverty is
exploitation by the core countries in the capitalist world systems (Cardoso,
1972; Emmanuel, 1974; Evans, 1979; Frank, 1967, 1969, 1972; Sunkel,
1969; Wallerstein, 1974). The means to develop is found both externally
and internally.

Externally, the unfavorable assignment of the precapitalist mode of
production to the LDCs has to be changed. As a result of LDCs' pressure,
the United Nations adopted a declaration in 1974 to establish a New
International Economic Order (NIEO), which would correct inequalities,
redress existing injustices, and eliminate the widening gap between developed and developing countries (United Nations,1974). Internally, the LDCs
are urged to dissociate themselves from the core countries in order to
develop independently (Hamelink, 1983). The delinkage argument, however,
has been weakened by the fact that development in LDCs has occurred with
dependency in the past several decades (Cardoso, 1972; Cardoso &
Falleto, 1979; Evans, 1979).

ROLES OF INFORMATION IN DEVELOPMENT

Corresponding to the three models of underdevelopment are three different conceptions of the media's role in development. Under the individual deficiency model, information and communication are important components for cultivating a "mobile" personality or "empathy" necessary for transforming a traditional society into a modern one (Lerner, 1958). Empathy is the capacity of an individual to project himself into the role of another and identify new aspects of his environment. Mass communication serves a role of mobility multiplier which "discipline Western men in those empathetic skills which spells modernity" (p. 54). Information has a role to play in the introduction of innovations and the persuasion of people to adopt new behaviors.

Under the social-institutional deficiency model, information plays a secondary role to structural reforms or revolutionary changes. Information is, however, needed to facilitate change in institutions and organizations. Information can help to improve organizational performance, government administration, and economic efficiency. It is especially important for decision makers in LDCs. As Hirschman (1958) noted, the capacity to take and implement decisions is itself a key input to the development process.

Leff (1984) detailed the benefits brought to organizations, government bureaucracies, and markets by information inputs. He pointed out that markets themselves are special institutions whose emergence depends, among other things, on relative prices. Two of the key prices that determine whether or not markets emerge in specific activities are the cost of acquiring information and the cost of negotiating transactions. In other words, without the adequate supply of information, it is difficult for a market to emerge.

On the other hand, with more information and participants, market prices are likely to become informationally efficient. Leff pointed out that modern telecommunications reduces information costs. With lower transmission costs, the market size for information expands. This then becomes an incentive for generating more and better information. A benevolent cycle may result from the increase in the quantity and quality of information.

Under the international deficiency model, the role of information in development is limited. However, in some instances the supply of quality information may be crucial. For example, in trade negotiations the control of timely and accurate information is important for obtaining favorable trade terms. Information products themselves, as commodities for trade, also have an impact on an LDC's foreign exchange. Foreign media products may not only affect the LDC's cultural autonomy, but also the trade balance and development of indigenous cultural industries.

The earlier discussion indicates that no matter what development model one accepts—individual, social-institutional, or international—information has a role to play in development. Its roles are more obvious and significant at the individual and social-institutional level and less influential at the international level. As modern telecommunications help to reduce the time and distance in information transmission, and improve efficiency in synthesizing and generating new information, telecommunications has an important role to play in development.

Leff (1984) stressed that the fall in the costs of obtaining accurate and timely knowledge is particularly important in the LDCs because of uncertainty in their economies. Lower transaction costs and reduced uncertainty can increase the efficiency both of markets and of administrative organizations, which are two major mechanisms for resource mobilization and factor allocation in economic development. With full development of satellites, cables, digitization, and compression technology, information costs will probably be reduced further.

Telecommunications, however, is important not only in improving economic efficiency, but in creating employment and reducing inequality. On an a priori basis, Leff (1984) reasoned that telecommunications expansion may lead to a more equal distribution of income through employment creation and price changes that favor the poor. The capital-intensive nature typical of telecommunications projects means that relatively few people are directly employed in their construction. However, the greater availability of telecommunications improves the performance of product and factor markets. Output and investment are likely to increase in response to new opportunities and reduced uncertainty. As a result, higher employment can be expected, improving the situation of the poor.

Expanded communications and increased quality in access of information will intensify competition and improve the market performance. These developments imply a reduction in the monopoly power that penalizes the poor. Increased availability of telecommunications is likely to accelerate the diffusion of new production-related knowledge and technology, for example, in agriculture. Such information may lead to prices benefiting the poor more as they usually spend a relatively larger share of their income on food. Better telecommunications may make a pattern of development better that is geographically more dispersed, and in which the comparative advantage of diverse regions is given greater importance. The relatively poor areas' productive advantages can be utilized to the fullest extent.

Parapak (1993) summarized eight roles of satellite communications in national development. These roles can be conceived as telecommunications' contributions to development:

1. *Accelerating national development*—Availability of high-quality telecommunications systems improves LDCs global competitiveness.

2. *Modernizing and integrating society*—Telecommunications provides easy access to information. Such access is important for
   industrialization, education, commerce, and sociocultural development.
3. *Improving efficiency and productivity*—Timely availability of information and a speedy response to social demands are made possible by modern telecommunications.
4. *Enhancing equitable distribution*—Telecommunications make rural
   and isolated areas more attractive to investment.
5. *Conserving energy*—Good communication decreases the need
   for traveling and improves the speed of decision making. Travel
   reduction means conservation of energy.
6. *Eliminating isolation of remote areas*—Telecommunications provides a fast and economical means to link remote areas with a
   nation's business, political, and cultural center.
7. *Expanding market opportunities*—Global networks facilitate service expansion and the introduction of new products.
   Decentralized corporate management is then possible.
8. *Attracting capital for infrastructure*—Good telecommunications
   attract capital flows and investment through global linkage.

TELECOMMUNICATIONS MODEL OF DEVELOPMENT

Taking the Modernization theorists' path without the "trickle-down" assumption, Parker (1992) viewed economic growth as the basic core of development. The foremost priority of a country is to create wealth; all other social
desirables are either causes or corollaries of economic growth. He correctly
pointed out that simple redistribution of wealth in the LDCs without wealth
creation merely makes everyone poor because there is not enough to go
around. Without enough wealth, investment in health or education is not feasible. In addition, wealth creation is not only essential to the satisfaction of
basic needs and improvement of living standard, but also positive in amelio-
rating class as well as ethnic cleavages.

　　　The obvious problem of the lower class in all societies is their inability to obtain material benefits enjoyed by the upper class. Wealth creation may
help to alleviate the class division through the market mechanism or state's
redistribution measures. Ethnic strife also often expresses itself because of
unequal distribution of wealth. if there is enough to go around, both the majority and minority, ruling and ruled, will surely have fewer conflicts.

　　　Parker (1992) believed that the key to wealth creation is mobilizing
the resources of the country, whatever those resources may be. He identified three key factors in the mobilization process: investment in human capi-

tal, investment in basic infrastructure, and institutional reform. These three factors permit the people of a society to have access to the infrastructure and use their labor and brain power in a way that creates new wealth for the society. He further argued that the unleashing of brain power must be the central focus if sustainable development is to be achieved. However, this leads to a dilemma: To invest in human capital we need to create wealth, to create wealth, we need to invest in human capital. It is difficult, if not impossible, to get out of this vicious circle.

All LDCs have the problem of insufficient capital for investment. To solve this problem, they can do two things: generate capital from within the country, or borrow capital from outside through aid, joint ventures or other forms of foreign investment. To generate capital from within, people must have earnings and savings. There are three types of resources from which earnings can be derived from within LDCs: depletable natural resources, labor, and brain power. The latter two are renewable and abundant in LDCs.

Parker (1992) favored the use of brain power and emphasized the importance of telecommunications infrastructure to develop brain power in the process of wealth creation. He posited that telecommunications can increase human information power and intelligence, just as electrification increases human labor power. Figure 1.1 is a schematic model of development from a telecommunications perspective.

Telecommunications infrastructure can help to utilize the human brain power by the rapid transmission of information across long distances. Information and intelligence can help unleash human initiative and creativity, improve management, reduce decision errors, facilitate organization, enable both centralization, and decentralization of work, and increase the efficient application of production technologies. The development of human brain power will help generate capital. After generating capital for investment and wealth, the goals of basic needs, higher living standards, equality, democracy, and national security can be met. The increase in wealth enables reinvestment in all sectors, strengthening the telecommunications as well as other infrastructure. This leads to a self-sustaining process of development.

TELECOMMUNICATIONS AND ECONOMIC GROWTH

Thus far, telecommunications is assumed to have beneficial effects on development. A review of the literature, however, shows that empirical studies are few and the findings are far from conclusive. There is a major interest in the causal effect of telecommunications on economic growth. The plain old telephones (POTs) became a center of interest in telecommunications studies in the 1980s when fiber optics, digitization, computerization, and satellite technology greatly expanded the capabilities of telephone. The telephone has

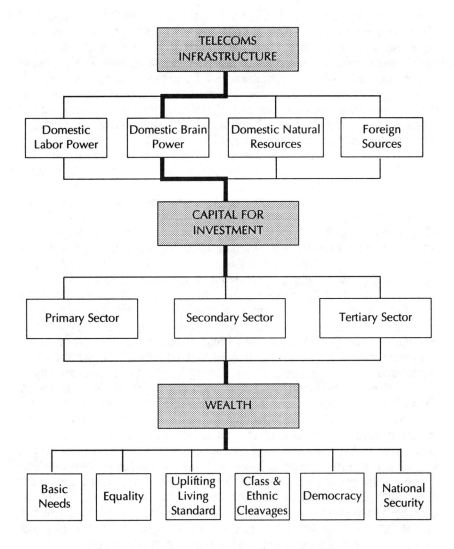

Figure 1.1. Telecommunications model of development

been used as an indicator for telecommunications development and a measuring stick for the extent of a society's information capacity.

Early studies on the relationship between telecommunications and development were generally correlational or crude regression studies of gross national product per capita and telephones per 100 people. Hardy (1980) attempted to establish an empirical causal relationship between telecommunications and economic growth. He ran a cross-sectional time-series regression analysis of telephones per million and GDP per capita of 15 developed and 45 developing countries, with a one year time lag. GDP per capita at time T-1, telephones per million at T-1, and radios per 1,000 people were used as predictors of GDP per capita at time T. The results showed that both GDP per capita at time T-1 and telephones per million at T-1 were significant in predicting the growth of GDP per capita one year later. Radios per 1,000, however, was not. Hardy cautioned that his language of causal inference referred to a "facilitating" or "contributory" cause rather than a "sufficient" or "necessary" cause.

Saunders, Warford, & Wellenius (1983) examined more than 300 World Bank reports on telecommunications, some of which partially quantify telecommunications benefits. A strong correlation between telecommunications and economic growth was noted. These authors favored an expansion of telephone service in developing countries, especially in rural areas. On the basis of this World Bank book, Wellenius (1984) argued that evidence for the relationship between telecommunications and economic growth was generally consistent. One could no longer use lack of empirical results as an excuse to give low priority to telecommunications development.

Hudson (1984) reviewed some other studies in LDCs and found that telecommunications may be particularly beneficial at certain key points in the process of rural development. The Maitland (1984) report commissioned by the International Telecommunication Union stressed the importance of the telephone in development. It indicated that countries that lag behind in telecommunications development will also lag behind in economic growth.

Parker & Hudson (1992) contended that upgrading telecommunications infrastructure was necessary to improve the depressed rural economy after their study of the relationship between economic indicators and telecommunications improvements in the United States as a whole, and within two states, Washington and Oregon. They used the unemployment rate as an indicator of rural economic health and found a causal link between economic quality and improvements in telecommunications. Using Singapore data, eight components of GDP and overall GDP, Ang (1993) tested the causality between telecommunications and economic growth. He found that overall GDP was significant but its components were not. This finding indicates that the relationship is not as simple as commonly thought.

In response to criticism of single regression equation and ignorance of two-way relations between telecommunications and economic growth, Cronin, Parker, Colleran, & Gold (1991) conducted a study in the United States testing two hypotheses: (a) economic growth is a cause of telecommunications investment at a later point in time, and (b) telecommunications investment is a cause of economic growth at a later point in time. Using the Granger Test and Modified Sims Test, they found that both hypotheses were supported. They further tested the two hypotheses at the state and county level, whereby both hypotheses were again supported. They noted that the results bear out the significance of telecommunications in economic growth, even in small geographical areas (Cronin, Parker, Colleran, & Gold, 1993). Zhu (this volume), however, replicating Cronin & colleagues' study in China, found that telecommunications contributed to development in China as a whole, but not in the industrial city of Shanghai.

In a study of four countries, namely Brazil, Costa Rica, Indonesia, and Singapore, Stone (1993) also found that telecommunications investments are relatively more effective in upper-middle income countries than in lower-middle income countries. This finding indicates that telecommunications investment not only has various effects in different stages of development, but also casts the "diminishing return" thesis in doubt.

According to this thesis, the size of the effect of telecommunications investment was inversely related to the prior level of telecommunications development. The largest effect of telecommunications investment on GDP was found in the least developed economies and the smallest effect was found in the most developed economies (Cronin et al., 1991). Stone's (1993) study may indicate that research on the link between telecommunications and economic growth is still too young to draw conclusions.

TELECOMMUNICATIONS AND OTHER RELATED ISSUES

Apart from the relationship between telecommunications and economic growth, there are other related issues in the study of telecommunications and development. One major issue is whether the LDCs should adopt a public utility model or marketplace model for telecommunications development. In the public utility model, the state maintains a telecommunications monopoly, either privately or publicly owned. The basic feature of a public utility is to provide universal service to all people at a regulated price. Cross-subsidization from profitable sectors to unprofitable ones is needed. Part of the monopoly profits will be reinvested for expanding and improving the service.

The marketplace model encourages competition of services, which reduces the price for larger users and eliminate cross-subsidization to small users. Competitors will operate only in a profitable sector. In telecommunications, market competition usually results in a price reduction for long-distance calls, benefiting large commercial users. Meanwhile, there is often a price increase for local and small users.

Whether the monopoly or marketplace model is more beneficial to an LDC's development is a question that has not been studied at length. The breakup of telecommunications monopolies is a relatively new phenomenon; it is thus too early to tell if the marketplace model is more suitable for LDCs than the public utility model. Drawing from the experience of deregulation in the United States, Great Britain, and Japan, Hills (1993) cautioned that market competition provides no incentive for telecommunications operators to expand coverage to the poor or expand new services to less wealthy geographical areas. She argued that the rationale for deregulation since the 1980s shows itself to be no more than an ideology in favor of one set of consumers—large business.

Another major issue in telecommunications study is the role played by telecommunications in democracy. Hills (1993) took a "neutral technology" position by pointing out that telecommunications, as part of the state, can be used to control citizens or to increase their access to economic and political resources, thus providing more choices and freedom. Beniger (1986), basing observations on a historical analysis, pointed out that the information revolution in the 20th century originated from the need for political and economic control.

With the aid of modern communications technology the central authority has rebuilt its control, which was lost in the decentralizing process inherent in the Industrial Revolution. Nevertheless, international direct dial and the audio cassette were known for their subversive role in overthrowing the authoritarian regime of the Shah Pahlavi in Iran and facsimile machines rendered the news blackout of the Tiananmen Massacre by the Chinese communists futile.

After reviewing the electronic mail networks in China, McIntyre (this volume) concluded that authoritarian control over telecommunications is not likely to succeed with the proliferation of independent private electronic mail services such as Fidonet, MCI Mail, Sprint Mail and ATTMail in China.

Rural telecommunications is also an important area of concern for telecommunications study. This area is often tied to the issues of financing, privatization, cross-subsidies, and transmission technology. LDCs are usually characterized by a huge rural population lacking access to modern telecommunications. The widely scattered rural population and light use of telecommunications do not justify investment in rural telecommunications in economic terms; hence, there are problems of financing that necessitate the maintenance of a monopoly to cross-subsidize from urban to rural areas. Some would favor the strategy of attracting capital by privatization, but such a policy may bring services only to profitable areas; the government still needs to intervene to provide services for unprofitable areas.

Stone (1993) thus proposed a public-private cooperation in which the private enterprise provides the profitable local area network, while the government provides the unprofitable trunk links. The question to be asked regarding such a "cooperation," however, is why should government take up only the money-losing part and let private enterprises take the profits? Lee (chapter 5, this volume) pointed out that, given the state's limited financial resources for rural telecommunications, an alternative to develop rural telecommunications is privatization. Through privatization, some local or foreign entrepreneurs will put up capital to invest in rural telecommunications, will be entirely responsible for the risks. Private firms may at least provide some services to potentially profitable rural areas, which are better than none at all.

Because of the scattered population in rural areas, satellite and cellular technologies are often viewed as the most "appropriate" technologies. For instance, Parapak (1993), the Secretary General of the Department of Tourism, Post, and Communications of Indonesia, was very satisfied with the Palapa satellite system of his country. He claimed that the satellite links to the global network have played a vital role in the economic and sociocultural development of Indonesia.

Apart from the aforementioned issues, studies on telecommunications and development also focus on micro- and practical issues such as access charges, tariffs, international accounting rates, numbering and interconnection among competitive networks and price controls, etc. At the end of the 20th century, the telephone has been transformed into an important telecommunications medium as a result of technological advancement. It is now not only a consumer good, but a producer good. In the eyes of many communication researchers and government officials, telephony and other telecommunications functions have become an important tool in economic growth, development, and national power.

CRITICISM ON THE TELECOMMUNICATIONS-GROWTH STUDIES

A review of the literature of telecommunications and development shows that the relationship between telecommunications and economic growth is one of the most frequently tested areas (Snow, 1988). Despite the increase in empirical evidence that supports the existence of a causal relationship between telecommunications and economic growth, however, four criticisms can be made of these studies. First, all of the studies on telecommunications and economic growth tend to ignore the negative impact of telecommunications development, both theoretically and empirically. For instance, although telecommunications allows a large chain store to rationalize the cost of expansion for the benefit of the rural economy, it also leads to the closing of the local retail outlets (Sieber, 1993). Improved infrastructure in urban areas will result in a brain drain from rural areas, depriving them of a valuable resource. The studies on telecommunications and economic growth are generally uncritical of the application of modern communications, assuming that telecommunications is a "risk free" activity in development. The simple assertion that telecommunications investment results in economic growth provokes critical comments. Mueller (1993) stated that "if the relationship is really that simple, we would all be better off if businesses ordered two or three telephone lines even if they needed only one" (p. 156).

The second major criticism of telecommunications and economic growth studies is leveled against the failure to examine the mechanism through which telecommunications effects work. In the studies, results often show only the statistical relationship between telecommunications and growth, but whether this growth is achieved through market rationalization, improved organizational efficiency, or better decision making is not known. Very few studies consider the mechanisms through which telecommunications exerts its effects on economic growth.

The third criticism of telecommunications-growth studies regards the issue of priority. The literature shows that these studies seldom examine the relative priorities of telecommunications investment vis-a-vis other infrastructural developments such as electricity, transportation, water, and health. These studies usually point out only the causal effects of telecommunications on economic growth, then argue for its priority in investment. Comparisons between benefits from investing in telecommunications and other infrastructural sectors are seldom made. Without detailed analysis of the relative costs and benefits of investments in various sectors, the high priority given to telecommunications development is often a "disciplinary bias" rather than an "informed" recommendation.

Finally, the studies on the relationship between telecommunications and economic growth fall short in examining the conditions under which developing countries should invest in telecommunications. Even if we know that there is a causal link between telecommunications and economic growth, we still cannot make an "informed" decision regarding when, where, why, and how an LDC with limited financial resources should invest in telecommunications. If the theory of telecommunications and economic growth is to withstand the challenges of time and LDCs' development needs, the conditions under which telecommunications can or cannot have positive effects on economic growth must be studied fully. Because empirical studies on the relationship between telecommunications and development have just begun, we can expect more empirical studies in the future to enrich our understanding of telecommunications' role in development.

TELECOMMUNICATIONS AND DEVELOPMENT IN CHINA

China is a vast land of 9.6 million square kilometers, inhabited by 1.2 billion people. In 1992, 72% of the population lived in rural areas. According to the 1990 Census, about 21% of people aged 6 or older were illiterate. Since the Open Door policy was adopted in 1978, China has witnessed tremendous economic growth. In the period between 1978 and 1992, it registered an average annual GNP growth of 8.5% (Statistical Bureau, 1993). In 1993, its GNP per capita was US$435 (*Yazhou Zhoukan*, 1994).

The growth of telecommunications is equally impressive. In 1980 there was a total of 4.1 million telephones in China, representing a density of .4%, or .4 telephones per 100 persons. By the end of 1992, the overall telephone density reached 1.6% and 70% of local switching in urban areas was digitized (Chen, 1993).1t is expected that by the year 2000 telephone density will reach 5% (Wan, 1993).

Although China remains a regional power in the international arena, its success or failure in development will certainly affect the world's economy and political alignments. If China's economy improves and the country becomes more democratic, the world will certainly be a more peaceful place. Today, the Chinese people are eager to improve their standard of living, taking great pains to raise their industrial as well as agricultural productivity. In the process, they realize that telecommunications infrastructure, among other things, is important to the success of their development. However, they are handicapped by the lack of financial resources, incompatible institutions, and bureaucratic inefficiency.

This volume attempts to provide a basic understanding of China's telecommunications, with particular attention being paid to the roles of telecommunications in development. Apart from providing a comprehensive picture of current telecommunications in China, the readings also aim to shed light on various issues related to telecommunications development and its social, economic, and political impact.

All of the works collected here do not presume to be complete, or conclusive. Because the role of telecommunications in development has not been given much attention by social researchers until recently, the analysis and discussion are only preliminary. Having more than one fifth of the world's population within its borders, China's success or failure in development has repercussions for the world and other LDCs.

Our understanding of the agents for development is still limited. Many people are starting to view telecommunications as "another" agent for development, after being disappointed by the failure of mass media in development in the past several decades. It is hoped that this collection will be a timely and useful reference for those who are interested in communication and development and that the readings can serve as a platform for further discussion and research on China's telecommunications and development.

REFERENCES

Ang, P. (1993). The causal relationship between international telecommunications and economic development: Cause for reanalysis? In A. Goonasekera & D. Holaday (Eds.), *Asian communication handbook* (pp. 341-358). Singapore: AMIC.

Beniger, J.R. (1986). *The control revolution: Technological and economic origins of the information society.* Cambridge, MA: Harvard University Press.

Cardoso, F.H. (1972). Dependency and development in Latin America. *New Left Review, 74,* 83-89.

Cardoso, F. H., & Falleto, E. (1979). *Dependency and development in Latin America*. (M.M. Unquidi, Trans.). Berkeley: University of California Press.

Chen, Y. (1993, July). Driving forces behind China's explosive telecommunications growth. *IEEE Communications Magazine*, 20-22.

Contreras, E. (1980). Brazil and Guatemala: Communications, rural modernity and structural constraints. In E.G. McAnany (Ed.), *Communications in the rural Third World: The role of information in development* (pp. 107-145). New York: Praeger.

Cronin, F.J., Parker, E.B., Colleran, E.K., & Gold, M.A. (1991). Telecommunications infrastructure and economic growth: An analysis of causality. *Telecommunications Policy, 15*(6), 529-535.

Cronin, F.J., Parker, E.B., Colleran, E.K., & Gold, M.A. (1993). Telecommunications infrastructure and economic development. *Telecommunications Policy, 17*(4), 415-430.

Emmanuel, A. (1974). Myths of development vs. myth of underdevelopment. *New Left Review, 85*, 61-82.

Evans, P. (1979). *Dependent development: The alliance of multinational, state and local capital in Brazil*. Princeton, NJ: Princeton University Press.

Frank, A.G. (1967). *Capitalism and underdevelopment in Latin America*. New York: Monthly Review Press.

Frank, A.G. (1969). *Latin America: Underdevelopment or revolution*. New York: Monthly Review Press.

Frank, A.G. (1972). *Lumpenbourgeoisie—Lumpendevelopment*. New York: Monthly Review Press.

Ghai, D.P., Khan, A.R., Lee, E.L.H., & Alfthan, T. (1977). *The basic needs approach to development* Geneva: International Labor Organization.

Hamelink, C.J. (1983). *Cultural autonomy in global communications*. New York: Longman.

Hardy, A.P. (1980). The role of the telephone in economic development. *Telecommunications Policy, 4*(4), 278-286.

Hills, J. (1993). Telecommunications and democracy: The international experience. *Telecommunication Journal, 60*(1), 21-29.

Hirschman, A.O. (1958). *The strategy of economic development*. New Haven, CT: Yale University Press.

Hudson, H.E. (1984). *When telephones reach the village: The role of telecommunications in rural development*. Norwood, NJ: Ablex.

Inkeles A., & Smith, D.H. (1974). *Becoming modern: Individual change in six developing countries*. Cambridge, MA: Harvard University Press.

Kuznets, S. (1955). Economic-growth and income inequality. *American Economic Review, 65*(1), 1-30.

Leff, N.H. (1984). Externalities, information costs, and social benefit-cost analysis for economic development: An example from telecommunications. *Economic Development and Cultural Change, 32*(2), 255-276.

Lerner, D. (1958). *The passing of traditional society.* New York: The Free Press.

Lewis, W.A. (1988). Reflections on development. In G. Ranis & T. P. Schultz (Eds.), *The state of development economics: Progress and perspectives* (pp.12-23). Oxford: Basil Blackwell.

Lipton, M. (1977). *Why poor people stay poor: Urban bias in world development.* London: Temple Smith.

Maitland, D. (1984). *The missing link. A report of the Independent Commission for Worldwide telecommunications development.* Geneva: ITU.

McAnany, E.G. (1980). The role of information in communicating with the rural poor. In E. G. McAnany (Ed.), *Communications in the rural Third World: The role of information in development* (pp. 3-18). New York: Praeger.

McClelland, D.C. (1961). *The achieving society.* New York: D. Van Nostrand.

Mouzelis, N. P. (1972-73). Modernization, development and peasants. *Development and Change, 4*(3), 73-88.

Mueller, M. (1993). Telecommunications as infrastructure: A skeptical view. *Journal of Communication, 43*(2), 147-159.

Palmer, R.R., & Colton, J. (1978). *A history of the modern world.* New York: Knopf.

Parapak, J.L. (1993). The role of satellite communications in national development. *Media Asia, 20*(1), 24-29, 32.

Parker, E.B. (1992). Developing Third World telecommunications market. *The Information Society, 8,* 147-167.

Parker, E.B., & Hudson, H.E. (1992). *Electronic byways: State policies for rural development through telecommunications.* Boulder, CO: Westview.

Polanyi, K. (1944). *The great transformation.* New York: Farrar & Rinehart.

Rogers, E.M. (Ed.). (1976). *Communication and development: Critical perspectives.* Beverly Hills, CA: Sage.

Saunders, R.J., Warford, J., & Wellenius, B. (1983). *Telecommunications and economic development.* Baltimore: Johns Hopkins University Press.

Schramm, W. (1964). *Mass media and national development.* Stamford, CA: Stanford University Press.

Sieber, R. (1993). A book review on electronic byways: State policies for rural development through telecommunications, written by E.B. Parker & H.E. Hudson. In *Journal of American Planning Association, 59*(3), 392-393.

Snow, M.S. (1988). Telecommunications literature: A critical review of the economic, technological and public policy issues. *Telecommunications Policy, 12*(2), 153-183.

State Statistical Bureau. (1993). *China statistical yearbook 1992*. Beijing: China Statistical Press.

Stone, P.B. (1993). Public-private alliances for telecommunications development: Intracorporate Baby Bells in the developing countries. *Telecommunications Policy, 17*(4), 459-469.

Streeten, P. (1984). Basic needs: Some unsettled questions. *World Development, 7,* 973-978.

Sunkel, O. (1969). National development policy and external dependency in Latin America. *Journal of Development Studies, 6*(1), 23-48.

United Nations. (1974). Declaration on the establishment of a New International Economic Order, G.A. Res. 3201, Sixth Special Session, U.N. Supp. (No.s) UN Doc. A/9559.

Wallerstein, E. (1974). The rise and future demise of the world capitalist system: Concepts for comparative analysis. *Comparative Study in Society and History, 16*(4), 387-415.

Wan, S. (1993, July). An overview of telecommunications in China. *IEEE Communications Magazine,* 18-19.

Wellenius, B. (1984). On the role of telecommunications in development. *Telecommunications Policy, 8*(1), 59-66.

Yazhou Zhoukan. (1994, June 12). p. 12.

CHAPTER 2

LEARNING FROM THE EVOLUTION OF TELECOMMUNICATIONS IN THE DEVELOPED WORLD

BENJAMIN J. BATES

The development of electronic forms of communication—or telecommunications—began in Europe and North America, and was rapidly adopted there. From the initial developments of telegraphy in the early 1800s to today's satellite and fiber-optic communications systems, these early adopter nations have led the way in developing and utilizing telecommunications technologies and systems. They are also the home of many of the world's most advanced economies. Telecommunications undeniably contributed to the process of economic and social development in these areas, just as the development of an industrial base fostered that continuing rise and adoption of telecommunications. This symbiotic relationship between telecommunications and "development" continues, promising (or threatening) to lead societies into a new age of economic and social development, sometimes referred to as the "Information Age."

It should be no surprise that telecommunications emerged in Europe and North America. These areas had already experienced the early stages of the shift from being an agricultural to an industrial society, providing a strong industrial, social, and political foundation for the development of electronic forms of communication. Industrialization expanded the world of trade and commerce, creating new needs for fast and efficient communication. The transition contributed to urbanization and more complex forms of social organizations, with their needs for new and efficient communications (Cherry, 1977, 1985), and the growth of a middle class that could afford it

On the political front, the growth of nations and empires had also contributed to a healthy demand for fast, efficient communication. The rise of Protestantism, positivism, and democratic ideals provided the social, philosophical, and political conditions for promoting faster and more efficient systems of communication and the sharing of information (Badham, 1986; Varma, 1980; Webster, 1984). As Beniger (1986) summarized, a wide variety of social, economic, and political changes were creating a need for new forms of communication and control; needs that telecommunications systems could fairly easily meet.

This growing demand for information and communication prompted numerous efforts at creating fast and efficient mechanisms for communication from the 18th century on. A wide variety of communication systems and techniques were experimented with throughout the world. However, when the notions of using electricity to send messages began developing, it was the more developed states of Europe and North America that possessed the necessary scientific, technological and industrial base to make such telecommunications practicable, and the rising industrial, social, and/or political demand for information and communication that would make telecommunications economically viable (Czitrom, 1982; Dills, 1941; Winston, 1986).

This should not be taken as suggesting that successful telecommunications development required a full industrial base—many early developments of telecommunication systems, in the United States in particular, occurred before industrial and economic development was widespread. Rather, it suggests that industrialization and telecommunications both benefited from a similar set of economic, technological, and social conditions. Further, the initial steps towards industrialization and the initial developments of telecommunications benefited each other.

As much as the rise of industry and railroads fostered the demand for telecommunications, telecommunications helped to fuel the fires of economic and social growth (Czitrom, 1982). Telecommunications linked distant lands, helping to create and open new markets for industrial goods (Melody, 1988; Saunders, Warford, & Wellenius, 1983). The rise, and adoption, of telecommunications systems enabled social, economic, and political systems to grow in size and scope (Beniger, 1986). The expansion of mass media via broadcasting arguably promoted the rise of new values, including consumerism (Pool, 1983; Williams, 1975). The creation, and further development and implementation, of telecommunications thus can be argued to have fostered industrial, economic, and social development.

Thus, in most of the industrializing world there was a concurrent rise of economic and social development and telecommunications. This seemed to suggest a causal link between the two, often leading to the perception, expressed in a number of international forums, that investment in telecommunications promoted economic and social development (see

Hamelink, 1988; Hilewick, Deak, & Heinze, 1978; Hudson, 1982, 1984; Saunders et al., 1983). There was also a general perception that information, and the ability to process and distribute information through telecommunications, is critical to organizational and cultural development (Beniger, 1986; Hudson, 1984; Pool, 1977). Early developmental theories (e.g., Lerner, 1958), and numerous quantitative studies seemed to link telecommunications and economic and social development (see chapter 1, this volume, for a review of the literature of telecommunications and development—for summaries of research, also see Hudson, 1984, 1988; Middleton & Jussawalla, 1981; Saunders et al., 1983).

These results seemed to fit in with the general economic growth paradigm, which focused on capital investment and technological innovations as the source of economic development (Arndt, 1978). However, Hamelink (1988), Mowlana & Wilson (1988), and others have noted that there seemed to be a lack of predictive theory about the impact of telecommunications, and that the results of economic studies were not always conclusive.[1] However, there seemed to be a clear relationship that the most developed nations also tended to have the best, and most extensive, telecommunications systems.

There was not, however, necessarily a standard experience among the nations adopting and developing telecommunications. Telecommunications systems evolved differently in different states, reflecting differences in social and economic conditions, divergent policies. Further, these variations can be linked to differences in how those states "developed." Scholars also began challenging the dominant development paradigm (Badham, 1986; Mowlana & Wilson, 1988; Rogers, 1976; Varma, 1980) and its narrow conceptualization of development. The new paradigms also integrated an awareness that local social and political factors could significantly influence the process of change and development. This reconceptualization was occurring in the economic growth paradigm as well, led by Rostow's argument that economic development was also dependent on appropriate social institutions and value systems (Arndt, 1978).

These new paradigms of development argued for more focused consideration of the context of development. They emphasized the importance of examining some of the variations in systems and impacts, and the policies and factors that contributed to those differences and called for a more individuated examination of the reciprocal links among society, telecommunications, and development.

---

[1]Hudson (1984) suggested that one reason for the lack of conclusive economic results might be due to the fact that many of the benefits of telecommunications came in the form of externalities, which were not picked up in the general aggregate statistics on which most studies relied. This argument is reinforced by Melody's (1993) and Bates' (1988a) examinations of the economics of information, and Cherry's (1985) argument that the economics of information is an economics of sharing, rather than the economics of exchange upon which modern economic theory is built.

The link between telecommunications and development is not purely historical, however. Today, many nations are critically examining the role of telecommunications in development, with an eye towards determining how they can best use telecommunications to enhance and foster their own development. They seek to learn from the experience of the early and heavy adopters of telecommunications, as well as the experience of other parts of the world. Meanwhile, neither telecommunications nor development are standing still; states continually face the necessity of dealing with new technologies and systems and maintaining policies to promote continued economic, social, and political development.

Nevertheless, there are several reasons to take a historical look at the relationship between telecommunications and development. Aside from the general value of knowledge and understanding, insights into the connection between telecommunications, society, and development can help current and future policy makers to determine how to best shape and promote development to meet their specific needs. However, the interrelationship of these factors is rarely clear and direct; they rarely provide clear signals as to how to design and implement telecommunications so as to achieve specific social and/or economic goals. There have been a number of different approaches to telecommunications development and policy in various states around the world, with a range of implications and results. Examining some of these differences, and how such distinctive developments have influenced general economic and social development can, however, help to illustrate some of the possible relationships among telecommunications and the social and economic factors promoting development.

With that goal in mind, this chapter focuses on the historical connections between telecommunications and development in several ways. First, the general, more theoretical, relationship of telecommunications and development are explored. The beginnings of telecommunications development in several countries of North America and Europe are then examined, identifying some of the different factors at work shaping the structure and focus of the emerging telecommunications networks and considering their implications for development in those countries. This section focuses primarily on the evolution of telecommunications in the United States, Great Britain, France, and Germany, although some consideration will be given to other North American and European nations. Finally, some of the current telecommunications policy issues shaping the future evolution of telecommunications, and their likely impact on future development, are briefly examined.

GENERAL PERSPECTIVES ON
TELECOMMUNICATIONS AND DEVELOPMENT

Economists generally suggest that development is predicated on two primary factors: capital acquisition and invention (Arndt, 1978). Sociologists, on
the other hand, suggest that development is as much a social process as an
economic one; thus, certain values, norms, and organizational structures
have also contributed to the development of the West. They suggest that the
rise of certain social and psychological factors—such as the emphasis on
education and innovation, a growing emphasis on individualism and equality,
and what Weber called "rationalization" and the Protestant ethic—form a
basis for the Western notion of development (Badham, 1986; Etzioni, 1986;
Varma, 1980; Weber, 1947; Webster, 1984).

Cherry (1985) argued that the hallmark of development was the creation of a host of increasingly complex social organizations, which required
communications if they were to be effective. Woods (1993) expanded this
notion by recently arguing that a key component in successful development
is human development. Economists began to recognize the role of social
and cultural factors in fostering development (Arndt, 1978). Therefore, it
would seem that development is just as much a social process as an economic one. In considering how the rise of telecommunications, as both technologies and as systems for communication, can affect development and
have social effects, we need to encompass more than a narrow consideration of aggregate economic impact.

There is a second reason to expand this consideration of
impact.Certainly, as telecommunications itself is an industry, it is self-evident
that the development of telecommunications as a sector contributes something to overall development, regardless of the way in which telecommunication develops. However, communication is generally held to be more than the
technology it employs; its impact results primarily from its use. The patterns
of use of communication, as well as the structures of telecommunications
systems, can influence economic values (Bates, 1988a), as well as cultural
values (e.g., Katz & Szecko, 1981; Mulgan, 1990; Slack, 1984; Williams,
1976) and society at large (Bates, 1990, 1993; Innis, 1950, 1964). This
suggests that any thorough examination of the impact of telecommunications
on development must also consider the impact of the use of telecommunications, and how that use can have social and economic impacts.

The most obvious, and immediate, source of economic value arising
from the rise and diffusion of telecommunications derives from the technology itself, which must be manufactured and maintained. The investment in
telecommunications plant and related materials can be quite substantial, yet
the contribution of the infrastructure can be outweighed by the value of the
services provided. Whatever the source, though, telecommunications as an

industry is a direct source of considerable revenues and benefits. However, in the grand scheme of things this source of value is perhaps only the smallest part of the contribution of telecommunications to an economy and a society.

What is probably a more important contribution to development and the overall economy in the long run is the ability of telecommunications to promote communication and the transmission and storage of information. In considering this aspect of the economic and social impacts of telecommunications, we first need to consider what differentiates telecommunications from other possible sources of communication, what makes telecommunication more than just communication. The essence of what differentiates telecommunications from earlier communication systems is that the rise of telecommunications finally separated communication from transportation, increasing the flow of information in efficiency, scope, and speed.

Communication is also different from other forms of technological innovation in the way in which value is created. Cherry (1985) noted that the economics of communication is an economics of sharing, rather than an economics of exchange. This suggests the presence of value in ways other than the consumption of goods and services.[2]

TELECOMMUNICATIONS IMPACT

The separation of communication from transportation through the rise and development of telecommunications had three general impacts. First, telecommunications expanded the geographical scope of practical communications. Telecommunications could reach isolated areas where transportation was problematic, costly, or slow. The second general impact was to speed the flow of information and communication. Communication was no longer tied to travel times. The third was in increasing the scope of information; expanding the amount and variety of information, and information services, available. The reduced cost and increased capacity of telecommunications encouraged the development of new uses, and the dissemination of greater amounts, and more diversity, of information. What the rise and continuing development of telecommunication did was essentially expand the range, speed, and scope of information and communication in society and, thus, its impact.

These three basic impacts each had the potential for influencing social and economic development, both singly and in combination. There are several ways in which the expanding geographic scope of telecommunications was thought to have impact. Pool (1990) argued that telecommunications' expanded geographic range impacted social geography, enabling and

---

[2]Also see Melody (1993), Bates (1988a) and Wolpert and Wolpert (1986) for discussions of the economic contributions of information and communication.

encouraging not only the process of suburbanization, but also the ability to expand vertical scope in the form of skyscrapers, enabling the growth of urban centers. In fact, Pool argued that telecommunication was most successful where it was offered as a means of disseminating access (through expanding the reach of communications), rather than as a means of disseminating messages.

The separation of communication from transportation meant that telecommunications could be used to improve transport efficiency. Telecommunications could coordinate supply and demand regionally, and improve transportation scheduling (Saunders et al., 1983). This could not only contribute to regional development, but telecommunications could also improve links to other nations and areas, thereby improving coordination of international activities, and expansion of markets. Hudson (1984) and others expanded on this notion of using telecommunications to broaden access by focusing on the ability of telecommunications to assist in rural development. Here, telecommunications was seen as helping to integrate rural areas, thereby expanding the benefits of development.

TELECOMMUNICATIONS AND ORGANIZATION

The increased range, speed, and efficiency of telecommunications made it acceptable for use as a mechanism for control. Beniger (1986) and others have demonstrated that telecommunications enabled and encouraged the formation of larger and more complex organizations by expanding the capacity to control them. Telecommunications, by providing information quickly and efficiently, simultaneously permits both the centralization and decentralization of control that larger, more complex, organizational forms require. This increased capacity for communication and control was not unwelcome in most developing societies. The rise of more complex, industrial societies brought with it the rise of a new level of complexity in the problems facing society.

The ability of telecommunications to extend coordination and control, particularly in a decentralized manner, provided the capacity to deal with many of these problems (Utsumi, 1978). This ability to extend control through telecommunications is an organizational function (Cherry, 1977), one that permits order to be extended throughout larger social organizations. As Weber (1947) argued, it was the rationalization of organization that made industrialization, and development, possible (Varma, 1980; Webster, 1984). Larger organizations were able to take advantage of the economies of scale resulting from industrialization and related technological advances. One general consequence of the expansion of communication and control was that it permitted the development of larger and more diverse corporate structures. This stimulated the rise of monopoly structures (DuBoff, 1983; Melody, 1988) and transnational corporations (Schiller, 1981).

It is important to note, however, that control can be exerted in several directions. Mulgan (1990) noted that with the rise of networked telecommunications, patterns of control also shifted. The technology and design of networks permitted and encouraged horizontal communication, and extension of forms of control other than the traditional "top-down" form normally associated with the concept of control. Mulgan and others (cf. Masuda, 1981; Radojkovic, 1984; Smith, 1983) suggested that such extensions can contribute to the advance of democratization and the decline of authoritarian values.

Although it was the telegraph that first provided the means for extending control, it was the telephone network that promoted not only organization, but whole new types of organizations and social institutions (Cherry, 1977). The network aspect of the telephone started to shift the emphasis from vertical to horizontal communication flows. This brought forth new efficiencies and new sources of value, as well as considerable social impacts (Pool, 1977).

TELECOMMUNICATIONS AND MARKETS

Increasing the speed of communications also aided in making the larger markets and organizations of the Industrial Age more efficient and manageable, thereby assisting in coordinating the expanding markets for goods and labor (Melody, 1988; Saunders et al., 1983). The increased speed of information flows reduced the degree of risk in trade and commerce. This further encouraged economic growth and development in these areas. In the world of business and economics, expansion of markets helped to provide the increased demand that initially made industrial mass-production techniques feasible. The larger, more complex, organizational forms fostered by telecommunications also provided the mechanism for overseeing and controlling industrial production. Both the growth in markets and the growing capacity to handle larger organizations fostered the growth of capital acquisition, one of the two prime components of economic development.

The increase in scope and speed meant that more information and knowledge was available to more people. There are two primary consequences with regard to development. First, information about new goods and services can increase demand, fostering additional capital investment as industry expands to meet the higher levels of demand. Second, science and invention build on existing knowledge in a synergistic manner. Expanding the information base can contribute to human development through improved education (Woods, 1993). Greater information bases and information flows also promote discovery and invention; invention, then, with capital acquisition, promotes development. In these ways, telecommunication can contribute to economic growth and development.

TELECOMMUNICATIONS AND SOCIETY

Development is also said to be, in large part, a set of values. As the area of people's experience expands from the community, nations must be built, and they are built on the basis of shared values, shared history, and shared experience. WIlliam and Pearce (1978) suggested that a fundament of society is its "literature": the myths and stories shared by its members; the product of the society's communications and socialization. This concept of literature does not refer to its writings, but rather embodies the shared values and history of a culture as symbolized in its stories and myths (in whatever form they are presented). Acquiring this "literature" provides the common experience and background necessary for membership in that culture. Telecommunications, particularly the development of broadcasting, helped to spread these stories and myths further and more comprehensively than ever before, bypassing both distance and limits of literacy. In addition, as many media critics point out (e.g., Curran, Gurevitch, & Woolacott, 1979; Katz & Szecko, 1981; Williams, 1975), radio and television can also hasten and contribute to shifts in social values, often creating values seeming to be coincident with those promoting development (Etzioni, 1986; Lerner, 1958).

There is a common thread weaving throughout these considerations of the various ways in which telecommunications can have an impact on development: the notion that whatever the source of influence, the impact is greater when the system is most widely diffused. The economic benefits of sector development are increased when the system is larger. The economic benefits of efficiency and extended scope are greatest when there is uniform, total coverage. The educational, social, and political benefits are maximized when the system is extended to incorporate all members of society.

This general impact provides a mechanism for examining the general impact of the development of telecommunications on overall development without having to consider in detail specific economic and social impacts. We can get an idea of the contribution of a particular telecommunications system by examining how well it has achieved the general goal of universal service and can consider how the specifics of the evolution of telecommunications encouraged, or discouraged, the expansion of the system and its ability to meet the goal of universal service.

There is often a tendency to think of technology as a simple causal agent; in this case, to think of telecommunications as causing development. Although certainly there are consequences of technological development and adoption, we also have to remember that social forces influence whether and how any technology is used. In the age of the inventor, these forces can even influence what gets invented and created. Scholars such as McAnany (cited in Hudson, 1984), Slack (1984), and Williams (1975) argued that technologies depend as much on the development of appropriate social and economic conditions as on inventive and creative genius.

Rogers (1983), in his review of diffusion research, amply illustrated the range of social, political, and economic forces that can influence the adoption of new technologies. Marxists and structuralists have both suggested that social forces influence the utilization of telecommunications, as well as other media. The growth and performance of the telecommunications sector are also affected by the political and economic environment in which it operates (Hudson, 1984; Noll, 1986). Both democracies and free market economies tend to place greater emphasis on making information widely available, fostering both the growth and diffusion of telecommunications as communication media.

Therefore, we should consider how the other social forces mat promote development might have aided, limited, or otherwise interacted with the rise of telecommunications systems. One way to do this is to examine the early stages of the innovation process and compare them with the eventual structures and uses. This can often reveal the underlying social forces at work. Initial implementations are likely to be based more on the entrepreneur's own notions of the uses of a system than on the needs of the society that adopts it. This can often be at odds with what the underlying social factors encourage and develop, which is evidenced more by what the systems evolve into. Virtually every telecommunications system has undergone a significant shift in perceived value, uses and structure during its lifetime.[3] The evolution and utilization of telecommunications have also differed somewhat from state to state, in the face of differing social and economic conditions.

The next portion of this chapter considers some of these differences and influences in the evolution of telecommunications systems and their ability to provide universal access and service. However, a detailed examination of the factors affecting the evolution of telecommunications, and their implications for development, in even one Western nation is beyond the scope of this chapter. Therefore, rather than launch into a history of the evolution of telecommunications, emphasis will be placed on the examination of the influence of several sociopolitical factors and policies that shaped the development of telecommunications in the United States and several European states. Specifically, the following sections consider how those factors impacted on the speed in which those systems were able to comprehensively diffuse telecommunications and, thus, their ability to achieve the full potential of the impact of telecommunications on development. This will allow the consideration of how different factors and/or policies had different impacts in other countries of the developed world.

---

[3]For example, many early telephone innovators envisioned the telephone as a mass communication device. (see Briggs, 1977; Marvin, 1988).

TELECOMMUNICATIONS AND DEVELOPMENT
IN THE UNITED STATES

As the United States is generally acknowledged to be one of the world's most "developed" nations, as well as a leader in the development and diffusion of telecommunications, it seems appropriate to begin our examination with a consideration of the interaction between telecommunications and development there.

Numerous factors have shaped the development of telecommunications in the United States, and have thus also influenced the impact of telecommunications. Although some factors are related to the nature of the country and its citizens, several are the results of government policy, and are therefore of greater interest. The key policies discussed in this chapter are the preference for private ownership, the role of patents, and the nature of government regulation, particularly in determining the mechanism for funding telecommunications.

One basic area of both social and economic influence lies in the patterns of the ownership and financing of telecommunications. It is a general tenet of critical analysis that owners control organizations and, thus, behavior. Structural approaches are somewhat less conspiratorial, yet generally concur that the need for funds gives power to those who influence or control funding. Although this may be obvious for private firms, even public and cooperative organizations must be concerned with behaving in a way that is satisfactory to those who control needed resources. Telecommunications firms, with substantial and continuing investment requirements, are particularly susceptible to the need to ensure a continuing flow of funds.

The emphasis on private ownership for telecommunications media in the United States is an outgrowth of the First Amendment to the U.S. Constitution and prevailing social attitudes (Pool, 1983). The inherent distrust of governmental power, particularly over forms of communication, kept a focus on private ownership and operation. The combination of a general capitalistic economy and this emphasis on private ownership has meant that the funds for telecommunications have predominantly needed to come from the provision of services to users. In general terms, the long term survival of telecommunications has been based on the need to identify and serve some customer base. Additionally, growth and/or expansion of telecommunications came from some combination of the growth of the customer base and/or the provision of new or improved services. Thus, there was a continuing motivation for telecommunications to expand and innovate.

The telegraph was first implemented in the United States in 1844, with funding supplied in part from a federal subsidy. In spite of several early appeals to the state to assume ownership and control of this new communications technology, the state left development and expansion to the private sector (Brock, 1981, Czitrom, 1982). Despite some early skepticism, the concept of instantaneous communication with the more distant regions of the country and the dream of forging a new nation together fed the development and extension of the telegraph.

The early visions of individuals communicating directly with one another over the telegraph did not manifest itself. Early telegraph systems found themselves relying heavily on a few key users: merchants, traders, railroads and the newspapers (Brock, 1981; Czitrom, 1982). Although the initial direct contribution of the telegraph to extending markets and knowledge was limited, the benefits accruing to the early heavy users fostered expansion of both the system and the markets. The heavy use of the telegraph by newspapers was instrumental in the evolution of the modern mass newspaper, which in turn further promoted the rise of mass society and mass markets. The efficiencies gained by the early merchants and traders also promoted the development of mass markets and mass-marketing techniques. The impact of the telegraph on the developing markets, however, extended further than the creation of demand. DuBoff (1983) argued that the telegraph, by improving the functioning of markets, and enhancing competition, stimulated and strengthened the social forces promoting monopolization.

The success of the telegraph in serving the newspaper industry, and the realization of the contribution made by the expansion of access to information and knowledge, further contributed to the rise of an educated middle class and a further demand for knowledge. The impact of the telegraph on newspapers also had a secondary impact on economic development, as the shift to mass orientation, and advertising, contributed to the development of a consumer culture in the United States.

AT&T

The emphasis on innovation was augmented by U.S. patent policy. Slack (1984) argued that the patent policy of the United States had a profound impact on both the initial development of telecommunications and the way in which the new forms of telecommunications firms were organized and operated. Certainly, patents have played a key role in the development of U.S. telecommunications systems. The evolution of AT&T and the U.S. telephone system provides several examples of the impact of patents—the granting of the initial patent on the telephone gave the Bell system a virtual monopoly on telephony in the United States, at least during the life of the patent. AT&T was notorious in the early years for pursuing competitors for patent violations (Brooks, 1976; Dills, 1941; Garnet, 1985; Goulden, 1968).

However, the early AT&T did not learn one key lesson from their initial patent; they devoted their energies to legal battles and maximizing profits rather than continuing to invent and innovate. Thus, when the key patents expired in the 1890s, competitors rushed into the field and had gained 51% of the market by 1907 (Faulhaber, 1987). By failing to continue to innovate, and patent, AT&T relinquished their control of the U.S. market. Later recognizing this failure, AT&T, under the leadership of Theodore Vail, sought to regain control of the technology. Vail did this by emphasizing the emerging area of long-distance service, where the link between technological innovation and the quality of service was stronger, and where AT&T was able to use their technology to establish a competitive advantage. Determined to not again fail to control technology, AT&T later established and funded Bell Labs as a major research & development lab to serve as a continuing source of system and corporate vitality (Temin, 1987).

Because the telephone company was not a state monopoly in the United States, it had to use means other than state power to try to maintain its monopoly status. One clear way was through the patent process. The legal rights given patent holders, and the short term of those rights, provided considerable benefits to those who not only innovated, but who continued to innovate. The short terms of those rights meant that the greatest advantage was afforded those who continued to innovate, who could string together a sequence of pivotal patents. If AT&T could control the key patents, they could control the industry, and assure its place. This meant that AT&T had to be continually engaged in research and development to ensure a stream of key patents. Unlike state monopolies, AT&T had two clear incentives to encourage further development of equipment and standards: the patent laws of the United States, and its funding patterns.

However, this time AT&T's attempt to expand and rebuild its earlier monopoly position came in conflict with changing social mores. In the early 1900s both popular sentiment and public policy against monopolists had strengthened. In 1912, AT&T was threatened with an antitrust suit and an investigation by the overseeing federal regulatory agency, the Interstate Commerce Commission (ICC). AT&T was also facing increasing local regulation by states and local communities. AT&T fought these developments by accommodation, by acceding to regulation with certain protections. In fact, this seemed to be more than mere accommodation: AT&T more or less attempted to forge a partnership with the public sector (Faulhaber, 1987; Temin, 1987).

After a period of strong competition, AT&T made a deal with the federal government (Brooks, 1976). AT&T accepted the status of a regulated monopoly, in return for guaranteed returns that would facilitate its ability to attract capital. AT&T saw itself as a "benevolent giant," developing a "powerful corporate culture framed in terms of service and technological progress" (Temin, 1987, p. 17). Regulators at the state level would limit competition and set prices that guaranteed a reasonable rate of return. The fact that rates were set by public bodies helped to ensure a customer-service orientation and that investments in equipment were appropriate.

There was a subtle interplay between regulation and economics at work. Regulators preferred investments in technology and plant with long service lives, and thus long depreciation schedules, which can help keep rates low (Cherry, 1985, Faulhaber, 1987). AT&T, although seeking to maintain control through innovation, was also concerned about the possible impact of unanticipated innovation, of too rapid technological change that could destroy the value of existing capital assets. These factors fostered a preference for relatively slow, but steady, innovation. It also tended to emphasize the single policy goal of achieving universal service (Faulhaber, 1987). Both factors contributed to the rise of a high-quality, widely available basic service.

Further, Temin (1987) has suggested that the differing rate-setting mechanisms utilized over the years have also had significant, and differing, impacts on society and the evolution of the U.S. telephone system. Temin suggested that there were three basic pricing strategies: rate of return pricing, uniform pricing, and what was known as the "separations process" of assigning costs to separate portions of the system.

Rate of return pricing, based as it was on historical trends of investment, promoted steady, consistent, planned investment. This funding mechanism, basing returns on capital investment, provided an incentive to innovate and upgrade equipment on a regular, continuing basis. The shift to uniform pricing mechanisms after World War I tended to promote telephone use throughout the country by averaging costs. This mechanism did provide the opportunity for competitors to jump into areas where service costs were lower.[4] However, this would have a negative impact on many of the groups regulatory bodies sought to serve, creating tensions between the regulatory body and existing operators. The existing operators would pressure the regulatory body into barring new entrants in fear of competitors' cream-skimming behavior. Uniform pricing then also had the effect of encouraging regulators to restrict competition.

The third pricing mechanism developed in 1943 in response to the growing complexity of the U.S. telecommunication system (Temin, 1987). It was, in particular, a response to the issue of how to price long-distance calls. Because long-distance calls utilized local facilities as well as the long-distance lines, regulators faced a quandary in determining the basis for long-distance charges. Basing charges solely on the long-distance segment would keep long-distance prices low, but would pass on the local segment costs to local users. This seemed unfair, and thus the "separations process"

---

[4]This refers to the notion of cream skimming. If prices for some service to a particular market segment are significantly higher than actual costs, a competitor could elect to serve only that segment, charge lower prices, and remain profitable. The existing company could not match those prices and maintain profits while continuing to serve more costly segments. The original firm, to compete, would have to lower prices in the less costly sector, which would benefit that group, but would also have to either raise prices in more expensive segments or stop serving those segments altogether.

was designed to include some portion of local basis in the long distance costs. This had the effect of reducing local service costs while increasing long-distance charges. It contributed to the cream-skimming problem, but also had the advantage of promoting universal service by keeping basic local service prices low (Temin, 1987).

The various pricing mechanisms, working on a private, profit-oriented operator had an additional impact. All of the pricing mechanisms were based heavily on the historical and on the capital, fixed-cost basis of telephone operations. Private telephone firms could take advantage of this by trying to expand demand for services, the additional revenues contributing highly to profits. It was thus in the phone companies' interest to work to continually expand demand for their services. Further, the flat-rate pricing prevalent throughout this period for most public customers also encouraged additional use of the system.

The regulation of the telephone industry after the Kingsbury agreement[5] occurred primarily at the state level. State regulatory boards were loath to include investments and costs incurred outside their service areas in the bases for rate calculations, which tended to promote both decentralization and state-wide consolidation (Garnet, 1985). On the other hand, the continuing need for large amounts of capital encouraged a degree of horizontal development—the rise of a single corporate structure that had the resources to obtain the best rates for investment capital. Garnet suggested that these conflicting influences lead to the rise of AT&T as an amalgamation of regional service companies.

The emphasis on expansion also contributed to social development, as firms sought to maximize their customer base by including as many segments of the population as possible and encouraging maximum use of the system. This was encouraged even further in the United States by policies designed to promote extension of telecommunications services to rural areas by underwriting construction of telecommunications by land grants (for the telegraph), and by cheap loans (for telephone companies). In urban areas, states and cities used pricing policies to further this goal of equal access and uniform service (Brooks, 1976). This emphasis on inclusion has profound social and political ramifications, helping to empower citizens and groups in a democracy (Pool, 1983). Both are social values often associated with the concept of development (Badham, 1986; Etzioni, 1986).

---

[5]The Kingsbury agreement was reached between AT&T officials and U.S. government representatives. In essence, AT&T agreed to being a regulated monopoly with a guaranteed rate of return and, in exchange, agreed to not enter into competition with other existing phone companies or acquire other existing phone companies. The agreement also stated that AT&T would interconnect and offer its long-distance service to all other phone companies. The agreement provided the foundation for the U.S. notion of a regulated monopoly offering universal access.

THE BREAKUP OF AT&T

U.S. policies placed the nation in a strong position to be able to react to, and take advantage of, technological change, which today seems to be the driving force in modern telecommunications markets (Baughcum, 1986). Nevertheless, as discussed previously, the monopoly structure and high capital investment requirements of telecommunications combined to create a tendency to slow down innovation. The pace of technological advance had so accelerated by the 1960s, however, that the tendency towards slow but steady innovation started to become a problem rather than an advantage. Technological advances were lowering entry barriers, and encouraging more competitive markets. These growing competitive forces, in fact, led to the rise of major competitors for the regulated telecommunications monopolies in the United States. This eventually led to the breakup of the AT&T in 1984 (Horwitz, 1989).

The court case resulting in the divestiture, and residual fears of monopolies, however, have some potential implications for the future development of telecommunications in the United States (Baughcum, 1986; Faulhaber, 1987; Horwitz, 1989). The courts and other federal policies have severely restricted the ability of the component telephone companies to enter new telecommunications fields, and have resulted in limiting their ability to adopt new technologies and provide new services. At a time when U.S. politicians and academics are calling for the development of a high capacity information infrastructure, regulators are hampering the ability of those firms most interested in, and most suited for, the development of such an infrastructure from building such a network (Faulhaber, 1987; Lansing & Bates, 1992).[6]

The early development of telecommunications in the United States clearly benefited from three aspects of industrial structure and policy. Perhaps the single most important aspect was the emphasis on private ownership, and the reliance on providing private customer service. This heavy reliance on private customers put an emphasis on providing a broad range of high-quality services, and on expansion to universal service. This drive for adding customers helped to spur expansion of telecommunications outside urban areas (Brock, 1981). This notion of universal service as a major goal was supported both directly and indirectly through various state policies (Borchadt, 1970; Pool, 1983). The second aspect promoting the development of telecommunications was U.S. patent policy, which rewarded continuing innovation. Finally,

---

[6]As this book went to press, the U.S. Congress has passed a rewrite of telecommunications law which would remove almost all of the business entry restrictions imposed on a variety of telecommunications firms (broadcasters, cable companies, and telephone companies), allowing each to enter each other's markets and to provide new services, thereby fostering competition, innovation, and the development of new communication systems through the removal of some artificial barriers.

the funding systems underlying much of U.S. telecommunications rewarded both innovation and the expansion of services (Faulhaber, 1987). These three factors combined to place a strong emphasis on providing high quality, innovative networks and services to the whole nation.

Although these factors promoted the rise of telecommunications networks, two other factors contributed to their impact. The common carrier status of the primary telecommunications networks, and the philosophical foundations of the First Amendment's emphasis on freedom of speech, opened the network to a wide range of uses, many of which were unforeseen at the time (Pool, 1983). It freed users of the network to take the fullest, broadest advantage of telecommunications. This has helped to broaden the impact of telecommunications in the United States.

Second, the fact that the telegraph and the telephone were two separate private monopolies aided in the early expansion of telecommunications. In countries where telephone and telegraph services were operated by the same organization, telephone service, particularly long-distance service, was often delayed in attempts to preserve telegraph revenues and protect investment in telegraph systems (Brock, 1981). In the United States, as both firms were private, the telephone system was free to compete and eventually largely superseded the telegraph system.

The general impact of the regulated private monopoly structure of the American telephone industry, and the various mechanisms for pricing services, was to foster an innovative network geared to maximizing diffusion and use of the system. This emphasis on universal service was also encouraged directly by a series of government policies. The effectiveness of these influences is clearly seen in the fact that telephone penetration and usage rates in the United States, particularly in rural areas, was among the world's highest throughout the 1900s (Saunders et al., 1983). It is also reflected in the general perception that the United States had perhaps the world's best telephone system.

However, as Baughcum (1986) noted, the United States is unique in its institutional structure, mix of privatization and regulation, and range of local, state, and national regulatory agencies. The development of telecommunications in the United States, although certainly contributing to the rise of the country as an industrial and economic power, was also influenced by the special character of the country, and some appropriate, or lucky, policy choices. Although an examination of this history can provide some insights to other nations, it should be remembered that the U.S. approach is not necessarily a prescription for development.

TELECOMMUNICATIONS AND DEVELOPMENT IN WESTERN EUROPE

The initial stages of telecommunications development in Europe often paralleled those in the United States. In most cases, initial investments in telecommunications were made by private entrepreneurs. Initial development was further fostered by the proximity of large cities and the expanding rail network. However, due to differences in social and economic needs, the further development of telecommunications in Europe tended to differ in fundamental ways from that in the United States, with different implications for continuing development. Contrary to the evolution of U.S. telecommunications, most European countries soon shifted telecommunications from private to public control (Brock, 1981; Noam, 1992). This pattern started with the telegraph, whose ability to deliver written messages over distances was seen in part as a threat to the existing state postal monopoly.

The pattern of early development was generally repeated with the telephone (Brock, 1981; Noam, 1992). Telephone service was initiated in many European countries by private firms. However, in many parts of Europe the initial advantages of numbers of large cities close to one another was offset by the lack of a sizable middle class, and a large number of dialects (Dills, 1941). The lack of a sizable middle class reduced the market for what was still a moderately expensive service in the early days of telephone service, and the diversity of languages and dialects further reduced the efficiency of a communication system that relied on the spoken word. These factors tended to reduce initial overall demand for telephone service in many parts of Europe.

Despite these handicaps, there was considerable early interest in telephony, and many states soon sought to protect both their postal and telegraph services by restricting telephony—long-distance service in particular (Brock, 1981). As interest in the telephone expanded, most European states continued to try to maintain control and limit competition, usually by incorporating telephone services into the existing state public communication monopoly, forming the basic structure known as the Post, Telephone, and Telegraph (PTT). The various PTT administrations gained tremendous power over time, partly through the expansion of telecommunications, and partly because they were able to establish alliances with key political and economic constituencies in society (Noam, 1992).

The development of the PTT structure had a number of implications for telecommunications diffusion and innovation. In the early years, expansion of telecommunications networks and services was often geared towards serving certain political or economic ends, rather than meeting customer needs (de Gournay, 1988; Dills, 1941; Noam, 1992). The desire to protect existing telecommunications systems, and their considerable capital investment, tended to discourage the development of competing services (Brock, 1981; Noam, 1992). Becker (1993) argued that this led the PTTs to engage in a conscious strategy to suppress competitive technologies, such as the telephone. Finally, the need to rely on public funds for financing expansion and innovation could also work to slow adoption of new services and technologies as the state's priorities shifted.

Within this general framework, however, various differences in the structure, funding, and evolution of the PTTs have set European nations down a number of distinct paths in the development of telecommunications systems. These differences can also be linked to variations in the economic and social development of these nations. More importantly, they can be fairly clearly linked to the speed in which various systems reached the goal of universal service.

UNITED KINGDOM

Early telecommunications development in the United Kingdom actually outpaced that of the United States, in part due to its more developed state. Many of the early innovations in telegraphy were made in the United Kingdom, and telegraph lines quickly spread throughout the country. British interests were also behind the early and rapid diffusion of undersea cables. Quite similarly, British interests quickly recognized the communication potential of Marconi's radio telegraph and financed much of the early development of radio—there seemed to be no lack of interest in new communications systems.

This early focus resulted from the existence of clear uses for the new media. The developed economy had already created demands for information and control systems. Unlike the United States, the business community in the United Kingdom recognized early on the usefulness of the telegraph and eagerly adopted that innovation. Both the emerging British rail system and the developing newspaper industry supported early telegraph systems, entering into a symbiotic relationship (Brock, 1981) like that in the United States (Czitrom, 1982).

In the early years, the telegraph system in Great Britain was private, with a second private firm entering the market in 1850. Competition between the two firms reduced prices and stimulated demand; so much so that profits remained high and a third firm entered the market in 1862. By 1865, the three competitors had formed a cartel. The formation of the cartel stabilized the system, and led to a period of profit maximizing at the expense of system and service improvements (Brock, 1981).

Growing dissatisfaction with the cartel, particularly by newspapers, led to an interest in nationalizing the telegraph industry. The British government bought out the existing private operators in 1868, at what was arguably a highly inflated price amounting to 20 times the 1868 profits (Noam, 1992). The new Post Office monopoly expanded service and reduced prices, quadrupling demand over the next 10 years (Brock, 1981).

However, the revenues from telegraph operations were often not able to cover its expenses, creating an inability to retire the considerable debt incurred in the purchase of the system.

The introduction and development of telephony in Great Britain began in 1878, and was accomplished primarily by private firms. The Post Office, burdened with debt from the acquisition of the telegraph industry, expressed little interest in establishing a second telecommunication system, although as the legal monopolist the Post Office soon reserved long-distance service in order to protect its telegraph operations (Brock, 1981; Noam, 1992). Private firms were granted limited licenses to provide local service.

Initially, high prices, the lack of connections to nearby systems, and the limited range of local exchanges kept demand low. The existing telegraph and transportation networks provided cheap and reliable alternatives. The early private firms, however, concentrated their efforts on serving the new industrial regions and rapidly expanded. Much of this success was attributed to the British policy of granting regional licenses to private firms (de Gournay, 1988). The emphasis on regional systems integrated the network with the local economy, placing more emphasis on commercial and industrial uses and adoption of the telephone by the growing middle class.

The fact that the early development of the telephone system in Britain was, in contrast to the United States, fairly slow actually falls in line with the argument that telecommunications was seen as essentially a message-sending system at this early stage. By the time that the telephone had been developed, the value of a fast and efficient communication system had been recognized, and fast and efficient postal and telegraph systems were in place. The presence of what many saw as the world's best communication system mitigated the demand for an alternative—the telephone (Perry, 1977). This led to a general lack of public interest and investment in telephony, and quite a poor telephone system, initially. This lack of interest was perhaps furthered by the Post Office's initial view that the telephone was a competitor to its telegraph monopoly. However, with the growing recognition of the intrinsic value of the telephone, particularly with regard to its ability to interconnect, the British government stepped in to promote it.

In 1884, the Post Office began to install telephone exchanges itself and provide interconnecting and long-distance service to other local exchanges. As the legal monopolist, the Post Office also began licensing competing service providers in many areas. Although some competition ensued, there was also considerable consolidation among the private telephone companies leading to the creation of the National Telephone Company (NTC). With attempts to control the NTC through competition and regulation being largely unsuccessful, the Post Office arranged to buy out private firms at the expiration of their license. In 1911, the unification of the public communication system under a state monopoly was complete.

The early period of private competition in both telegraphy and telephony did work to promote and diffuse telecommunications services. Even after the telephone system was nationalized, telephone penetration rates in the United Kingdom remained among the highest in Europe (Noam, 1992). However, growth rates did slow initially, as the PTT kept telephone tariffs high, and telegraph rates low. The PTT did pursue a strategy of universal service, but seemed to define it more in terms of universal access to reliable and high-quality service. Pricing and cross-subsidization tended to keep penetration rates, particularly among some sectors of the population, fairly low for most of the 20th century (Noam, 1992).

As with most of Europe, Great Britain seemed to recognize the growing importance of achieving true universal service and integrating all segments of the population, and all sectors of the economy, into the telecommunications system. In the 1980s, it began a series of moves designed to privatize the telecommunications sector, and introduce competition, as spurs to more rapid development and diffusion of telecommunication services (Noam, 1992). With these moves, penetration rates did substantially increase.

FRANCE

Development of the telephone in France was also fairly slow, and until the 1970s, the French telephone system was considerably less advanced than the systems in Great Britain, Germany, and the United States. As with the British, the French recognized early the power of telecommunications to extend communications and the impact that could have on society. However, they seemed to be somewhat more concerned with its implications for political power and control than with economic power and value. Attali & Stourdze (1977) suggested that the process of communication was seen somewhat differently in France, as a mechanism for state control rather than as a tool for economic development. The telegraph, and later the telephone, were seen as important devices to be controlled by the state, and that meant that their use would be restricted. Its value as an aid to economic development was secondary.

The French government was an early adopter of distance communication systems, having established by 1837 a national optical telegraph system as a government monopoly within the postal monopoly (Noam, 1992). The first electrical telegraph line was constructed in 1845, but was maintained for government use only. Over time the telegraph system expanded, even allowing limited public access after 1851, although it remained primarily for governmental use (Brock, 1981).

Telephony in France began as a private enterprise in 1878, following the pattern in the United States and much of Europe. At the time, the ruling government was advancing the concept of economic liberalism in public services—seeking to shift the burden of risk and investment to the private sector (Noam, 1992). Restrictive licenses were granted to several firms. However, beginning in 1884 the private company resulting from the merger of these various early competitors became involved in a series of disputes with the public administration, which virtually halted progress in the private development of telephony until the system was nationalized in 1889 (de Gournay, 1988). After nationalization, several factors seemed to further slow development. Nationalization of the telephone industry seemed to result in a policy for telephony that did not allow for business needs or the development of lateral networks. Extension of long-distance lines tended to reinforce the traditional centralization in Paris (de Gournay, 1988).

The slow growth of those networks was further hampered by a financing strategy that required those seeking service not only buy to their own sets, but to pay in advance for the full cost of extending the service and to be reimbursed (without interest) only from whatever profits the line generated that were not otherwise absorbed by the state system, which would also maintain ownership (de Gournay, 1988). This tended to overemphasize service to those with the necessary funds: local government officials and the land owning elite. Between the administrative emphasis on using telecommunications as a mechanism to further centralized state control and a financing system that imposed significant costs to potential users, the early structure of French telecommunications began to set barriers between the telephone system and the vast majority of the French people. Although the national PTT seemed to be aware of these problems as early as 1900, de Gournay argued that "the weight of political considerations and social differentiation seems to have outweighed economic rationality or functional rationality" (p. 337).

Despite an awareness of these difficulties, a problematic political situation and financing difficulties prevented the PTT from obtaining either the appropriations or the outside funding necessary to build and expand a very capital-intensive telephone system. The lack of funds for innovation and expansion not only kept the system smaller than many others in the United States and Europe, but the system that was in place was expensive, congested, and very unreliable. Early statistics showed, for example, that on one single long-distance line there were more than 200 interruptions in a single year, with an average duration of more than 14 hours (Noam, 1992).

The slow start in telecommunications development in France was exacerbated by two world wars and the French government's underinvestment in telecommunications. In the period of economic conservatism in the 1920s, the considerable capital requirements of the telephone network prompted consideration of denationalization: a return to private operations (Noam, 1992). Although political considerations prevented privatization, the PTT was reorganized with a directive to serve industrial and commercial purposes, and to cover its costs. The reorganization also allowed the PTT access to special loans, which enabled it to begin to slowly expand and update the system. However, the French system still lagged behind most of Europe. The pattern of underinvestment continued for nearly 30 years following the World War II. The unreliable and inadequate telephone network became a stumbling block in the otherwise rapidly developing French economy (Noam, 1992).

A government commissioned report by Nora & Minc (1980) suggested that France's current, relatively poor telecommunications sector was likely to prove to be a significant hindrance to further economic development, particularly in the information sector. Hudson (1984) indicated that this underinvestment resulted in reduced levels of productivity and competitiveness in the French economy, amounting to a loss of 2% of GNP in 1972. The losses due to poor or nonexistent telephone facilities in the early 1970s were estimated to amount to at least twice the total amount invested in telecommunications during that period.

As a result of these and similar studies, the French government embarked on a massive effort to bring its telecommunications systems up to world standards. Huge investments were made in updating and extending the telecommunication network. The goal was not only to bring the French telecommunications up to par with the rest of Europe, but to develop a high technology industrial base strong enough to compete in a global market (Noam, 1992; Nora & Minc, 1980). The government also invested quite heavily in certain leading edge technologies and systems, such as public packet-switched networks and videotext. This brought state investment in France up to the level of other major European nations (Noam, 1992; Voge, 1986).

It can be argued that until recently France has been fairly slow to recognize the economic value of telecommunications. Whereas the Nora and Minc (1980) report did emphasize the importance of telecommunications for the future economy, some have argued that the thrust of this report was to prompt development of telecommunications manufacturing industry, rather than promote the use of telecommunications (Bates, 1988b). It is, however, in the use of telecommunications that the strongest benefits originate.

However, whatever the initial motivations, France seems to have recognized the increasing importance of telecommunications in the new information age. In recent years, France has greatly upgraded basic telecommunications services, and has been at the forefront of developing new networks and services (Voge, 1986). They have also been privatizing and deregulating the more mass-oriented segments of telecommunications. Voge, however, has argued that the French efforts are directed more towards decentralization than U.S.-style deregulation; resulting, perhaps, from the continuing French emphasis on political aspects of control.

GERMANY

Germany's involvement with telecommunications began with the development of a military electrical telegraph in 1846. The Prussian government
soon extended the system, which was opened to public use in 1849 (Brock,
1981), although the government maintained strict control through the monitoring of private messages. Other German states soon introduced their own
state telegraph systems, and with the unification of these states the systems were integrated under the auspices of the postal system in 1876
(Noam, 1992). The telephone was introduced shortly thereafter, with the
Bundespost offering telephone services. In fact, telephone service in
Germany was initially seen as a means of offering telegraph service to smaller post offices that might not be able to afford me full-time services of a
trained telegraph operator (Dills, 1941; Noam, 1992).

Private interests were also interested in developing the telephone.
Several German industrialists, seeing the potential in equipment manufacturing, sought to create and expand the public market for telecommunications.
In conjunction with the Reichspost (with part of its mandate being to serve
the interests of the German economy), the emerging telecommunication
equipment manufacturers began a close alliance with government and business interests (Noam, 1992). After a false start by private interests in
Stuttgart, the Post Office declared a state monopoly and began constructing
urban exchanges in 1881 (Brock, 1981).

The growth of the telephone system in Germany was slowed, however, by several factors. First, local exchanges were built only after the
accumulation of sufficient long-term service commitments to ensure the economic success of the service. Similarly, long-distance lines were constructed only after communities guaranteed profitability. Brock (1981) noted that
although this financing method was not as restrictive as that of the French, it
imparted a conservative bias that impeded rapid development.

In addition to the financial restrictions, the German PTT only built
long-distance lines where demand exceeded the capacity of the existing telegraph service. Through this means, and the setting of fairly high service
rates, the Reichspost was able to control the growth of the telephone system's competition with its postal and telegraph services. In fact, the investment and development strategy seemed to be designed to replace new telegraph investment with telephone investment, rather than displacing existing
telegraph investment (Brock, 1981). The Reichspost treated the telephone
as a supplement to telegraph services, rather than as a competitor.

Both factors tended to slow the early expansion of telephone services, and to concentrate it in urban, high demand areas and in the provision
of local service. The emphasis on urban development put the early focus on
local, rather than regional or supraregional, services, which tended to reduce

the value, and thus demand for, telephone services. The alliance with equipment manufacturers, however, placed an emphasis on equipment acquisition, on continuing innovation and expansion of the network. Because most of the destructive force of World War I occurred outside of its borders, Germany tended to benefit from this period of increased innovation and the expanded exposure the general population had to the benefits of long-distance telecommunications. The 1920s was a period of steady expansion, when the telephone began to assert itself as a social and economic force (Becker, 1993).

Unlike during World War I, much of the telecommunications infrastructure in Germany was destroyed or damaged during World War II. With the end of the war, the German PTT was reconstructed as a separate administration, existing to support and foster industrial policies as much as to meet public and private telecommunications needs. The Bundespost continued to operate an equipment procurement quota system dating from 1933, which, along with the steady growth of capital investment, facilitated recovery and production planning by those firms (Noam, 1992).

The emphasis on promoting and protecting existing industry and infrastructure was beneficial to those sectors, but tended to slow overall growth. Tariffs were also used to limit demand and regulate growth. The policy of slow but steady development hindered the growth of telecommunications among the general public until the 1970s. At that time, however, under the Social Democratic government, there was considerable expansion in the public sector and a restructuring of the tariff structure, helping to reduce the considerable variation in penetration among social and economic classes (Brock, 1981).

Although the German PTT is financed independently from the federal budget and is required to cover its own costs, the setting of rates and tariffs is highly influenced by political concerns. Neumann (1986) suggested that the prices for telecommunications services in Germany are political prices, and have very little to do with economic efficiencies or costs. An analysis of the 1979 rate structure showed considerable cross-subsidization to meet social goals. Further, Neumann noted that the revenues from telecommunications provides considerable subsidies to postal operations, as well as to the federal government. He indicated that the postal subsidy alone contributes some 15% to the price of telephone services in Germany. Dissatisfaction with the pace of change and pressure from within and without the system forced Germany to reconsider the nature of its telecommunications system in the 1970s and 1980s. After a great deal of political wrangling and several false starts, the Bundespost was restructured in 1989. The reform created three separate public corporations, separating telecommunications from postal services and removing the system from direct government control. After some complaints that the new telecommunications arm was still using its high tariffs and its ability to limit access to block competition, stronger legislation was drafted (Noam, 1992).

However, the unification of Germany in 1990 shifted the focus of governmental concerns by creating an urgent need to upgrade East Germany's antiquated infrastructure. The East German PTT was merged into the Western entity, which then undertook a massive effort to bring the telecommunications network in East Germany up to par with the West by 1997. A key component of the plan was to use cellular service to reduce pressure on the standard network while it was rebuilt and extended (Noam, 1992). The scope of the high financial demands placed on the system by unification, taking place at the same time as revenue-eroding liberalization, enhanced the arguments of some traditionalists debating slowing down the pace of change.

The structure and pricing mechanisms of German telecommunications seemed to have been developed primarily to meet industrial and, to a lesser extent, political goals. The history of state monopoly operation of telecommunications in conjunction with postal services, almost from the beginning, meant that development of new, competitive services was hampered by the need to protect and subsidize existing services. This was accomplished by keeping early tariffs high and by restricting investment in new systems. Further, when development occurred, it was driven more by the needs and capacities of equipment manufacturers than by the needs of the service consumers. Although the relationship with the telecommunications industry probably helped to ensure that the German telecommunications system was of fairly high quality, it did slow growth. The high tariffs aided in restricting the size and scope of the potential market, limiting the ability of telecommunications to contribute in that way to general development, at least until the rate structure was revised in the 1970s.

TRENDS IN TELECOMMUNICATIONS DEVELOPMENT

In all four of the states considered, the early competitive telecommunications systems evolved into monopoly structures. There are several factors behind this general trend, the two biggest of which being the efficiencies of scale and the need for sizable capital investment (Brock, 1981; Noam, 1992). The tendency toward monopoly, and its underlying contributing factors, had several broad impacts. First, the sizable capital investments had a tendency to slow down innovation, to prevent existing infrastructure from being devalued. Second, the existence of a single firm providing a range of services allowed for a pricing mechanism to engage in cross-subsidies, leading to distortions that can impact on the size and shape of the market. There was also an incentive for the monopolist to act to maximize the market served, either to prevent competition or mollify public concerns. Monopolists are more likely to be risk-adverse than competitive firms can allow themselves to be. This can be seen in the monopolists' tendency to rely on internally generated capital for investment. As Brock (1981) noted, "the conservative internal financing used by both private and public monopolists made high prices and slow growth appear attractive even if it was not the route to maximum profits" (p. 46). Finally, as a single provider the actions and evolution of the system were heavily tied to the specific motivations of the monopolist. This suggests that the impact of a telecommunication monopoly may vary, and allows for the consideration of how different motivating factors influenced the evolution of telecommunications systems.

One key distinction is between private and public monopolies. The United States developed separate private, regulated monopoly systems for both the telegraph and the telephone, whereas most of Europe followed the route into a public (state) monopoly, usually integrating several forms of communication. Although private monopolists are likely to charge higher prices than those having competition, they must also keep prices low enough to satisfy existing demand and remove any incentive for other firms to enter the market. The regulation of the telecommunications industry in the United States did tend to control prices while maintaining sufficient profitability to allow for fairly rapid development.

On the other hand, a public monopoly with legal barriers to entry has little economic motivation to develop rapidly through the provision of good service and low prices. In Europe, the public monopolists tended to use their market power to protect themselves from risk. Slow development and high tariffs ensured that the monopolist would not find itself with unusable capital investments; this applied especially when the monopolist controlled competing communication systems. Technological innovations were restricted in order to protect established rights in existing methods and high tariffs were often used to limit demand and slow growth.

The various pricing mechanisms and the subsidies and cross-subsidies involved also had a considerable impact on how telecommunications impacted development. For most of its history, rate structures (and public policy) in the United States promoted expansion of telecommunications to all communities. In contrast, until recently most pricing mechanisms among the public monopolies favored those with the most political clout: urban, industrial, and upper- and middle-class users. This tended to slow the expansion of telecommunications under public monopolies, with the consequence that the full value of telecommunications was rarely achieved. In some cases, such as was seen in France, the weakness of the telecommunications system actually seemed to restrict development.

Although eventually moving to monopolies, both the United States and the United Kingdom benefited from extensive periods of intense competition. Under competition, the striving for competitive advantage through innovation and/or low prices led to rapid development—it allowed firms to test demand elasticity, and to find that lower prices significantly increased demand for telecommunication services. The search for competitive advantage promoted innovation in technology and services and ensured the rapid diffusion of practicable innovations.

The existing monopolies have largely done an adequate job of extending their telecommunications networks so that services are available universally. However, outside of the United States the achievement of high levels of network penetration is a very recent phenomenon. As Becker (1993) noted, "the universality hoped for with the beginnings of telephony proved to be correct, but only as a potential and not as a concrete fact" (p. 119). With the growing recognition of the value of telecommunications in the global marketplace (Akwule, 1992; Masuda, 1981; Noam, 1992; Pool, 1990) and the increasing speed of technological innovation, many states are reconsidering the benefits of competition in telecommunications.

In recent years, Western Europe and the United States appear to have recognized the growing importance of telecommunications to continuing economic and social development (Noam, 1992; Snow, 1986). Governments and PTTs have undertaken a wide range of policies in recent years all geared to improve telecommunications networks and services and to better position operators to respond to the continuing rapid changes in the field.

There have been three key policy thrusts: development and expansion of high capacity digital networks (usually under the rubric of ISDN and/or fiber-optic); the development of computer-based information services, such as videotext; and the promotion of privatization and deregulation, with the expansion of service providers and a competitive focus that will drive consumer demand and adoption. Although the first two policies appear to be designed to develop specific aspects of telecommunications, and to rectify existing deficiencies, the emphasis on deregulation is aimed towards providing greater incentives for innovation and expansion. These policies are geared, therefore, to traditional industrial economic development as well as the development of human capital (Woods, 1993) and new information services. These actions seem to be positioning the United States and Western Europe for rapid future development in an era of global competition.

LESSONS FOR FUTURE PLANNING

Planning the development of telecommunications to meet specific needs or goals can be a problematic exercise. The history of past telecommunications policy amply illustrates the pitfalls of presuming that we know all of the factors involved in shaping the final effects of our attempts to design systems to meet specific needs. However, although there have been numerous failures, there have also been successes. We may not know everything required to accurately predict specific successes, but we can generate lessons from examining past efforts.

Several such lessons can be learned from this chapter's discussion. Applying these to the construction of specific policy, however, depends on knowing what the basic underlying goal of the policy is. Although these may certainly vary, for the sake of this analysis I will assume that the basic goal of telecommunications policy is to maximize long-term economic and social benefits, to maximize development.

The basic lesson to be learned is that those long-term benefits are maximized when the full potential of universal service is realized. Benefits arise from use of the system, not merely from construction of the network. Further, those benefits are maximized when all sectors of the society are fully integrated into the system. The greater the reach and the more comprehensive the scope, the greater the value of telecommunication services to individual users as well as to society at large. Thus, if one is seeking to maximize benefits, policy should be designed to maximize both the diffusion of the network and the adoption of its various services.

The question of how this can be accomplished still remains. Here, again, lessons can be learned from the history of telecommunications development. One is to not confuse social policy with industrial policy. Often, policy is designed to protect or promote specific industries or firms. History indicates that whereas such policy may well be effective in those specific goals, it also tends to retard expansion and development in other areas. The lessons of state monopoly protection of earlier technologies and the history of German industrial connections suggest that such policies retard development and the achievement of the goal of universal service.

A related lesson comes in the form of considering the structure of telecommunications systems. History certainly shows that policy can shape structure, both directly and indirectly. There has been a continuing debate over the relative benefits of competition versus monopoly in telecommunications; there do seem to be some natural monopoly aspects to many telecommunications technologies, which suggest certain benefits of monopoly structures. Among the benefits are greater integration and interconnection, ease of raising the often substantial capital needed for construction of the network, and the facilitation of cross-subsidization. On the other hand, there are also several benefits to competitive structures. Competitive firms have stronger motivation to engage in innovation and expansion of networks and services, as well as to minimize prices.

The consideration of the various structures in this chapter does suggest several general lessons. First, there should be competition, at least between competing technologies. A monopolist controlling competing technologies has strong incentives to restrict newer systems. The history of telecommunications in Europe shows a consistent pattern of monopolists retarding the development of telephony to protect the telegraph and postal systems. In contrast, the battle between the telegraph and telephone monopolies in the United States stimulated the growth of telephony. Second, competition encourages diffusion and adoption of telecommunication, as long as there are sufficient profits to acquire the funds necessary for capital investment. However, a perfectly competitive marketplace in networks may not, long-term, be in the best interest of society. A competitive oligopoly structure or a regulated private monopoly may achieve many of the benefits of both structures.

The third basic lesson is that tariffs and pricing policy can have a significant impact in promoting or retarding system expansion, the achievement of high penetration rates, and the goal of universal service. Tariff structures have often been used to limit demand. They have also been used to stimulate demand, often through the use of cross-subsidies, however. This is most clearly demonstrated in the fact that whereas the telecommunications systems in Germany and Great Britain had largely achieved the potential for universal service by the 1960s, penetration rates remained low until the revision of tariff structures. Similarly, the removal of hidden cross-subsidies in U.S. tariff structures after the breakup of AT&T had a slightly negative effect on telephone penetration rates.

These lessons can provide guidance for states seeking to maximize the potential benefits of telecommunications. How they are applied in a specific social, political, and economic context, however, needs more research.

REFERENCES

Akwule, R. (1992). *Global telecommunications: The technology, administration, and policies.* Boston: Focal Press.

Arndt, H. W. (1978). *The rise and fall of economic growth: A study in contemporary thought* Chicago: University of Chicago Press.

Attali, J., & Stourdze, Y. (1977). The birth of the telephone and economic crisis: The slow death of monologue in French society. In I. S. Pool (Ed.), *The social impact of the telephone* (pp. 97-111). Cambridge, MA: The MIT Press.

Badham, R. J. (1986). *Theories of industrial society.* New York: St. Martin's Press.

Bates, B. J. (1988a). Information as an economic good: Sources of individual and social value. In V. Mosco & J. Wasko (Eds.), *The political economy of information* (pp. 76-94). Madison: University of Wisconsin Press.

Bates, B. J. (1988b). The role of social values in information policy: The cases of France and Japan. In B. D. Ruben (Ed.), *Information and behavior: Volume 2* (pp. 288-307). New Brunswick, NJ: Transaction.

Bates, B. J. (1990). Information systems and society: Potential impacts of alternative structures. *Telecommunications Policy, 14*(2), 151-158.

Bates, B. J. (1993, May). *The macrosocial impact of communication systems: Access, bias, control.* Paper presented at the 43rd International Communication Association conference, Washington, DC.

Baughcum, A. (1986). Deregulation, divestiture, and competition in U. S. telecommunications: Lessons for other countries. In M. Snow (Ed.), *Marketplace for telecommunications: Regulation and deregulation in industrialized democracies* (pp. 69-105). New York: Longman.

Becker, J. (1993). The political economy of early telephony in Germany. In J. Wasko, V. Mosco, & M. Pendakur (Eds.), *Illuminating the blindspots: Essays honoring Dallas W. Smythe* (pp. 111-131). Norwood, NJ: Ablex.

Beniger, J. R. (1986). *The control revolution: Technological and economic origins of the information society.* Cambridge, MA: Harvard University Press.

Borchadt, K. (1970). *Structure and performance of the U.S. communication industry: Government regulation and company planning.* Boston: Division of Research, Harvard Business School.

Briggs, A. (1977). The pleasure telephone: A chapter in the prehistory of the media. In I. S. Pool (Ed.), *The social impact of the telephone* (pp. 40-65). Cambridge, MA: The MIT Press.

Brock, G. W. (1981). *The telecommunications industry: The dynamics of market structure.* Cambridge, MA: Harvard University Press.

Brooks, J. (1976). *Telephone: The first 100 Years.* New York: Harper & Row.

Cherry, C. (1977). The telephone system: Creator of mobility and social change. In I. S. Pool (Ed.), *The social impact of the telephone* (pp. 112-126). Cambridge, MA: MIT Press.

Cherry, C. (1985). *The age of access: Information technology and social revolution.* London: Croom Helm.

Curran, J., Gurevitch, M., & Woolacott, J. (Eds.). (1979). *Mass communication and society.* Beverly Hills, CA: Sage.

Czitrom, D. J. (1982). *Media and the American mind: From Morse to McLuhan.* Chapel Hill: University of North Carolina Press.

de Gournay, C. (1988). Telephone networks in France and Great Britain. In J. Tarr & G. Dupuy (Eds.), *Technology and the rise of the networked city in Europe and America* (pp. 322-338). Philadelphia: Temple University Press.

Dills, M. M. (1941). *The telephone in a changing world.* New York: Longman, Green & Co.

DuBoff, R. (1983). The telegraph and the structure of markets in the United States, 1845-1890. *Research in Economic History, 8,* 253-277.

Etzioni, A. (1986). The American way of economic development. In O. F. Borda (Ed.), *The challenge of social change* (pp. 57-74). London: Sage.

Faulhaber, G. R. (1987). *Telecommunications in turmoil: Technology and public policy.* Cambridge, MA: Balinger.

Garnet, R. W. (1985). *The telephone enterprise: The evolution of the Bell system's horizontal structure, 1876-1909.* Baltimore: Johns Hopkins University Press.

Goulden, J. C. (1968). *Monopoly.* New York: G. P. Putnam's Sons.

Hamelink, C. J. (1988). *The technology gamble: Informatics and public policy: A study of technology choice.* Norwood, NJ: Ablex.

Hilewick, C. L., Deak, E. J., & Heinze, E. (1978). Investment in communications and transportation: Socio-economic impacts on rural development. In A. S. Edelstein, J. E. Bowes, & S. M. Harsel (Eds.), *Information societies: Comparing the Japanese and American experiences* (pp. 135-145). Seattle: International Communication Center.

Horwitz, R. B. (1989). *The irony of regulatory reform: The deregulation of American telecommunications.* New York: Oxford University Press.

Hudson, H. E. (1982). Toward a model for predicting development benefits from telecommunication investment. In M. Jussawalla & D. M. Lamberton (Eds.), *Communication economics and development* (pp. 159-189). Elmsford, NY: Pergamon Press.

Hudson, H. E. (1984). *When telephones reach the village: The role of telecommunications in rural development.* Norwood, NJ: Ablex.

Hudson, H. E. (1988). *A bibliography of telecommunications and socio-economic development.* Norwood, MA: Artech House.

Innis, H. A. (1950). *Empire and communications.* Toronto: University of Toronto Press.

Innis, H. A. (1964). *The bias of communication.* Toronto: University of Toronto Press.

Katz, E., & Szecko, T. (Eds.). (1981). *Mass media and social change.* London: Sage.

Lansing, K. P., & Bates, B. J. (1992). Videotex as public information systems: The French and American experience. *Southwestern Mass Communication Journal, 7*(1), 22-34.

Lerner, D. (1958). *The passing of traditional society.* Glencoe, IL: The Free Press.

Marvin, C. (1988). *When old technologies were new: Thinking about electric communication in the late nineteenth century.* New York: Oxford University Press.

Masuda, Y. (1981). *The information society as post-industrial society.* Bethesda, MD: World Future Society.

Melody, W. H. (1988). Dealing with global networks: Some characteristics of international markets. In G. Muskens & J. Gruppelaar (Eds.), *Global telecommunications networks: Strategic considerations* (pp. 59-73). Dordrecht, Holland: Kluwer Academic Publishers.

Melody, W. H. (1993). On the political economy of communication in the information society. In J. Wasko, V. Mosco, & M. Pendakur (Eds.), *Illuminating the blindspots: Essays honoring Dallas W. Smythe* (pp. 63-81). Norwood, NJ: Ablex.

Middleton, K. P., & Jussawalla, M. (1981). *The economics of communication: A selected bibliography with abstracts.* New York: Pergamon Press.

Mowlana, H., & Wilson, L. J. (1988). *Communication technology and development.* Paris: UNESCO.

Mulgan, G. J. (1990). *Communication and control.* Cambridge: Polity Press.

Neumann, K. (1986). Economic policy toward telecommunications, information, and the media in West Germany. In M. S. Snow (Ed.), *Marketplace for telecommunications: Regulation & deregulation in industrialized democracies* (pp. 131-152). New York: Longman.

Noam, E. (1992). *Telecommunications in Europe.* New York: Oxford University Press.

Noll, R. G. (1986). The political and institutional context of communications policy. In M. S. Snow (Ed.), *Marketplace for telecommunications: Regulation & deregulation in industrialized democracies* (pp. 42-65). New York: Longman.

Nora, S., & Minc, A. (1980). *The computerization of society.* Cambridge, MA: MIT Press.

Perry, C. R. (1977). The British experience 1876-1912: The impact of the telephone during the years of delay. In I. S. Pool (Ed.), *The social impact of the telephone* (pp. 69-96). Cambridge, MA: MIT Press.

Pool, I. S. (Ed.). (1977). *The social impact of the telephone.* Cambridge, MA: MIT Press.

Pool, I. S. (1983). *Technologies of freedom: On free speech in an electronic age.* Cambridge, MA: Harvard University Press.

Pool, I. S. (1990). *Technologies without boundaries: On telecommunications in a global age.* Cambridge, MA: Harvard University Press.

Radojkovic, M. (1984). Eight considerations on new information technology and the development of democracy. *Gazette, 33*(1), 51-58.

Rogers, E. M. (Ed.). (1976). *Communication and development: Critical perspectives.* Beverly Hills, CA Sage.

Rogers, E. M. (1983). *The diffusion of innovations.* New York: The Free Press.

Saunders, R. J., Warford, J. J., & Wellenius, B. (1983). *Telecommunications and economic development.* Baltimore: Johns Hopkins University Press.

Schiller, H. I. (1981). *Who knows: Information in the age of the Fortune 500.* Norwood, NJ: Ablex.

Slack, J. D. (1984). *Communication technologies and society: Conceptions of causality and the politics of technological intervention.* Norwood, NJ: Ablex.

Smith, A. (1983). Telecommunications and the fading of the industrial age. *Political Quarterly, 54*(2), 127-136.

Snow, M. S. (Ed.). (1994). *Marketplace for telecommunications: Regulation & deregulation in industrialized democracies.* White Plains, NY: Longman.

Temin, P. (1987). *The fall of the Bell system: A study in prices and politics.* Cambridge: Cambridge University Press.

Utsumi, T. (1978). Need for a global information system. In A. S. Edelstein, J. E. Bowes, & S. M. Harsel (Eds.), *Information societies: Comparing the Japanese and American experiences* (pp. 79-83). Seattle: International Communication Center.

Varma, B. N. (1980). *The sociology and politics of development: A theoretical study.* London: Routledge & Kegan Paul.

Voge, J. (1986). A survey of French regulatory policy. In M. S. Snow (Ed.), *Marketplace for telecommunications: Regulation & deregulation in industrialized democracies* (pp. 106-130). New York: Longman.

Weber, M. (1947). *The theory of social and economic organization.* Glencoe, IL: The Free Press.

Webster, A. (1984). *Introduction to the sociology of development.* London: Macmillan.

William, P., & Pearce, J. T. (1978). *The vital network: A theory of communication and society.* Westport, CT: Greenwood Press.

Williams, R. (1975). *Television: Technology and cultural form.* New York: Shocken Books.

Williams, R. (1976). *Communications* (3rd ed.). Hammondsworth, Middlesex, England: Penguin.

Winston, B. (1986). *Misunderstanding media.* Cambridge, MA: Harvard University Press.

Wolpert, S. A., & Wolpert, J. F. (1986). *Economics of information.* New York: Van Nostrand Reinhold.

Woods, B. (1993). *Communication, technology and the development of people.* London: Routledge.

CHAPTER 3

A HISTORY OF TELECOMMUNICATIONS IN CHINA: DEVELOPMENT AND POLICY IMPLICATIONS

ZHOU HE

INTRODUCTION

From the mid 1870s to the early l990s, China's telecommunications under went a long and rough process of development featuring four recurring themes. The first was China's persistent struggle for its own sovereignty in telecommunications. Despite differing and even conflicting political ideologies, the successive rulers of China—the Qing imperial court, the Nationalists, and the Communists—all waged dogged struggles to maintain their absolute control over telecommunications in the face of foreign encroachment.

The second theme was the telecommunications industry's outcry for adequate funding to fuel its development. From its early start to the 1980s, China's telecommunications industry constantly labored under insufficient funding—sometimes because of limited national resources, other times because of the government's low priority in telecommunications. Even when China's economy took off in the late 1980s and amassed enormous capital from both domestic and international sources, only relatively marginal investment was injected into the capital~starved telecommunications industry.

The third theme was the monopolistic control over the posts and telecommunications business by a national official organization. From Li Hongzhang's Directorate General of Tianjin-Shanghai Telegraph in the Qing Dynasty to the Ministry of Posts and Telecommunications (MPT) in the

People's Republic of China, the Chinese government always has strived to monopolize the telecommunications market in one form or another. Although conducive to the integration and standardization of a national telecommunications network, this monopoly obviously impeded the development of a viable and competitive telecommunications market.

The fourth was the orientation to the elite assigned by or imposed on the telecommunications industry. Owing its birth and growth to official backing, China's telecommunications almost always put service to the elite, especially the political elite, as its top priority. This orientation manifested both at a time of mandated feudal rule and in an era of presumably mass-oriented rule.

This chapter traces these themes through major historical junctures over the past century and a half, with a special focus on the interplay of international relations, China's sociopolitical environment, new technologies, and governmental telecommunications policies. It presents a broad overview of the major developments in China's telecommunications and, more importantly, points out several policy implications. The areas that obviously lend themselves to policy considerations include: the monopoly of the telecommunications market by the Ministry of Posts and Telecommunications or similar organizations, the separation of the public and private networks, the mix of the postal service and telecommunications, a fee scheme of extremes, prohibition of foreign involvement, uneven development and the information gap, and insufficient funding.

THE EARLY DEVELOPMENT OF TELECOMMUNICATIONS IN CHINA: TORN BETWEEN SOVEREIGNTY AND MODERNIZATION

For centuries before 1840, China had existed in a self-contained system, always proud of its advanced agricultural cultivation, arts and literature, early inventions such as paper and printing, military power, sophisticated bureaucracy, and centuries-old postal service. Indeed, it had viewed itself as the Central Empire (Zhongguo) of the world and looked down on all other "barbarians" outside the Empire.

All of this changed in 1840 when the first Opium War broke out. Equipped with advanced weaponry and steam gunboats, the industrializing and globally expanding Western powers waged aggressive wars against China in an effort to secure their lucrative opium business and conquer the world's largest market. In battle after battle, the Qing military, equipped mainly with medieval spears and sabers, was defeated; and in one treaty after another, the Qing court was forced to surrender sovereignty over its territory, politics, foreign trade, and telecommunications rights.

In 1842, the Qing court signed the Treaty of Nanking with Britain. The treaty provided for the cession of Hong Kong, the opening of five trading ports, indemnity of 21 million silver dollars, and the tariff on exports and imports on British goods to be fixed by mutual agreement. In the following year, the Qing court signed the Supplementary Treaty of Hoomun Chai, granting Britain the privileges of consular jurisdiction and a unilateral most-favored-nation status in China. These treaties were soon followed by other similarly unequal and humiliating ones: the Treaty of Wang-hea with the United States in 1844, the Treaty of Whampoa with France in 1844, the Treaty of Aigun in 1858 and the Treaty of St. Petersburg in 1881 with Russia, the Treaty of Tientsin with France in 1885, the Treaty of Shimonoseki with Japan in 1895, and the International Protocol of 1901 (Bai, 1982). These treaties not only gave privileges to the signing countries but also granted other foreign powers the right to claim the same treatment stipulated in any of them.

Confronted with these technologically advanced aggressors and an increasing danger of colonization, some Qing officials realized the importance of new technologies and advocated a Westernization drive to learn such technologies from the West. Represented by Prince Gong (personal name Yixin), Zeng Guofan, Li Hongzhang, and others, the Westernization group set up machinery factories to manufacture rifles and ammunition, build shipyards, and form modern navies modeled after those in the West. The group's attitude toward the West, as that of an increasing portion of the Chinese populace, was ambivalent. It wanted only the technologies from the West, not the values, ideology, and systems that lay at the roots of the technologies. This ambivalence was well reflected in two popular maxims at that time: "Learn the superior technology of the barbarians in order to control them" and "Chinese learning for essential principles; Western learning for practical applications." It also demonstrated itself in the form of a swing from xenophobia to subordination in China's later encounters with the West, which were often accompanied by wars, unequal treaties or concessions, and a struggle for national sovereignty and integrity.

THE START OF TELECOMMUNICATIONS IN CHINA: ENCROACHMENT BY WESTERN POWERS

It was against this background that China began its adoption of telecommunications technologies: first telegraph, then telephone, and finally radio and others. As in other areas, this adoption process was often dominated by aggressive foreign encroachment on China's telecommunications sovereignty.

On April 30, 1870, British ambassador Thomas Francis Wade presented a memoir to the Qing court's Zongli Yamen (foreign ministry), demanding the permission to lay a submarine cable from China's five open ports through other port cities to Shanghai by the Eastern Extension Australasia and China Telegraph Co. Ltd. (EEACT), a British company. Under tremendous diplomatic pressure and threat of potential warfare, Prince Gong, then head of the Zongli Yamen, granted permission in writing on May 19. He attached only two conditions: First, the terminal of the cable should not land on shore; second, China did not accept responsibility for protecting the submarine cable (Posts & Telecommunications History Compiling Office [P&THCO], 1984). This was the first written government policy on telecommunications involving foreign countries, and it opened China's marine territory to foreign telecommunications business with a loophole: no time limit on foreign companies' rights to submarine cables.

Before the EEACT started the construction of the cable, another foreign company, The Great Northern Telegraph Company (GNTC), took advantage of Prince Gong's decree and began the construction of a 2,200-knot cable from Haicenwei through Nagasaki to Shanghai and Hong Kong. The GNTC, a Danish company with major stock holders from Britain and Russia, had earlier struck a deal with the EEACT that divided China into two business turfs: The territory north of Shanghai belonged to the GNTC, the territory south of Hong Kong went to the EEACT, and the territory between Hong Kong and Shanghai was under their joint control. On June 3, 1871, the GNTC's cable was connected to Shanghai and went into operation. Completely ignoring Prince Gong's condition, the GNTC landed the cable in two places in Shanghai and even connected it to its transmission station in the concession area. Furthermore, it landed the cable in Xiangmen (P&THCO, 1984). This cable started China's international telecommunications, but its ownership and operation were completely in the hands of a foreign company. As a result, China's sovereignty in international telecommunications through submarine cable was encroached on from the very outset.

In June 1881, when China was preparing to build its own telegraph networks and needed imported equipment and expertise, the GNTC presented a proposal to Li Hongzhang, which contained the following: (a) The exiting cable owned by the GNTC enjoyed exclusive rights to profits in China, and no other countries should set up marine cable in Chinese territory in 20 years; (b) within the 20 years, China should not install any submarine or land cables in places where the GNTC already had one; (c) when China built new cables, the GNTC should be given the contract if its bidding was lower than others; and (d) the GNTC offered free services to first-class official telegrams for 20 years as a compensation. Taking the bait of the free services, Li Hongzhang approved the proposal. His approval virtually ensured the GNTC's monopoly of China's international telegraph communications and restricted the development of China's own effort in this regard—for only 33,300 silver yuan a year (P&THCO, 1984).

Unhappy about this agreement, the British government demanded the right to lay another cable from Hong Kong to Shanghai. Despite resistance from the Qing government, the British EEACT went ahead and completed the cable in 1883. When the EEACT requested the permission to land the cable in Shanghai, the Qing court refused. In the following rounds of negotiations, the British government proposed raising the tariffs for opium imported into China as a trade off for the right to land cable in China. Attracted by this offer and frightened by the diplomatic pressure, the Qing government signed the Agreement on the Methods of Shanghai-Hong Kong Telegraph on March 31, 1883, and the Supplementary Regulations on Shanghai-Hong Kong Telegraph on May 7 of the same year. These agreements allowed British cable to land in Shanghai. In September of the same year, Britain pressured the Qing government again to permit the EEACT's cable to land in Fuzhou (P&THCO, 1984).

With those deals, foreign companies obtained the right both to lay submarine cable and to land it on shore in China. The only right the Qing government was able to maintain was the right to continental cable.

In 1900, the joint army of Britain, Russia, Japan, the United States, Germany, France, Italy, and Austria attacked and occupied Beijing. After the defeat of the Chinese army, the joint force imposed the International Protocol of 1901 on the Qing court. By the terms of the treaty, the Qing court would apologize to the powers and punish the officials who had "offended" them, pay an indemnity of 450 million taels of silver in 39-year installments that amounted to about a billion taels of silver with interest, allow the powers to control China's maritime customs and salt bagelle, and establish in Beijing a "legation quarters" where foreign troops were to be stationed (Bai, 1982).

During the war, the GNTC and EEACT took advantage of the chaotic situation and the damage to the Chinese telegraph network to expand their operations in China. Supported by the Western powers, the two companies took the repair of the damaged Chinese Yantai-Dagu-Shanghai submarine cable into their own hands. The Qing court attempted to stop their work, but its attempts were completely ignored. In August 1900, the Chinese Directorate General of Telegraph was forced to sign the Shanghai-Dagu Submarine Cable Contract with the two companies. According to the contract, China had to pay 210,000 British pounds (twice as much as the actual costs) for the repair service it did not order and to relinquish all its rights to the two companies for 30 years before it paid off the bill with 5% interest.

In addition, all of the previous contracts China signed with the two companies were automatically extended to the end of 1930. The two companies also encroached on China's land cable. They approached the Qing Court with a "proposal" to repair the damaged Tianjin-Beijing cable for China. Left with no choice, the Qing Court signed a contract with them. Under the contract, the two companies would be responsible for repairing the cable, could hire foreign employees and set up bureaus, could bill all costs to the Directorate General of Telegraph, and should return the operation to China after a peace agreement was reached by the belligerent parties.

After the war, however, the two companies made all kinds of excuses to delay the return of the cables to China. After nearly a year of negotiations, the two companies agreed to return the cables on one condition: The Qing court should lease two other cables to them, namely the Beijing-Qiaketu cable to the GNTC and the Beijing-Dagu cable to the EEACT. Because of the importance of the Beijing-Tianjin line and the two companies' protracted delay, the Qing Court reluctantly agreed to the conditions. With the Beijing-Qiaketu cable gone, China not only lost the most direct line to Europe through Russia but also relinquished its last control over international telegraph communications (P&THCO, 1984).

CHINA'S EARLY EFFORTS (1871-1911)

In 1871, Russia attacked and occupied Ili, a region in Xinjiang, west China. It took several weeks for the traditional Chinese official Yizhan (official postal service) messengers to send word to Beijing through express horse delivery. It took another 8 years for the Qing court to send envoys back and forth to negotiate with Russia on the return of the occupied territory. In October 1879, Chonghou, an official envoy sent by the Qing court to Russia, signed an extremely unfavorable treaty to cede a large portion of territory to Russia without fully consulting the court—partly because of his eagerness to appease the expansionist Russia and partly because of communication difficulties. When news of the treaty finally reached China, the entire nation was outraged, and the Qing government had to send another envoy to St. Petersburg for a new round of negotiations. Russia immediately deployed troops and naval fleets both along China's west border and off the east coast for an imminent invasion (P&THCO, 1984). Pressured on both sides and lacking speedy communication with its border garrisons, the Qing Court was forced to sign the unequal Treaty of St. Petersburg in 1881, which ceded a large portion of Chinese territory to Russia as a tradeoff for Ili (Bai, 1982).

Upset by inadequate communication in this and other incidents, Li Hongzhang, then head of the Northern Navy, ordered the installation of a telegraph line to link his office in Tianjin with the Dagu and Beitang fortresses and the Tianjin weaponry factory in 1879. This line, the first on the mainland, inaugurated China's serious efforts to build up its own telecommunications industry. In fact, a 47-kilometer-long telegraph cable was installed between Taipei and Gaoxiong two years earlier in Taiwan. However, because of its remote location, this cable was not as important as that in Tianjin.

Telegraph. After completion of the telegraph cable in Tianjin, Li Hongzhang established the Tianjin Directorate General of Telegraph in October 1880. In April 1881, the Qing Court began the construction of a 1,500-kilometer cable from Tianjin to Shanghai and completed it in 8 months. This telegraph trunk line tremendously improved China's south-north communication. After this project, the Directorate General of Tianjin-Shanghai Telegraph was set up.

Before and during the Sino-French War along China's southwest border and southeast coast in the early 1800s, the Qing government sped up its construction of telegraph facilities. Three major trunk lines were built during this period: the Tianjin-Beijing trunk; the Yangtze River trunk that linked Zhenjiang and Hankou; and the Guangzhou-Longzhou trunk. These trunk lines played an important role in thwarting the advance of French troops into China. After the war, Li Hongzhang had this comment on China's newly established telegraph network:

> When the French created a crisis along the borders, the generals' war information to the court and the court's commands all flowed instantaneously with very little barrier. Never in Chinese history has military maneuvering been so smooth and fast. (P&THCO,1984, p.64)

In the following 15 years, China's own telegraph business made some headway. From 1884 to 1899, 27,500 kilometers of cable was laid, and by 1908, there were 45,448 kilometers of telegraph cable in the country. A marine cable connecting Taiwan and Fujian was finally installed after years of planning and debating.

Telephone. The telephone was introduced to China in the early 1880s. As in the case of the telegraph, foreign companies first set up telephone services in China. On February 22, 1882, the GNTC opened a switchboard service in the common concession area in Shanghai. Two months later, the Shanghai Mutual Telephone Association, an organization established by British businesses, opened a second switchboard to compete with the GNTC. Because the two companies were not connected with each other and the quality of their service was poor, another British company, the China and Japan Telephone Company, bought the GNTC switchboard and merged it with that owned by the Mutual Telephone Association in 1883. This new company served as the sole telephone company in the concession areas in Shanghai for 18 years until it lost the bidding to the Shanghai Mutual Telephone Company in 1900.

In 1900, Care H.O. Poulson of Denmark took advantage of the invasion of Beijing by the eight Western powers and set up China's first long-distance telephone line between Tianjin and Beijing. In 1904, the Beijing Directorate General of Telegraph contacted Poulson and demanded that he hand over the telephone service to the Chinese government. After several rounds of negotiation, the Qing Court agreed to pay 50,000 silver yuan to purchase the service. Based on this service, China set up a Beijing telephone directorate general and a similar institution in Tianjin.

By this time, China had already spent 5 years in building its own telephone facilities. In 1899, Sheng Xuanhuai, then director of the Directorate General of Telegraph (DGT), submitted a report to the court suggesting that some profits from telegraph services should be used to develop China's own telephone networks and that the telephone industry should be managed by the DGT. This report was soon approved by the Qing Court, and Sheng began the construction of some state-run telephone facilities. From 1900 to 1906, telephone services were established in some big cities such as Nanjing, Suzhou, Wuhan, Guangzhou, Beijing, Tianjin, Shanghai, and Taiyuan. Some of them were run by the government, and others were managed by private individuals.

In 1905, Yuan Shikai, then the minister in charge of telecommunications, submitted another report to the court suggesting that all telephone services be controlled by the state. In the report, he stated:

> Recently, foreign businessmen have set up unauthorized telephone facilities in concession areas in the open port cities, making these facilities a fait accompli. Furthermore, they have even extended their lines to the inland to reap our profit. This is too much. I hereby suggest to your Majesty to declare that all telephone facilities in China should be administered by the Directorate General of Telegraph. Except for the exiting telephone facilities in the open port cities, no telephone facility by anybody anywhere is permitted unless it is authorized by the Directorate General of Telegraph. This is for the purpose of protecting our profit in telecommunications and national sovereignty. (P&THCO,1984)

However, the Ministry of Transportation, which was in charge of posts and telecommunications, had been operating in the red for a long time and could not afford any funding for the telephone business. As a result, the development of the telephone in China was virtually halted for a long time, with only marginal development by business people in some medium-and small-sized cities.

Management. At the outset of China's telecommunications buildup, almost all of the projects were funded and run by government organs, such as the Directorate General of Tianjin-Shanghai Telegraph. The money mostly came from the government's military budget, which was exhausted from consecutive wars. In fact, the Tianjin-Shanghai cable was built with 170,000 taels of silver borrowed by Li Hongzhang from the payroll for his troops. As the government-run cables went into operation, operational funds were nowhere to be found, and the services lost money year after year. From 1881 to 1882, for example, the services' revenues were about 6,000 taels of silver, but their expenditures ran as much as 19,000 taels.

Pressured by the shortage of investment funds, the Qing Court decided to adopt a policy of "commercial management under official supervision." Under this policy, individuals could run telegraph businesses with official authorization and backing of the Directorate General of Telegraph. This system worked fairly well in the early stage of China's telecommunications development. The official backing provided protection and convenience for the projects, and commercial impetus ran the operations in an efficient fashion. This system lasted for about 20 years until 1908.

After the invasion of Beijing in 1900, there was an uproar in the country and widespread discontent with the Qing Court. To appease the increasingly alienated populace and to consolidate its rule, the Qing Court began to carry out some institutional reforms under a "new administration." One of the reforms was to establish the Ministry of Posts and Transportation. On November 6, 1901, the court approved a report submitted by a group of officials who had toured several countries and set up the ministry. However, in the next 6 years, the ministry remained an empty frame, and the minister changed several times. In August 1907, the ministry finally set up its own organizational framework and organized five departments—navigation, road transportation, telecommunications, the postal service, and administrative affairs. Under this framework, the department of telecommunications was separate from the department of postal service and responsible for the regulation and administration of state run telecommunications bureaus, commercial telecommunications companies, submarine and land cables, and even the installation of urban telephones and electric lighting (P&THCO, 1984).

Beginning in 1908, the Ministry of Posts and Transportation began to nationalize the fledgling telecommunications industry. It first bought over the commercial operations and then took over all of the provincial official bureaus. Within a year, the country's telecommunications were nationalized. Under the centralized administration of the Qing Court, however, the industry was in chaos, and its quality deteriorated rapidly. There were numerous stories of telegrams traveling more slowly than mail.

THE POLITICALLY CHAOTIC ERA (1911-1949)

With the overthrow of the Qing Dynasty in 1911 after its reign for nearly 300 years, China entered an era of political instability. There were wars among warlords, the invasion and occupation of China by Japan, and the protracted civil wars between the Nationalists and Communists.

During this period, the new telecommunications technologies introduced to China earlier increased in quantity and coverage. The most noticeable progress was made in the adoption of wireless telegraph and radio.

Wireless telegraph was introduced to China around 1904 when France set up an antenna in Qinhuangdao, Hebei province. In July 1905,

Yuan Shikai sponsored a wireless technology training seminar in Beijing, which was taught by an Italian technician. In the same year, Yuan purchased some quenched spark gap wireless telegraph machines and had them installed in his provincial military commands and warships (P&THCO, 1984). Later, Jiangsu province and Shanghai began to operate their own wireless telegraph stations.

It was not, however, until the downfall of the Qing Court that wireless telegraph was quickly adopted and diffused. In fact, as different ministries of the Beiyang (Northern) government vied with each other to secure foreign loans for their wireless operations, an organizational and later international conflict erupted. In 1912, the Ministry of Transportation ordered five wireless machines from Germany. In 1918, the Ministry of the Army secured a loan of 600,000 British pounds from the British Marconi Company for the purchase of military wireless telegraph machines. However, half of the money went to other uses. In the same year, the Ministry of Transportation also borrowed 170,000 pounds from Marconi for three wireless stations. To compete with its counterparts, the Ministry of Navy signed a contract with a Japanese bank for a 30-year loan of 8 million yen at an annual interest of 8% to construct a wireless telegraph station in Shuangqiao near Beijing. According to the contract, the station was to be operated by the Japanese bank for international and offshore communication for 30 years, and no other country, not even China, could build wireless international stations within the period.

This contract immediately drew a ferocious protest from other industrialized powers, especially the United States. Before construction started, the U.S. Federal Telegraph Company signed an agreement with the Ministry of Transportation in 1921 to build five wireless stations in China. Under this agreement, all of these stations had the right to conduct international communication; therefore, the United States was unhappy with Japan's monopoly, condemning it as a violation of the principle of equal opportunities and the "open door" policy in China. Japan, in turn, condemned the United States and China for violation of a legal contract. This fight dragged on for several years without any solution even after the downfall of the Beiyang government in 1927.

In 1928, the Nationalists led by Chiang Kai-shek established a new government in Nanjing after defeating the Beiyang warlords in two expeditions from 1926 to 1927. Pressured by the upsurge of anti-imperialism, an awakening nationalism and militant labor movements, the Nationalist government began to take steps to restore China's control over its domestic and international telecommunications.

In the same year, the Shenyang international radio station, which was first introduced in 1924, was expanded with the installation of two 20-kilowatt short-wave transmitters and extended its communication from Germany to other countries. This operation broke the foreign monopoly of China's international telecommunications, especially the GNTC and the EEACT. In 1930, the

Nationalist government built another international short-wave station (20 kilowatts) in Shanghai, which soon began communication with almost all Asian and European countries. From June 1928 to February 1929, the new government also set up 27 short-wave stations in China's major cities.

At the same time, the government began negotiations with the GNTC and EEACT to reclaim the leased cables and terminate the 30-year submarine cable contracts. In 1929, the Nationalist government issued a notice to the two companies, informing them that their contract would not be renewed after its expiration. The two companies responded aggressively, saying that China had no right to unilaterally terminate the contracts and that China had not paid off the loans. To repay the loans, the Nationalist government planned to issue 10 million yuan of bonds and use half of it to clear the debt. However, the negotiations went on and off for three years. In April 1933, the Ministry of Transportation finally struck a deal with the two foreign companies. Under the agreement, China revoked the exclusive right of foreign submarine cable to land in China, set a time limit on the landing of licensed submarine cable, and took back the right to direct transmission and reception. In May 1934, China paid off all the loans and reclaimed all the "leased" cables. However, the two foreign companies were still given a 14-year license for their land connected cables.

From 1934 to 1936, the Nationalist government built a nine province telephone network. By June 1936, the Ministry of Transportation had 47,000 kilometers of long-distance open wire and, in the same year, introduced carrier-wave technology.

Under the Nationalist government, the telecommunications sector was first administered by the Construction Commission; however, this commission could not control all the radio stations owned and operated by different government departments, military divisions and provinces. A year later, the Nationalist government decided to put telecommunications under the supervision of the Ministry of Transportation in a department separated from the department of postal service. Japan began a full-scale invasion of China in 1937 after occupying Northeast China for 6 years. It soon took over the bulk of Chinese territory and started an 8-year occupation. Under Japanese rule, telecommunications development in China came to a halt and even went downhill. In 1936, there were 55,683 intracity telephone subscribers and 52,245 kilometers of long-distance lines. By the end of 1944, these figures dropped to 7,918 and 4,085.

After World War II, the Communists and Nationalists entered a 4-year civil war. During this period, there was only a brief period of revival in the telecommunications sector when the Nationalist government started a "reform of the postal service" in 1946. The reform was carried out after years of financial losses in the postal service and telecommunications sector. In the first 8 months of 1945, for example, the postal service lost 3.9 billion yuan (inflated currency at that time). The objectives of the reform were to improve service, enhance efficiency, and increase revenue. Although the reform was intended in the postal service, it also spilled over to the telecommunications sector. Under the reform program, the telecommunications sector added some new services and set up standards for telecommunications delivery. However, this reform did not last long before it was interrupted by the Communists' winning march toward power.

DEVELOPMENT OF TELECOMMUNICATIONS IN CHINA AFTER 1949: A LONG AND ROUGH BUILDUP

THE FIRST 3 YEARS OF THE PEOPLE'S REPUBLIC

When the Chinese Communists took power and founded the People's Republic of China in 1949, they inherited little in telecommunications from the preceding government. In the entire country, there were about 260,000 telephones with a 310,000 line exchange capacity in the cities, 62,000 telephones in the countryside, and some 2,000 long-distance telephone lines. The telephone penetration rate was only .05% (Gong, 1993). Most of these telephones were in big cities, such as Beijing, Shanghai, Nanjing, and Tianjin, and the majority of the "long-distance" lines did not go any farther than 200 kilometers. There were only 35 short-wave transmitters that served as the main means of real long-distance communication. The infrastructure was fragmented, managed by a variety of conflicting interest groups. The facilities were incompatible with each other because of the various equipment used (Xie & Luo, 1990).

The newly founded government was not all ready to plan, run and build up a telecommunications network in a vast and war-torn country. Though seasoned in wars, the Communists had very limited experience in running and managing telecommunications on a large scale. Their endeavors in the field started about 20 years earlier with the establishment of a small and primitive open-wire telephone network in the "Hai-Lu-Feng Revolutionary Base" in Fujian province between November 1927 and February 1928. As the base fell under the attack of the Nationalist troops, the network was soon dismantled. In 1928, the struggling Chinese Communist Party held a clandestine training seminar in Shanghai to train some wireless communication technicians. It was this barely trained group who later became the backbone of a small intelligence network and started communication in 1930 between the Communist central leadership in Shanghai and the Red Army in south China. In 1931, the Red Army in Jiangxi province formed its first "Wireless Communication Brigade," equipped with communication facilities captured from the Nationalist (Kuomintang) army (Directorate General of Telecommunications [DGT], 1986). In the late 1940s, as the Communists consolidated and expanded their territories, they began to establish regional postal and telecommunications networks. However, these networks were not connected in any integrated fashion, and they were mostly war-oriented and temporary. The personnel came from two vocational schools—the Northeast China School of Posts and Telecommunications and the East China School of Posts and Telecommunications (Gong, 1993).

As battles against the Nationalist armies were still going on in Southwest China and some southern coastal areas in 1949 and early 1950, the imperative for the ascending leaders of the new republic apparently was to set up a network that could connect different army units fighting to take power in various cities. In May 1949, the Liberation Army established a "Directorate General of Telecommunications of the Chinese People's Revolutionary Military Committee" in Beijing to manage all telecommunications businesses in North China. On November 1, 1949, the 1-month-old Chinese People's Government formed the Ministry of Posts and Telecommunications, which supervised two departments: the Directorate General of Telecommunications (DGT) and the Postal Service (DGT, 1986). Under the original setup, those two departments were independent institutions, each responsible for its own operations under the umbrella of the MPT (Gong, 1993). Soon afterward, posts and telecommunications bureaus were established at regional, provincial, and municipal levels.

In March 1950, the MPT held its first national conference on telecommunications and formulated a strategy for the development of domestic telecommunications: to construct "a national network based on wire communication and supplemented by wireless communication." In the same year, about 15,000 technicians and workers gathered from around the country to form eight construction teams. They worked for 8 months to lay about 8,000 kilometers of new long-distance wire, restore 4,000 kilometers of old lines, and install some 10,000 carrier-wave telephones. This project enabled Beijing to have direct telegraph and telephone communication with regional government headquarters. In December 1950, a line from Beijing to Moscow was put into operation. By the end of 1952, all provincial capitals, except for those in Tibet and Ningxia, were hooked up to Beijing through open wire (DGT, 1986).

In July 1950, the MPT held a meeting of directors of regional telecommunications and posts bureaus. Advised by Soviet experts, the meeting made an important change in its administrative structure and formulated the principle of "centralized leadership, division of specialties, combination of telecommunications and postal service, and merging of postal service and distribution of periodical publications." It decided to break down the original two departments under the MPT into four departments: a directorate general of postal service, a directorate general of long-distance telecommunications, a directorate general of urban telephone service, and a directorate general of wireless communication. These departments were no longer independent administrative institutions but functional units of the MPT (Gong, 1993).

On November 7, 1950, the State Council issued a document that stipulated, "All telecommunications, except for those for the military and railways, should be managed by the Ministry of Posts and Telecommunications." This document established the MPT's monopoly of the Chinese telecommunications market and, at the same time, authorized the military and railway system, two most important institutions in the country's national defense and economy, to run their own private telecommunications networks (Gong, 1993). Although not stipulated in the document, the departments of the central government and Party also enjoyed a privilege; namely, red-colored telephones for top leaders should be connected first at any time.

Two other major policies were also formulated in this period that would have a long-term impact on the development of China's postal service and telecommunications. One concerned foreign involvement: Driven by their long anti-imperialist tradition and concern with national sovereignty, the Chinese Communists declared on their ascent to power that foreign companies were not allowed to run posts and telecommunications businesses in China. The other concerned mail rates. In July 1950, the new government standardized mail rates for the entire country: local mail at 4 fen (in 1953 money), per piece under 20 kilograms, and out-of-town mail at 8 fen per piece (Gong, 1993). These rates remained unchanged for 40 years. The government also attempted to standardize the rates for telecommunications but failed because of the different levels of development in various administrative regions.

When the Korean War broke out, a major part of China's military, manpower, and financial resources went to the war effort. This obviously tied the new government's hands in telecommunications development. In the 1949-1952 period, the only two other major accomplishments in telecommunications were the standardization of telephone numbers for police emergency, fire emergency, and telephone directory service, and the establishment of a telephone message relay system in 16 major cities (DGT, 1986).

THE FIRST FIVE-YEAR PLAN PERIOD (1953-1957)

After the smoke of the Korean War cleared and the world entered a protracted cold war, the Chinese government began to draw blueprints for its national economic development by drafting its First Five-Year Plan for the 1953-1957 period. Under this plan, the state would invest RMB$8.1 billion (Renminbi [People's Currency]) in transportation and communications. Of this amount, only RMB$361 million went to telecommunications and posts, accounting for only .08% of the total investment in the economy for that period (The First Five-Year Plan, 1955; Liu, 1988). The plan was ambitious and favored the construction of a heavy industry that centered around 156 major industrial projects designed and aided by the Soviet Union and 694 large- and medium-scale supplementary projects (Wei & Dai, 1993). Posts and telecommunications, however, were given a back seat. The plan called for the construction of 63,000 kilometers of long-distance telephone and telegraph lines, the addition of some carrier-wave channels to the trunks from Beijing to a handful of major cities, and the installation of 91,000 intracity telephones. No new investment was made in telephone systems in rural areas. Only where there were enough local funds and an extreme need could rural areas engage in innovations and new construction (The First Five-Year Plan, 1955).

The modest goals of the plan for postal service and telecommunications were fulfilled and even surpassed. In the 5-year period, 250,000 intracity telephones were installed, 25 cities expanded or built automatic exchange telephone systems, and about 2,000 county seats had telephone connections. The most important project was the construction of the Beijing Telegraph Office Building, a hub of China's telegraphic communication (DGT, 1986). In all, RMB$478 million was invested (Liu, 1988). Also in this period, all the privately owned and operated telecommunications businesses were bought out by the state and incorporated into the state-run system (DGT,1986).

The First Five-Year Plan had a tremendous impact on future 5-year plans and on the development of telecommunications in China. Though considered one of the best for its design and implementation, it set a bad precedent for proportionally low investment and slow development of the postal service and telecommunications in China. Critics would late call this a result of a "misunderstanding of the role of communication in national economic development" (MPT, 1984, p. 3). An important report by the MPT to the State Council in 1984 even attributed the persistent low investment in telecommunications starting with the First Five-Year Plan to a mistranslation of the word "communication" in Marx's classics. "In the past," the report said, "the word 'communication' used by Marx to mean both transportation and communication has been wrongly translated from English as 'transportation,' thus resulting in a long-time neglect of the important role of communication." (MPT, 1984, p. 3) However, the main reason appeared to be the elitist orientation that was woven in the planning and development of China's telecommunications from the very beginning. Communication needs of the elite, especially the party apparatus, were given top priority and ensured by a system of private networks, courier services, red telephones, and preferential connection. As a result, the leaders did not feel the imperative for rapid development of telecommunications. When they had very limited financial resources, as they did in the early years of the Republic, they gave telecommunications the back seat. Even when their resources increased, they habitually gave low priority to telecommunications.

THE SECOND FIVE-YEAR PLAN AND THE ADJUSTMENT PERIOD (1958-1965)

The success of the First Five-Year Plan, especially the rapid economic growth in the last 2 years of the plan, encouraged excessive optimism and impatience in economic development among Chinese leaders. In September 1956, the Chinese Communist Party's Eighth National Conference approved a Draft of Suggestions for the Second Five-Year Plan based on the implementation of the First Five-Year Plan. Like the previous plan, the Draft emphasized the development of the heavy industry while planning only modest growth in light industry, transportation, and telecommunications.

The Draft was never used to formulate specific plans and was soon completely ignored as the country suddenly plunged itself into a "Great Leap Forward Movement"—a movement that was supposed to enable China to catch up with the United States and Great Britain in 15 years and to "run into the ideal world of communism." Ad hoc and fantastic goals were set and reset at the whims of leaders, unrealistic plans were devised and implemented, and unaffordable projects were carried out. In addition, the national investment in basic construction ran amok: RMB$13.8 billion in 1957, RMB$26.7 billion in 1958, RMB$34.4 billion in 1959, and RMB$38.4 billion in 1960. As millions of farmers entered the cities to produce low-quality iron and steel, agricultural production plummeted at an annual rate of 9.7% from 1959 to 1961 (Wei & Dai, 1993). When a series of droughts hit the country, a great famine came— and remained for 3 years. Worse still, the Soviet Union broke relations with China, stopping its aid, withdrawing its advisers, and demanding payment of its loans with interests. The national economy collapsed. Cut off from the rest of the world and its important Eastern Bloc allies, China had to adopt a "self-reliance" policy in its development. In 1962, the Chinese government was forced to cut investment in basic construction down to RMB$670 million, the smallest amount since 1953 (Wei 8 Dai, 1993).

The development of telecommunications in this period was caught by the same craze that permeated other economic sectors. Although there were no specific goals for the investment in and development of telecommunications in the Draft for the Second Five-Year Plan, the postal and telecommunications industry managed to get RMB$771 million in investment, which, although larger in absolute terms than the investment in the previous 5 years, represented only .6% of the national investment, down by .2 percentage points from the First Five-Year Plan (Liu, 1988). Most of the money went to the construction of long-distance telephone lines because of the MPT's new strategy to prioritize long-distance communication. In 1957, China began the construction of a giant project—the Beijing long-distance telephone building—with a prospective budget of RMB$40 million. As one of the major projects in this 5-year plan period, the building was designed to be the most important long-distance telephone hub in the country; however, after the foundation was laid and the basement was finished in 1960, state funding dried up. The whole project had to be canceled (Gong, 1993).

As the country swirled in a mass movement of decentralization and mass participation in industrial management in 1958, MPT lost its control over the nationwide network. Most of its subordinates were decentralized within a month, and what was left for MPT's direct supervision was three P&T enterprises in Beijing, eight P&T colleges and vocational schools, and nine factories. Consequently, national coordination was severely damaged. As provinces and cities struggled to manage the newly decentralized enterprises, tremendous chaos occurred in the country's telecommunications. This forced the State Council to reinstate MPT's monopolistic management system in 1961.

Not everything in this period was negative. Some noticeable achievements were made in the development of telephone facilities. From 1958 to 1960, long-distance telephone lines doubled thanks to the increased investment. Research and development of 60-channel carrier-wave and 600-channel microwave telephonic and telegraphic facilities were underway, some factories were built to produce China-designed, automatic-exchange telephone equipment, and MPT finally standardized telecommunications rates. Most importantly, China, faced with dwindling sources of foreign imports, began a serious buildup of a domestic industry to manufacture telecommunications facilities (DGT, 1986).

In 1963-1965, the country entered an era of damage control and conservative development. As investment went down in all economic sectors, so did it in the P&T industry. For the 3 years, the total state investment in the P&T industry was RMB$137.2 million, accounting for only .5% of the total national investment (Liu, 1988). Such an investment was less than half of that in the First Five-Year Plan period and less than one-third of that for the Second Five-Year Plan era.

Despite the smaller investment, the industry made some progress— mainly by better absorbing and utilizing the investment. By the end of 1965, growth was seen in these areas: short-wave transmitters to 6510 from 4502 in 1962; microwave trunk lines to 120 kilometers from zero; open wire to 500,955 pair kilometers from 468,325; carrier-wave terminal capacity to 16,021 lines from 14,282; telegraph lines to 6,995 from 5,992; telephone cable in the countryside to 1,057 kilometers from 379; and city telephone exchange capacity to 1.1 million lines from 0.97 million (Industrial Transportation Department of State Statistics Bureau [ITDSSB], 1989).

THE CULTURAL REVOLUTION (1966-1976)

After three years of readjustment from 1962 to 1965, China's national economy went back to the track of the First Five-Year Plan and made some progress. In 1964, the National Planning Commission submitted a preliminary outline of the Third Five-Year Plan to the State Council and the Party Central Committee. Based on the experience in the readjustment period, the outline put forth some solid and realistic suggestions for the Third Five-Year Plan.

However, before the outline materialized into a specific plan, the Cultural Revolution broke out and paralyzed China's economy. As "revolutionary rebellions," "power takeovers," and armed factional wars spread throughout the country, factories stopped production, management broke down, transportation foundered, and industrial and agricultural production plummeted. In 1967, China's industrial and agricultural output dropped to RMB$210.5 billion, down by 10% from 1966; in 1968, it fell again to RMB$201.5 billion, down by 4% from 1967. GNP plunged by 7.2% in 1967 over the previous year and again by 6.5% in 1968 (Wei & Dai, 1993).

The chaos in the country was so great that there was not even an economic plan for 1968. From 1969 to 1970, some extreme measures were taken, such as military takeovers, and the economy picked up a modest recovery (Wei & Dai, 1993). However, political and economic disorders resurged and lasted well into the late 1970s.

Surprisingly, a relative large amount of investment was put into the P&T industry. For the 1966-1970 period, the total investment was RMB$1.37 billion, almost double that of the ambitious Second Five-Year Plan. For the first time in 30 years, the investment broke through the 1% ceiling in total national investment to reach 1.4% (Liu, 1988). However, where all this money went remained a mystery. A careful check on the statistics revealed that there was only marginal progress in most of the important fields and even regress in some.

From 1965 to 1970, for example, only marginal development was recorded in these fields: long-distance public switched network capacity went up by only 17% from 2,669 to 3,136 lines; short-wave transmitters by 9% from 6,510 to 7110 units; short-wave receivers by 9% from 2,287 to 2,506 units; the number of long-distance telephone lines by 18% from 9,913 to 11,696; city telephone exchange capacity by 5% from 1.1 million to 1.16 million circuits; the number of city telephone sets by 4% from 1.27 million to 1.32 million; and the length of open telephone wire in the countryside by 15% from 1.6 million pair kilometers to 1.86 million. A modest growth was seen in the following: the length of long-distance open wire up by 27% from 500,955 to 637,531 pair kilometers; the length of long-distance cable by 24% from 1,346 to 1,665 kilometers; and the number of telex machines by 40% from 3,585 to 5,019. A decline was found in the following: telephone penetration rate down by .02 percentage points from 0.29 percent; telegraph lines by 11% from 6,955 to 6,498; and the number of fax machines by 6% from 88 to 83 (ITDSSB, 1989).

The most noticeable increase in this period was in microwave trunks (up six times from 120 in 1965 to 6,952 kilometers in 1970), rural telephone cable (up 11 times from 1,057 to 12,033 kilometers), and carrier-wave terminal capacity (up 71% from 16,021 to 27,487 lines).

In 1969, the Ministry of Posts and Telecommunications was dismantled. Postal service was merged into the Ministry of Transportation and the Ministry of Railways, and telecommunications was taken over by the military. The management of the two systems at local levels was also decentralized and handed over to provinces and cities (MPT, 1986a).

After the Third Five-Year Plan ended messily, the Chinese leadership was forced to do something about the economy. In March 1971, the Chinese Communist Party Central Committee handed down *An Outline of The Fourth Five-Year Plan for 1971-1975*. Based on the moderate economic recovery in 1970, the Committee thought that another peak in "socialist construction" was coming and set unrealistically high goals for the 5 years, including the completion of a complete industrial system in the "third frontline" (inland areas in west and southwest China) that was first started in the previous period in preparation for envisioned wars with either the United States or the Soviet Union. These wishful goals stretched all national resources and caused a tremendous disorder in the economy. By the end of 1971, the number of employees in state-run enterprises broke through the ceiling of 50 million, salary payment exceeded RMB$30 billion, and food consumption surpassed 40 million tons—dangerous all-time highs (Wei & Dai, 1993). Although damage-control measures were again taken in 1972, the adverse impact was felt throughout the whole period. Moreover, ferocious political struggles were waged again, causing dramatic ups and downs in the economy.

For those 5 years, RMB$1.51 billion, or .8% of the total national investment, was injected into the P&T industry (Liu, 1988). Despite the dramatic fluctuation over this period, some progress was made across the board in the industry. At the end of 1975, China's telephone penetration rate rose from .27% in 1970 to .33%, long-distance open wire grew by 10% from 637,531 to 700,042 pair kilometers, long-distance telephone lines increased by 37% from 11,696 to 15,981, and intracity telephone exchange capacity expanded by 26% from 1.1 million to 1.5 million lines.

The most noticeable development took place in carrier-wave communication and long-distance telephone cable—obviously a result of the government's strategic priority for those technologies. From 1970 to 1975, China's carrier-wave terminal capacity more than doubled from 27,484 to 64,686 lines, and the length of long-distance cable almost tripled from 1,665 to 4,590 kilometers. For the first time in history, China installed 345 kilometers of long-distance coaxial cable (ITDSSB, 1989).

In 1973, the Ministry of Posts and Telecommunications was reestablished. However, the new MPT lacked the power it used to have and could only control the technical aspect of the business. Decision-making power in personnel, financing, and administration of PT bureaus at and below the provincial level still remained with provincial governments. Another important development in this period was the introduction of satellite communication. In 1972, when U.S. President Richard Nixon visited China, his staff brought two mobile satellite stations with a 10-meter-diameter aerial to ensure communication with the United States. After Nixon's visit, China purchased the two stations and kept the satellite line to the United States open. In late 1972, China started the construction of two permanent international satellite earth stations imported from the United States and Japan. Those two stations, one in Beijing and the other in Shanghai, were completed in 1974 and hooked up to international satellites over the Pacific Ocean.

THE FIFTH FIVE-YEAR PLAN PERIOD (1976-1980)

In 1976, the three most important political leaders in China—Zhu De, Zhou Enlai and Mao Zedong—died successively. As Hua Guofeng took power and arrested the "Gang of Four" headed by Chairman Mao's widow Jiang Qing, the new leadership needed to show its ability in national economic development. Based on the *Draft Outline of the Plan for Ten-Year National Economic Development from 1976 to 1985*, it finalized a master plan for the next 10 years. Ignoring the problems of the past few years and the weaknesses of the national economy, the plan set ambitious goals, such as the construction of 120 major projects that would use an equivalent of the total investment in the past 28 years, an annual 7.5-8.1% increase in industrial and agricultural output, and a total of RMB$203 billion in investment for the first five years (Wei & Dai, 1993).

As in the previous 5 years, the unrealistic goals—and their mandatory power—threw the economy off balance and stretched resources. When Deng Xiaoping and his reform-minded colleagues came to power in 1979, the plan was abandoned.

Despite the ambitious investment goals, which were mostly for the heavy and petrochemical industries, the investment in postal service and telecommunications was marginal: RMB$1.8 billion for 1976-1980, or .8% of the national total (Liu, 1988). However, because of the increase in the total amount of investment, the telecommunications industry made some accomplishments, especially in cable and long-distance telephone communication. Compared with 1975, statistics in 1980 showed that the total length of long distance cable rose by 74% from 4,590 to 8,019 kilometers, including a six fold increase in coaxial cable; telephone penetration rate rose from .33 to .43; rural telephone cable rose by 178% to 1 million kilometers; the number of city telephones rose by 48% to 2.8 million; subscriber telephone exchange capacity rose by 75% to 2.2 million lines; long-distance telephone lines rose by 37% to 22,011 lines; long-distance public switched exchange capacity rose by 64% to 7,085 lines; and carrier-wave terminal capacity rose by 68% to 109,129 lines. Most noticeably, automatic long-distance telephone exchange capacity started from zero to reach 1,969 lines (ITDSSB, 1989).

However impressive these accomplishments might be, they did not significantly increase the capability of China's telecommunications to meet the growing demand. Instead, the gap between demand and supply grew even wider because of the development in other sectors, and the lack of communication facilities became so grave that other measures had to be taken. Starting in 1976, several ministries, such as Aerospace, Transportation, and Energy Resources, were authorized to construct and operate their own private communication networks for their internal communication. These networks, along with those already in existence for the military and Ministry of Railways, formed a giant invisible kingdom that would later become a tremendous source of tension in the industry.

In 1979, the MPT (1986a), no longer tolerant of the administrative structure that fragmented its management, filed a report to the State Council to fight for its lost administrative power. Within 3 months, the report was approved, and the MPT became a monopolistic institution again. However, provincial authorities still retained the power to oversee Party work and review major personnel changes.

As the mechanisms of a market economy began to seep into China's centrally planned economy in the late 1970s, telecommunications bureaus at provincial and municipal levels started to charge fees for telephone installations in order to overcome the shortage of state funding. In 1980, the MPT officialized such a practice and issued a joint circular with the Ministry of Finance and State Price Administration to standardize such fees, setting the charges at RMB$1,000 to RMB$2,000 per installation (MPT, Ministry of Finance, & State Price Administration, 1986).

THE REFORM ERA (1981-1993)

When the Fifth Five-Year Plan period ended, a new era unfolded in China— this was an era of economic reforms. The "four modernizations" drive, flirted with by Chinese leaders since the founding of the People's Republic and formally put forth by the late Premier Zhou Enlai in the mid-1970s, became the imperative and official goal of the country. Political struggles stabilized, dramatic changes took place in the economic structure, the door was open to the outside world, market mechanisms were introduced into many sectors, and, most important, the entire country embarked on a road toward "state capitalism" that would make its economy one of the most viable in the world. The telecommunications industry experienced a quick takeoff during this period. The changing trends can be seen in the following areas.

Strategies and policies. After three decades of ignoring the P&T industry, the Chinese leadership finally felt the pulling impact of an insufficient industry on the national economy. In the Sixth Five-Year Plan for 1981-1985, the government made the industry a development priority. The plan said:

Transportation and postal service and telecommunications are a con-
spicuously weak area in the current economy. In the Sixth Five-Year Plan
period, a concentrated effort should be made to reinforce the construction of these industries, to improve their management and to raise their
capabilities and efficiency so that they can meet the needs of energy
development and stable economic growth. (The Sixth Five-Year Plan,
1983, p. 360)

The Seventh Five-Year Plan also positioned the P&T industry as one
of the key strategic sectors in the nation's economic development (The
Seventh Five-Year Plan, 1986). To ensure and implement the strategic shift,
several policies and regulations were made.

In October 1984, the Standing Committee of the State Council and
the Secretariat of the Chinese Communist Party Central Committee issued
the Six-Point Instructions after hearing a report by the MPT. The Instructions
stipulated, among other things:

1. The P&T industry should be positioned as a priority industry,
    enjoying the same weight as the energy and transportation indus-
    tries;
2. The industry should focus on major cities and economically devel-
    oped coastal areas, and should avoid the pursuit of a nationally
    even development;
3. The state budget for the industry is changed to state loans to the
    industry, and the payment time can be extended longer than for
    other industries;
4. The industry can borrow foreign currency from the state and
    repay in Renminbi (Chinese currency);
5. The industry needs to readjust service fees;
6. The industry should be given a preferential package in taxation
    (Gong, 1993).

Another important policy is the Three Reversed 90%s. This was a
policy concerning the financing of the P&T industry. The essence of the policy was:

1. The P&T industry can keep 90% of its profit, meaning that it has
    to pay only 10% profit tax, a rate much lower than the 55% for
    other industries;
2. The industry can retain 90% of nontrade foreign exchange earn-
    ings;
3. The industry is exempted from repaying 90% of the state loans.

The first two 90%s were first considered in February 1982 at a
State Council meeting and became official State Council Directive No. 40 in

the same year and the Standing Committee meeting in October 1984. The third 90% was approved by the State Council on a report by the MPT (Gong, 1993).

A Sixteen Word Policy on the development of the P&T industry was first suggested by the State Council at a national conference on P&T work in June 1988. It was later formalized and written into the State Council Directive No. 54 in 1990 and A Ten-Year Plan and Outline of the Eighth Five-Year Plan for National Economic and Social Development in the People's Republic of China. The policy stipulated that the P&T industry should adhere to the principles of "central planning, vertical and horizontal coordination, management responsibility at various levels, and joint construction." The main idea of this policy was to mobilize all resources in society to boost the development of the P&T industry under the supervision of MPT. Specifically, the policy stipulated:

1. The MPT is responsible for the overall planning of the industry and for the development of international telecommunications and A-grade trunk lines, including long-distance trunk lines and facilities for communication from the central government to regional centers and provincial capitals.
2. Provinces, cities and counties were responsible for the development of B~grade trunk lines and facilities, including intracity telephone lines and intraprovince communication (Gong, 1993).

State statutes regarding telecommunications. Despite numerous internal regulations issued by the MPT, there was no state statute on any aspect of telecommunications for more than 30 years. In September 1982, the State Council and the Military Commission of the Central Party Committee passed the *Regulations on the Protection of Telecommunications Lines.* These regulations, the first set that had the power of a state statute, defined the boundaries of telecommunications lines and facilities, acts of damage to telecommunications lines, and the criminal liability of offenders (State Council, & Military Commission of Central Party Committee, 1986). In 1980, the MPT started the drafting of the Telecommunications Law of the People's Republic of China, which was similar in mandatory power to the Posts Law of the People's Republic of China that was passed in 1986. The first draft was submitted to the State Council for review in 1982 and failed to be finalized. Another draft was submitted to the State Council and the relevant military departments for suggestions in July 1990. After some revisions and consultation, a third draft was again sent to the State Council in December 1991. As of this writing, it has not yet been approved.

Policy on foreign involvement. The "open door" to the outside world and numerous joint ventures did not make China liberalize its telecommunications market, as one would assume. Instead, the door of this market remained tightly shut. Several documents and directives were issued in this period, all reaffirming that telecommunications was a matter of national sovereignty and should never fall into the hands of foreigners. In 1981, the State Council approved and forwarded the joint report by the Foreign Investment Management Commission and the MPT on the prohibition of foreign express mail businesses in China (Gong, 1993). In 1984, the State Council approved another report by the MPT to forbid joint ventures in postal service and telecommunications. In Directive No. 54 issued in 1990, the State Council reiterated that no foreign businesspeople should operate or be involved in the management of postal service and telecommunications. In Directive No. 55, the State Council decreed that even in lump development areas by foreign developers, P&T businesses should be planned, constructed and managed by China's P&T departments. Finally, in a 1992 circular, the MPT reiterated the prohibition of any joint ventures with foreign businesses in the P&T market (MPT, 1993).

   Administrative structure. Although the administrative structure of the telecommunications industry remained largely a monopolistic and vertical hierarchy, some changes and challenges did occur from within and without. From 1980, Posts and Telecommunications Bureaus (PTBs) at the prefecture, municipal, and county levels began to merge into one administrative institution. By 1987, 63 cities and 492 counties completed the mergers. In 1984, the MPT granted more power to its enterprises in 12 administrative functions, including management development, use of funding, institutional setup, and personnel (Jing, 1987). In 1986, the MPT and its subordinates started an independent accounting system, in which all the enterprises operated under the concept of network revenue. Intracity telephone networks were authorized to have a separate accounting system from the rest of the business. Under this system, they had the right to retain all profits and telephone installation fees for further investment and development. To a certain degree, these internal changes and measures helped streamline the giant bureaucracy and improve its efficiency.
   Also in this period, the MPT's monopoly was seriously challenged by outside forces. The two strongest challengers were the Lian Tong Corporation and the Ji Tong Communication Corporation. In 1992, the Ministry of Electronic Industries (MEI), the Ministry of Electric Power and the Ministry of Railways submitted a joint proposal to the State Council for the establishment of the Lian Tong Corporation (China United Communications Corporation). The purpose of the corporation was to interconnect their private networks and compete with the MPT in long-distance communications (He, 1994). The corporation was approved in December 1993, seriously challenging the MPT's monopoly in the telecommunications industry. Ji Tong was another corporation running an alternative network in China. Its major

shareholder was the Liberation Army ("Tripartite Competition," 1994). The aims of this corporation were to compete with the MPT in radio, paging, cellular, and CT2 networks, and the operation of public data and value-added network services by utilizing the facilities of private networks.

Rapid development in special economic zones and coastal "open" cities. After 1980, five special economic zones and 14 coastal "open" cities were established by the Chinese government—partly to implement Deng Xiaoping's policy of "letting some people get rich first," partly to experiment with a market economy, and partly to attract foreign investment. Thanks to the central government's preferential policies and the dramatic inflow of foreign capital, those privileged areas recorded an astonishing development in their telecommunications. By 1991, intracity exchange capacity in those areas reached 1.84 million lines, accounting for 22.5% of the national total, and long-distance lines amounted to 41,822, representing 37% of the national total. The average telephone penetration rate grew to 5% in the coastal cities and 18% in the special economic zones, far higher than the national average of 1.29%. In Shenzhen, the penetration rate was 28.35%, the highest in the country (Di & Liu, 1994; Gong, 1993).

Overall telecommunications capabilities. By 1990, China had a national telecommunications network that incorporated various technologies, including microwave, fiber optics and satellites. A nationwide trunk long-distance telephone system was almost completed, reaching 97% of townships. About 321 cities and counties could directly dial 180 countries. All together, there were 12.73 million telephone sets in the country, 112,437 long-distance lines and an intracity exchange capacity of 8.2 million lines.

However, demand still far exceeded what the telecommunications industry could provide. The telephone penetration rate rose only slightly to 1.29% in 1991 and to 1.63% in 1993, far below the world average of 12% in 1983 and even below the average 3.3% in Asian countries (12% if China is excluded) in that year (MPT, 1984). Long-distance lines in south and central China were so congested that only about 15% of the calls got through. The successful rate of intracity calls was about 60%. The waiting period for telephone installation was about 2 years (Di & Liu, 1994).

POLICY IMPLICATIONS

From the xenophobic period in the late Qing Dynasty to the reform era at the end of the 20th century, China's telecommunications industry has undergone a long and rough development, sometimes depressing and at other times astonishing. No matter how deeply the Chinese bury Li Hongzhang or the

"Great Leap Forward" in their memories, the legacies of history remain, and they render several policy implications.

STATE CONTROL OVER TELECOMMUNICATIONS

Despite the ups and downs and challenges from without and within, telecommunications in China has remained an undertaking tightly controlled by the state. From a historical point of view, state control has served several good purposes in a vast country like China. It has helped lay the foundation of a national telecommunications network, integrated local and long-distance services, standardized public networks, funneled funds to key projects, and devised nationwide plans for the overall development of the industry.

However, its legitimacy is very questionable in a rapidly developing economy driven by market forces. Growing out of a quasi-military institution, the telecommunications administration has become a large, inefficient bureaucracy. Its functional departments are overlapping and redundant, its vertical command hierarchy severs horizontal ties among services within itself, and its employees are poorly trained, with only 10% of them having an education higher than vocational school (Zheng, 1988).

Furthermore, it stifles competition from outside the system and, therefore, impedes the improvement of service quality. This situation is definitely detrimental to a booming telecommunications market. Despite the obvious drawbacks of such a control, however, the Chinese government is unlikely to loosen its long tradition of unified planning and concern over national sovereignty in communication.

THE SEPARATION OF PUBLIC AND PRIVATE NETWORKS

The expedient development of private telecommunications networks over the past 4 decades has created a monstrous invisible kingdom and tremendous tension between this kingdom and the public network. Currently, there are more than 30 private networks run by about 20 ministries and major state enterprises using both fixed-wire and radio-based facilities (Ure, 1994). According to one estimate, of China's 32 million lines of total network capacity, 12.74 million are for private and specialized use. This means that about 40% of the country's network capacity is in the hands of private networks, and most of these networks are poorly connected to the public network and compete with the public network for limited resources and the lucrative telecommunications market.

Even the Chinese authorities recognize this problem. The assessment of the situation in a MPT report to the State Council in 1982 well summarizes MPT's official view—the report said:

> Because of the severe backwardness of the posts and telecommunica-
> tions sector and the sector's inability to meet the urgent needs of vari-
> ous institutions, some of them have set up communication facilities of
> their own (such as microwave trunk lines and large- and medium-sized
> radio stations). Meanwhile, because we don't have a set of management
> measures to regulate them, there have been redundant projects,
> tremendous waste and chaos. As those facilities are separately con-
> structed to be self-containing systems, their technical standards are not
> compatible, their frequencies and bands overlap, and their management
> conflicts with each other. Consequently, underground cables overlap
> and mess up each other, open-wire poles are everywhere in a chaotic
> fashion, and airwaves interfere with each other. (MPT, 1986b, p. 346)

After several rounds of state directives and hard bargaining, especially since the State Council Directive No. 54, some private networks have
been connected to the public network. However, the tension has not eased;
in fact, it has grown in recent years with the advent and imminent establishment of such joint private network operators as the Ji Tong and Lian Tong.
Despite the repeated warning against private networks' service provision to
the public, several of them have already entered the market in such businesses as paging and long distance services.

THE "ARRANGED MARRIAGE" OF THE POSTAL SERVICE AND TELECOMMUNICATIONS

Since the founding of the People's Republic in 1949 the postal service and
telecommunications have been tightly bound together under the MPT, separated only for two brief periods of time. Although always a pride on the part
of the MPT, this "arranged marriage" has been a long-term thorn. It has
impeded the development of both the postal service and the telecommunications sector and has made people on both sides unhappy.

The postal service people are unhappy because they think their
plight has been covered up by their joint membership with the telecommunications sector in the MPT. For more than 30 years, rates for postal service
have remained unchanged, and the postal service has been in the red most
of the time. However, because of the joint membership the MPT's overall
accounting book has often shown a profit, thus covering up the loss and the
urgent need of the postal service. Moreover, 90% of the modest state
investment in the P&T industry has gone to the telecommunications sector,
leaving only 10% for the postal service. "From the viewpoint of telecommunications," said Gu Lianyu, associate director of Postal Networks &
Automation Committee of the China Telecommunications Association, "even
all the 100 percent for telecommunications is not enough. As a result, this
bondage makes the urgency of the postal service always lesser than that of

telecommunications and renders it impossible for the postal service to develop" (Gu, 1988).

The telecommunications people are unhappy because they think the postal service has dragged them down. They have had to make up the losses suffered by the postal service, share limited state funding with it, send its cadres to help run the postal service, and provide equipment for local telecommunications offices whose revenues all go to the postal service (Jing, 1987). For both groups, the best way out of this unhappy relationship seems to separate the postal office and telecommunications, leaving the former with the state and the latter liberalized (Gu, 1988).

A FEE SCHEME OF EXTREMES

Over the past few decades, the fee scheme of the telecommunications industry has swung from a super-stable, low-rate system to an extremely high-rate system. During the early days of the People's Republic, low fees were charged for the use of telecommunications facilities under the policy of "being fast, accurate, safe and convenient"—for the elite. In fact, those who had direct access to facilities such as telephones and telegram machines did not pay out of their own pockets. They were the Party and government officials, and their use of those facilities was covered by their offices. In 1958, the State Council further slashed telegram fees from 13.5 fen per character to 3 fen and cut long-distance telephone fees by 40% (Gong, 1993).

For the 25 years up until 1983, those low rates remained unchanged despite inflation and increasing costs of telecommunications operations. In 1980, when local Posts and Telecommunications Bureaus (PTBs) began to charge an installation fee, they suddenly found a gold mine that was not restricted by any conventions or consumer pressure. The fee went quickly from RMB$500 to RMB$2,000, and there were long lines of people eager to pay the hefty fee in order to get a telephone. Organizations were willing to pay because the money came from collective and, most often, state funds. Those who became rich quickly were willing to pay because a telephone gave them a status symbol they had never dreamed of—after all, it was a seller's market. By the end of the 1980s the fee soared to RMB$6,000 and, in some places, RMB$20,000, or about US$3,000. The same thing happened to cellular phones. The latest estimate is that a handset and registration would cost US$4,000—about an average worker's 10-year salary. Those two types of fees are probably the highest in the world relative to the modest per capita income in China (Ding, 1994).

All those fees have been set by local PTBs, and the profit thus generated has gone to them, with only 10 to 20% handed over to the MPT. Although the MPT has set caps for the fees over the years, they have often been ignored. By charging those fees, the PTBs have undoubtedly collected some needed money for reinvestment and higher salaries and benefits for the employees. However, those obviously inflated fees have also affected the rates of other services. With those fees serving as a baseline for the calculation of material and labor costs, other locally set rates such as rentals, data transmission, and fax fees have also shot up. In addition, those fees have given rise to an expanding profiteering private industry of "street phone services." Operators in this industry are owners of the high-price telephones. They lease their phones out and charge a hefty fee for the use, thus transferring the installation fees to consumers and causing chaos in telephone rates.

Because of the huge profits from installation fees, some PTBs have grown addicted to them. For example, one-fourth of Shanghai's investment in network expansion from 1980 to 1991 came from installation fees. In fact, the entire telecommunications industry has become fairly dependent on those fees. It is estimated that 36% of the total investment in fixed assets in the Eighth Five-Year Plan period from 1991 to 1995 will come from those fees (Di & Liu, 1994).

There has also been a growing concern that the high fees would one day dry up the quick-rich and elude the ordinary wage earners, thus driving telephone services into a no-man's land. Some people have suggested that compulsory bond purchase be used as an alternative. However, given the importance of such a seemingly endless source of revenue today, very few people in the MPT appear to be concerned about the establishment of a stable, reasonable, and long-term pricing scheme.

PROHIBITION OF FOREIGN INVOLVEMENT

At a time when land, stock, factories, and even political decisions are being traded for foreign capital, the concept of national sovereignty sounds extremely obsolete. However, it is not so in China's telecommunications industry, where national sovereignty is still the buzzword. Indeed, it is the last border the ever-present foreign businesspeople should not cross.

Ever since Li Hongzhang's first encounters with foreign telegraph companies, China has held that border firmly in the face of foreign encroachers, sometimes successfully, other times not. As recently as 1992, the Chinese government issued another document to reiterate the policy of prohibiting foreign businesses from operating telecommunications services in China. Such a policy is perfectly understandable when one looks at China's traditional xenophobia, its humiliating experience with Western powers in the 19th century, its occupation by the Japanese in the 1930s and 1940s, and its breakup with the Soviet Union in the 1950s.

However, given China's urgent need for foreign capital and management expertise, the policy clearly stands as an impediment to the development of the telecommunications industry, especially its service sector. From

1980 to 1990, China obtained US$1.2 billion of foreign capital for the telecommunications industry, most of which was spent in the purchase of intracity program-controlled switchboards (Gong, 1993). Compared with foreign investment in other infrastructure industries such as land development, transportation, and airlines, this is not an impressive amount.

In light of the rapid development of other industries and the experience of liberalization of the telecommunications market in other developing countries, some people have raised doubts about the wisdom of the "closed-door" policy in China's telecommunications service market. Others have even suggested foreign contribution to the introduction of new services and improvement of quality might eventually override concerns about national sovereignty and security (Tan, 1994).

UNEVEN DEVELOPMENT AND THE INFORMATION GAP

Over the years, China's telecommunications have developed in an extremely uneven fashion. Cities have developed far faster than rural areas, and special economic zones and open coastal cities have outpaced the rest of the country.

This uneven development has obviously stemmed from two strategic, or expedient, considerations. In the early years, it was the cities, especially the cities where the political, industrial, and commercial power was concentrated, that had the top priority for telecommunications development. In the reform era, it was the special economic zones and open coastal cities that got the lion's share of investment. Underlying these two considerations were, of course, the limited national resources. Because of the limited resources, the government had to be selective in granting development funds.

However valid the strategic considerations were at the time, the uneven telecommunications development has created and widened an information gap between the telecommunications rich and the telecommunications poor (see Chapter 5, this volume). Because information is not only a consumer product but an asset, such an information gap has contributed to the economic polarization of the cities and rural areas and the special economic areas and the rest of the country.

Unfortunately, the impact of such an information gap has not been fully recognized by the Chinese leadership. Judging from what is planned for the Eighth Five-Year Plan period and the years approaching the 21st century, priority in telecommunications investment and development is still given to the already privileged areas—and there is no sign of any plan to narrow or bridge the fast-growing gap. As the gap grows wider in the future, it may become a major source of economic conflict and political tension.

INSUFFICIENT INVESTMENT

Since 1950, China's investment in the P&T industry has averaged only about 1% each year—an extremely low percentage even compared with the rates of 2% for Pakistan, 2.6% for India and 7% for Malaysia in the early 1980s (MPT, 1984). Obviously, this low investment has been a root cause of China's slow and rough telecommunications development throughout history.

This problem was recognized in the early 1980s, and the telecommunications industry has since been positioned as a priority sector in the country's economic development. More investment has been injected, and more is expected in the latter part of the 1990s. The MPT has even set an ambitious goal to triple all telecommunications facilities by 2000 from the 1980 baseline.

Despite the attitudinal change and rhetorical emphasis, however, actual investment in the telecommunications industry has risen only marginally, and the state, obviously tied up with the needs from other sectors, has not promised any significant increase in its funding for the industry in the near future. Instead, it has imposed a major part of the fund-raising burden on the industry itself. The only two major sources of investment capital for the telecommunications industry are telephone installation fees and mobile communication revenues.

Even with the combination of state funds and industry revenue, there is still not enough money to finance the planned boost in the telecommunications industry. As the revenue from telephone installations dwindles, the shortage of investment will become even more acute. Unless the state is willing to make a significant commitment, China's telecommunications industry is going to be haunted by the shortage of needed investment, as it has been over the past century.

REFERENCES

Bai, S. (Ed.). (1982). *An outline history of China.* Beijing: The Foreign Languages Press.

Di, A., & Liu, J. (1994). Telecommunications development and economic growth in China. *Telecommunications Policy, 18*(3), 211-215.

Ding, L. (1994). The management of China's telecommunications industry. *Telecommunications Policy, 18*(3), 195-205.

Directorate General of Telecommunications. (1986). An outline of telecommunications development in China. In Editorial Board of China Transportation Yearbook. (Ed.), *China transportation yearbook 1986* (pp. 28-32). Beijing: China Transportation Yearbook Press. (in Chinese)

Gong, D. (Ed.). (1993). Post and telecommunications. In H. Ma & S. Sun (Eds.), *A compilation of major events in contemporary Chinese economy* (pp. 1843-1920). Beijing: China Finance and Economics Publishing House. (In Chinese)

Gu, L. (1988, October 4). Separate postal service and telecommunications, get out of the current plight. *Economic Reference News*, p. 1. (In Chinese)

He, F. C. (1994). Lian Tong: A quantum leap in the reform of China's telecommunications. *Telecommunications Policy, 18*(3), 206-210.

Industrial Transportation Department of State Statistics Bureau. (1989). *The development of transportation and posts and telecommunications in China: A compilation of statistics on transportation and posts and telecommunications from 1949-1987*. Beijing: China Statistical Press. (In Chinese)

Jing, Y. (1987, July 2). To reform in exploration, and to develop in reforms. *People's P&T*, p. 2. (In Chinese)

Liu, T. (1988). *Transportation and communication in national economy*. Chongqin: Chongqin Publishing House. (In Chinese)

Ministry of Posts and Telecommunications. (1984). To ensure a two-fold national economic development by a three-fold development of posts and telecommunications: A report outline to the State Council. *Posts and Telecommunications Management, 4*, 1-7. (In Chinese)

Ministry of Posts and Telecommunications. (1986a). MPT report on the reorganization of the management system of posts and telecommunications 1979. In Editorial Board of China Transportation Yearbook (Ed.), *China transportation yearbook 1986* (pp. 342-343). Beijing: China Transportation Yearbook Press. (In Chinese)

Ministry of Posts and Telecommunications. (1986b). MPT report on speeding up the construction of postal service and telecommunications to relieve the tension in telecommunications, 1982. In Editorial Board of China Transportation Yearbook (Ed.), *China transportation yearbook 1986* (p. 346). Beijing: China Transportation Yearbook Press. (In Chinese)

Ministry of Posts and Telecommunications. (1993). The MPT circular on the reaffirmation of non-foreign involvement in joint ventures in postal service and telecommunications, 1992. In Editorial Board of China Transportation Yearbook (Ed.), *China transportation yearbook 1993* (p. 445). Beijing: China Transportation Yearbook Press. (In Chinese)

Ministry of Posts & Telecommunications, Ministry of Finance, & State Price Administration. (1986). A joint circular on intra-city telephone installation charges by the MPT, Ministry of Finance and State Price Administration, 1980. In Editorial Board of China Transportation Yearbook (Ed.), *China transportation yearbook 1986* (pp. 344-345). Beijing: China Transportation Yearbook Press. (In Chinese)

Post & Telecommunications History Compiling Office. (1984). *A history of contemporary Chinese postal service and telecommunications.* Beijing: The People's Posts and Telecommunications Publishing House. (In Chinese)

State Council & Military Commission of Central Party Committee. (1986). The state council and military commission of central party committee regulations on the protection of telecommunications lines, 1982. In Editorial Board of China Transportation Yearbook (Ed.), *China transportation yearbook 1986* (pp. 347-348). Beijing: China Transportation Yearbook Press. (In Chinese)

Tan, Z. (1994). Challenges to the MPT's monopoly. *Telecommunications Policy, 18*(3), 174-181.

The First Five-Year Plan for national economic development of the People's Republic of China. (1955). Beijing: The People's Publishing House. (In Chinese)

The Sixth Five-Year Plan for national economic development of the People's Republic of China. (1983). Beijing: The People's Publishing House. (In Chinese)

The Seventh Five-Year Plan for national economic development of the People's Republic of China. (1986). Beijing: The People's Publishing House. (In Chinese)

Tripartite competition in China's telecommunications. (1994, March 14). *Hong Kong Economic Journal,* p. 2. (In Chinese)

Ure, J. (1994). Telecommunications, with Chinese characteristics. *Telecommunications Policy, 18*(3), 182-194.

Wei, L., & Dai, G. (1993). An outline of economic development. In H. Ma & S. Sun (Eds.), *A compilation of major events in contemporary Chinese economy* (pp. 1843-1920). Beijing: China Finance and Economics Publishing House. (In Chinese)

Xie, M., & Luo, Y. (Eds.). (1990). *Forty years of China's economic development.* Beijing: The People's Publishing House. (In Chinese)

Zheng, G. (1988, January 21). A preliminary analysis of the characteristics of our Country's P&T sector in the initial stage of socialism. *People's P&T,* p. 3. (In Chinese)

CHAPTER 4

THE POLITICAL ECONOMY OF THE COMMUNICATION SYSTEM IN CHINA

LEONARD L. CHU

INTRODUCTION

Reforms in China in the 1980s and their acceleration in the 1990s have brought about many fundamental changes in China. These changes are gradually, though not always unwaveringly, moving the country away from the total politicization that characterized the Cultural Revolution era. Although generally considered the slowest and most difficult sector to change, China's media and communication have seen dramatic changes as a result of the introduction of a market economy and administrative restructuring since late 1978. What are these changes in China's communication system? What about resistance to these changes? This chapter is aimed at providing a macrohistorical understanding of the continuity and change of the political economy of China's communication. It focuses on three aspects: ideologies, structure, and content. Forces resistant to changes are identified and discussed. It should be noted that although these factors are considered in separate sections, they intertwine and interact.

ORTHODOX IDEOLOGIES UNDER CHALLENGE

In all Communist countries, the fundamental ideology regarding the functions of communication follow the tenets of Marxism and Leninism as interpreted by those in power. Since the inception of Communism in China, the Communist media, whether mass or interpersonal, have had to propagate the ideals of the Chinese Communist Party (CCP), advance its ideological line, and execute its policies. As champion of the proletariat's interests, the CCP uses communication as an instrument of struggle against the bourgeois. It is assumed that through serving the Party which represents the people, communication is also serving the people. Because truth is assumed to have already been found in Communist ideals, communication thus functions to propagate and elaborate this truth and never question it or seek alternative interpretations.

POST-MAO RETHINKING ON COMMUNICATION FUNCTIONS

To ensure that communication systems perform what the Party plans and wants, all forms of communication, whether or not technologies are used, are integrated within its bureaucracies and with its policies. This arrangement has meant that communication has had to operate in accordance with the Party's guidance and supervision. Thus, between the 1920s and the 1940s the major task facing Communist communication was to win popular support and mobilize mass efforts in the Party's struggle against the ruling Nationalist government. After the CCP's proclamation of the People's Republic of China in 1949, mobilization of communication was shifted to focus on national reconstruction and the creation of "new socialist men" in the Communist ideal. This has been well documented by researchers.

Underlining all CCP ideologies and policies is the assumption that the media and communication are powerful weapons of class struggle. This conviction—and its enforcement—culminated in the Communist's successful struggle against the Nationalists with the proclamation of the Communist government on October 1, 1949. However, once remnants and sympathizers of the Nationalists had been effectively silenced and crushed in the 1950s, the CCP found itself in want of an enemy to struggle against. The events that unfolded from the late 1950s until the late 1970s show that this enemy was presumed to have resided within the CCP itself.

The antirightist rectification campaign in 1959 and the 12-year Cultural Revolution (1965 to 1977) saw the purge of many Communist leadership cadres and endless ideological campaigns in the general populace to eradicate these class enemies. As later developments indicate, the various campaigns against these "phantom" class enemies were futile and did great damage to economic and intellectual development. As powerful weapons of class struggle and policy instruments under the Party's tight control, media and communication were active partners in the hundreds of campaigns since 1949 (Yu, 1980). Although post-Mao Chinese leaders and scholars lamented, in retrospect, the conspiring roles played by the media and communication in implementing the CCP's many counter-productive policies and destructive campaigns, very few would argue that media and communication could have done otherwise. The media had been ideologically obliged and organizationally compelled to play an activist role.

Although the death of Chairman Mao Zedong in September 1976 and the subsequent arrest of his close associates, known as the Gang of Four, meant a new opportunity for change, the prescribed functions of communication have not only persisted but been reiterated by post-Mao Chinese leaders, whether Hua Guofeng, who immediately succeeded Mao, Deng Xiaoping, who masterminded the current reforms, or Jiang Zemin, who ascended to power after the military crackdown of the 1989 prodemocracy movement (Journalism Institute of Chinese Academy of Social Science [JICASS], 1980-1993). In short, in the eyes of CCP leadership communication has always had the role of educating and mobilizing the people to understand and execute the Party's goals and policies. This is best summarized in a 1981 CCP Central Resolution, which outlined six major duties for the mass media ("The Party Central's," 1982):

1. To follow strictly the Party line, its guiding principles and policies as laid out at the 3rd Plenary Session of the 11th Party Central Committee;
2. To earnestly carry out the propaganda for the persistence of the four basic principles (taking the socialist road, a people's democratic dictatorship, the Communist Party's leadership, and Marxism-Leninism-Maoism);
3. To publicize and promote the highly developed socialist spiritual civilization;
4. To correctly handle the relationship between praise and criticism;
5. To insist on the direction of serving the people and socialism and correctly and thoroughly carrying out the guiding principle of "letting a hundred flowers bloom and a hundred schools contend";
6. To strengthen the organization and discipline of the mass media as they are the Party's opinion organs.

DEBATES ON COMMUNICATION'S ROLES

Although the aforementioned duties have, up to the present, determined what mass media and communication must or must not do, there are differences in interpretation and changes in emphasis regarding these duties. Post-Mao CCP policies have concentrated on economic development rather than the ideological purification enforced since the late 1950s. This fundamental ideological and policy shift to economic development has meant that the media and communication now have more room to maneuver in carrying out their assigned duties. Before the current reforms, all communication forms and media were viewed as weapons in class struggle and tools of the Party. Now, focus on communication's role as a weapon of class struggle has shifted to that of viewing it as an instrument of the CCP's reform and open-door policies. The current reform and open-door policies have emphasized economic rationality; this requires knowledge of the latest market changes and the learning of new market techniques. Media and communication are being compelled for the first time by the changing circumstances to provide the latest information. On the other hand, because the CCP leadership also recognizes that hard work without relaxation may be counter-productive, communication and media are also encouraged to provide the people with entertainment. This shift has given rise to the official prescription of two new functions for communication; namely, to inform and to entertain, in addition to serving the CCP.

This change and persistence in the CCP's ideologies are encapsulated in two important documents—the talk given by the late Party Secretary General, Hu Yaobang (1985), on the Party's journalistic work delivered on February 8, 1985 and the Seventh Five-Year Plan adopted in the same year. Although generally regarded as a CCP liberal, Hu, in his address to journalistic leaders and cadres, unequivocally ruled out freedom for the Party's media and urged the media to serve the Party unswervingly and observe an "8 to 2" ratio in their praise and criticism of current policies. This explains in part why media criticism, though on the increase, still largely applies to low-ranking cadres and requires the approval of supervising Party committees. Criticism of high-ranking leaders is mostly sporadic and in response to instructions from above (Chu, 1983).

In addition to affirming Hu's position, the Seventh Five-Year Plan also promulgated the media's information and entertainment roles. It stated that journalistic units must accurately propagate the Party's line, principles, and policies while satisfying the people's multifarious needs for information dissemination, knowledge diffusion, cultural entertainment, etc. (JICASS, 1987).

Such an unequivocal declaration of the media's information and entertainment roles, unprecedented in CCP history, has not only ushered in the rapid expansion of communication media but also increased the diversity of its content. It has also brought about relentless challenges against orthodox ideologies regarding the function of communication. Whereas the CCP leadership wants the media to provide guidance for the public so as to ensure public support of its policies, reformists want the media to play a more critical role by reflecting public opinion whether or not it supports CCP policies. In short, although CCP leaders want the media to be docile "lap dogs," the reformists want the media to be the society's dutiful "watch dogs."

It is against this background that the media's prescribed role in guiding, rather than reflecting, public opinion, in supporting, rather than criticizing, policies, and in serving the Party's policies rather than the people's needs, has come under mounting ideological and operational challenges (Gan, 1994).1t is also against this background that Gan (1993) proposed his "one direction many voices" to urge the Party to allow the media and its practitioners to have greater autonomy in their reporting and criticism so long as they supported socialism (one direction). Because all communication media are run by the Party or government organs, the support of socialism is assumed and does not have to be established, according to Gan. The pros and cons of press freedom for economic and social development, a taboo topic, was at last hotly debated (Hu, 1988).

Although the debate has not yet been resolved, it has meant changes in thought and in action. For example, when the 13th Party Congress was convened in late 1987, then-CCP Secretary General Zhao Ziyang announced that policies of the central government and the Party would be made more "transparent" and that all levels of society should be encouraged to engage in "consultation and dialogues" (Yan, 1991). At the conclusion of the Congress some of the usually silent Chinese journalists began to ask critical questions.

To cater to the varied needs of society, non-Party, though not truly private, media have appeared. Many such local radio and TV stations as well as publications carry nothing but consumer information or entertainment. The increasing adoption of such technologies as telephones and fax machines, media that serve individuals and the market economy, can also be understood in this shifting ideological context.

It is true that perceiving the media and communication as weapons of class struggle has been reiterated on such occasions as the antispiritual pollution campaign of 1983, the anti-Western bourgeois liberalization campaign of 1987, and the antipeaceful evolution campaign in the aftermath of the military crackdown of the prodemocracy movement in 1989. However, this thinking has lost much of its clout. Rapid and widespread marketization of the economy has brought about decentralization and separation of the Party from enterprises, although the process is still incomplete.

Although contradictions exist, ongoing overt and covert debates over the functions of the media and communication have opened the minds of China's journalists and intellectuals. The spring of 1989 illustrated this clearly when millions of ordinary people either sympathized or supported the prodemocracy movement and more than 1,000 journalists joined the ranks of protesting university students and marched in Beijing to vent their yearning for "press freedom" (Liu-Jernow, 1993). Such a demonstration speaks of the ideological fermentation among Chinese intellectuals and journalists. In summary, communication, although remaining a tool under the CCP's tight control, has changed so much that it should no longer be understood as merely fulfilling the Party's propaganda goals. Communication in China now serves more varied functions, including not only transmitting the CCP's instructions, but providing consumer information, linking up business partners, and even peddling sex and crime. Although truly dissenting views still have tremendous difficulty in gaining access to the mainstream media, the room for maneuvering has enlarged.

THE EXPANDING AND LOOSENING COMMUNICATION STRUCTURE

Prior to the adoption of reform and open-door policies in late 1978, China's communication system was not only tightly controlled, it was truly underdeveloped in the sense that mostly primitive technologies, including wired loudspeakers or posters on makeshift bulletin boards, were adopted. Besides, access to or ownership of such personal media as telephones was almost nonexistent. All media, whether personal or mass, operated under the watchful eyes of the Party. This situation has been changing; the Chinese communication structure is now "externally" expanding and "internally" loosening. In addition, an "off-shore" extension of the structure is emerging thanks to adoption of modern communication technologies such as satellites, short-wave radio sets, videotape recorders, and so on. These modern communication technologies further expand and stretch China's communication structure.

THE EXPANDING STRUCTURE

Scholars used to note and applaud China's adroit blending of modern media and traditional folk media in the country's development (Rogers, 1976). Before the present reform and open-door policies, although adoption of communication technologies was extremely low the CCP was efficient in conducting its communication activities. For example, rural wired broadcasting networks and small groups were coordinated to extend the reach of such urban communication services as the telephone, wireless broadcasting or telecasting, and the print media. Because of centralized economic planning, societal need for communication services was kept at a minimum. The primitive communication technologies were adequate in serving the country's then limited need for information. As a result of the open-door policy and economic growth, the demand for information is increasing—this necessitates the expansion of the communication structure. The adoption of modern technologies in newspapers, radio, television, telephones, fax machines, videos, satellites, and so on has been rapid since the late 1970s. The growth of modern media effectively shifts the country's dependence on such traditional technologies as posters and loudspeakers as communication means.

    As can be seen in Table 4.1, all major media in China have experienced quantum jumps during the 1980s. The number of newspapers increased by nearly two thirds, radio stations almost tripled, and television

Table 4.1. Development of Selected Media in China Prior to Consolidation in 1990.

	1981	1985	1989
Newspaper (all)	476	1,170	1,496
Total yearly circulation (in thousands)	15,917,645	23,099,900	20,619,200
Dailies	—	231	263
Per 1,000 circulation	—	44.7	35.5
Radio stations	b125	213	531
MW/SW relays, transmitter	b482	568	a(1990)673
Radio receiving sets (in thousands)	b150,000	241,810	a368,000
Per 100 ownership	b14	23.1	a33.2
Loudspeakers (in thousands)	d90,000	82,710	82,370
% of households	49%	42.1%	38.3%
TV stations	c39	c202	a469
Over 1,000-watt transmitters/relays	c238	c514	a(1990)673
Satellite earth stations	c3	c1,598	a13,753
TV receiving sets (in thousands)	c10,000	c69,650	a166,000
Per 100 ownership	c1	c6.7	a14.9
Cable TV stations	—	—	e1,069
Subscribers (in thousands)	—	—	11,100
Films			
Features	f105	f144	f136
Science/education	f33	f45	f53
Documentaries	f276	f399	f256

Notes. Unless otherwise noted, see Journalism Institute of Chinese Academy of Social Science. (1982, 1986, 1990). Note that after the military crackdown on June 4,1989 there has been a tightening up of control over all media.
aSee Xun Xupei, "Functions and Operation of China's News Media during the New-era Decade" (xinshiqi shinian zhongguo xinwen meijie de gongnun yu yunzuo) in L. L. Chu & J. M. Chan. (1992).
bRadio statistics in "1981" column are those for 1982. See Journalism Institute of Chinese Academy of Social Science (1983).
cTelevision statistics for 1981 and 1985 are obtained from Editorial Board of China Broadcasting and TV Yearbook (1988).
dThe number of loudspeakers peaked in 1980 to 120 million. The drop wad due to adoption of radio receiving sets.
eCable statistics are for the year 1990 as reported in Y.L. Liu (1994).
fAll film statistics from Executive Yuan (1991). The final column statistics were those of 1989.

stations increased more than 10 times. In contrast, the use of loudspeakers began to decline as a result of rising ownership of radio sets in rural areas. In fact, during the early part of the 1980s the most sought-after household item was a television set (Chu, 1980/81). It is also reported that nearly one new newspaper was launched every other day (Sun, 1992). Film production also increased. Cheng (1986) noted that in the first 4 years after adoption of reform the production of feature films nearly doubled, jumping from 63 in 1979 to 115 in 1982.

Another noticeable sign of the expanding communication structure is the adoption of cable technologies. Official Chinese statistics in 1990 showed that there were 782 cable systems operated by various state enterprises and another 314 systems operated by local district governments. It was estimated that more than 12,000 stations were capable of relaying programs. The number of cable TV subscribers is estimated to be around 11.1 million (Liu, 1994).

Although consolidation measures after the crackdown of the prodemocracy movement in the Spring of 1989 have slowed down the expansion, modern communication technologies continue to be adopted. It is now a common scene in centers of economic success like Beijing, Guangzhou, Shanghai, and Shenzhen to see people using mobile telephones. There is no doubt that during the past 15 years tremendous progress has been made, but one only needs to consider China's 1.2 billion population and land area of more than 9,596,960 square kilometers to realize the diminutive proportions of China's "huge" communication structure. For instance, the addition of 12 million telecommunications lines in 1993 brought China's total to 42 million, accounting for only 3.5 lines per 100 people ("China Says," 1994)—this is still the world's lowest rate. However, it is already a great improvement. China has set the target of 140 million lines by the year 2000. That would be 1 line per 10 people, which still allows great room for development.

THE "LOOSENING" STRUCTURE

Media organizations in China, as in all Communist countries, are staffed by Communist members and supervised by cadres. In fact, journalists themselves are referred to as "journalistic cadres." Organizationally, there is also a clear media hierarchy or division of labor. For example, the *People's Daily* is a central level medium directly supervised by the Department of Propaganda and serves as the mouthpiece of the CCP's Central Committee. In addition, there are *China Youth, China Peasants, China Workers, Guangming Daily,* the *Liberation Army Daily,* and so on, which are published to serve different readers. Correspondingly, there are the Central People's Radio Station and the China Central Television Station. Although these national media are aimed at the whole country, each provincial or municipal Party committee also has its respective daily newspaper, radio station, and/or television station.

Because media are considered policy tools, profit making is not the primary concern. The move to a market economy, however, has meant that even the media have to become self-sustaining. As a result, mainstream newspapers under the supervision of the Party committees have launched lively supplements in order to attract an audience and advertising dollars. Some even go so far as to carry nude photos or lurid descriptions of sex or crimes. The more serious ones venture into exposes of corruption or social problems, which are not always condoned by the leaders.

With respect to radio and television, as counties and enterprises are being allowed to operate their own channels there has been a further loosening of the Party's tight control. For instance, in Shanghai and in the Pearl River Delta there are stations that model their format and style of programming after Hong Kong's. As media are required to become self-sufficient, they must increasingly become attuned to the needs of their audience. It is not that the CCP is relinquishing its control of the media; rather, the CCP has found it increasingly impossible to control them.

THE ALTERNATIVE STRUCTURE

The adoption of modern technologies has meant that the Chinese people now have access to an alternative "off-shore" media structure, which is not always to the liking of their leaders. For instance, Star-TV, Asia's satellite television service launched in October 1991, revealed that by mid-1993 China was already its largest market, claiming that 4.8 million of its 11.3 million Asian household receivers were in China (Karp, 1993). Reception of its Mandarin Chinese entertainment, BBC, and MTV, a popular music channel, was so popular that the CCP had to ban the purchase, installation, and use of dish antennas by individuals even if the ban may be unenforceable (Kaye, 1993). To placate CCP leaders, Rupert Murdoch, who acquired Star-TV's holding shares in 1993, decided to scrap both the BBC and MTV from the existing five channels as he contemplated expansion into China's media market ("Murdoch Says," 1994; "Star-TV Signs," 1994).

Listening to the Voice of America (VOA) has become another popular pastime or must for China's intellectuals. Estimates of its audience are put at 100 to 300 million (He & Zhu, 1994). VOA's impact culminated in the prodemocracy movement of 1989 and was one major factor in the American Congress' recent provision of US$10 million to establish a new Radio Free Asia to beam newscasts and programs into China and other Asian countries ("House Adds," 1994).

CONSEQUENCES OF THE CHANGING COMMUNICATION STRUCTURE

The expanding and loosening communication structure described earlier is also witnessing a restructuring of information flows in China. In the past, communication was basically vertical, dominated by a flow of information from the top down. Now more attention is being given to feedback, the flow from the bottom up. The increasing frequency of audience surveys and opinion polls is one indication (Chen & Mi, 1989). There has also appeared a greater horizontal flow of communication; namely, information exchange among individual enterprises and administrative units on the same administrative level. The return of advertising to the media is but one of many signs (Chu, 1979/80). In the past, much of the flow of information took place in the form of "covert" communication through bureaucratic channels (Oksenberg, 1974). Because of the separation of the Party from enterprises, easier access to private telephones and fax machines, and the need for efficient and timely trade transactions, the proportion of bureaucratic to overall societal communication has now been on the decline. The flow of information is thus much more overt and horizontal. In addition, the new communication structure also allows greater "exchange" flow of information with foreign countries.

In the long run, these changes may have the unintended impact of alleviating the burden on the country's already overloaded transportation system as the need to dispatch personnel to handle business in person is reduced. Needless to say, the changing communication structure also means greater capacity for a greater variety of messages and information.

INCREASINGLY VARIED AND UNRULY CONTENT

Changes in the media were observed shortly following the arrest of the Gang of Four in 1976. Restoration of the public's trust in the media was considered essential by the new leadership for future use of the media in propagating its policies. At first, the media were called on to criticize their performance under the Gang of Four's reign. Some major newspapers, including the People's Daily, went on at length to admit their own mistakes for having engaged in untruthful reporting (Yiu, 1983). Soon, calls for shorter and more timely news articles appeared. This was followed by improved page layouts and calls for more letters to the editor and criticism as well as more exposes of corrupt cadres who had abused their power for political or economic gains. Such changes made the People's Daily the most popular paper in the late 1970s and early 1980s as the paper succeeded in righting many of the wrongs committed during the Cultural Revolution (Chu & Chu, 1981).

WIDER AND LIVELIER COVERAGE IN PRINT MEDIA

Adaptation to the changing political economy was swift indeed. Comparing the content of the *People's Daily* in 1975-1976, me year before Mao's death and the purge of the Gang of Four, and 1979-1980, the first year after the introduction of reforms, Lee (1981) reported marked differences in the two periods. She noted that some 30 new topical categories being reported in 1979-1980. In addition, news was depoliticized. In 1975-1976, 83.2% of the news was political in nature, compared to only 36.4% in 1979-1980.

There was also more local news. In the 14 sampled issues of 1975-1976, there were 161 stories whereas 3 years later the count was 357. Economic news was on the rise, increasing from 6.2% to 42% and editorials commenting on economics also increased sharply, from 26.7% to 48.3%. Western countries receiving negative coverage were given positive reporting, with the United States recording the most dramatic change. Positive reporting leaped from 8.3% to 82.8%. Letters to the editors increased, as did the space devoted to art and literature. This trend has certainly continued into the 1990s with additional attention to sports and business.

Since reforms and the open-door policy were adopted in late 1978, China's highly centralized media have had a taste of market forces. Although the media continue to be owned by the state, the market is left to decide the life and death of most. Forced to become self-sufficient, many Party media, government institutions, Party organizations, and enterprises launched their own "supplementary" publications with the sole goal of making profits. The content of these tabloids is devoid of the political or ideological dullness usually found in publications directly supervised by the Party committees. Although some pluck the interests of women and youths, others focus on the consumer market or science and technologies. Life styles of popular entertainers and movie stars as well as radio and television programming are other major genres ("Pluralized News Channels," 1991).

To boost their sales, a few tabloid publications have turned to yellow journalism, peddling crime and sex stories. For instance, under the pretense of popularizing "legal knowledge" one tabloid in Hunan province printed a voluminous number of detailed descriptions of rapes, adulteries, and other violent crimes. Around mid-1985 there were more than 100 such tabloids, with circulation varying from tens to the hundreds of thousands (Pu, 1985). Although the Chinese authorities issued strict decrees to clamp down these publications, they have continued to dominate China's street-side and terminal newsstands. Popularity of these lively tabloids has contributed to the further decline of dull-reading official publications (Zhasiduo, 1993). In early 1993, the official English *China Daily* reported that the country's 18 major newspapers and magazines suffered an average 14% decline in subscriptions (Murphy, 1993). Circulation of the *People's Daily*, the CCP's mouthpiece, was reported to have dropped by 20% in 1993 ("CCP Oppresses," 1994).

Daring and Entertaining Electronic Media

On radio, the most dramatic changes occurred in 1993 when stations began to host phone-in programs. In Shanghai, for instance, listeners to East Radio can call up their midnight program hosts to share everything from traffic congestion to family spats, sex confessions, and accounts of crimes with them. The Beijing Broadcasting Station even went so far as to engage a popular Hong Kong radio host to take the calls. In spite of its popularity, the program was later dropped on the grounds that nonresidents were not permitted to do live broadcasting in China (Frankel, 1993).

In China, expansion of television since the late 1970s has meant an education for millions who had been deprived of such opportunities during the Cultural Revolution. In the mid-1980s, some 1,150,000 students were estimated to be attending television courses and another 400,000, radio courses—all were offered by the Central Radio and Television University in Beijing. In addition, similar courses were being offered by many provincial and municipal broadcasting universities. The courses included science, physics, chemistry, plant physiology, agricultural management, English, etc. (Zhang, 1986).

As China's most popular medium, television has responded swiftly to change, enlivening its screen with programming of more international news, dramas, foreign series, and films. The Biannual TV Festival held in Shanghai in 1988 best illustrated the CCP's unmistakable affirmation of the new functions of television. Popular singers and entertainers from Hong Kong, Japan, the United States, France, and the former U.S.S.R. were invited to attend its opening ceremony, which was officiated by Shanghai's mayor. During the one-week gala, 51 foreign soap operas and 79 documentaries were screened on television. Other provinces and more than 20 foreign countries provided a total of 500 films and programs. The event attracted a total audience in the hundreds of millions (Cheng, 1994). Although heavy propaganda continues to dominate the main evening newscasts, entertainment on television has become lively and diversified. Soap operas, historical dramas, variety shows, and pop music programs as well as series from Hong Kong and Taiwan have now become the usual fare on the evening screen. Such variety has meant "a rich resource for the construction of an alternative reality and a new political consciousness" (Lull, 1991, pp. 76-77) and has undoubtedly "opened the minds" of the Chinese (p. 170).

Films have also contributed to this "mind-opening" phenomenon. Used to serve ideological indoctrination in the past, films are now being produced to provide entertainment and relaxation, and even to satirize social problems. During the initial period of reform, feature films still served political goals such as condemning the disgraced Gang of Four, promoting Communist values, or extolling people to build China's four modernizations, but love and romance as well as humor, denounced as bourgeoisie during the Cultural Revolution, also began to reappear (Cheng, 1986). It did not take much time for films produced either inside China or jointly with Hong Kong or Taiwan producers such as the "Old Well," "Hibiscus Town," "Farewell My Concubine," "Alive," and "Blue Kite" to become not only excellent aesthetically, but also serious social commentaries provoking reflection on the Communist system and problems brought about by marketization of the economy. These films are either banned or severely criticized in China but they are winning international acclaim. This explains in part why the Ministry of Culture has decided to reassert its control of joint film ventures with overseas producers (Halligan, 1994).

RETURN AND GROWTH OF ADVERTISING

Prior to the 1980 reforms, advertising had been condemned as a decadent bourgeois practice. The return of advertising to China has contributed to horizontal information flow and consolidation of marketization of the economy. The content of advertising has also become much more varied, shifting its focus from wholesale industrial goods to retail consumer goods (Chu, 1979/80). With economic growth and improved living standards, approaches to advertising are also changing. Format and styles have become more lively—not only do glamorous women now appear frequently in advertisements, warmth and joy associated with the products or services are also being emphasized more than mere descriptions of the services or products (Chan, 1994). *Yazhou Zhoukan,* a Chinese version of *Asiaweek,* reported that in 1992 there were already some 20,000 advertising companies in China. The demand for advertising time or space is so high that clients usually have to wait 3 to 6 months, because both TV time and newspaper space are extremely scarce. For instance, the China Central Television's national channels broadcast 33 hours a day, but only 70 minutes of advertising is allowed. *China Advertising* (*Zhongguo Guanggao*) estimates that from 1981 to 1992 advertising volume grew at an annual rate of 40% (quoted in Chan, 1994). *Yazhou Zhoukan* estimated that total advertising revenue for 1992 would reach US$730 million, nearly 35 times that of 1981 ("Advertising's New Continent," 1992).

With advertising came multinational advertising agencies and consumerism, spreading an ideological climate favoring foreign products and services (Kim, 1987). For example, in the Summer of 1984 China's Central Television contracted with CBS to broadcast 60 hours of programming. CBS was to collect commercials from American manufacturers—ABC and NBC soon followed. As one commentator stated, "the Gang of Four is nothing compared with the Gang of Three" (Postman, 1985, p. 169).

In the early 1980s, commercials were selling products beyond the reach of the average Chinese. In the 1990s, brand-name advertising and people who can afford brand-name products have become common (H. Ming, 1991). *The Chinese Industry and Business Times* (*Zhonghua Gongshang Shibao*) reported that in Beijing expensive brand-name fashions ranged from RMB$6,800 for a man's business suit to RMB$71,000 for a woman's short mink coat. Such is the current state of conspicuous consumption that the former "xenophobia" that characterized the Cultural Revolution has now become "xenophilia." *The People's Daily* also noted a decline in spending on knowledge products for consumer and recreational products (Wang, 1992).

In addition to Chinese language advertising, English language advertisements are also allowed on the radio. In a 10-year joint venture with China Radio International, an Australian radio station named Easy FM/AM was slated to begin broadcasting advertisements on October 1, 1994 in English for 6 minutes per hour, 7 hours a day and 7 days a week selling Coca-Cola, McDonald's, Panasonic, and foreign automobiles (Masters, 1994).

As demand for advertising space and time far exceeds supply, advertising in the form of news has frequently crept into the pages and on the screens. "Cash journalism" with the sources paying the media or the reporters for favorable coverage of their activities or products has become so widespread that a journalistic code of ethics and numerous other measures were adopted or considered to stop this practice (Chang, 1991; "Strengthen Ethical," 1993). Shady public relations practices, from which even capitalist news media try hard to distance themselves, have become a major sideline frequently conducted and openly sanctioned by the Chinese Communist media. Such practices include organizing press conferences or exhibits on behalf of industries and businesses in return for cash compensation (Fang & Yang, 1991; "Strengthen Ethical," 1993). To ensure their attention, reporters at press conferences are now routinely paid US$10 to US$50 by the news sources. An article in national newspapers may fetch US$175 or even more. TV crews get even better deals. Entire front pages of newspapers may also be rented to advertisers for as much as US$200,000 per day. In addition, many news organizations run their own public relations or advertising affiliates (Benjamin, 1993).

POPULAR GENRES GETTING OUT OF CONTROL

Watching programs and singing songs from Hong Kong, Taiwan, and the West are now among the most popular recreational activities in China. In 1992 in Shanghai alone, Hong Kong and Taiwan singers gave 32 concerts ("Hong Kong, Taiwan Stars," 1993). In Guangdong province alone, audio cassettes of some popular singers sell more than one million copies ("Singing Out," 1994). Singers from overseas, many of whom enjoy cult status, have made so much money and are so popular that many of China's own singers have been driven out of the market. In December 1993, the Chinese government banned concerts by overseas singers, finally allowing local singers and entertainers an opportunity to recover.

Sex and violence have also crept into the media. As video tape recorders spread, so have vulgar videos. Politics has been yielding to commercialism. Similar trends can be observed in the former Soviet Union and Communist countries in Eastern Europe. No sooner had political control subsided, then commercialism stepped in. The newly gained freedom is certainly being put to the service of making profits.

Although still lacking complete freedom, the loosened communication system in the changing political economy has produced many thought provoking publications. Their circulation may be small, but their influence with the elites can be tremendous. For example, in June 1990, *Megatrends 2000: Ten New Directions for the 1990s* by Naisbitt and Aburdene was translated by none other than the Foreign Military Affairs Research Division of the Military Science Academy and published by the Central Party School. The translation is edited, but the world it presents can be very eye-opening.

The most iconoclastic publication is perhaps *Snow White and Blood Red* (*Xuebai xuehong*), a historical account of the barbarous battles fought between the Communists and the Nationalists in Northeast China from 1945 to 1948. Written by a People's Liberation Army lieutenant colonel born in the same year the People's Republic was founded, it takes a humanistic perspective in lamenting the human sacrifices while praising the bravery of both Communist and Nationalist troops. The author also unequivocally contrasts the backwardness of life on the Mainland under the Chinese Communists with the much higher living standard and greater freedom enjoyed in Taiwan under the defeated Nationalists.

Ruined Capital (*Feidu*), issued in December 1993, is another example. In addition to profuse use of vulgar language and sex scenes, this fiction is unmistakably a satire against current social phenomena punctuated by jeers at leaders. Other nonconformist titles include *The Trends of History* (*Lishi di chaoliu*), *Anti-Leftist Memoranda* (*Fanzuo beiwanlu*), *China's Leftist Catastrophes* (*Zhongguo di zuohuo*), and *Deng Xiaoping in 1976* (*Deng Xiaoping zai 1976*). All contain unmistakable criticism of the Communist system and Chairman Mao. These unwelcome titles are banned officially, but this has only boosted their sales on the black market.

The 5 years following the military crackdown of the 1989 prodemocracy demonstrations have seen intermittent tightening of controls over the "big" media. However, "small" media like books and tabloids as well as local radio and television stations often carry unapproved messages. Entertainment has not only survived but prospered (Chan, 1993; Chu, 1991). These media have continued to experiment with and model themselves after the successful formats practiced overseas. Although Chinese leaders like CCP Secretary General Jiang Zemin continue to demand that the media be tightly "held in the hands of true Marxists" and that public opinion be shaped to better serve Party policies, their words are drawn out by economic pressures. Whereas the mainstream "big" media continue to parrot official lines, the tributary "small" media, the tabloids, the telephones, the video houses, the books, etc., outside the watchful eyes of the Party, have found ways and means to develop popular genres of their own. This trend will definitely have a scathing impact on the development of China's politics and society.

CONCLUSIONS AND DISCUSSION

In spite of the rapid development of China's communication brought about by reform and the open-door policy, China's overall communication system remains underdeveloped and tightly controlled. The CCP continues to expect the major mass media to toe the Party line and serve its propaganda goals. However, adoption of modern communication technologies is making this control increasingly difficult, as evidenced in the proliferation of small media that cater to the needs of their clients rather than the Party. Satellite communication and the availability of telephone services to individuals and to private enterprises are also improving the efficiency of China's trade and business transactions, which is also beginning to spill over into bureaucratic administration.

Technologically and economically, the backwardness of China's communication is not all that negative. In June 1994, the Telecommunications Minister Wu Jichuan was reported to have observed that "China's telecommunications construction can leap over some development stages and technical levels which Western countries had gone through and directly adopt highly efficient new technology and equipment" ("China Says," 1994). In short, China can consider adopting the latest communication technologies without having to worry about phasing out "usable technologies," because in many cases they simply do not exist. As reform continues, so will China's development of communication. Despite the impressive growth observed in the past 15 years, China's low beginning means that it still has a long way to go before becoming a true information society.

As discussed in this chapter, several distinctive features of the changing political economy of China's communication can be identified. First, although the CCP's grip on media remains tight despite economic restructuring, depoliticization and commercialization of communication have been taking place. Second, there has been a rapid adoption of modern media in place of primitive technologies. This development, along with marketization of the economy, has forced CCP leaders and communication practitioners alike to rethink the functions of communication. The expanding communication structure has made it nearly impossible for the CCP to keep a close eye on the operation of the media, whether mass or individual. As the

CCP is no longer capable of controlling all media, Party leaders can only have their eyes on the major television stations and dailies directly supervised by ministerial or provincial Party committees. Now the CCP can only set the parameters for its executives and practitioners. As the economy continues to liberalize and grow, even the parameters the CCP sets from time to time are being stretched farther and farther.

Aside from its political impact, Chinese society is also incurring a cultural cost stemming from changes in the communication system. Once hailed as a model capable of defending the onslaught of Western culture (Pickowicz, 1974; Smythe, 1973), China is now experiencing the fate of many developing countries. Whereas depoliticization during the past 15 years has emancipated the Chinese from the CCP's rigid regimentation, commercialization has subjected them to a different kind of control. Decreasing popularity of indigenous Chinese cultural genres, such as the exquisite Beijing opera and classical music, and vulgarization and Westernization of the culture have worried many. These are vital issues that demand to be addressed but cannot be easily answered.

Writing in the early 1970s, Pool (1973), a communication scholar at MIT, observed that the change from a word-of-mouth system to a mass-media system of communication has made it very difficult for any government to control the circulation of unofficial information among the people. Pool accurately foresaw the changes in Eastern Europe, the former Soviet Union, and China. Although Communist regimes in these regions reacted at different stages of liberalization with bloody crackdowns or purges, access to small media and international broadcasts have made information control by the government futile. The communication system eventually contributed to the downfall of regimes in Eastern Europe and the Soviet Union as well as the furthering of reforms and the open-door policy in China. There is no doubt that the CCP is still firmly entrenched, but its authority has been persistently eroded as the country's political economy changes.

China is determinedly set on the track of adopting more technologies. Writing in two 1991 consecutive issues of *Newsfront*, a monthly published by the *People's Daily* to coordinate the media, two Chinese scholars (Jia, 1991; A. Ming, 1991) can hardly hide their admiration of the wonders of the latest communication technologies, which include DBS, HDTV, ISDN, optical fiber, teletext, PostScript (computer graphics), robots (to operate printing presses), TCS-lite (a mobile satellite earth receiving station), etc. They see great potential in these technologies to raise work efficiency and living standards as well as make contributions to social and economic development. In fact, plans to develop China's telecommunications infrastructure by providing telephone, facsimile, and telex services in economic centers and satellite communication to remote areas were spelled out about a decade ago in the 7th Five-Year Plan of 1986-1990 (Zhang, 1986).

In November 1992, the *Chinese Culture Daily*, official organ of the Ministry of Culture, suggested that the press be recognized as a commodity, that administrative interference be reduced, and that the media's survival be left to market forces ("CCP Media's Call," 1992). The April 1993 issue of *Mirror*, a pro-China, current affairs monthly in Hong Kong, reported that Deng Xiaoping had urged that press reform be bolder and remarked that even private newspapers might be allowed.

In terms of adopting technologies, in cooperation with a Taiwan-financed company, two communication satellites, APT Star 1 and APT Star 2, with a life span of 10 years, were scheduled for launch in December 1994 ("Taiwan Stake," 1994). All of these developments indicate China's unequivocal commitment to developing her communication infrastructure.

However, there are also retreats from this commitment. In the Spring of 1994 the editor of *China Youth Daily* was dismissed for his exposes of social problems and labor disputes. Yuan Hongbing, a Beijing University philosophy lecturer and a coauthor of the iconoclastic *Trends of history* was arrested ("Beijing University," 1994; "Beijing Youth," 1994). A set of new rules was also drawn up to limit film coproductions and stamp out joint ventures in films with overseas producers and stars (Halligan, 1994). Around this same time, the Central Propaganda Department's Deputy Director demanded that Chinese journalists strengthen their propaganda work in shaping public opinion to support Party policies ("Central Propaganda Department," 1994). These are, of course, very disturbing developments. However, when people in the future look back at these attempts at control, they will most likely view them as temporary, unsuccessful measures to forestall the process of further liberalizing China's communication structure.

For many centuries, human beings have struggled hard to emancipate themselves from political domination by dictators. Increasing liberalization in Asia, Africa, and South America as well as the collapse of Communist regimes in Europe all seem to be pointing to the completion of this process. However, during this process of political emancipation communication that used to be regimented to perpetuate political indoctrination is now being organized to sustain commercial messages, frequently at the expense of society's cherished values. Can this price be reduced or regulated? The swing from total political regimentation to market domination in China in the past 15 years, as well as similar changes in other former Soviet states, seems to say that, more than ever, we need to seek answers to this question. It also demands that we monitor continuously the impact of communications on human life.

REFERENCES

Advertising's new continent. (1992, May 31). *Yazhou Zhoukan (Asiaweek)*, pp. 50-51. (In Chinese)

Benjamin, R. (1993, August 9). *No free press in China—In more ways than one*. Baltimore Sun. (Obtained from e-mail)

Beijing University lecturer Yuan Hongbing arrested. (1994, April 30-May 1). *Sing Tao Daily*, p. 5. (Australian edition in Chinese)

Beijing Youth Daily editor-in-chief dismissed. (1994, May 2). *Sing Tao Daily*, p. 5. (Australian edition in Chinese)

CCP media's call for journalistic reform has become more progressive. (1992, November 7). *Central Daily News* (Overseas edition), p. 4. (In Chinese)

CCP oppresses liberal publications. (1994, May 7). *Central Daily News* (Overseas edition), p. 4. (In Chinese)

Central Propaganda Department demands strengthening of public opinion work. (1994, April 29). *Central Daily News* (Overseas edition), p. 4. (In Chinese)

Chan, J. M. (1993). Commercialisation without independence: Trends and tensions of media development in China. In J. Y. S. Cheng & M. Brosseau, (Eds.), *China review 1993* (pp. 1-21). Hong Kong: The Chinese University Press of Hong Kong.

Chan, K. W. (1994, May 17). Information content and problems of China's advertising. *Ming Pao*, Hong Kong, p. D7. (In Chinese)

Chang, G. (1991, July). Serious self-profiting by the Chinese press (dalu xin-wen hangye mousi yanzhong), *The Nineties*, p. 19. (In Chinese)

Chen, C. S., & Mi, X. L. (Eds.). (1989). *A perspective study of media communication effects in China*. Shenyang: Shenyang Press.

Cheng, K. H. (1986). *Social reality as reconstructed in Chinese cinema under Deng Xiaoping*. Unpublished master's thesis, Department of Journalism and Communication, The Chinese University of Hong Kong.

Cheng, Y. (1994). *A critical biography of Zhu Rongji*. Hong Kong: Ming Pao Publishing House. (In Chinese)

China says it's leaping onto telecom superhighway. (1994, June 21). *Reuter.*

Chu, G. C., & Chu, L. L. (1981). Parties in conflict: Letters to the editor of the *People's Daily*. *Journal of Communication, 31*(4), 74-91.

Chu, L. L. (1979/80). Advertising returns to China. *The Asian Messenger,* 4(2/3), 55-56.

Chu, L. L. (1980/81). Changing faces of China's TV. *The Asian Messenger,* 5(1/2), 34-36.

Chu, L. L. (1983). Press criticism and self-criticism in Communist China: An analysis of its ideology, structure, and operation. *Gazette, 31,* 47-61.

Chu, L. L. (1991, June 4). The good and the bad situation of the Chinese Communist media. *China Times*, p. 27. (In Chinese)

Chu, L. L., & Chan, J. M. (Eds.). (1992). *Communications and societal development*. Hong Kong: The Chinese University of Hong Kong. (In Chinese)

Chue, C. P. (1994, January 13). Official publications feel the threat. *Central Daily News* (Overseas edition), p. 4. (In Chinese)

Editorial Board of China Broadcasting & TV Yearbook. (Ed.). (1988). *China broadcasting & TV yearbook 1987*. Beijing: Beijing Broadcasting Institute.

Executive Yuan. (1991). *A survey of mass media and their management organizations in the Mainland*. Taipei: Government Information Office.

Fang, J. L., & Yang, W. (1991, July). How we banned paid journalism. *Newsfront* (*Xinwen zhanxian*), p. 16. (In Chinese)

Frankel, M. (1993, August 31). All the nudes that fit to print. *Bulletin*, pp. 58-59. (Australia's edition of *Newsweek*)

Gan, X. F. (1993). New situations call for reform of the press system. *Vision Points, 2*, 27. (In Chinese)

Gan, X. F. (1994). Debates contribute to the development of the journalistic science. *Journal of Communication, 44*(3), 38-51.

Halligan, F. (1994, January 27). Beijing cuts back on film projects. *South China Morning Post*, p. 4.

He, Z., & Zhu, J. (1994, February). The "Voice of America" and China. *Journalism Monographs*, No. 143.

Hong Kong, Taiwan stars blinding China's youth, report. (1993, December 13). Agence France Presse [AFP].

House adds funding for Radio Free Asia. (1994, June 28). *Reuter*.

Hu, J. W. (1988). The freedom to discuss "press freedom." In Chinese Journalism Society (Ed.), *Collection of essays on press freedom* (pp. 1-6). Shanghai: Wenhui Press. (In Chinese)

Hu, Y. B. (1985, May). On the Party's journalistic work. *Newsfront*, pp. 2-5.

Jia, S. P. (1991, July). Adoption of hi-tech by the American press. *Newsfront*, pp. 45-46.

Journalism Institute of Chinese Academy of Social Science. (1980-1993). *Chinese Journalism Yearbook*. Beijing: Chinese Social Science Press. (In Chinese)

Karp, J. (1993, October 21). Prime time police: China tries to pull the plug on satellite TV. *Far Eastern Economic Review*, pp. 72-73.

Kaye, L. (1993, October 21). Shooting star: Peking may find ban is unenforceable. *Far Eastern Economic Review*, pp. 73-74.

Kim, S. S. (1987). *The communication industries in modern China: Between Maoism and the market*. Unpublished doctoral thesis, Centre for Mass Communication Research, University of Leicester, Leicester, UK.

Lee, Y. L. (1981). Changing faces of China's press. *The Asian Messenger, 5*(3), 32-35.

Liu, Y. L. (1994). A research on cable television laws and regulations in mainland China. *Journalism & Communication, 1*(1), 69-87. (In Chinese)

Liu-Jernow, A. (1993). *"Don't force us to lie": The struggle of Chinese journalists in the reform era.* New York: Committee to Protect Journalists.

Lull, J. (1991). *China turned on: Television, reform, and resistance.* London: Routledge.

Masters, R. (1994, June 30). Chinese jingle has Singo atingle. *The Sydney Morning Herald,* p. 3.

Ming, A. X. (1991, August). Prospects of next generation new communication technologies and new media. *Newsfront,* pp. 40-43.

Ming, H. (1991, December). Brand-name surges in the mainland. *The Nineties,* pp. 26-27. (In Chinese)

Murdoch says he broke BBC contract to appease Beijing. (1994, June 14). *AFP.*

Murphy, P. (1993, June 23). State grip on media tight despite economic liberalization. *Inter Press Service.*

Oksenberg, M. (1974). Methods of communication within the Chinese bureaucracy. *China Quarterly, 57,* 1-39.

The Party Central's resolution concerning current guiding propaganda principles for newspapers, periodicals, news, and broadcasters. (1982). In *Selected documents since the 3rd plenary session* (Vol. 2, pp. 681-689). Beijing: People's Press. (In Chinese)

Pickowicz, P. (1974). Cinema and revolution in China: Some interpretive themes. *American Behavioral Scientist, 17*(3), 328-359.

Pluralized news channels break through monopoly. (1991, September 22). *Yazhou Zhoukan,* pp. 26-27.

Pool, I. S. (1973). Communication in totalitarian societies. In I. S. Pool, W. Schramm, F. W. Frey, N. Maccoby, & E. B. Parker (Eds.), *Handbook of communication* (pp. 462-511). Chicago: Rand McNally.

Postman, N. (1985). *Amusing ourselves to death.* New York: Penguin.

Pu, S. H. (1985). Monsters in magic bottles: Yellow tabloids in Mainland China. *United Monthly* (Lianhe Yuekan), 46, 115-119. (In Chinese)

Rogers, E. M. (Ed.). (1976). *Communication and development: Critical perspectives.* Beverly Hills, CA: Sage.

Singing out one's own popularity. (1994, May 29). *Yazhou Zhoukan,* pp. 60-61.

Smythe, D. W. (1973). Mass communications and cultural revolution: The experience of China. In G. Gerbner, L. Gross, & W.H. Melody (Eds.), *Communications technology and social policy: Understanding the new "cultural revolution"* (pp. 442-465). New York: Wiley.

Star-TV signs up prime-time China football. (1994, July 4). *AFP.*

Strengthen ethical construction of the journalists' team to stop "paid journalism." (1993, October). *Newsfront,* pp. 4-8.

Sun, X. P. (1992). Functions and operation of China's news media during the new era decade. In L.L. Chu & J.M. Chan (Eds.), *Communication and societal development* (pp. 63-81). Hong Kong: The Chinese University of Hong Kong.

Taiwan stake in China launch. (1994, June 29). *Associated Press.*

Wang, X. Y. (1992, January). Beijing files. *The Nineties*, pp. 66-67. (In Chinese)

Yan, Z. X. (1991, August). *From supervision by public opinion to guidance by public opinion: An anatomy of two perspectives on public opinion.* Unpublished manuscript, Department of Journalism and Communication, The Chinese University of Hong Kong.

Yiu, H. (1983). Falsehood, exaggerations, and empty talks in the Chinese Communist press. In *Academic Journal 1983 of the Society of Journalism and Communication* (pp. 24-29). Hong Kong: Chinese University of Hong Kong. (In Chinese)

Yu, Z. J. (1980). On the nature and duties of the press after shift of the Party's work focus. *Treatises on Journalism, 1*, 1-10. (In Chinese)

Zhang, S. Q. (1986). Solving problems of national development through communication technology. *Media Development, 33*(1), 6-7.

Zhasiduo. (1993, August). From "orioles sing and swallows dart" to "flower-decorated streets and willow-lined alleys": The flooding of popular tabloids. *The Nineties*, pp. 12-13. (In Chinese)

SURVEY OF TELECOMMUNICATIONS IN CHINA

Part II offers a survey of the current state of telecommunications in China. Uneven development is a common phenomenon in LDCs; the "backward" sector often drags the feet of overall development, whereas the "advanced" sector exploits the manpower and resources of the backward sector. The advanced-backward gap is widened instead of narrowed in time. Paul Lee examines this phenomenon in regard to telecommunications in "Uneven Development of Telecommunications in China." He analyzes the "engulfing" and "uplifting" strategies to narrow this gap. The former aims at expanding the urban core into the rural and remote areas, whereas the latter resorts to massive injection of capital into the rural areas. Lee suggests that the "engulfing" strategy should be accompanied by the "uplifting" one to reduce the dualistic nature of telecommunications. Various means of obtaining capital for investment are also discussed.

Using the data of China, Jianguo Zhu examines the causal relationship between telecommunications and economic growth in "Telecommunications and Economic Development in Shanghai: A Case Study." To his and probably many people's surprise, he finds support for the contribution of telecommunications to China's economic growth as a whole, but fails to find such a contribution in the industrial city of Shanghai. He seeks to explain the result through the forms of social structure and postulates that in an industrial structure which is characterized by economies of scale and enormous centralization in labor, material, capital, plant, and equipment, telecommunications plays a less important part in economic growth. In agrarian and information societies, however, the scattered production units and different work patterns require efficient communication. Telecommunications' contribution to growth is more obvious in the decentralized setting.

111

An important component of telecommunication services is electronic mail. Bryce McIntyre gives a report on the current state of electronic mail in "China's Use of the Internet: A Revolution on Hold." He discusses the financial and language issues involved in the use of electronic mail networks. He thinks that the development of these networks will weaken authoritarian control in China.

Junhao Hong, in "China's Satellite Technology: Developments, Policies, and Applications" gives a detailed account of satellite development in China since the 1970s. He analyzes satellite policies from the past three decades, showing a shift of emphasis from national security and prestige to commercialization and socioeconomic uses. Hong identifies three weaknesses in China's satellite programs: political orientation, lack of infrastructural support, and neglect of social applications.

For a long period of time, China has used Hong Kong as an important outlet not only for trade, but for communication to the outside world. Hong Kong has played a significant role in China's telecommunications development, a fact that is often ignored. In "The China-Hong Kong Relationship in Telecommunications," Zhaoxu Yan discusses the contribution of Hong Kong to China's telecommunications development and vice versa. Yan also examines the possible relationship between Hong Kong and China in telecommunications after 1997 when control of Hong Kong reverts to China.

The inclusion of a chapter on Taiwan in this book serves a purpose; namely, to contrast the capitalist mode of telecommunications development with the "socialist" mode. Before the 1970s, mainland China's telecommunications development was rather slow compared to Taiwan. In 1981, mainland China reached .45% telephone density (CSSB, 1982), whereas Taiwan already had 17.6% in 1980 (see Chapter 10).

In "The Beginning of a New Era: Privatization of Telecommunications in Taiwan," Georgette Wang and Fan-Tung Tseng attribute the growth of Taiwan's telecommunications to continued investment in this sector under a series of "Four-Year" plans. In 1950 Taiwan had only .2% telephone density, but in four decades' time, it now has 42% telephone density. In contrast, China may reach only about 5% in the year 2000. Taiwan is currently engaged in telecommunications reforms through liberalization and privatization. Wang and Tseng analyze the background for liberalization and point out that after the security issue disappears, economic rationale takes precedence in telecommunications development. The pressure from the General Agreement on Tariffs and Trade (GATT) is also a force behind liberalization of telecommunications, yet the liberalization process is dragged by government's heavy bureaucracy. The Taiwan experience may provide some useful reference for the Mainland.

REFERENCE

State Statistical Bureau. (1982). *China statistical yearbook 1981*. Beijing: China Statistical Press.

CHAPTER 5

UNEVEN DEVELOPMENT OF TELECOMMUNICATIONS IN CHINA

PAUL S.N. LEE

INTRODUCTION

The 1980s was an important period for Chinese political and economic development—during this time, Deng Xiaoping rose to power. The 3rd Plenum of the 11th Central Committee of the Chinese Communist Party (CCP) held in 1978 made modernization the highest state goal; this reformist line has since dominated the political scene. Despite the tragic crackdown of the democratic movement in Beijing in 1989, China has continued its open-door policy and economic reforms. In the period between 1979 and 1991, China had an average annual GNP growth of 8.7%; its per capita GNP rose from RMB$375 in 1978 to RMB$2,063 in 1992 (State Statistical Bureau [SSB], 1993).

However, the growth rate is uneven. The coastal provinces and cities grew much faster than inland areas. In 1991, Shanghai had the highest per capita national domestic product (GDP) (RMB$6,675), followed by Beijing (RMB$5,781), Tianjin (RMB$3,944), Guangdong (RMB$2,823), Liaoning (RMB$2,707), and Zhejiang (RMB$2,310) (SSB, 1993). On the other hand, the per capita national income of Guizhou, Guangxi, Anhui, and Gansu were RMB$890, RMB$1,052, RMB$1,058, and RMB$1,133, respectively. Apart from the disparity between coastal and inland regions, uneven development also exists between rural and urban areas. For instance, in Guangdong, one of the fastest developing provinces, about 4 million people

113

in the mountainous areas still lead a poor life and 30 counties are living on state subsidies (Cao, 1992).

Before 1984, rural-urban migration was severely restricted by the state. Despite the growth of industry that accounted for 70% of the national product in 1978, the rural-urban ratio was maintained at 8:2. The surplus labor was kept in rural areas, resulting in low production rates and low incomes. In the early years of reform, the rural-urban income disparity was reduced, with the ratio reaching its lowest level of 1:1.71 (Han & Li, 1994). In recent years, however, the labor absorption ability of rural industries has been reduced by their modernization efforts using capital intensive technologies. For example, during 1978-1984, when the value of rural industries increased by 1%, job opportunities increased by .57%. In 1992, however, the job opportunity rate was reduced to .15%.

From 1978-1984, rural industries on average absorbed 12.6 million rural workers per year. But from 1989-1992, they could on average absorb only about 2.6 million rural workers per year (Commentator, 1994). Accompanying this drop in rural employment is increasing income inequality. Such inequality is growing within the rural population. In 1983 the Gini coefficient in rural areas was 0.3, and rose to .31 in 1989 and .33 in 1993 (Han & Li, 1994). This growing inequality in society is reflected in telecommunications.

CORE-PERIPHERAL DISPARITY

Uneven development in telecommunications most obviously exists between the coastal and inland regions. The coastal region has become the economic core, whereas the inland and remote areas have become an economic periphery. This is, in part, due to physical and historical differences, but is also a result of the state policy of opening up certain cities and special economic zones along the coast. The open cities and special economic zones have greater flexibility in handling foreign investment, taxation, and bureaucratic red tape. In 1991 there were 19 open cities and special economic zones.

Table 5.1 shows that in 1992 Guangdong had the largest number of telephones (2,630,790), followed by Jiangsu (1,504,899), Beijing (1,236,868), Shanghai (1,156,859), Liaoning (1,066,674), Shandong (1,036,411), and Zhejiang (1,036,353). These seven provinces and cities possessed 51% of the telephones in China, whereas Tibet (18,717), Ningxia (70,352), Qinghai (71,921), Hainan (117,266), Guizhou (168,842), Yunnan (257,318), and Xinjiang (244,942~the seven least developed provinces—accounted for only 5%.

It is evident that the peripheral areas are lagging behind in telecommunications investment. In 1988, although Tibet and Xinjiang recorded RMB$9 million and RMB$8 million capital investment respectively in telecom-

Table 5.1. Telephone and Paging Service by Province, 1992.

Province	Total	Of which rural telephones	%	Paging Subscribers	Mobile Telephone Subscribers
National total	18,888,188	3,438,810	18.2	2,220,238	176,943
Beijing	1,236,868	19,218	1.6	91,587	11,333
Tianjin	428,608	29,434	6.9	30,684	4,714
Hebei	790,694	111,577	14.1	44,062	3,071
Shanxi	425,916	44,701	10.5	25,035	1,790
Inner Mongolia	363,537	50,905	14.0	8,246	636
Liaoning	1,066,674	135,506	12.7	137,810	4,779
Jilin	603,208	106,852	17.7	35,677	2,747
Heilongjiang	745,924	82,153	11.0	79,388	3,916
Shanghai	1,156,859	129,011	11.2	156,225	11,479
Jiangsu	1,504,899	394,161	26.2	88,278	985
Zhejiang	1,036,353	344,509	33.2	126,446	6,084
Anhui	456,665	70,271	15.4	26,878	1,994
Fujian	564,359	88,152	15.6	143,851	10,862
Jiangxi	331,911	62,519	18.8	20,026	1,510
Shandong	1,036,411	215,588	20.8	84,458	
Henan	639,550	75,224	11.8	45,932	3,948
Hubei	611,231	115,619	18.9	59,377	5,825
Hunan	531,636	130,518	24.6	68,601	2,571
Guangdong	2,630,790	855,236	32.5	705,935	2,061

Table 5.1. Telephone and Paging Service by Province, 1992 (cont.).

Guangxi	309,267	54,067	17.5	48,507	82,987
Hainan	117,266	13,647	11.6	27,163	2,019
Sichuan	803,510	115,621	14.4	70,095	1,013
Guizhou	168,842	24,141	14.3	11,345	5,169
Yunnan	257,318	56,979	22.1	32,356	
Tibet	18,717	320	1.7	298	
Shaanxi	400,779	48,802	12.2	19,573	4,357
Gansu	263,182	23,010	8.7	9,071	1,085
Qinghai	71,921	3,134	4.4	1,069	
Ningxia	70,352	4,780	6.8	3,737	
Xinjiang	244,942	33,155	13.5	18,528	8

Note. Data compiled from State Statistical Bureau (1993).

munications, more than that of Jiangsu (RMB$5 million), Zhejiang (RMB$5 million) and Shandong (RMB$5 million), three core areas—Guangdong (RMB$197 million), Beijing (RMB$143 million), and Shanghai (RMB$132 million—accounted for nearly 60% of total capital investment in telecommunications (SSB, 1989). In 1991, the total investment in posts and telecommunications was RMB$1,450 million in Guangdong and RMB$702 million in Liaoning, but only RMB$75 million in Guizhou and RMB$44 million in Tibet (Editorial Board of China Transportation Yearbook [EBCTY], 1992).

This unbalanced pattern in development is due to the rapid growth of business activities and quick return on investment in the coastal regions. As of 1990, it cost only RMB$0.04 for a 3-minute call (China Posts & Telecommunications, 1990). The set-up cost for a telephone in 1992 was about RMB$2,000—RMB$5,000 (Zhou, 1992), which installation charges could not cover until recently. Only with frequent usage can telephones recover an investment and earn a profit. Rural telephones in Guangdong, for example, made a profit of RMB$28.63 million in 1987, whereas those in Gansu, a northwestern province, earned only RMB$42,000. In 1986, Gansu's rural telephones were still losing money (EBCTY, 1988). In 1991, the total number of long-distance calls in Guangdong was 457.9 million, accounting for 26% of the national total, whereas that of Gansu was 14.7 million, accounting for less than 1% (EBCTY, 1992, p. 492).

The coastal regions also had the fastest development in mobile communication. In 1992, Guangdong had the largest number of paging (705,935) and mobile telephone subscribers (82,987), accounting for 32% and 47% of the national total respectively. The next three places having rapid development in mobile communication were Shanghai, Beijing, and Liaoning (see Table 5.1). Telecommunications development in Guangdong outpaced all other provinces in the early 1990s.

A major reason for Guangdong's rapid growth is its remarkable success in attracting capital investment, both from internal and overseas sources. Between 1980 and 1991, total capital investment in state-owned enterprises amounted to RMB$183.6 billion, with an average annual increase of 26%. The state budget only contributed about 5% of this total capital investment—the majority of capital was invested by local and foreign investors (Guangdong Statistical Bureau, 1993). Hong Kong was the most important source of external investment in China, accounting for about two thirds of the total. In 1993, around 3 million people were working for Hong Kong companies either through joint ventures or work commissioned by Hong Kong companies (Hong Kong Government, 1994).

In sharp contrast are the northwestern provinces. Ningxia province, for example, had a population of 4.7 million in the 1990 census, but only 23,571 urban and 1,826 rural households had telephones. For some counties, there were less than 30 telephones (Ningxia Statistical Bureau, 1991). Tibet is another example. Its telephone density rose from .24% in 1980 and

.39% in 1985 to .67% in 1990. Despite this progress, as of 1992, 50 of its 76 counties had no long-distance phone service ("Rapid Growth," 1992.

RURAL-URBAN DISPARITY

Apart from the difference between coastal and inland areas in telecommunications development, China also exhibits a serious rural-urban disparity. In 1992, only 18% of telephones were in rural areas; 81% of two-way communication facilities were located in urban areas. Among all provinces, only Zhejiang (33.2%), Guangdong (32.5%), and Jiangsu (26.2%) had more than a quarter of their telephones serving rural areas. In some provinces, such as Tibet (1.7%), Qinghai (4.4%), and Ningxia (6.8%), less than 10% of telephones served rural populations (see Table 5.1).

In terms of telephone subscribers, the rural-urban gap is even greater. The figures for 1992 show that there were 3.5 times more urban than rural subscribers (see Table 5.2). Such a disparity is due to low levels of investment in rural telecommunications as well as financial losses from their telephone operations. In 1990 more than one third of the provinces and administrative areas lost money in rural telephony, the total loss amounted to RMB$309.4 million (EBCTY, 1992). This financial loss is a disincentive for provincial or local governments to invest in rural telephones

The time series data in Table 5.2 shows that with the growth of national economy the rural-urban gap has not narrowed; on the contrary, the gap has widened over time. In 1965, when there were .29 telephones per 100 persons, the rural-urban ratio was 1:1.6. A quarter century later, when the number of telephones had increased to 1:61 per 100 persons in 1992, the rural-urban gap had widened to 1:3.5. This indicates that the growth of rural telephone services is not catching up with urban services. Such rural-urban disparity is not a problem if the degree of urbanization is high. For example, cities like Beijing, Tianjin, and Shanghai only have a small proportion of rural telephones (see Table 5.1), yet the majority of people in these cities live in urban areas with easy access to telephone service. In 1992, the nation, however, was still 72% rural (SSB, 1993). The lag in development of rural telecommunications services implies that a huge number of people being denied the opportunity to interact with others instantly over long-distance lines. This lack of instant access through telecommunications will drag the nation's overall development for the years to come.

Table 5.2. Development of Telecommunications Services in China, 1965-92.

Year	Telephones (per 100 persons)	Long-distance calls (10,000) subscribers)	Urban telephones (10,000 subscribers)	Rural telephones (10,000
1965	.29	8,869	77.11	49.22
1970	...	8,570	78.41	52.74
1975	...	15,151	103.28	65.92
1981	.45	22,049	142.64	79.45
1982	.46	23,574	153.87	80.38
1983	.50	26,556	168.86	81.90
1984	.53	31,553	191.07	86.36
1985	.60	38,254	218.96	83.07
1986	.67	42,303	250.51	99.87
1987	.75	51,525	293.04	97.68
1988	.86	64,617	362.30	110.39
1989	.98	85,300	439.62	128.42
1990	1.11	116,771	538.45	146.58
1991	1.29	172,921	670.83	174.23
1992	1.61	287,380	920.57	226.34

Note: Data not available. Data compiled from State Statistical Bureau (Various years).

IMPACT OF UNEVEN DEVELOPMENT IN TELECOMMUNICATIONS

Although the relationship between telecommunications and economic growth is far from conclusive (see chapters 1 and 6, this volume), quite a few studies (Cronin, Parker, Colleran, & Gold, 1991; Hardy, 1980; Wellenius, 1984) show that telecommunications development has a positive impact on the economy. The Ministry of Posts and Telecommunications (MPT) of China also estimated that from 1981-1983, every dollar invested in telephone construction brought about RMB$6.7 in macroeconomic benefits (Xiao, 1993). Another study showed that in 1988 an additional investment of RMB$100 million in the posts and telecommunications industry, after a lag of three years, would result in RMB$1.38 billion in macrobenefits in terms of technical progress and national income growth from the 4th to 10th years. In other words, it had a macro benefit ratio of 1:13.8 in 10 years (Di, 1993).

In 1990, it was estimated that development of telecommunications could reduce existing vehicle traffic volume in China by one third. This would save RMB$10 billion a year. If satellite communications worked efficiently with ground communications, the traveling time of capital to and from banks could be saved by 20%, increasing capital save by RMB$10 billion per year (Gu & Tang, 1990).

A huge rural sector deprived of effective communication and immediate information will remain poor and drag down the modernization of the whole country. It will become a heavy burden for the advanced urban core to develop. The urban core will face increasing economic and political pressures from the rural periphery. Even if the urban core can ignore or resist the economic and political pressures from the rural periphery, its economic integration with the periphery makes it difficult to ignore the poor telecommunications facilities there Without efficient communication with the rural periphery, the urban core's development will be hindered by an inefficient flow of information.

A survey on Hunan peasants in 1993 showed that 64% of the peasants expressed their need for production, technology, and market-related information; only 6% said they did not need such information. When they were asked about their grievances, lack of information ranked fourth after heavy taxation, chaotic markets, and crime (Yang & Liu, 1994). This survey shows that improvement of information will help the peasants increase their productivity and produce products the market needs. Telephone is different from mass media in its interactive nature. The users of mass media usually cannot get an immediate response from the information source, but peasants can reach out for the information they need through the use of the telephone. The telephone and other interactive media put control into the hand of the users.

A backward rural periphery usually generates less return on investment. A survey in southern Shaanxi showed that the input of RMB$1 labor in rural industries generated RMB$0.02 profit, but the same input of RMB$1 dollar labor (migrant labor) in urban cities garnered a profit of RMB$2.0 (Han & Li, 1994). The total macro benefits realized in the urban core may be reduced if telecommunications investment was directed to the inefficient markets of the rural periphery through state appropriations. However, the low return on investment in telephony in rural areas is an obvious disincentive for the state to use the scarce financial resources in rural areas. The peasants cannot place much hope in the state to finance the development of rural telephony.

"UPLIFTING" VERSUS "ENGULFING" STRATEGY

In face of a vast backward telecommunications sector, China has two options: an "uplifting" strategy and an "engulfing" strategy. The first option is to inject massive capital into the rural-peripheral sector to speed up its telecommunications development. The second strategy is to use the model of unbalanced growth (Baumol, 1967; Hirschman, 1958) that continues to develop the urban core and only some strategic sectors in the rural periphery where the interdependent links between telecommunications and other economic activities are strong. The " uplifting" strategy attempts to eliminate disparity by pulling up the rural periphery, whereas the "engulfing" strategy aims at eliminating disparity by expanding the urban core. With the expansion of the urban core into the rural and inland areas, disparity between the rural periphery and urban core disappears.

The "uplifting" strategy is similar to the "big push" model of development (Lewis, 1954; Nurkse, 1953; Rosenstein-Rodan, 1957). It maintains that the LDCs continue to have low levels of per capita income because of interlocking vicious circles. Piecemeal attempts to promote economic growth are defeated by these vicious circles, which only a massive injection of capital on all fronts can possibly break. Uneven development is to be avoided and the idea of a "Big Push" is to introduce a comprehensive and integrated program.

Myint (1980), however, pointed out that the crucial practical question which faces the LDCs is not how to plan their development programs as if they had unlimited supply of resources, but what sort of choices they should make when their currently available resources are insufficient for comprehensive balanced growth programs. Hirschman (1958) argued that even if the balanced growth approach were successful, it would merely achieve a once-and-for-all increase in national income, leveling at the higher plateau that represents the balanced growth equilibrium.

According to Hirschman (1958), economic development is a continuous dynamic process, kept alive by the tension of shortages and excess supplies and by the disequilibria in the strategic sectors that are capable of responding to these pace-setting pressures. In Myint's (1980) words, "The balanced-growth theorists would like the two complementary industries A and B to expand simultaneously to their 'full' equilibrium level which would exhaust the external economies possible in the initial situation" (p. 105). Hirschman (1958), on the other hand, hoped that either A or B would over shoot the equilibrium point; the resulting pressures of excess demand or excess supply would thus change the initial situation and lead to further economic development in a series of "leap frog" movements.

In using the "uplifting" strategy, China is constrained by its lack of financial capital. Like most of the developing world, China has to face the problem of insufficient capital for investment in its infrastructure. In 1992, total capital investment in China was RMB$301.2 billion. Only RMB$5.52 billion could be given to posts and telecommunications, which accounted for 1.8% of the total (SSB, 1993). This 1.8%, however, was the highest percentage the state has ever invested in posts and telecommunications since the founding of the People's Republic (see Table 5.3).

Table 5.3. Capital Investment in Transport, Post & Telecommunications, 1952-1992 (RMB $100 Million).

Year	All Infrastructural Investments	Total Investment in Transport, Post & Telecomms	Post & Telecomm Investment	% of All Investment
1952	43.56	7.78	.30	.68
1953	90.44	11.50	.54	.60
1954	99.07	15.91	.63	.63
1955	100.36	18.28	.57	.57
1956	155.28	26.21	.80	.52
1957	143.32	20.50	.70	.49
1958	269.00	38.03	2.00	.74
1959	349.72	56.79	2.43	.70
1960	388.69	56.14	2.46	.63
1961	127.42	15.59	.45	.35
1962	71.26	5.62	.24	.33
1963	98.16	8.81	.22	.23
1964	144.12	17.46	.39	.27
1965	179.61	32.54	.67	.37
1966	209.42	34.03	...	...
1967	140.17	26.07	...	...
1968	113.06	18.30	...	...
1969	200.83	34.32	...	...
1970	312.55	60.45	...	...
1971	340.84	61.61	...	...
1972	327.98	62.34	2.28	.70
1973	338.10	66.05	2.25	.65
1974	347.71	72.32	2.55	.73
1975	409.32	75.50	2.65	.65
1976	376.44	56.99	2.62	.70
1977	382.37	50.32	2.20	.58
1978	500.99	69.47	3.35	.67
1979	523.48	70.96	3.33	.64
1980	558.89	60.90	3.14	.56
1981	442.91	39.87	3.56	.80
1982	555.53	70.09	4.09	.74
1983	594.13	82.07	5.23	.88
1984	743.15	119.95	7.52	1.01
1985	1074.37	133.59	11.33	1.05
1986	1176.10	148.17	12.30	1.05
1987	1343.10	163.65	15.20	1.13

Table 5.3. Capital Investment in Transport, Post & Telecommunications, 1952-1992 (RMB$100 Million) (cont.).

1988	1525.80	175.92	16.60	1.09
1989	1551.70	186.15	21.70	1.40
1990	1703.80	218.85	23.30	1.37
1991	2115.80	330.62	30.78	1.46
1992	3012.65	448.25	55.13	1.83

Note: Data Not Available. Data compiled from Editorial Board of China Transportation Yearbook (1991) and State Statistical Bureau (1992).

The "engulfing" strategy seems to be more "affordable" to China. From the experience of the "four little tigers" of Guangdong province; namely, Dongwan, Chongshan, Shunde, and Nanhai, this strategy seems to work well. These four Guangdong counties in 1990 already produced a per-capita GNP of about US$3,000 in 1990. They made use of outside capital, mainly from Hong Kong, to develop rural industries. With the growth of these industries, basic infrastructure including electricity and telephones was gradually extended from rural townships to villages (Tang & Liu, 1993).

The strategy of developing the urban core and some strategic rural peripheral sectors, however, has its limitations. It is constrained by the pressures of rural-urban and peripheral-core migration. Although capital constraint also exists in the urban core, it generally has less of a problem in attracting capital because the returns on investment are usually better. On the other hand, telephones as well as cinemas, television, tap water, hospitals, easy transportation, and other conveniences are available in the urban core. These conveniences already make urban-core life attractive to rural-peripheral people. Increased development of telecommunications in urban areas could exacerbate the rural-urban migration problem.

Unplanned rural-urban migration leads to urban unemployment. Guangdong province and many coastal cities have been perplexed by this problem in recent years. The large influx of unemployed rural laborers to Guangzhou, the capital city of Guangdong, from other provinces has created living, health, and public security problems. Other big cities also face the problem of the so-called "blind flow"' It was estimated that in 1993, Shanghai had a mobile population of 2.5 million every day. Sichuan was the largest supplier of surplus labor; about 5 million people migrated from Sichuan to the coastal cities in 1993 (Shao, 1993). If rural industries fail to absorb surplus rural labor in proportion to labor growth, it is estimated that by the year 2000 there will be 200 million surplus laborers. In 1994 the figure was about 60 million (Han & Li, 1994).

The "engulfing" strategy may accelerate the rural-urban migration up to a point where the expanding urban core cannot sustain it. An exodus of the rural peripheral population to the urban core may occur if state planners chose to develop only the urban core. The talents and resources in the rural periphery will flow to the urban core, making the rural periphery even poorer. A study on migration labor patterns in Anhui in 1994 showed that 94% of the migrants are between the ages of 20-40, and more than one third of them have received upper-secondary education (Qing, 1994). They are indeed the most valuable resource in rural areas. Although the "engulfing" strategy may eliminate the rural periphery in the end, the social and economic costs may be too great to pay. In the "engulfing"process, there is a danger of nullifying the development achievements of the urban core if the demands of rural immigrants for housing, medical care, public security, energy, water, and transportation are beyond the urban core's resources.

Nevertheless, the impact of developing telecommunications in the urban core on rural-urban migration should not be exaggerated. Telecommunications facilities are only one of many factors contributing to the urban-core's attraction. Economic reasons (i.e., the "push" from subsistence agriculture, the "pull" of relatively high urban wages and the potential "push-back" of high urban unemployment) offer better explanations for rural-urban migration (Todaro, 1977). Uneven development of telecommunications facilities only helps perpetuate rural-urban migration. In sum, the choice of unbalanced development will widen the rural-urban gap in the short run, while in the long run the urban sector "engulfing" the rural sector may not be realized. On the contrary, there is a danger of disrupting the urban core's development by the influx of surplus labor from the rural periphery.

At present, telecommunications investment by the state is directed more to profitable developed areas. The less profitable regions are encouraged to find their own financial resources. The present policy requires the villages themselves to accumulate funds for the development of rural telephones (EBCTY, 1988), of which the state supports only a small proportion. In 1990, only RMB$21.1 million was invested in the capital construction of rural telephones, accounting for 1.2% of the total investment in telecommunications. In sharp contrast, RMB$1,238 million was invested in urban telephones, accounting for 70% of the total; the rest was invested in long-distance cables and radio links. In 1991, investment in rural telephones increased only marginally to about 4% (RMB$64.1 million) of China's total capital construction in telecommunications (EBCTY, 1992).

The meager investment in rural telephones is probably due to a perception that telecommunications investment, particularly in rural areas, confers direct benefits only on a relatively narrow and privileged portion of the population. Low investment returns in rural areas is another reason, but as Saunders, Warford, & Wellenius (1983) argued, well-focused investment might in fact modify the demand for travel and conserve energy. Balanced development of telecommunications might also slow down rural-urban migration because it would reduce the disadvantages of living in rural-peripheral areas. With better job information, the rural-urban migration might also be better planned, reducing the problem of urban unemployment.

The state planners seem to have chosen the "engulfing" option while relying on local resources for "uplifting" the rural-peripheral sector. This strategy has widened the rural-urban gap over the years, partly due to the prohibition of rural-urban migration. The rural-peripheral areas lag behind the telecommunications development in the urban core after four decades. In view of the greater percentage of people in rural-peripheral areas, the strategy of "uplifting" the poorer sector must be given more attention.

The main problem in uplifting the rural sector is availability of capital. Although the state encourages local capital investment in telecommunications, the initiatives have to be made by collective enterprises under state control. Private ownership and operation of telephone services is not allowed. Foreign investors can only participate in joint ventures in manufacturing telecommunications equipment and facilities. Direct involvement of foreign capital in the construction of telecommunications infrastructure is forbidden. This restriction cuts out an important source of funding for telecommunications development. Recently, the government started to seek multiple sources of funding for telecommunications. Due to its short history of openness to foreign capital, the utilization of foreign loans by China's rural sector is relatively low compared with other developing countries. Bilateral loans, for instance, take only about 33% of their capital from foreign governments, 8% below the average of 41% for all developing countries (Tan, 1993). With further opening up of China, the use of loans from abroad will probably increase.

Foreign loans, however, may not be able to meet the goals of the project due to inefficient administration. For example,the World Bank provides loans to China's agriculture free of interest, with a repayment period of 35 years, in addition to an extension of 10 years. However, the Chinese government usually charges the local area or administration 3-5% interest, with a repayment period of 15-20 years and an extension of 5 years. Sometimes, when the interest rate is too high, peasants will lose incentive to complete the project (Tan, 1993). Loans borrowed from other governments or private banks usually have more stringent terms—borrowing capital is not a good means to finance home investment.

China prefers joint ventures and processing industries in order to obtain capital and skills for investment. In the telecommunications sector, however, joint ventures are not allowed except for the provision of equipment and facilities—no foreign interests are allowed in service operations. Such insistence has deprived China of a very important source of funding in telecommunications. In order to quicken the pace of telecommunications development in rural areas, thus reducing the dualistic nature of its telecommunications, China might need to reconsider three options: The first is the use of Build, Operate, and Transfer (BOT) schemes; the second is allowing minority foreign interests in the operation of telecommunications services; and the third is privatization of telecommunications.

First, BOT schemes are most appropriate for the rural periphery where the government will not be likely to invest much. Foreign or local entrepreneurs might find some areas profitable if they can be connected with metropolitan cities. With careful calculation and negotiation, the nightmare of losing telecommunications sovereignty as in the Qing Dynasty (see chapter 3, this volume) should not recur. Second, prohibiting foreign interests in the joint operation of telecommunications service resulted from psychological scars from the past rather than real necessity. China can restrict foreign interests to a small fraction, but that small fraction will be a great relief for the shortage of funds in rural development. Third, if the government does not want any foreign participation in telecommunications services, it might rely on private Chinese citizens or corporations to pool the resources for rural development. However, due to the limited development of capital markets in China the capital collected from internal markets may not be enough for large-scale projects.

At present, privatization of telecommunications services at the corprate level seems to be the most viable and acceptable way of raising capital to the Chinese government. In privatization, the government may hold a certain amount of shares so that it can continue to exercise some influence. In addition, it can legislate against "undesirable" activities of the private operator.

PRIVATIZATION OF TELECOMMUNICATIONS IN RURAL PERIPHERY

In order to attract local and foreign capital to rural-peripheral regions, more incentives need to be introduced. Privatization of services is a way to raise capital for rural investment. At present, the rural market is not attractive because it is not profitable, but one reason for its unprofitability is the use of nonmarket approaches for rural telecommunications development. For example, after a plan for telephone development is fixed, a quota on telephones is allotted to various levels. The development plan is devised on the basis of the "conceived needs" of the planners, not necessarily reflecting the real needs of consumers. In addition, the markets are tightly controlled by the government.

If ownership restrictions are relaxed, local as well as foreign entrepreneurs will be more interested in investing in rural telephones. It is inevitable that the new capital interests will give priority to the profitable rural sectors, ignoring the backward and unprofitable ones. However, to develop some potential rural sectors is better than not to develop any, delaying further rural development. Moreover, in some profitable rural-peripheral sectors the government might be able to impose a universal service requirement on the private operators, allowing nonprofitable areas to be served through cross-subsidies from profitable areas. Giving out local franchises in rural areas for private operators will accelerate the development of rural telecommunications. The government can still have control over private operators through franchise regulations, franchise period, and periodic reviews of the franchisee's performance.

In view of the lack of capital for telecommunications in China, privatization of telecommunications construction and operation in the form of franchising at the local level is probably the most viable and desirable means to raise capital for rural telecommunications. Privatization will attract enterprising individuals to invest and develop rural telecommunications. Without privatization, the funds for rural development are unlikely to increase because the government is usually conservative in rural investment Government officials generally consider rural investment only in political and social terms—seldom do they consider it on a commercial basis. As a result, the government is unwilling to venture into risky rural sectors that have a high risk of losing money although some may turn out to be profitable. Government is less willing than private enterprises to take such investment risks.

As a rule, public utilities under state control are characterized by inefficient and poor services. This is probably due to greater bureaucratic inefficiencies in nonprofit-oriented organizations. State officials are seldom rewarded directly for improving the services they provide; their pay is seldom cut because of losing money, either. Private organizations, however, are profit-seeking—they are ever-conscious of the cost structure and efficient utilization of resources so as to garner maximum profit. They are also more responsive to customers' needs, especially when there is competition. This explains why private enterprises usually provide better services than the government. Private organizations also sustain less political pressure from the public when they adjust prices. Governments, on the other hand, must pay a political cost for a price adjustment. Low prices tie the service provider's hand in providing better service. Privatization in short, shifts the investment decision from the state to private individuals who will allocate their resources more efficiently to get the best return for their investment.

CONCLUSION

If China is to develop its rural sector faster and consolidate its achievements in the urban core, the "engulfing" strategy should be accompanied by the "uplifting" strategy. Lack of capital is the chief obstacle to China's telecommunications development. Although privatization may be the most acceptable means for the Chinese government to obtain additional funding for rural areas, the government should seriously consider the possibility of BOT schemes and joint ventures, especially in the rural-peripheral areas to increase the pace of telecommunications development.

REFERENCES

Baumol, W. J. (1967). Macroeconomics of unbalanced growth: The anatomy of urban crisis. *American Economic Review, 57*, 415-426.

Cao, Y. H. (1992). The possibility for Guangdong to become a "dragon" *Economic Quarterly, 48*, 69-72. (In Chinese)

China posts and telecommunications. (1990). Beijing: New Star. (In Chinese)

Commentator. (1994, April). The tide of migration labor: A cross-century difficult question. *Chinese Rural Economy*, pp. 8-10. (In Chinese)

Cronin, F. J., Parker, E. B., Colleran, D.K., & Gold, M. A. (1991). Telecommunications infrastructure and economic growth: An analysis of causality. *Telecommunications Policy, 15*(6), 529-535.

Di, A. Z. (1993, June). *Development of Chinese post and telecommunications and its effect on national economy*. Paper presented at Conference on Telecommunications and the Integration of China: Telecommunications, Trade and Economic Development in Hong Kong China, and Taiwan, Hong Kong University, Hong Kong.

Editorial Board of China Transportation Yearbook. (Ed.). (1988). *China transportation yearbook 1988*. Beijing: China Transportation Yearbook Press. (In Chinese)

Editorial Board of China Transportation Yearbook. (Ed.). (1991). *China transportation yearbook 1991*. Beijing: China Transportation Yearbook Press. (In Chinese)

Editorial Board of China Transportation Yearbook. (Ed.). (1992). *China transportation yearbook 1992*. Beijing: China Transportation Yearbook Press. (In Chinese)

Gu, M. N., & Tang, H. (1990, April 23). *The star of the republic*. Liaowang, p. 13. (In Chinese)

Guangdong Statistical Bureau. (1993). *Guangdong statistical yearbook 1993*. Jiangxi: China Statistical Press. (In Chinese)

Han, J., & Li, C. (1994, May). The tide of migration labor A cross-century question in China. *Chinese Rural Economy*, pp. 3-11. (In Chinese)

Hardy, A. P. (1980). The role of the telephone in economic development. *Telecommunications Policy, 4*(4), 278-286.

Hirschman, A. O. (1958). *The strategy of economic development*. New Haven, CT: Yale University Press.

Hong Kong Government. (1994). *Hong Kong 1994*. Hong Kong: Government Printer.

Lewis, W. A. (1954). Economic development with unlimited supply of labour. *The Manchester School, May*(2), 139-191.

Myint, M. (1980). *The economics of developing countries* (5th ed.). London: Hutchinson.

Ningxia Statistical Bureau. (1991). *Ningxia statistical yearbook 1991.* Ningxia: China Statistical Press.

Nurkse, R. (1953). *Problem of capital formation in underdeveloped countries.* London: Oxford University Press.

Qing, D. W. (1994, April). The investigation and reflection of the return of migration labor in Fouyang Area. *Chinese Rural Economy,* pp. 11-14. (In Chinese)

Rapid growth of Tibet's telecommunications undertakings. (1992). *China Market, 6,* 29.

Rosenstein-Rodan, P. N. (1957). *Notes on the theory of the "big push."* Cambridge, MA: MIT, Center for Industrial Studies.

Saunders, R. J., Warford , J. J., & Wellenius, B. (1983). *Telecommunications and economic development.* Baltimore, MD: Johns Hopkins University Press.

Shao, L. (1993, December 7). New features of labor migration in Mainland. *Tin Tin Daily,* p. 7. (In Chinese)

State Statistical Bureau. (1989). *China statistical yearbook 1989.* Beijing: China Statistical Press. (In Chinese)

State Statistical Bureau. (1993). *China statistical yearbook 1993.* Beijing: China Statistical Press. (In Chinese)

Tan, J. C. (1993, November). The experience and strategies of using foreign capital by Chinese agriculture. *Chinese Rural Economy,* pp. 16-20. (In Chinese)

Tang, J. H., & Liu J. Y. (1993, November). The industrialization and urbanization of rural villages: From the rise of "four little tigers" in Guangdong. *Chinese Rural Economy,* pp. 41-47. (In Chinese)

Todaro, M. P. (1977J. *Economics for a developing world.* London: Longman.

Wellenius, B. (1984). On the role of telecommunications in development. *Telecommunications Policy, 8*(1), 56-66.

Xiao, B. Y. (1993). Techno-economic analysis of P&T construction projects. *China Telecommunications Constructions, 5*(2), 5-53. (In Chinese)

Yang, G. J., & Liu, N. N. (1994, February). The mind and behavior of peasants entering the market economy for the first time. *Chinese Rural Economy,* pp. 44-47. (In Chinese)

Zhou, C. F. (1992, November). *The future development of cable television.* Paper presented at the International Symposium on Prospects and Challenges in Chinese Language Television Broadcasting, Television Broadcast Ltd., Hong Kong. (In Chinese)

CHAPTER 6

TELECOMMUNICATIONS AND DEVELOPMENT IN SHANGHAI: A CASE STUDY

JIANGUO ZHU

INTRODUCTION

It is widely believed that telecommunications plays a positive role in economic development (Strover, 1989). With an improved telecommunications infrastructure, production activities can be efficiently organized and market information can be promptly delivered, thus generating more benefits (Parker, 1984). In addition, telecommunications itself is a highly profitable service sector. The introduction of new technologies such as optical fiber and satellite communication along with increasing economy of scale, has lowered the unit price and made telecommunications a cost-declining industry (Saunders, Warford, & Wellenius, 1983).

Many studies have been done to examine the benefits of telecommunications services. Most of the earliest studies were conducted by engineers and economists. Some international organizations like the International Telecommunication Union (ITU), the Organization of Economic Cooperation and Development (OECD), and the World Bank strongly encouraged these initial efforts (Hudson, 1984). Until the early 1980s, the ITU continued to sponsor such studies. In 1983, the Maitland Commission was founded to explore ways to encourage worldwide investment in telecommunications (see Introduction, Hudson, 1988). That year was also designated as World Communication Year by the United Nations (see Preface, Saunders et al., 1983). Since 1980, the Chinese government has paid more attention to the role of telecommunications in development and investment in telecommunications has expanded rapidly (Wang, 1989; also see Chapter 3, this volume).

TELECOMMUNICATIONS AND ECONOMIC DEVELOPMENT

Studies of telecommunications and economic development primarily concentrate on three areas: communication in development, the information economy, and sector structure analysis. In the 1960s, telecommunications was ignored by development communication scholars. At that time, the mass media were regarded as the most important and effective means to develop lagging countries (Schramm, 1964). The telephone, as a means of communication was rarely studied. At the end of the 1960s, scholars believed that the mass media could directly bring about higher GDP per capita and a higher quality of life (Rogers & Svenning, 1969). They reasoned that by exposure to mass media, people would become modernized and favor social change (Inkeles & Smith,1974). However, this theory was questioned and strongly criticized in the 1970s (Golding, 1974)—communication researchers realized that the effects of the mass media were limited and indirect (Rogers, 1976).

In the late 1970s, the role of telecommunications in economic development was examined and some positive results were discovered. For example, a study by Hardy (1980) confirmed that telephones contributed to GDP, but radios did not. Researchers started to examine the role of telecommunications in development.

In the meantime, Porat (1977) observed a shift of production pattern from industrial manufacturing to information production in the United States. He found that the information related sector; that is, the service or tertiary sector, was engaging more laborers than the industrial sector. In an attempt to measure the value of various information activities, he distinguished the "primary information sector" from the "secondary information sector." The primary information sector includes media such as books, newspapers, and telecommunications, and the services dealing with information such as commerce, education, accounting and other consulting services. The secondary information sector refers to information internally consumed by government and private enterprise. Porat's (1977) research found that the primary sector, of which telecommunications is a part, increased dramatically during the 1960s, whereas the secondary information sector increased at a much lower rate. More systematic research in this respect was conducted in the analysis of sector structures.

In the 1980s, information was believed to play an important role in modern society and the idea of "information society "emerged. Information society is characterized by the dominance of economic activities of producing, distributing, and consuming information The labor force in postindustrial society (Bell, 1976) is increasingly shifting from agricultural and industrial production to information services. There are data giving support to the important role played by information in modern society. Table 6.1 shows the relative change of American labor distribution in industry and information sectors from 1950 to 1987. In 1950, 17% of American laborers were engaged in the service sector whereas 65% were in the industrial sector. In 1987, the percentage of service workers increased to 73%, whereas that of industrial workers was reduced to 24%.

The three primary classifications of an economy into agriculture, industry, and services is accepted worldwide; China adopted these classifications in 1985 (Xinhua News Agency, 1985). Telecommunications falls into the service sector. Some popular concepts like the "postindustrial society" (Bell, 1976) and the "third wave" (Toffler, 1980) stress the service sector. Some even proposed to derive the information sector from services and named it "the fourth sector" (Li, 1989).

The share of labor, investment and products (GNP or GDP) of every sector are used to measure the sector structure. In developed countries, both the share of labor and that of products in the tertiary sector exceeded the other two sectors (Zhu, 1983, p. 74). It is not unusual that the rate of increase of telecommunications is higher man that of the national economy. From 1960 to 1980, the annual increase of world GNP was 4.7%, and the annual increase in telephone penetration during that period was 6.6%. In China, however, the increase of telephone penetration was only 60% of its GNP (Chen, 1990a). It is impossible to figure out the share of telecommunications in China's GDP because postal service and telecommunications service are combined together in the available statistics. However, an interesting finding shows that telecommunications service stably accounts for 6% of GDP in most of the advanced countries. In a study of the United States, Great Britain, France, West Germany, Italy, Canada, and Japan, Zhu (1992) found that for all countries in all years (1975, 1980, 1982-1986), the share of the posts and telecommunications in GDP was 6%, except for Italy (5% in 1980, 1982, 1983) and Great Britain (7% in 1975).

Table 6.1. Change of Labor Distributions in Industry and Service Sector (US: 1950, 1980, 1987).

Year	Labor in Industry	Labor in Service
1950	65%	17%
1980	30%	55%
1987	24%	73%

Note: Data compiled from Editorial Board of World Economic Yearbook (1991) and Liu (1988).

THE MACRO-AND MICROECONOMIC BENEFITS OF
TELECOMMUNICATIONS

Studies of telecommunications and economic development are broken down into two major areas: macro- and microeconomic benefits.

At the macro level, telecommunications serves as an input to nearly every other sector in the economy. Benefits accrue to the whole economy by the penetration of information in other economic sectors. With the help of telecommunications, information is effectively transmitted, stored, and utilized, so that economic activities can be efficiently organized. In other words, insufficient investment in telecommunications hinders the economy. This is usually referred to as the bottleneck effect. According to Jequier (1984), the loss due to insufficient investment is estimated to be 2% of GNP.

Some efforts have been made to quantify these macroeconomic benefits. For example, researchers have attempted to determine ways in which telecommunications can substitute for transportation and reduce energy consumption. One study by the Ministry of Posts and Telecommunications of China showed that 84% of business trips could be replaced by long-distance calls and 69% of commuting could be substituted by local phone calls. Improved telecommunications is estimated to be able to reduce one third of the current passengers using various transportation means. With respect to energy savings, it is calculated that the energy consumption ratio between local phone calls and public bus use is 1:29; between local phone calls and taxi use is 1:504; between long-distance calls and train use is 1:90; and between long-distance calls and long-distance public bus use is 1:140 (Chen, 1990a).

The other area of study is the micro level, which focuses on the revenues directly realized from telecommunications service. In 1952, the service revenue of posts and telecommunications in China was only RMB$1.64 billion. It increased very slowly in the 1960s and 1970s, and in 1978 it reached RMB$11.65 billion. In recent years, revenue has soared with the telecommunications industry boom. For example, revenue in one year jumped from RMB$81.65 billion in 1990 to RMB$204.38 billion in 1991 (Editorial Board of PRC Yearbook, 1993). Whether it is the micro or macro level, researchers share the same aim: to determine whether telecommunications really facilitates economic development.

PREVIOUS STUDIES ON TELECOMMUNICATIONS
AND ECONOMIC DEVELOPMENT

Studies on the macroeconomic benefits from telecommunications began in the 1960s, but only in the past decade are these studies bearing fruit. Due to efforts over the past three decades, the relationship between telecommunications and economic development is now better understood (Wellenius, 1972, 1984).

The most commonly employed method in such studies is correlation analysis; that is, to correlate measures of telecommunications availability and use with measures of national economic performance. Recently, some efforts have been made to test the causal relation between telecommunications and economic development (Hudson, 1984). According to the data used, these studies can be classified into three categories.

CROSS-SECTIONAL ANALYSIS

This kind of study examines the relationship between telecommunications and economic development using data from different countries at a single point in time In 1963, Jipp pointed out the strong relationship between telephone density and national wealth. Telephone density was defined as the number of phones per 100 persons. Since then this relationship has been a topic of much public debate.

One year later, ITU's International Consultative Committee on Telephone and Telegraph (CCITT) set up a group to study this issue. Based on the telephone density and GNP per capita of 30 countries (both developed and developing) in 1965, the study group found a strong linear relationship between telecommunications and economic development. Furthermore, they analyzed the data between 1955 and 1960, and obtained the following equations from regression analysis:

$$1955 \ \log D = -3.0932 + 1.444 \ \log G$$
$$1960 \ \log D = -3.1171 + 1.432 \ \log G$$
$$1965 \ \log D = -3.1329 + 1.405 \ \log G$$

(Where D is telephone density, and G is GDP per capita.)

The correlation coefficients in these studies were all between .91 and .92, which indicated high correlation (Saunders, Warford, & Wellenius, 1983). Similar results were recently replicated with updated data by Kudriavtzev and Varakin (1990). When the telex replaced the telephone as the telecommunications indicator, such results still held (Saunders et al., 1983).

Bebee and Gilling (1976) used a "telephone index" and an "economic performance index" to study the relationship. The telephone index combined the following factors: number of telephones per 100 literate persons over 15 years of age, number of business telephones per 100 nonagricultural persons, and the average annual number of telephone calls per telephone. The economic performance index is constructed using a number of variables such as population, education, and intake of calories. Data from the 1970s for 29 countries was calculated and the results once again supported the previous findings. No matter whether GDP or GNP is used as an economic indicator or the telephone or the telex is used as the telecommunications indicator, a strong correlation between telecommunications and economic development always exists.

TIME SERIES ANALYSIS

This type of study analyzes the data for a specific country over time. CCITT examined the data from 1900 to 1965 in Sweden. The following linear relationships were found by regression analysis:

1900-1915 logD = -10.4106 + 3.1935 logG
1920-1965 logD = - 4.6445 + 1.5476 logG

(Where D is telephone density, and G is GDP per capita)

The coefficients of correlation obtained were as high as .99, which indicated an extremely strong relationship between these variables. However, the slope for 1920-1965 (1.55) was smaller than that for 1900-1915 (3.19), which showed a less significant relationship when the countries became more developed (Saunders et al., 1983).

So far, the high correlation between telecommunications and economic development has been well documented, but it is still far from conclusive. It is questionable whether telecommunications or a national economy can be represented by such simple indicators as telephone density or GDP per capita. Another criticism is that causal direction cannot be determined by correlation studies (Wellenius, 1984). In response to these criticisms, some modifications have been made to later studies.

CROSS-SECTION TIME ANALYSIS

In 1980, Hardy analyzed 1960 1973 data from 60 countries. He found that the telephone did contribute to economic development. Hardy used a 1-year time lag between dependent and independent variables to test the relationship. Telephone density and GNP per capita in the previous year were used to predict the current year's GNP per capita. Two significant research results were found:

1. Based on the analysis of the data from 35 countries, he found that if telephone density increases one percent in the previous 5 years, it will lead to a 3% increase in national income per capita in the next 7 years.

2. In countries with low telephone density, the telephone contributes more to economic development.

Although Hardy's (1980) study showed a causal relationship, some critics were still not satisfied. Their criticism focused on the study's failure to take into account the mutual relationship between telecommunications and economic development (Chen & Kuo, 1985).

In order to test the mutual relationship between telecommunications and development, Cronin, Parker, Colleran, & Gold (1991) did a study based on data from 1958 to 1988 taken from the United States. Two hypothesis were proposed:

H1: American economic level at one time can be used to predict its telecommunications investment at a later time.

H2: American telecommunications investment at one time can be used to predict the country's economic level at a later time.

Economic level was indicated by GNP and the total output of 432 industrial sectors. The Granger Test (for details, refer to Cronin et al., 1991) was employed and the results are shown in Table 6.2. Both of the hypotheses were supported.

In recent years, some studies were also conducted in China. The Ministry of Aeronautics and Aerospace undertook research based on more than 30 years of data. It showed that a 1% increase in telecommunications revenue per capita led to a .14% increase in national income (Chen, 1990b). Another study sponsored by the Ministry of Posts and Telecommunications concluded that a RMB$1 investment in telecommunications yielded RMB$6.78 for the national economy (Chen, 1990b). However, these results were not very convincing because causal conclusions were drawn from a simple Ordinary Least Squares (OLS) regression.

Table 6.2. Causal Relations Between Telecommunications Investment and American Economic Level.

Relations	F value by Granger Test
	df = 2/26
GNP on telecom investment	6.52
Total output on telecom investment	3.45
Telecom investment on GNP	3.87
Telecom investment on total output	2.58

Note. time lag = 2 years; $p < .10$; data from 1958-1988. Data complied from Cronin et al. (1991).

Growth in telecommunications also requires input from other economic sectors. In this sense, investment in telecommunications can stimulate other economic activities It is calculated that RMB$1 investment in telecommunications yields RMB$2.38 for other economic sectors (Chen, 1990b).

THE CASE OF SHANGHAI

RESEARCH SUBJECT AND HYPOTHESES

So far, only aggregate indicators at a national level have been used to explore the relationship between telecommunications and economic development. Indicators below the national level are rarely used; to a large extent, this is due to the unavailability of local data. A question arises: Can the results and conclusions drawn from national data be projected to smaller territorial units?

The comparability between developed and developing countries also raises questions. Developed countries have diverse and complete telecommunications services, but the largest concern for developing countries is the lack of facilities and services. Telephone density can mean different things in each of these countries, and can hardly be treated equally (Saunders et al., 1983). In China, when we use aggregates at the national level, geographical disparities are also hidden. Lee (1991, also see chapter 5 this volume) pointed out that there was a dualistic nature in Chinese communication—a backward sector exists alongside an advanced sector.

This study will test the relationship between telecommunications and economic development for both Shanghai and China as a whole. The Granger Test is used to determine if causality exists.

Two hypotheses are proposed:

H1:   In Shanghai, telecommunications contributes to economic development.

H2:   Compared with Shanghai, telecommunications' contribution to economic development in China as a whole is greater.

In the second hypothesis, Shanghai is treated as a relatively developed region, whereas the whole of China is regarded as a developing region. If Hardy's theory that in countries with low telephone density the telephone contributes more to economic development is correct, then support should be found for the second hypothesis in this study.

A BRIEF BACKGROUND OF SHANGHAI TELECOMMUNICATIONS

Shanghai used to be the telecommunications center of China before 1949. The first telecommunications operating entity in China originated in Shanghai, and the first telephone station was set up only 6 years after Bell's invention. After 1949, telecommunications development in Shanghai was disrupted by frequent political movements. Telephones, especially residential telephones, were accused of being "bourgeois toys" during the Cultural Revolution between 1966 and 1976.1t was not until 1979, that telecommunications resumed development. Table 6.3 shows investment from 1949 to 1988.

In recent years, with the expansion of investment, telecommunications facilities have improved quickly. Table 6.4 shows the telephone density of Shanghai between 1949 and 1990.

From the tables 6.3 and 6.4, we can see that telecommunications increased gradually between 1979 and 1981. After 1982, it increased dramatically; however, the large increase still cannot meet the demand. Registered unmet service applicants increased from 23,626 in 1981-1983 to 86,000 in 1987 (Shanghai Statistical Bureau, 1992).

DATA COLLECTION

The data used in this study were mainly obtained from the *China Statistical Yearbook, Development of Transportation, Posts and Telecommunications in China*, and *Shanghai Statistical Yearbook*. The raw data taken from these books include GNP, telephone quantity and populations, and so on. GNP per capita is used to compare with measures used in previous studies. However not until 1978 did the Chinese Statistical Bureau begin to calculate and record GNP. Telephone density in Shanghai is defined as the number of telephones per 100 persons. For all of China, it is the number of telephones per 10,000 persons. Time series data of GNP per capita and telephone density from 1978 to 1990 were collected.

When using time-series data, we should take into account four factors: long-term trends, cyclical effects, seasonal effects, and random variations (Zhang, 1990). Cyclical effects and seasonal effects were not detected from the plot of data. Random variations were eliminated by the least-squares method. After examining the data, it has found that a long-term trend exists.

Table 6.3. Telecom Investment in Shanghai (1949-1988).

Year	'40-'78	'79~'82	'83-'85	'86	'87	'88
Investment (million yuan)	230	120	225	204	250	340

Note. Data compiled from Shanghai Academy of Social Science (1983), Shanghai Academy of Social Science (19083-1992), and Shanghai Statistical Bureau (1992).

Table 6.4. Telephone Density of Shanghai (1949-1988).

Year	Telephone Density (per 1,000 persons)
1949	2.0
1952	1.9
1957	1.7
1962	1.2
1965	1.3
1970	1.2
1975	1.5
1978	1.7
1979	1.8
1980	1.8
1981	1.9
1982	2.0
1983	2.2
1984	2.5
1985	2.8
1986	3.0
1987	3.2
1988	3.6
1989	4.8
1990	6.2

Note. Figures were calculated by the author. Data compiled from Shanghai Statistical Bureau (1992).

The Granger Test[1] can be quantified thus:

$H0: Gt = aGt\text{-}1 + ct + d + u$
$H1: Gt = aGt\text{-}1 + bTt\text{-}1 + ct + d + u$

Where: G is GNP per capita;

Gt is the GNP per capita at time t;
Gt-1 is GNP per capita at time t-1;
T is time
d is constant;
b and c are coefficients;
u is a residual.

[1]In Cronin & his colleagues' study, both the Granger and Modified Sims Test were employed. According to Guilkey, the Granger Test is superior to the Modified Test for small samples. For further information, please refer to Guilkey & Salemi (1982). Please also note that the formulas used here are simplified for the convenience of this study. For a general formula, readers may refer to Granger (1963).

The sum of the residuals can be obtained from regression for H0 and H1, respectively. Then the F value is calculated by:

$$F = \frac{SEE_0 - SEE_1}{SEE_1/(n-4)}$$

$$df = (1, n-4)$$

If the calculated F is larger than the criteria F ($p < .05$), then H0 is rejected, and H1 accepted.

RESEARCH RESULTS

The correlation coefficient for Shanghai is 0.818 and for China as a whole it is 0.957. These results are consistent with the current literature—the linear relationship between them is quite clear. Similar to CCITT's findings, two equations are obtained:

Shanghai $logG = 3.03 + 1.21 logT$
China $logG = 1.28 + 0.84 logT$

After such a strong correlation was verified, causality was tested by the Granger Test. Mutual directions; that is, from telecommunications to development and vice versa, were tested. The results are summarized in Table 6.5.

It is clear in this table that we are not able to support the hypothesis that telecommunications contributes to economic development in Shanghai. However, such a relationship holds for the whole of China.

We can also see that telecommunications depends on economic development. This relationship holds for both Shanghai and the whole of China.

Table 6.5. Causal Relation (1978-1990).

Place	Telecom on GNP	GNP on Telecom
Shanghai	1.14	6.78*
China	8.47*	14.12*

Note. $p < .05$.

DISCUSSION: SHANGHAI AS AN INDUSTRIAL SOCIETY

The economic situation in Shanghai is different from that of the whole China and the United States. In 1988, Shanghai had a GNP per capita of RMB$5,161, whereas China had RMB$218 and the United States had RMB$73,916.[2] The GNP per capita in these three places differed by more than 10 times (Shanghai Statistical Bureau, 1992; State Statistical Bureau, 1992). Based on this, we can divide these places into three categories: developed, middle level, and underdeveloped. With respect to the causal relationship between telecommunications and development, we might say that for both the developed and underdeveloped areas, there is a positive relationship, but for middle-level areas, the relationship is not found. The present study shows that telecommunications stimulates economic development in both well-developed and underdeveloped countries, but in some middle-level areas like Shanghai, such a relationship does not exist.

A look at the labor distribution across different sectors in these three places may throw light on this finding. Table 6.6 shows that most of the laborers in Shanghai are industrial workers, whereas most of the laborers in China as a whole are engaged in agriculture and most of the laborers in the United States work in the service sector. Based on this data, we may propose that telecommunications plays different roles in different stages of social development.

In an agricultural society like China, telecommunications may boost economic development. In agricultural societies, information cannot flow

Table 6.6. Labor Distribution in China, Shanghai, and USA.

Sector	Agriculture			Industry			Service		
Year	China	SH	USA	China	SH	USA	China	SH	USA
1960[a]	75.0	40.4	7.0	15.0	35.2	36.0	10.0	24.4	57.0
1965	81.0	41.0	5.0	8.0	34.9	35.0	11.0	24.1	60.0
1978	62.0	34.5	2.0	25.0	44.1	33.0	13.0	22.4	65.0
1980	69.0	29.2	2.0	19.0	48.8	42.0	12.0	22.0	66.0
1985	62.5	16.6	3.0	21.1	57.9	26.9	16.4	25.5	70.2
1987	60.1	13.2	2.9	22.5	59.5	23.5	17.4	27.3	73.6

Note. Figures are percentage of sectoral employment relative to total workforce in the economy. Data compiled from Editorial Department (1991). Shanghai Statistical Bureau 1992.
[a]1962 data were used for Shanghai.

[2]The RMB$ values of the U.S. GNP per capita in 1988 was calculated on the basis of the Chinese official exchange rate that year

smoothly because of the self-sufficient structure. In such societies, the development of telecommunications facilitates the flow of information and coordination of economic activities. Consistent with this explanation, Hudson (1984) found a positive effect on economic growth from setting up satellite earth stations and telephones in isolated rural areas. Hardy (1980) also found that telecommunications contributed more in less developed countries

In information or postindustrial societies, information is treated as a commodity—one will lose the competitive edge if one does not get information in time. It is not surprising, therefore, that Cronin et al. (1991) found that telecommunications contributed to economic development in America

In industrial societies like Shanghai, although information is also used to organize economic activities, generally speaking, the effect of telecommunications may not be so direct and obvious as in postindustrial and agricultural societies. There is one example that may shed some light on this question: In the 1950s and 1960s, the French telecommunications infrastructure lagged behind other Western countries, but the economy still grew at a 6% rate during these years. In other words, telecommunications did not become a bottleneck of economic development. Scholars thought that it was because the French economy depended on industry, not on the service sector at that time (Saunders et al., 1983). French labor statistics at that time showed that labor in industrial sector outnumbered other sectors until 1967 (see Table 6.7). However, a question naturally arises: Why is the role of telecommunications in industrial societies different from that in agricultural and postindustrial societies?

EXPLANATION AND CONCLUSION

The differences in production patterns may offer some clues. In agricultural societies and postindustrial societies production is decentralized, but in industrial societies it is centralized. In a highly centralized production context, the contribution of telecommunications to economic development is

Table 6.7. Labor Distribution in France (1950s-1960s).

Year	Agriculture	Industry	Service
1957	16.90	47.4	35.7
1960	14.0	49.1	36.9
1965	11.1	49.6	39.3
1967	16.3	39.1	44.5

Note. Figures are percentage of sectoral employment relative to total workforce in the economy. Data compiled from International Labor Office (1965).

less obvious than that in a decentralized context. Telecommunications is probably more important for scattered productions patterns.

Naisbitt (1982) made an observation on the decentralized trend in the United States, and remarked:

> The growth of decentralization parallels the decline of industry, America's industrial machine was probably history's greatest centralizing force. The mechanical blueprint of industrial society required enormous centralization—in labor, material, capital, and plant. This is because mass industrialization was organized according to the principle of economics of scale: the more you produce in one place, in one way, the cheaper each individual unit will be. (p.82)

In a postindustrial society, one of the main characteristics is decentralization. This is also true for an agricultural society. It is obvious in China, especially after 1978 when the land was distributed to every single family, that telecommunications had become an important means of organizing and coordinating the scattered autonomous units in rural areas.

The exception in Shanghai seems to be related to its sector structure. The major portion of Shanghai's economy is in industry and the production pattern of an industrial society is its centralization. In agricultural societies such as China and in postindustrial societies such as the United States, however, decentralization is the main characteristic of the production system. In decentralized societies, telecommunications are more important for the coordination of economic activities. Because the causal relationship between telecommunications and economic development doesn't exist in Shanghai, but exists in the whole of China, it is inferred that telecommunications contributes more to the whole of China than to Shanghai

This study obtained unexpected findings. It found that telecommunications does not stimulate economic development in Shanghai. Shanghai is in the middle economic level, and previous studies simply divided the countries into developed and underdeveloped categories, resulting in the neglect of the middle-level stage. It is suggested that the exception of Shanghai is due to its centralized production pattern. Telecommunications plays a more important and obvious role in economic development in societies with decentralized production patterns.

Of course, the present discussion and explanation is very tentative. Because the result is based on a case study, caution must be taken before making generalizations. Moreover, this study is based on a small sample size—the results may not be reliable.

This study also has some policy implications. In developing countries such as China, it is very important to allocate limited resources in an optimal way. Given the result of this study, policy makers should consider giving high priority to telecommunications development in underdeveloped areas.

REFERENCES

Bebee, E. L., & Gilling, E. J. W. (1976). Telecommunications and economic development: A model for planning and policy making. *Telecommunication Journal, 43*(8), 537-543.

Bell, D. (1976). *The coming of postindustrial society: A venture in social forecasting.* New York: Basic Books.

Chen, H. T., & Kuo, C. Y. (1985). Telecommunications and economic development in Singapore. *Telecommunications Policy, 9*(3), 240-244.

Chen, Y. Q. (1990a). The socio-economic benefits of Chinese telecommunications. *China Telecommunications Constructions, 2*(3), 6-7. (In Chinese)

Chen, Y. Q. (1990b, June). Speed up the development of telecommunications. *Modernization*, p. 5. (In Chinese)

Cronin, F. J., Parker, E. B., Colleran, D. K., & Gold, M. A. (1991). Telecommunications infrastructure and economic growth: An analysis of causality. *Telecommunications Policy, 15*(6), 529-535.

Editorial Board of PRC Yearbook. (Ed.). (1993). *People's Republic of China yearbook 1992/1993.* Beijing: PRC Yearbook Ltd. (In Chinese)

Editorial Board of World Economic Yearbook. (Ed.). (1991). *World economic yearbook 1990.* Beijing: Chinese Social Science Press. (In Chinese)

Editorial Department. (Ed.). (1991). *Abstract of international economy and social statistics 1990.* Bejing: China Statistical Press. (In Chinese)

Golding, P. (1974). Media role in national development: Critique of a theoretical orthodoxy. *Journal of Communication, 24*(3), 39-53.

Granger, C. (1963). Economic processes involving feedback. *Information and Control, 6*(1), 28-48.

Guilkey, D. K., & Salemi, M. K. (1982). Small sample properties of three test for Granger ordering in a bivariate stochastic system. *Review of Economics and Statistics, 64*(4), 668 680.

Hardy, A. P. (1980). The role of the telephone in economic development. *Telecommunications Policy, 4*(4), 278-286.

Hudson, H. E. (1984). *When telephone reaches the village: The role of telecommunications in rural development.* Norwood, NJ: Ablex.

Hudson, H. E. (1988). *A bibliography of telecommunications and socio-economic development.* Norwood, NJ: Ablex.

Inkeles, A., & Smith, D. H. (1974). *Becoming modern: Individual change in six developing countries.* Cambridge, MA: Harvard University Press.

International Labor Office. (1965). *Yearbook of labor statistics.* Geneva: International Labor Office.

Jequier, N. (1984). Telecommunications for development: Findings of the ITU-ECD project. *Telecommunications Policy, 8*(2), 84.

Jipp, A. (1963). Wealth of nations and telephone density. *Telecommunications Journal, 30*(7), 199-200.

Kudriavtzev, G. G., & Varakin, L.E. (1990). Economic aspects of telephone network development. *Telecommunication Journal, 57*(8), 537-543.

Lee. P. (1991). Dualism of communication in China. *Telecommunications Policy, 15*(6), 535-544.

Li, Z. (1989). The trend of world economic development. In Editorial Board of World Economic Yearbook (Ed.), *World economic yearbook 1989* (pp. 1-8). Beijing: Chinese Social Science Press. (In Chinese)

Liu, T. W. (1988). *Transportation, communications and national economy.* Sichuan: Chongqing Press. (In Chinese)

Naisbitt, J. (1982). *Megatrends: The new directions transforming our lives.* New York: Warner Books.

Parker, E. B. (1984). Appropriate telecommunications for economic development. *Telecommunications Policy, 8*(3), 173-177.

Porat, M. U. (1977). *The information economy.* Washington, DC: U.S. Department of Commerce.

Rogers, E. M. (Ed.). (1976). *Communication and development: Critical perspectives.* Beverly Hills, CA: Sage.

Rogers, E. M., & Svenning, L. (1969). *Modernization among peasants: The impact of communication.* New York: Holt, Rinehart & Winston.

Saunders, R.J., Warford, J.J., & Wellenius, B. (1983). *Telecommunications and economic development.* Baltimore: The Johns Hopkins University Press.

Schramm, W. (1964). *Mass media and national development.* Stanford, CA: Stanford University Press.

Shanghai Academy of Social Science. (1983). *Shanghai economy 1949-82.* Shanghai: Shanghai People's Press. (In Chinese)

Shanghai Academy of Social Science. (1983-1992). *Shanghai economy yearbook.* Shanghai: Shanghai People's Press. (In Chinese)

Shanghai Statistical Bureau. (1992). Shanghai statistical yearbook 1991. Beijing: China Statistical Press. (In Chinese)

State Statistical Bureau. (1992). *China statistical yearbook 1991.* Beijing: China Statistical Press. (In Chinese)

Strover, S. (1989). Telecommunications and economic development: An incipient rhetoric. *Telecommunications Policy, 13*(3), 194-196.

Toffler, A. (1980). *The third wave.* New York: Morrow.

Wang, H. J. (1989). *Studies on China's sector policy.* Beijing: China Finance and Economic Press. (In Chinese)

Wellenius, B. (1972). On the role of telecommunications in development of nations. *IEEE Transactions on Communications, 20*(1), 3-7.

Wellenius, B. (1984). On the role of telecommunications in development. *Telecommunications Policy, 8*(1), 59-66.

Xinhua News Agency. (1985, May 4). State council demands that value statistics of tertiary sector be done by all areas. *Economic Reference News,* p. 1. (In Chinese)

Zhang, Y. (1990). *Social statistics*. Nanjing: Nanjing University Press. (In Chinese)

Zhu, J. (1992). *The share of the posts and telecommunications in GDP and its impact on national development*. Unpublished paper, The Chinese University of Hong Kong.

Zhu, J. M. (1983). *Introduction to national economic structure*. Beijing: Knowledge Press. (In Chinese)

CHAPTER 7

CHINA'S USE OF THE INTERNET: A REVOLUTION ON HOLD*

BRYCE T. MCINTYRE

China has had the infrastructure in place to send and receive overseas electronic mail since 1990. For a number of reasons, however, China lags behind industrialized nations in its utilization of this emergent yet powerful communication technology.[1] Even now, many years after the adoption of computer networking technology by China, it is difficult—difficult to the point of seeming impossible—to carry out routine e-mail communications with Chinese citizens from overseas locations.

This must be disheartening news for proponents of the New World Information Order (Unesco, 1980), who have long called for more horizontal flows of information around the world. Computer networks, especially smaller, volunteer networks such as Fidonet, are ideally suited for this purpose (Bates, 1992), but such nets have only a toehold in China today.

Explanations of China's lag in this regard are the focus of much of this chapter. Before delving into the heart of the discussion, however, it is necessary to make several short digressions.

First, this chapter focuses on China's use of the Internet, as opposed to local area networks or wide-area networks within China. The reason for this focus is twofold: (a) network enthusiasts in the West view com-

*The author wishes to thank Dr. Benjamin Bates, Dr. Paul S. N. Lee, and Mr. Vincent Chau for their assistance in preparing this chapter.
[1]China leads some Southeast Asian countries in narrow applications of networking technology, however. This is taken up later in the chapter.

puter nets as powerful force for social change, and China is the last surviving major Communist state in the world; and (b) information on network use within China, where social science research is viewed with hostile suspicion, is not available, at least in the public domain. However, any discussion of access to the Internet would be incomplete without reference to wide area networks within China itself, so these will be mentioned in passing.

Second, information about e-mail to and from China is somewhat confused by nomenclature. This is due in part to the jargon of computer technology itself, in part to translation problems, and in part to the many perspectives that foreign visitors bring to Chinese computer networking facilities. This chapter points out some of the problems based on nomenclature and attempts to clarify some of the confusion.

Third, e-mail is, in most contexts, media content. The popular notion that the medium cannot be separated from the message applies here as much as it does to a discussion of film, television, or any other mass medium. The medium of e-mail is computer networking technology. It is the unique set of attributes of this medium that is so powerful and fascinating, not the contents of specific messages. In any case, if some of the references to e-mail in this chapter seem to include network technology, it is due to the inseparability of the medium from the message.

This suggests that a formal definition of electronic mail is needed. Electronic mail, or e-mail, is a human communication process that allows a single individual or organization to transmit text and graphics electronically to one or more individuals or organizations by using established computer networks, communication protocols and some combination of the following technologies: computers, modems, hosts, gateways, wide-area networks, local-area networks, conventional land-based communication systems, and satellites

An essential feature of this definition that may escape the casual reader—and one that enters into discussions about e-mail to and from China—is "established communication protocols": Successful employment of electronic mail requires users to adhere to internationally recognized protocols—or "procedures"—for addressing and routing communications, and these protocols have been spelled out in international agreements among supporters of e-mail communication networks. The supporters include groups such as Information Sciences Institute (ISI), the Internet Assigned Numbers Authority (IANA), and the Network Information Center (NIC), which is operated by Stanford Research Institute International (SRI).

Although network users can successfully use computer nets with a very simplistic understanding of protocols, they nevertheless use them—for example, in writing a network address. The significance of the protocols in a discussion of e-mail to and from China is made clear in the following section.

E-MAIL VERSUS FAX TECHNOLOGY

One of the reasons for providing a definition of e-mail is to make clear the distinction between e-mail and facsimile communications, or faxes, which play an important role today in China and other Asian nations whose language have large, complex character sets. The inherent properties of fax technology lend themselves well to communication in ideographic languages such as Chinese, Japanese, and Korean. Because the fax machine sends a visual image, ideographic languages can be written by hand and reproduced easily and quickly at a remote location.

The advantage of this is worth emphasizing: Keyboard entry of Chinese characters is an extremely complex task. On a conventional Western qwerty keyboard—and using any one of several commonly available Chinese text entry programs—it takes about four keystrokes to produce a single Chinese character. To do so, however, requires a more sophisticated understanding of the software than is required for ordinary word-processing programs available for Western languages. It takes from one to two years to become proficient at Chinese text entry, and once the skill is mastered, the process is still slow and cumbersome.

Hence, relative to the technologies required for e-mail, which demand users to have computer skills and an understanding of complex communication protocols, fax technology is simple and cheap, and it requires low levels of skill on the part of operators. The user needs only to replace the telephone set with a fax machine; the existing telephone network carries facsimile transmissions, and it is already in place. For these reasons, fax technology is popular in China, and the fax machine has come to occupy a "communications niche" similar to that of electronic mail.

One of the principal differences between facsimile communication and e-mail communication is that facsimiles are almost universally sent to a single destination—or "node," in e mail jargon—whereas e-mail systems are enormously flexible in permitting transmission of messages either to a single destination or, by using "mail reflectors" or "mail exploders," a very large number of receivers—literally thousands of destinations.[2] Communications also may be sent to any conveniently identified subset of a larger set of destinations.[3]

Another difference is that many e-mail applications use established local-area networks (LANs) and wide-area networks (WANs) without tying into the telephone network. Some WANs, on the other hand, engage in "lease-line" agreements with telephone networks. In addition, tax recipients receive

---

[2]It should be noted however, that some telephone companies such as Hong Kong Telecom provide a fax multiplex service that permits the sending of a single fax to several destinations. This service is not nearly as flexible as that of e-mail, however.

[3]A brief glossary is provided at the end of this chapter.

a "hard copy"—that is, a printed document—as the final message, whereas e-mail recipients receive a computer file that may be manipulated, merged with other files, printed, and retransmitted.

Another major difference between e-mail and facsimile transmissions is that the skillful e-mail user may access thousands of FTP (File Transfer Protocol) sites worldwide and download information from a vast number of databases.[4] Finally, e-mail may be used for "real time" interactive communication. This statement applies not only to machines (computers), but also to groups of people, who can use this interactive feature to conduct online, interactive computer conferences.

These differences aside, the distinctions between fax communications and e-mail today are blurred by innovative computer hardware and software applications that combine fax and computer technologies. Today it is possible for one computer user to send a computer fax—a fax created on a personal computer that combines text and graphics—to another computer user, and the communications links between the two machines will include modems, telephone lines, and other technologies outlined earlier in the definition of electronic mail.

In short, by the time personal computers have diffused enough in China to reach a critical mass (Markus, 1987) to see an explosive demand for e-mail, fax technology may have reached such a state as to reduce much of the demand for e-mail. Also, competing new technologies such as voice messaging may cut into the demand for computer network applications.

THEORETICAL PERSPECTIVES

The rapidly growing body of research on computer-mediated communication or CMC, provides a laundry list of hypothetical social and organizational effects of e-mail communications in China. These may be grouped into processes and effects in education, organizations, and interpersonal relations, and social, individual, and infrastructural issues (Bentson, 1993). In addition, diffusion theory (e.g., Rogers & Shoemaker, 1971) provides a theoretical context in which to explain the process of adoption of computer networking technology in China.

Turning first to the CMC literature, most research in this area deals with decision-making processes in professional settings (Walther, personal communication [e-mail], February 11, 1994), so most research in CMC is not directly relevant to China's use of the Internet. Also, there are significant differences in the Chinese experience that inhibit inferences based on research

---

[4]The exact number cannot be known. Some of these databases are catalogued by a program on the Internet called "Archie." As of this writing, Archie monitors 800 FTP hosts containing a total of more than 1 million databases.

from the West. First, e-mail to and from China is still a nascent form of communication. Even though the technology is in place, e-mail is only barely being used, for reasons discussed here later.[5] Broad areas of CMC research—for example, research on distance education (Duning, 1990) or on gender issues (Herring, 1993) are not yet relevant to Chinese use of the Internet. Second, almost all Chinese e-mail communications are in English, as are Internet information services, so proficiency in English is a prerequisite for use of the Internet. This restricts international e-mail to a small but elite group of scholars

From the extensive literature on the diffusion of innovations, one can confidently predict that the innovator—that is, the first 2-3% of adopters of computer networking technology in China—are venturesome and interested in new ideas. They are cosmopolitan enough that their intense interest in the technology will lead them outside of their local interpersonal networks of peers to wider social circles. They also have substantial financial resources and the ability to apply complex technical knowledge.

Although there are no data to support these observations about the adopters of computer networking technology in China, visits to Chinese computer networking sites by foreign scholars have revealed that many of the leading proponents have been educated at America's most prestigious universities.

Today tens of thousands of Chinese students and scholars are studying and teaching in the United States—estimates range from 80,000 to 100,000 scholars. As these people return to China, the demand for access to the Internet will undoubtedly be greatly accelerated.

COMPUTER NETWORKING INFRASTRUCTURE IN CHINA

As of this writing, nothing of substance has been published in conventional media about e-mail in the PRC. What little is known about e mail to and from China has come to light as a result of visits by interested foreign scholars and computer scientists. Most of what follows is based on e-mail communications with computer and telecommunications experts who have visited networking sites in China.

China adopted the Internet's domain naming system in 1990. In September of that year, the Institute for Computer Applications in Beijing registered "cn" (for "China") as the top level domain with the administration of the Internet. As a result, any computer host within China following the Internet's protocols must have "cn" as the final part of its address.

---

[5]Banks and airline companies make heavy use of computer networks for business transactions, so research on CMC in organizations may be relevant here; however, the focus of this chapter is on China's use of the Internet rather than CMC in general.

A survey in August 1992 revealed only two hosts with this suffix: ica.beijing.canet.cn and mam.tsinghua.cn. For remote computer sites within China itself, these hosts may be accessed through CNPAC—the China National Public Data Network—or through dial-up telephone links. The potential for dial-up access will increase dramatically under China's plans to improve telephone service. The Chinese Ministry of Posts and Telecommunications has set the ambitious goal of installing 100 million new telephone lines by the year 2000.

CNPAC, which is also referred to as CHINAPAC or ChinaPac, is the first public data network in China and is undergoing rapid development. For example, in February 1993, Northern Telecom, a Canadian firm, began installing advanced CNPAC switching systems in Beijing and provincial capitals as part of a US$9 million contract with the Chinese government. Today CNPAC principally serves the academic community, although other heavy users include the Bank of China, which uses the system for internal and external transfers of funds and for hooking up automatic teller machines, and airline companies, which use it for reservations and scheduling.

CNPAC was established at the end of 1989 and is run by the Ministry of Posts and Telecommunications. CNPAC had three node computers and eight multiplexers, located in 11 cities in China. As explained below, however, none of these is directly connected to the Internet. Eventually, CNPAC will link nodes in at least 32 of China's provinces, municipalities and autonomous regions.

One of the most comprehensive reports of a recent visit to Chinese networking sites is provided by Dr. Franklin F. Kuo, executive director of Asian Programs for SRI International in Palo Alto, California Dr. Kuo led a delegation of 24 people—known as the Networking Technology Delegation—to the People's Republic of China in May 1992. The group's express purposes were to exchange information on telecommunications and networking technology, and to solidify contacts among professionals in the computer and communications industries. The invitation had come from the China Institute of Communications.[6]

The delegation visited a number of research institutes and universities in Beijing, Shanghai, and Xian, where there was some interest in how to connect to the Internet One sentence in Dr. Kuo's report succinctly summarizes his visit: "There are a lot of local area networks in China, connecting many PC-clones, mostly Chinese-produced, to some older-generation mainframes such as Honeywells. What we did not see were operational wide-area networks, with the exception of a metropolitan demonstration network in Beijing" (Kuo, 1992).

---

[6]Dr. Kuo's complete report can be anonymously transferred using File Transfer Protocol from host arizona.edu, directory japan/kahaner.reports, filename china.net.

The only wide-area network in China that Dr. Kuo's delegation witnessed was CNPAC, which he referred to as a demonstration network in Beijing. The system was still under development and implementation in the Spring of 1992.[7] The hub of the system—the main hardware and the system's administrative staff is in Beijing and is administered by the Ministry of Posts and Telecommunications

The international connection to CNPAC is an X.25 link to the Internet using a store-and-forward system. This link is to the University of Karlsruhe in Karlsruhe, Germany. Computer users who send e-mail to China usually use "CANET as part of the address. The China Academic Network, as it is formally known, is not a computer network. According to Dr. Kuo, CANET is the name of the Beijing-Karlsruhe link; nevertheless, many Chinese networking specialists are unfamiliar with the term CANET, according to Dr. Kuo.

According to Qian Tian-bai, the ranking administrator at the Institute for Computer Applications (ICA), CANET was co-initiated by ICA and the University of Karlsruhe in 1986. Its purpose was to integrate Chinese academic communities with the worldwide computer network and to promote information exchange and technical cooperation with the rest of the world. The first connection with CANET was operational in September 1987.[8]

The e-mail link to China is not a direct link to the Internet. In order for a direct link to be established, China must agree to adopt a wide range of Internet protocols. It has not yet done this although negotiations have been in progress for some time. The author's queries to Beijing on the status of the negotiations were not answered, so additional details cannot be provided at this time.

SMALLER NETWORKS

There are many smaller public and private data networks in China. Examples of these are found in the railway system, the banking system, and in civil aviation (Kuo, 1992).[9]

Of the public networks, a leading example involves several research institutes of the Chinese Academy of Sciences that are connected to

[7]The system is an x.25 packet switched network capable of transmission speeds ranging from 1.2 to 9.6 kilobytes per second, which is quite slow for a modern network. Packet switches have been planned for Shanghai and Guangzhou, and packet switch concentrators have been planned for other cities as well. All packet switches, concentrators and packet assembly/disassembly devices, or PADs, were manufactured in China.

[8]The principal machine at ICA being a Siemens 7,760/BS2000 running PMDF/BS2000 software.

[9]SPRINT has made a major bid for the development of a new China Rail computer network, but its status was unclear at the time of this writing.

Tsinghua and Beijing Universities by means of the National Computing and Networking Facility of China (NCFC). This is a two-level system having the backbone and the network control center as the upper layer and the local campus networks as the lower layer.[10] Each of the universities and the Chinese Academy of Sciences has its own campus network (Kuo, 1992). The Computer Network Center of the Chinese Academy of Sciences is leading the development of the NCFC system and China's premier technical university, Tsinghua University, is the site of one of China's most impressive networks.

China leads most other Asian countries in bringing e-mail to school children, but this is due in large part to American benefactors. The Copen Family Fund, which sponsors the International Education and Resource Network, has funded 13 schools in Beijing with individual e-mail accounts to communicate with local schools in San Francisco. Initially, any message from the United States to Beijing would have had to be sent 13 times to reach all of the schools; however, in November 1992 Peter Copen gave the schools highspeed modems and a 486 file server—which is located at the Central Institute for Educational Research in Beijing—so the schools are now interconnected. Only one message needs to be sent to the file server, which can then redistribute it to all of the schools involved.[11] A few other similar arrangements exist between other schools and universities in the United States and China, but the overall quantity of e-mail communications is kept to a minimum in almost every case because of the costs.

OUTSIDE LINKS

E-mail can be sent to China on the public nets mentioned above, or on private nets. Fidonet is an amateur, private e-mail system that is run by volunteers. In 1991, Fidonet had 5,800 nodes on six continents and 800,000 users (Bates, 1992). Fidonet has a number of international gateways that connect it to other networks, inclincluding the Internet.

---

[10]The backbone of this system is a 10Mbps TCP/IP protocol system connecting the campus networks, and phone call for the system to be upgraded to a 100Mbps system using OS/ISO protocols.

[11]E-mail communications 30 January 1993 and 24 April 1993 from G. Ernest Anderson, Professor of Education, University of Massachusetts. As an aide, Prof. Anderson reported that the e-mail link between Beijing and San Francisco schools was dedicated by American Vice President Albert Gore during a demonstration at the Great Hall of the People in Tiananmen Square. "Our schools are no longer 10,000 miles apart, they are 10 seconds apart," said Mr. Gore in a broadcast of the demonstration. Prof. Anderson later noted, "From subsequent communications, I think the Chinese authorities were caught by surprise, or this dedication would not have been broad-cast".

In many ways, FidoNet seems to meet the idealized notions of an open international cooperative communication network with horizontal flows of information, as spelled out by the so-called MacBride Commission (Unesco, 1980)

Bates (1992) characterized FidoNet this way:

> What the (MacBride) Commission sought was an open international communication system; one in which control was minimized and access was maximized, one where messages and information flowed horizontally. The FidoNet system would seem to have been explicitly designed for such a purpose. The system uses basic, commonly available technologies in order to minimize costs and maximize access; The software to operate a FidoNet BBS, and to connect with the system, was provided free to interested users. Basing the system on local BBSs acted to maximize access through the provision of local access; further, the fact that the local BBS offered both their typical information services and FidoNet services provided local users with a wider range of incentives for use.

There are three FidoNet nodes in China: One is in Beijing (roy.luo@fl .n650.z6.fidonet.org); one is in Shantou (danleis.huang@ fl.n652.z6.fidonet .org); and one is in Shanghai (dean.lee@ fl.n651.z6.fidonet.org). E-mail communications with the sysops of these nodes indicate, however, that local usage is almost nil.

Large multinational corporations such as Shell Corporation maintain international computer networks with nodes in China. It goes without saying, however, that these are restricted to use by company employees. There also are independent online services that provide network connectivity to smaller corporations, and some of these services are available in China. AlphaGraphics corporation, for example, uses an American online service called Connect to link its American, Shanghai, Beijing, and Hong Kong offices.

Also, major U.S. telephone networks have all adopted e-mail services that may be accessed anywhere in the world with a computer, modem, and telephone line. These services include Sprint Mail, MCI Mail, and ATTMail.

FINANCIAL ISSUES

The principal roadblock to international e-mail communication with Chinese citizens is a simple one indeed: Individual users must pay for both incoming and outgoing messages.[12]

---

[12]It is for this reason that the author did not include any e-mail addresses in the chapter.

According to G. Ernest Anderson (personal communication [e-mail], April 24, 1993), a professor of education at the University of Massachusetts who visited the Institute for Computer Applications in Beijing in October 1991:

> ChinaNet is very small and very expensive. Costs are 8,000 yuan for join-ing and 2,000 yuan per month maintenance, and 10 yuan per kilobyte of information sent or received. For comparison, the average professor's salary in the PRC is 150 yuan per month. This explains why some Internet information Qian Tian-bai (vice-chief engineer at the institute for Computer Applications) wanted is being sent by regular mail rather than e-mail. Those of us who view internet as a big, free resource need to realize that casual communications elsewhere, and especially to China, may not be welcome by the recipient because of the cost.
>
> As an interesting aside, one of the major U.S. planners of the November conference (a November 1991 conference on telecommunications that was held in Beijing) also created a large share of international use of Chinanet in the previous month, and was pointed out to me as someone insensitive to what their costs were. My personal reaction was that action was needed to drive down costs, or get them subsidized, because what I saw represented to me exactly the kinds of interchanges the networks were designed to facilitate.

Unless and until this particular problem can be solved, the spread of net-working technology is bound to be greatly hampered in China.[13]

LANGUAGE ISSUES

As mentioned earlier, the People's Republic has not adopted the full suite of Internet protocols, so a direct connection to the Internet does not exist. The so-called CANET link between Beijing and Karlsruhe is the principal interna-tional link. Twice daily at the University of Karlsruhe, messages to and from China are exchanged, so there is a relatively long delay in sending and receiving messages to and from China. In a sense, the CANET link might best be thought of as an indirect link rather than a direct one.

When Dr. Kuo's delegation visited networking sites in China in May 1992, the group was frequently asked about the future of OSI/ISO versus that of TCP/IP. OSI is the abbreviation for Open Systems Interconnection, a set of standards developed by the International Organization for Standardization and TCP/IP stands for Transmission Control Protocol/Internet Protocol, a set of standards promulgated by the INTERNET Activity Board. Both of these sets of

---

[13]Similar financial barriers exist in other developing countries as well.

standards are fundamental to the operation of computer networks, and they are often seen as being in competition with one another.

The Internet uses TCP/IP protocols as the underlying technology, but China is moving toward the adoption of ISO/OSI.[14] OSI/ISO has no inherent advantages over TCP/IP for "lower-level" communication in the Chinese character set, but there are distinct advantages at another level These are outlined by S. Shaw (personal communication [e-mail], 15 February, 1993):

> I suppose two levels of networking standards should be distinguished. For the use of non-Latin character sets there is no particular advantage in the use of TCP/IP versus OSI for lower layer interconnection. However, at the application layer there are advantages in the use of OSI standards versus those associated with (but not part of) TCP/IP
>
> By contrast the applications associated with the Internet (using TCP/IP as underlying networking technology) are pretty well Latin-alphabet oriented, which follows from their North American origin.
>
> I discovered just last week that two Japanese standardization organizations communicate with each other in English because: (a) MHS is not yet deployed, so they use the Internet; and (b) internet applications only work with Latin character sets.

This may explain some of China's delay in adoption of the full suite of Internet protocols. However, the author's queries to Beijing and elsewhere on this matter were unanswered.

There are several systems in the public domain for encoding Chinese characters. Chinese computer users who prefer to communicate in the Chinese character set do so by using a computer language called GB, or GuoBiao (see Figure 7.1), which is an official standard in the PRC. Because of its popularity in China, it is heavily used by Chinese expatriates living abroad, and has become an unofficial standard in Singapore.

The principal drawback to GuoBiao is that it is based on simplified Chinese Characters. For this reason, in Taiwan the most popular system is called BIG5, which is based on the traditional Chinese character set and provides codes for more than twice as many characters. BIG5[15] has become an unofficial standard in other Chinese communities using traditional characters, such as Hong Kong.

---

[14]it is unlikely that ISO/OSI will completely replace TCP/IP; however, some ISO/OSI proponents believe otherwise. In any event, ISO/OSI is an international standard that proponents believe is significantly superior to TCP/IP. The most likely scenario is that TCP/IP and SO/OSI will "converge" through the adoption of additional protocols for TCP/IP and the development of patches, or short programs that will permit interfacing between the two sets of protocols.

[15]The origin of the term is unknown to the author.

```
M4&5O<&QE)W,@4F5P=6)L:6,@;V8@0VAI;F$-"M;0N?JQL;ZIRM"UVK;^O.#3
M_'T*S?6UI,_(R?K**UOT*#0I096]P;&4G<R!297!U8FQI8R!O9B!#:&EN80T**
MUM"UY^K&&QOJ\G`G*#*@T*+7:MOZ\X-/\#0K-];[\S,[[/R,GZ,GZZ]*R,ULG
M4F5P=6)L:6,@;V8@0VAI;F$-"M;0N?JQL;ZIRM"UVK;^O.#3_'T*L\+7T7\/W
MS\C)*LK5K5;#0H-"M;0N?JQL;ZIRM"UVK;^O.#3_'T*L\+70H-"M;0(052<&QE
MJ<KOM=JV_K64K_S@T_P_-"KGYJ.WY<_(R?K**UOT*#0I096]P;&4G<R!297!U8FQI
M8R!O9B!#:&EN80T**MM"UY^K&&QOJ\G`G*#*@T*+7:MOZ\X-/\#0K(SVVUU[J[/R,GS
M"@T**4F5P=6)L:6,@;V8@0VAI;F$-"M;0N?JQL;ZIRM#'V+/'
MO.#3_'T*L\+7:.-KL_IRM*MOT*#0I096]P;&4G<R!297!U8FQI8R!O9B!#:&5N
M8OT**UM"UY^K&&QOJ\G`G*#*@T?,8L\>\X-/\#0K(STL:%.9RP@*&4G]N.9;2F5
M"@T**4F5P=6)L:6,@;V8@0VAI;F$-"M;0U93RM"UY^K&&QOJ\G`G`G2<K.5#)OH-
M"@T**E!E.R?W;@T*+3LOOVN?0V..XL
MMT_P_-"TL$+BB.#0T7O(QML?E,,_(R?K**UOT*#0I096]P;&4G<R!297!U8FQI
M:6YA#0M8$8]R*'QG`G*#*@T?,8O@T?,8L\>\X-/\#0K(S
M)W,#0T*(%LO07!L:6,@;V8@0VAI;F$-"M;0U937;G[[+/=Q
MMT_P_-"TL$+2HOF5SY;65V5VMX\W?__=U]_1T]?/S<_Y]_Z?Z?Z?O
```

This text is the first part of a list of prisoners and their addresses in Chinese labor camps. The list was distributed on China-Net on December 8, 1992, and it may be converted into Chinese characters by means of software specially designed for this purpose, such as b2g or gb2ps. These programs are available by anonymous ftp in the src/unix subdirectory at ahkus.org [192.55.187.25]

Figure 7.1. Sample guobiao, or GB, text file

To communicate in these various encoding systems, the computer user requires a program to convert the computer codes into a readable script. There are several so called interpreters in existence, such as ChiRK which means "Chinese reader on Tektronics compatible graphics terminals."[16] However, their complexity required a rather high level of sophistication by end users.

These last observations point out some of the barriers to the spread of e-mail technology in China. Although it is possible to use e-mail networks strictly in English, to make full use of the system the Chinese user must also be familiar with the encoding process for Chinese characters, must know at least one—but preferably more—of about a dozen Chinese inputting systems, and must be quite sophisticated as a computer user.

---

[16]There are a number of FTP sites for Chinese related software the principal one being ahkcus.org (192.55.187.25). Others include crl.nmsu.edu (128.123.1.14), ftphost.cac.washington.edu (128.95.112.1), and hanuama.stanford.edu (36.51.0.16).

POLITICAL AND SOCIAL IMPLICATIONS

For an overview of the basic concerns of introduction of new communications technologies in society, see Bates (1990), who provides an extensive bibliography. With respect specifically to China, in the absence of scientific research on the subject one can only speculate about the effects of e mail technology on China's political and social institutions. However, the political and social effects of this new technology may have been harbingered by another new technology—the fax machine.[17] Fax machines played an interesting role in the 1989 Tiananmen Square event. According to Fredrick (1993):

> When the Chinese government fired on its citizens near Tiananmen Square, Chinese students transmitted the most detailed, vivid reports instantly by fax, telephone and computer networks to activists throughout the world. They organized protest meetings, fund raising, speaking tours, and political appeals. Their impact was so immense and immediate that the Chinese government tried to cut telephone links to the exterior and started to monitor computer networks where much of this was taking place. (pp. 235-236)

One outcome of these events was government regulation of fax machines in China. Special licenses and taxes are required to own a fax machine in China today, and this undoubtedly inhibits diffusion.

The political implications of e-mail for China are complex and far reaching, and we are ill-equipped to understand them. Many writers describe e-mail as a force for democratization of government and social change (see, for example, Perry & Adam, 1992). What they ignore is e-mail's potential as a tool of the state. As any subscriber to ChinaNet will attest, e-mail can be a channel for state propaganda as well as political debate, and the machinery of the networks is ideally suited to monitor the activities and messages of network users. Computers are far more efficient at compiling lists of names of dissidents—based, for example, on message content—than are offices full of bureaucrats.

In any case, it is wrong to assume that any effect of e-mail on China will come solely from within China itself. E-mail is a nascent technology in China, so its political and cultural effects are minimal. However, e-mail is fairly advanced in other nations, and it is clear already that e mail networks of expatriate Chinese in the United States have had significant effects on China's human rights policies. Examples of these effects follow.

---

[17]In fact, fax technology is at least 50 years old, but it only recently diffused into the consumer market. Edwin Armstrong's first FM demonstration in the early 1930s included a fax demonstration on the FM sideband, or that part of the radio band on either side of the carrier signal.

Wandesforde-Smith (Personal communication [e-mail] February 3, 1993) writes:

> There is absolutely no question but that new techniques and technologies for global communication will have a transforming impact. It's just a matter of time. As some previous comments suggest, the impacts will be uneven, because of language barriers that constrain attention and because of relative inattention among individuals and groups. The more interesting immediate question may be whether we are equipped to understand the nature and significance of the transformation, as it unfolds.

E-mail presumably accelerates democracy movements by: (a) increasing overall flows of information among dissidents and dissident organizations at remote locations, including international sites; (b) circumventing attempts by authorities to manage the infrastructure and to control message content; (c) focusing worldwide media attention on local and regional issues such as human rights abuses; and (d) making online databases available for research at remote locations.

E-mail discussion groups are organized in two basic ways: as either listserv or Usenet groups. A listserv group gets its name from a computer dedicated as a list server, or a computer that channels e-mail communications to everyone on a "list" People join the list by e-mailing a "subscribe" command to the list server.

In Usenet, each subscribing Internet site receives only one copy of each posting for a given discussion group, and the thousands of files that accumulate weekly are stored for access by subscribers. This system is more efficient but less personal than the listserv system.

At present, there are 1,200 Usenet discussion groups on the Internet. The groups' communications are coordinated by an Internet service with the same name, Usenet. In August 1992 Usenet reported that there were 12.4 million users with accounts. Discussion groups with interests in Chinese affairs include soc.culture.china, which has 86,000 readers; soc.culture.hongkong, 57,000 readers; soc.culture.taiwan, 56,000 readers; talk.politics.china, 8,000 readers; and aus.culture.china, 4,100 readers. Another organization, the Alliance of Hong Kong Chinese in the United States, publishes an electronic magazine titled China News Digest—known as CND on the net—which has 26,000 readers. The digest reports more news about China than Hong Kong. AHKCUS also maintains an FTP (File Transfer Protocol) site known as ahkcus.org, which serves as an archival database for CND.[18]

---

[18]One must not overlook other organizations that have interests in Chinese political affairs but are less parochial, such as Amnesty International, which has its own net, and various "Green" movements with nets.

An example of a Chinese listserv group on Internet is China-Net. China-Net, which had 800 regular readers in early 1993, is an excellent example of increasing flows of information among dissidents and dissident organizations[19] China-Net is a computer network of Chinese expatriate university students and faculty members in the United States. Various estimates put me total number of Chinese expatriates in the United States anywhere from 80,000 to 110,000. China-Net was created during the spring of 1989 at the height of the prodemocracy movement the main coordinators coming from New York University, the University of Florida, Stanford University, Case Western Reserve University, the University of Georgia, and Kent State University. According to the ChinaNet Management Committee, which over sees China-Net operations from an office at New York State University at Buffalo, the purpose then was "to provide a vital communication network for coordination of the world-wide prodemocracy activities as well as for exchange of information related to CSS (Chinese Students and Scholars) communities" (personal communication [e-mail] January 22, 1993).

In July 1989, the Independent Federation of Chinese Students and Scholars (IFCSS) was founded in the United States, and China-Net was devoted to serve IFCSS as a volunteer-coordination network. Today the network serves to coordinate IFCSS lobbying activities in the U.S. Congress on China-related legislation. A recent prominent example was Senate Bill 1216, The Chinese Student Protection Act, which was approved late in 1992 and is currently being implemented by the Immigration and Naturalization Service. The act gives political asylum to Chinese students and scholars who fear reprisals from Chinese authorities if they are forced to return to their homeland, and the INS expects to process 40,000 applications for political asylum in the first year alone. During the Congressional debates on the proposed law, letter-writing and telephone campaigns were meticulously coordinated on ChinaNet. Now that the act has been passed, the IFCSS has been lobbying the INS for details on the implementation of the act, and the organization has been posting progress reports on ChinaNet.

Through China-Net, IFCSS also coordinates lobbying activities in China. In early December 1992, ChinaNet distributed worldwide the names and addresses of dozens of political prisoners in China and urged recipients to send season's greetings to the prisoners (see Figure 7.1). China-Net claims some of the responsibility for the release of Chinese dissidents such as Beijing University student leader Wang Dan, who was released in mid-February 1993.

Turning now to the circumvention of authorities, it might be said that there are two attributes of computer networks that make them difficult to control or eliminate—decentralization and interconnectivity. It is these attributes that make e-mail communications so powerful as an agent of change.

---

[19]China-Net's Internet address appears in the glossary at the end of this chapter.

Crippling or otherwise controlling part of a network is largely ineffective because of the multitude of networks and channels, and because of the PAD—packet assembly and disassembly—technique utilized to relay messages across the nets. As the term implies, the PAD technique results in the dismembering of a message into small packets of data, consisting of a few kilobytes each, that are transmitted independently over computer networks. These are reassembled in the correct order on reaching their destination.

Chinese prodemocracy activists could profit from the Soviet experience during a crisis in Moscow in 1991:

> The "Emergency Committee" seized power as (Mikhail) Gorbachev vacationed in the Crimea. Yet communications had so developed under glasnost that the coup leaders were unable to "pull the plug". . . . Computer networks such as Moscow-based "GlasNet" telecommunicated with supporters outside the country. Information flowed through the vast underground communication network, which was first developed with mimeographed samizdat publications and was now interconnected in a decentralized web of electronics. The coup leaders did manage to send a surge through the electrical lines in a partially successful attempt to bum out fax machines, computers, and telephones. . . . [In] the end the abortive Soviet coup demonstrated that once the electronic gates are opened, it is hard to close them again. (Fredrick, p. 235)

One might predict a similar scenario during a time of crisis in China.

Authoritarian control of computer networks by oversight committees may be successful at controlling communications, but only to a limited extent. As long as the Chinese government limits the number of outside links to the rest of the world to a manageable number, it can record and randomly sample communications for subversive content.[20] However, with the proliferation of independent private e-mail services such as Fidonet, MCI Mail, Sprint Mail, and ATTMail, the government will lose its grip on control. The controls will be even less feasible within China itself. The example of FidoNet illustrates that it is simple and cheap to set up a network. However, the creation of "subversive" nets would be out of the question in China, because a net requires the use of a file server in a fixed location, and this could be easily identified by the authorities. Seized files would reveal the names and addresses of all users on the net. However—and this is where the powers of the nets outside of China really exert themselves—once a message from a foreign net gets into China, there is no limit on how many times it might be subversively passed around without detection. The only risk to the people involved would be the details in the headers, which indicate the origin and

---

[20]Many nations, including the United States and even Hong Kong, routinely do this for overseas telephone communications.

destination of a message and list the nodes and gateways through which it passes. Even a moderately sophisticated e-mail user would know enough to strip as much of this information out of a "subversive" message before for warding it to another individual.

GLOSSARY

AHKCUS (The Association of Hong Kong Students in the United States)—A discussion group interested in prodemocracy movements in China. To subscribe: send e-mail to REQUEST@AHKCUS.ORG(192.55.187.25).[21]

Archie—a computer program on the Internet that maintains a continually updated catalog of the contents of thousands of anonymous FTP archives.

backbone—major cable, software, and gateway linking a hierarchically organized system of local area networks. See also "gateway."

BBS (Bulletin Board Service)—file storage area available to all members of a net. They may post messages there—that is, save files—and read files that have been saved by others.

BIG5—This is the official Chinese language encoding system adopted by Taiwan, and it is an unofficial standard in places where traditional characters are used, such as Hong Kong. The system has codes for almost twice as many characters as GuoBiao. See also GuoBiao.

CASnet—the campus network of the Computer Network Center of the Chinese Academy of Sciences.

CCITT (International Telephone and Telegraph Consultative Committee)—a division of the International Telecommunication Union (ITU) comprised of representatives of worldwide national post, telephone, and telegraph administrations. CCITT issues recommendations on telecommunications standards.

CCNET (The Chinese Computing Network)—a computer network forum on technologies relating to the use of Chinese on computers. To subscribe: "SUB CCNET-L <your name>" to server CCNET-L@UGA.BIT-NET, or CCNET-L@UGA.UGA.EDU.

CHINA—A discussion group organized by scholars at Princeton University on topics related to Chinese studies. To subscribe: "SUB CHINA <your name>" to server LISTSERV@PUCC.PRINCETON.EDU.

CHINA-NT—a computer network serving the Independent Federation of Chinese Students and Scholars, a U.S.based association of Chinese expatriates. To subscribe: "SUB CHINA-NT <your name>" to server LISTSERV@UGA.BITNET.

---

[21]As this chapter was being written, there was some speculation on the Internet that ahkcus.org's FTP site might have become permanently disabled.

CHINANET—A network based at Texas A8M University with special interest in computer networking in China. To subscribe: "SUB CHINANET <your name>" to server LISTSERV@TAMVM1.BITNET.

Chinese Academic Network (CANET)—the name of the Beijing-Karlsruhe link between CNPAC and the Internet.

CND (China News Digest)—A daily electronic news digest about what is happening in China. There are several versions—U.S., Canadian, European-Pacific, and global. To subscribe to the global version, which is compiled and distributed from Arizona State University: "SUB CHINA NN <your name>" to server USTSERV~ASUACAD.BITNET.

CNPAC (China National Public Data Network)—a wide-area network headquartered in Beijing. CNPAC's link to the Internet is by means of the Chinese Academic Network, or CANET.

connection-oriented—a computer network in which there is no logical connection between the end user and the network until the moment that a transmission is made. The alternative is a so-called connectionless system, in which the end user is always connected to the network.

concentrator—a wiring closet or cabinet providing outlets for interconnecting computers in various configurations.

FTP (File Transfer Protocol)—an IP protocol for uploading and downloading computer files, usually anonymously, from remote computers. See also "IP and "protocol."

gateway— a computer that acts as a host for two or more networks. It can function as a "protocol translator" between two networks with different protocols. See also "host," "local area network."

GB (GuoBiao)—This is the official Chinese language encoding system adopted by mainland China, and it is an unofficial standard in Singapore and among many mainland Chinese living abroad. It is based on the simplified character set.

HKNet (Hong Kong Net)—A U.S.based bulletin-board service about Hong Kong. To subscribe, send mail to CST@HOBBES.CATT.NCSU.EDU or SO@CS.WISC.EDU. All postings should be sent to HKNET@CS.WISC.EDU.

host—a computer that acts as a file manager for other computers.

HXWZ (Hua Xia Wen Zhai)—A weekly electronic literary digest published in Chinese characters by China News Digest. To subscribe: "SUBCCMAN -L <your name>" to LISTSERV@UGA.BITNET.

Internet—the complete collection, now totalling more than 1,000, of all IP based networks. See also "Internet Protocol."

Internet Protocol (IP)—a layer of protocols between networks that was developed to allow "connectionless" interoperation of gateways and local area networks. See also "OSI," "TCP," "TCP/IP," and "OSI."

listserv group—a discussion group whose communications are managed by a list server, a computer that manages a mailing list.

local area network (LAN)—No or more local computers that can send and receive files to or from one another using a system of cables, software, and another computer dedicated as a file server.

mail exploder—See "mail reflector".

mail reflector—an electronic mailbox that resends a message to a list of other mailboxes, usually comprising a so called "interest group."

MHS (Message Handling System)—an e-mail system. The term comes from the International Federation of Information Processing.

NCFC (National Computing and Networking Facility of China)—a metropolitan network in Beijing Linking Tsinghua and Beijing Universities to several research institutes of the Chinese Academy of Sciences.

node—computer that acts as a local file server on a network.

OSI (Open Systems Interconnection)—a suite of nonproprietary protocols developed by the International Organization for Standardization and International Electrotechnical Committee (ISO/IEC) and the International Telephone and Telegraph Consultative Committee (CCITT). It is considered superior in many respects to TCP/IP. See also "protocol," "protocol suite" and "TCP/IP."

packet assembly/disassemby (PAD)—the process of dividing a message into discrete components, or packets—usually a few kilobytes—and then routing them through a network by means of switching devices.The process is performed by a computer that links the end user's computer to a network. The message is reassembled near its destination.

packet network—a computer network that breaks communications into discrete "packets" and transmits them in a switching system that contains many alternate routes.

protocol—a procedure or set of rules that computers with different hardware and software use to communicate with one another.

protocol suite—a set of protocols administered by a common body. See also "OSI" and "TCP/IP."

soc.culture.hongkong—An electronic news group with about 35,000 members interested in Hong Kong issues. It is most easily reached through Usenet, an Internet service. However, subscribers may be added to the SCHK mailing list by sending mail to POSTMASTER@AHKCUS.ORG asking to be added to the mailing list.

store-and-forward service—a message-handling system that sends messages from one user to another by means of a series of routers, where they may be spooled, or stored temporarily. This is the most common kind of e mail service, as opposed to the end-to-end service, which provides instantaneous communications.

sysop (system operator)—common title for the individual who manages a node, or computer acting as a file server in a network.

TCP (Transmission Control Protocol)—a "connection-oriented" file transport service. See also "connection-oriented."

TCP/IP (Transmission Control Protocol/Internet Protocol)—the Internet protocol suite, overseen by the Internet Activity Board. TCP/IP includes the
Simple Mail Transfer Protocol (SMTP), which most users employ when
sending e-mail; the File Transfer Protocol (FTP), for accessing files on
remote computers; the Domain Name System (DNS), which maps host
names to network addresses; and TELNET, which provides virtual terminal emulation service. See also "protocol and suite."

Unicode—This is an international standard for character representation. It
incorporates codes for simplified Chinese characters, traditional Chinese
characters, Japanese characters, and Korean characters. It is reportedly
flexible enough to encode any alphabet in the world.

Usenet—an Internet service that manages communications for discussion
groups. Postings to each discussion group are forwarded to each
Internet site and stored for access by discussion group readers.

X.25—a widely adopted set of CCITT-recommended standards for packet networks. Its principal function is to prevent congestion in a network by
switching messages to underutilized channels. See also "CCITT."

ZHONGWE—A discussion group based at the Royal Institute of Technology in
Sweden that focuses on Chinese computing. It maintains an ftp archive
of Chinese-related software. To subscribe: Send e-mail to server zhongwen request@nada.kth.se.

REFERENCES

Bates, B. J. (1990). Information systems and society. *Telecommunications Policy, 14*(2), 151-158.

Bates, B. J. (1992, May). *The new world of democratic communications: Fidonet as an example of the new horizontal information networks.* Paper presented at the 42nd Annual Conference of the international Communication Association, Miami, Florida.

Bentson, T. W. (1993). Editor's introduction: Computer-mediated communi-cation. *Electronic Journal of Communication/La Revue Electronique de Communication, 3*(2).

Duning, B. (1990). The coming of the new distance educators in the United States: The telecommunications generation takes off. *Distance Education, 2*(1), 24-49.

Frederick, H. (1993). *Global communication in international relations.* Belmont, CA: Wadsworth.

Herring, S. C. (1993). Gender and democracy in computer-mediated com-munication. *Electronic Journal of Communication/La Revue Electronique de Communication, 3*(2).

Kuo, F. (1992). *Networking in the People's Republic of China.* [On-line]. Available FTP: Host: cs.arizona.edu Directory: japan/kahaner.reports Filename: China.net.

Markus, M. L. (1987). Toward a "critical mass" theory of interactive media. *Communication Research, 14*(5), 491-511.

Perry, T. S., & Adam, J. A. (1992, October). E-mail: Pervasive and persuasive. *IEEE Spectrum*, pp. 22-23.

Rogers, E. M., & Shoemaker, F. F. (1971). *Communication of innovations: A cross-cultural approach* (2nd ed.). New York: The Free Press.

Unesco. (1980). *Many voices, one world.* New York: Author.

CHAPTER 8

CHINA'S SATELLITE TECHNOLOGY: DEVELOPMENTS, POLICIES, AND APPLICATIONS

JUNHAO HONG

INTRODUCTION

Nearly 30 years have passed since China started its satellite program. The three decades have witnessed significant progress in the country's development of satellite technology. As early as 1970, China became one of the five nations, after the United States, the former Soviet Union, France and Japan, to independently make and place a satellite in orbit with an indigenous rocket, making it the undisputed Third World leader in satellite technology ("Software Error," 1994). In 1975, China was one of the three countries which possessed the technology to retrieve satellites. In 1984, China became one of the three nations that could launch stationary satellites into the earth orbit. Now, China is one of four space powers in the world, along with the United States, Russia and the European Arianespace Consortium, that have the ability to manufacture, launch and operate satellites of various types for various purposes ("French Experts," 1993).

Any development in technology is not merely a technological development. Almost always, it is a result of political, economic and social factors interacting with each other, regardless of whether it is in the West or in the East. Grant (1992) observed, development of communication technology depends on the specific condition and content of five aspects of a particular society—its social system, organizational institutions, software, hardware, and individual use/social application. China's case also reflects this pattern.

171

Due to the differences in political environment, economic situation, and social context, the policies, purposes of applications and course of developments in China were quite different from other countries. This chapter, by reviewing the developments of China's satellite technology, examines why and how the satellite technology was adopted, developed and applied. The emphasis is placed on satellite policies and changes in applications. Historical and sociocontextual interpretations will be provided for tracing the factors that caused the changes. In addition, both the advantages and disadvantages from changing satellite policies for different periods will be discussed. Finally, the Chinese space program's future goals and strategies will be outlined.

A SHORT HISTORY, A RAPID DEVELOPMENT

China's satellite technology has existed for only thirty years. Yet, the country has experienced a rapid development in the field and now has one of the most advanced capabilities. In many aspects, its development speed exceeded the elite world satellite club's few members.

A SWIFT DEVELOPMENT OF SATELLITE: ONE AND HALF SATELLITES PER YEAR

The record of China's satellite technology shows a swift development. From 1970 when the country launched its first satellite to 1994 when the nation launched two satellites with one rocket, China has launched a total of 36 of its own manufactured satellites, nearly one and half satellites per year.

China launched its first low earth orbit scientific satellite PRC-1 in 1970 The satellite's instrument payload was a transmitter that broadcast a song entitled "The East Is Red," which had been used as a Chinese communist anthem since the 1930s. Although the first satellite made more of a political statement, its technological advancement and sophistication were also noticed by the world, because not only had China orbited a satellite on its own, but also the payload was heavier than the first Russian, American, French, and Japanese satellites combined (Gu, 1992). The advent of PRC-1 marked China's entry into the world's exclusive space and satellite club.

Just ten months later, PRC-2, a geodetic satellite powered by solar cells and carrying two telemetry systems was launched (Hsieh, 1971). The speedy pace disquieted the U.S. and the former Soviet Union, since the event signified that China had entered both the nuclear and space ages without assistance from either of the two superpowers and even became a potential competitor in the global space technology race.

Although almost all of China's industries in the 1970s were seriously damaged by the Cultural Revolution (1966-1976), satellite technology was spared. In fact, space technology grew very rapidly during the period. For example, in 1975 China launched its first recoverable scientific experimental satellite and two reconnaissance satellites. In 1976, two more reconnaissance satellites were launched (Kohler, 1989). In the 1970s, China also successfully developed the technology of retrieving satellites, three of which were recovered during the period (Gu, 1992).

Since the 1980s, China has been making more prominent achievements in satellite technology during which a total of 20 satellites were launched. In 1981, a triple payload satellite was launched for an atmosphere study; later that same year, two other satellites were launched for natural resources study; and in 1982, a recoverable satellite was launched for remote sensing. In 1984, the country's first geosynchronous experimental communication satellite and two other satellites including a recoverable satellite for photo reconnaissance were launched. In 1985, a more advanced recoverable geosynchronous domestic communication satellite for land resource study was launched (Kohler, 1989).

The second half of the 1980s was both a breakthrough and harvest season in China's satellite development. From 1986 to 1990, a total of 11 satellites of four sophisticated types were launched. Among them, 3 were domestic communication and broadcast satellites, five were recoverable satellites, one was a meteorology satellite, and the fourth type of satellite is now in synchronous orbit with the sun, producing high-quality cloud chart materials using scanning radiometers (Min, 1992). Table 8.1 shows the launching record of China's satellites from 1970 to 1990.

After entering the 1990s, China continues to maintain its rapid pace in satellite development. In the past 3 years, half a dozen of its own satellites have been launched. Most recently, in February 1994, the country launched a scientific satellite Shijian 4 and a simulated satellite with just one rocket newly developed to lift heavier loads (*Shijian* stands for World). Shijian 4, carrying six sound instruments, probes charged particles and their effects in near-earth space. With this satellite, the country's space scientists can calculate the parameter of the particles' distribution and their potential for charging satellite batteries. The use of the simulated satellite was a test run for the launch later this year of China's third-generation communication satellite—the 2.22 ton "The East is Red 3." The new telecommunications satellite will replace three experimental models already in orbit and provide more channels for television programs and telecommunications services than the existing three put together (Zhou & Li, 1994).

So far, China has launched a total of 36 satellites of its own, including small, medium and large satellites, to low, middle and high orbits. Xinhua News Agency, China's official news organization, referred to the latest launching as "another important achievement in China's high-tech space

Table 8.1. Launching Record of China's Own Satellites (1970-1990).

Type of Satellite	Launch Date
Dong Fang Hong 1	Apr-24-1970
Shi Jian 1	Mar-03-1971
Technical Experiment	May-11-1974
Recoverable	Nov-26-1975
Technical Experiment	Dec-16-1975
Technical Experiment	Aug-30-1976
Recoverable	Dec-07-1976
Recoverable	Jan-26-1978
Shi Jian 2	Sept-20-1981
Shi Jian 2A	Sept-20-1981
Shi Jian 2B	Sep-20-1981
Recoverable	Sep-09-1982
Recoverable	Aug-19-1983
Experimental	Jan-29-1984
Experimental GEO Communications	Apr-08-1984
Recoverable	Sep-12-1984
Recoverable	Oct-21-1985
Operational GEO Communications	Feb-01-1986
Recoverable	Oct-06-1986
Recoverable	Aug-05-1987
Recoverable	Sep-09-1987
Operational GEO Communications	Mar-07-1988
Recoverable	Aug-05-1988
Meteorological	Sep-07-1988
Operational GEO Communications	Dec-22-1988
Operational GEO Communications	Feb-04-1990
Meteorological	Sep-03-1990
Recoverable	Oct-05-1990

Note. All launches were successful except the January 29, 1984 launch, which was stated as partially successful by the authority. Data compiled from Space in China (1991).

research field," and "it will have a notable impact on efforts to accomplish China's strategic objective of developing a new generation of multipurpose satellites and expanding exchanges and cooperation with overseas in the space field" ("Asia-Pacific," 1994; "Central government," 1994).

THE SUCCESSFUL "LONG MARCH" CARRIER ROCKET FAMILY

China's most successful area in satellite technology probably lies in the carrier rockets. In fact, China's space technology started with this type of launch vehicle. Space activities can date back to the late 1950s when the country formulated a development plan for the space industry and the corresponding scientific research organizations. After a few years of preparation, China entered into the space age with its launch vehicles. In November 1960, the first short-range rocket was successfully launched. In March 1962, the first short-medium-range rocket was launched. In 1964, the country launched its first launch vehicle. In December 1966, a medium-range rocket was successfully launched. Four years later, in 1970 a two-stage, medium-long-range rocket was launched and in the same year the well-known "Long March" carrier rocket was manufactured. In April 1970, the first Chinese satellite was successfully launched with Long March 1 (*China Academy of Launch Vehicle Technology*, 1991).

Since 1970, China's rocket technology has rapidly developed. In 1971, a preliminary successful launch of an intercontinental rocket was conducted. In 1975, the first recoverable scientific experimental satellite was launched with Long March 2C. In 1980, an intercontinental rocket was launched, impacting the target area in the Pacific Ocean. In 1984, China's first geosynchronous experimental communication satellite was launched with Long March 3 (*China Academy of Launch Vehicle Technology*, 1991).

After entering the 1990s, launch vehicle technology reached a new level with an exceptional ability to launch heavy loads. In 1990, the first test flight of the Long March 2E cluster carrier, a high-capacity booster rocket, was successfully launched. With strap-on boosters, the low earth orbit capability of the launch vehicle was significantly increased up to 9000 kg. The launch added new dimensions to China's carrier rocket series and was an indicator of its ability to launch heavy satellites. The Long March 3, three-stage rocket has become the centerpiece of China's satellite launch technology. Its third stage booster adopted the crucial rocket technology of hydro-oxygen and hydro-hydrogen, high-energy, low-temperature fueled rockets. The technique, by which a three-stage rocket can be started twice under the zero gravity of space and a high vacuum, marked a breakthrough in overcoming the orbit control difficulties previously faced when launching earth stationary orbit satellites at a place far removed from the equator (Kohler, 1989; Xu, 1990).

Moreover, the even larger Long March 4 carrier rocket, which functions as a booster for small manned space vehicles has been in service for a couple of years. In 1990, a Long March 3 carrier rocket successfully launched AsiaSat I, a 24-transponder communication satellite manufactured by the US Hughes Group and jointly owned by a Hong Kong company, a

British company and a Chinese company. AsiaSat I was the first Pan-Asia satellite with a footprint covering half of the world's population in about 40 countries ranging from Egypt in the West to Japan in the East and from Russia in the North to New Zealand in the South (Ma, 1992).

The latest development in China's rocket technology is the success-ful launching of two satellites with a new-generation Long March 3A rocket in February 1994. Featuring many technological advances, Long March 3A can carry a 2.5-ton payload, nearly double the 1.4-ton capacity of Long March 3, which already ranks fourth in the world in terms of launching capabilities ("China Uses," 1994). The launching of Long March 3A was considered "a big, significant leap" in China's space technology development (Liu & Huang, 1994). In addition, the country is developing another Long March family member, Long March 3B, to be used to launch satellites manufactured abroad. It will be able to put a 4.8-ton satellite into space, well beyond the 2.5-ton capability of Long March 3A ("Big China," 1994). Table 8.2 shows the Long March Family of launch vehicles.

Using the growing Long March carrier rocket series, China has launched more than 40 satellites (including those launched for other coun-tries) with a very high success rate of 96%—better than that of any other rocket in the world (Xu, 1990). Only European Ariane rockets come close to the Chinese reliability rate with 92% Although there have only been five Ariane flops in 14 years of its operations, the rate is below China's. The advancement of China's satellite carrier rocket has made the country one of the most reliable for launching satellites. As Ma (1992) remarked, China is now recognized to have one of the best records for satellite launch ability and facilities in the world.

Table 8.2 Long March Family of Launch Vehicles.

Model	LM1D	LM2C	LM2E	LM3	LM3A
Overall Length (m)	28	35	51	43.9	52.3
Lift-off weight (ton)	80	191	464	202	240
Lift-off thrust (ton)	112	284	600	284	300
Payload capability (kg)	700-750*	2,500*	9,000*	1,500**	2,500**

Note. Data compiled from Space in China (1991).
*LEO/SSO (or Low earth orbit/sunsynchronous orbit).
**Geostationary transfer orbit

SATELLITE POLICIES IN THE 1970S

China's rapid development of satellite technology, in the 1970s, 1980s, and 1990s, is attributed to the country's particular social and political contexts at the time. The 1970s can be referred to as the first phase of China's satellite technology. The swift and successful development during that phase resulted from a variety of factors. Among them, the first and most important factor was China's national security needs.

A NATIONAL SECURITY-ORIENTED, SELF-RELIANCE POLICY

China's satellite program can be traced back to its military oriented research and development. As early as the late 1950s, China began to establish space program institutes, production plants and test bases. The initial efforts provided considerable knowledge and experience in manufacturing modern rocket motors, instruments, and ancillary equipment (Chen, 1991). These efforts were implemented under the assistance of the former Soviet Union. Ironically, however, the decision to build short-medium-range rockets was also made following the withdrawal of all Russian technical assistance for China's missile program. In 1961 China decided that it should establish independence from the Soviet Union. The pressure and difficulties caused by the withdrawal of Russian assistance stimulated China's resolve and pace of developing its own space technology. Mao's self-reliance policy became the guide which proved fruitful. For example, not long after the split between China and the former Soviet Union, in 1964 the first launch of a short-medium-range missile was made, and in 1966 the first fully operational medium-range missile was launched (Chen, 1991).

Sino-American relations in the 1950s were quite tense and the 1960s saw no improvement. To the Chinese leadership, the U.S. threat of an attack during this period was imminent, especially as the United States became increasingly involved in the war with China's neighbor—Vietnam. Meanwhile, on the Sino-Soviet side, disputes over ideology and the eventual break in relations gradually escalated to military tensions over territorial issues, culminating in 1969 in bloody armed clashes along the border. The Russians even moved missiles near the Chinese border, and installed long-range missiles to which nuclear warheads presumably could be fitted.

Under these circumstances, in 1968 China initiated a national defense-oriented satellite policy and a detailed plan to develop satellite manufacturing and launch capabilities. In the same year, the China Academy of Space Technology was set up under the approval of Mao. Thus, the country's satellite technology entered a new period of rapid development with well designed and organized plans (He, 1993). In 1970, the launch of the first satellite was proclaimed by the nation's press as an important step in the struggle against U.S. imperialism and Soviet socialist imperialism as well as an effective effort to forge human development in a safer environment (Hung, 1970). Soon after, China launched a total of six reconnaissance satellites in just two years.

Thus primary motive, then, behind China's satellite technology in the 1970s, was not economic, but as a sort of deterrence and a tranquilizer for a country surrounded by hostile forces. The major objective was to make the world aware that China was a military power to be reckoned with. As Hung (1970) puts it, the satellite was experimental in nature, and did not have specific military missions, but what was important was the significant impact of the unspoken message behind the experiment: China now had the capability of delivering atomic and hydrogen bombs to any point on the earth's surface. As claims Xinhua News Agency, "It is a powerful check to the moves of these imperialists to carry out nuclear war threats and re-divide their monopoly over nuclear weapons and rockets" ("China Launches Its," 1970).

A POLITICAL-PRESTIGE-ORIENTED POLICY

Besides national security considerations, the desire for political self-assertion and prestige in the international arena was also an important basis for satellite policy in the 1970s. Although China still had a long way to go to reach equality with the former Soviet Union and the U.S. after it launched its first satellite, the world had ceased to be as polarized. The launch of the first satellite promptly raised China's status to influence its neighbors and changed the perceptions of some underdeveloped countries that now looked up to China for leadership.

One of the goals of China's satellite program was to create global political prestige. Mao Zedong (1971) repeatedly made the statement that China, with its vast territory and unmatched human resources, ought to make greater contributions to humanity in fighting against all "reactionaries" in the world and in forging human development. Only six months after the former Soviet Union launched the world's first satellite in the 1950s, Mao claimed that "this is a good thing to socialism and human kind," and "China should also have its own satellites" (He, 1993, p. 1). As his congratulatory message for the launching of China's first satellite indicates, Mao saw the satellite program being able not only to help establish stability and order at home and to make contributions to the world but also to provide the country with a fresh source of nationalism (Mao, 1970). Specifically, China could pride itself that no foreigner took part in the work of, nor were any foreign-made articles used for the entire satellite project (Hsieh, 1971).

Zhou Enlai, the late Chinese Premier, was also a strong political supporter of and major policy-maker in the satellite program. He highly cherished the strength and prestige satellite technology conferred upon China in the international community (Nie, 1984). Deng Xiaoping, the currently retired but still most powerful person in China, also praised the political significance of the development of satellite technology. He recalled in 1990 that "if China had not exploded atom and hydrogen bombs in the 1960s and launched satellites, it would not have been considered one of the three big powers and would not occupy such a position in the world." He concluded that "these things can mirror the capability of a nation and symbolize a country's vigor and prosperity" ("China Space," 1990, p. 20).

SATELLITE POLICIES IN THE 1980S

The early 1980s marked a turning point for satellite policy. During the reform decade, China shifted its policy concerns from national security, self-reliance and political prestige toward economic and social development, openness and commercialization.

AN ECONOMIC AND SOCIAL-DEVELOPMENT-ORIENTED POLICY

Changes in satellite policy first centered around the application of satellite technology. Although military and political reasons were still salient motivating factors, economic and societal purposes also began to be noticed. In general, the development of China's satellite technology in the 1980s reflected a relatively more mature and balanced course.

In the late 1970s, Deng Xiaoping made known his practical, scaled-back view of the satellite program. He stressed that the satellite program must conform to the society's larger goal of economic development and that it should focus on the technology that would have economic value instead of just sending rockets to the moon (Chen, 1991). Deng emphasized the necessity and importance of readjusting China's space technology development strategies, saying that the country should put its space technology personnel, facilities and budget toward first developing badly needed applications (He, 1993).

The change in space technology development strategies was derived directly from China's new social context. Since the late 1970s, the country started economic reforms which resulted in significant increases in agricultural and industrial output as well as foreign trade. The authorities showed a willingness to extend the definition of self-reliance to permit substantial imports, foreign loans, investment, and joint ventures. During the 1980s, China opened five major provinces and 14 cities as special economic zones. By 1990, the country had attracted nearly 30,000 foreign-invested enterprises with a total investment close to US$20 billion (Rao,1991).

However, China's use of telecommunications facilities per capita was still 10% less than the world's average per capita consumption ("China's space," 1990). The outdated and saturated communications network became a weak link in the country's goal of attracting foreign investment and quadrupling the annual gross value of industrial and agricultural output by the end of the century. The policy makers realized that improved telecommunications facilities were crucial to China's ambitious modernization plans.

Under Deng's pragmatic guidance, China entered a period of rapid development of applied satellites. Since the early 1980s, technological spin-offs from the military research and development programs were incorporated in civilian industries and yielded tangible benefits in areas such as communications, natural resource surveys and meteorology. Moreover, the direction of space technology development was clearly set toward economic and social applications. For instance, in 1984 the country launched its first geosynchronous experimental communication satellite. By 1990, 12 recoverable remote-sensing satellites were placed in orbit, which helped the country to detect large coal deposits and oil fields. Timely information relayed from the weather satellite reduced losses from typhoons, floods, fires and other disasters (Li, 1991).

With a high capacity transponder, satellites were also used to serve telephone, telegraph, facsimile, VSAT, and many other economic and business purposes. By the end of the 1980s, a basic operational domestic satellite communications system had formed (Wu, 1988). In 1989, the leadership reiterated that satellite technology was one of the key sectors in development of the national economy. The authorities also declared that the development and advancement of satellite technology should focus on economic growth and the advancement of society (Song, 1991).

AN OPEN, COMMERCIALIZATION POLICY

Unlike other Third World countries where satellite technology was initiated in close collaboration with foreign countries, China's satellite technology started behind closed doors. It was not until the mid-1980s that the nation began to seek partnerships with the outside world. China has since taken steps to cooperate with foreign nations out of the realization that it can benefit from the valuable experiences of other countries, thereby saving time and financial resources (Tu, 1988). In other words, the space program is no longer an exclusively secret industry directly controlled by the topmost leaders, but an industry that functions basically in a normal fashion.

By nature, the open policy actually unfastened the hands and feet of the space program, which enabled it to absorb useful experiences from its counterparts and promote exchanges and cooperation with other more advanced countries. This ultimately made China's satellite technology more developed. Since the early 1980s, China has established space research collaboration or business partnership with more than 100 companies and organizations in 36 countries, including the United States, Japan, the Netherlands, Italy, Britain, France, Germany and the former Soviet Union. In 1993, China reached its first agreement with the U.S. to rent payload space in the U.S. space shuttle program for scientific research projects. Eight payload booths are to be used by China to carry equipment for experiments in space physics. In addition, China contracted with the European Space Agency to take part in the "Cluster Program," which also includes Britain, France, Germany, Austria and the United States. The project, considered the most advanced satellite research program in the 1990s, involves launching four satellites to conduct joint studies of the heliosphere ("China to Use," 1993; Qing, 1993; Yu, 1993).

In the meantime, foreign satellite companies were also allowed to enter China's market. A global telecommunications company that provides expert engineering, design and integration of satellite earth station facilities, IDB Communications Group Inc. will design and install Standard A and B Intersat earth stations for China. These technologies will be used to transmit video and telephone communications. The first major video project for the earth stations was the international 43rd Table Tennis Championship held in Tianjin in 1995 ("IDB Systems," 1994).

As an indicator of further openness, in the early 1990s China set up an office in the United States to provide consultation services related to satellite launch services and to seek to import U.S. space technology (Gu, 1992). Recently, it opened another agency in Hong Kong (Zhang, J., 1993). In 1993, for the first time the Chinese authorities allowed foreign correspondents and diplomats to visit its satellite manufacturing plants and launch centers. Beginning in 1994, even foreign tourists were given a chance to view a Chinese satellite launch on the spot. Although designed to make money, the tours also function to impress the world with the country's satellite technology ("China Organizes," 1993). China will also hold satellite exhibitions in the United States, Australia and Malaysia ("China to Aggressively," 1994).

Tightly bound to the shift from a closed-door to an open-door policy was the change in the financial structure of the satellite program from full state-subsidy to self-support. This change inevitably resulted in the commercialization of the space program.

In contrast to the 1970s, during the 1980s the Chinese authorities proclaimed that the nation's development of satellite technology was primarily intended to meet its domestic modernization needs, and if it had surplus capability, to simultaneously provide commercial services for the world market ("China Space," 1990). This alteration occurred out of a two-fold consideration. On the one hand, after years of development, China had attained an appreciable level of satellite technology which had the potential to make a profit. Profit-making as a concept became acceptable as compatible with socialism, and no longer labeled as a capitalist or bourgeois practice. Instead, it was regarded as a necessary means to promote economic development. On the other hand, the leadership believed that, by commercialization, the country's satellite technology would be put into an internationally competitive system, and thus would become stronger and more advanced.

As government support for the satellite program decreased, the satellite industry identified two sources of funding: domestic and international. At the domestic level, satellite plants were devoting part of their capacity to producing consumer and industrial goods. As Reuters reported, hoping to slash huge state subsidies to inefficient and often redundant munitions factories, the government encouraged the space industry to shift production to television sets, refrigerators, trucks, cars and hundreds of other high-demand consumer items, and even illegal satellite TV dishes (Parker, 1993). For example, according to The *New York Times*, one of China's satellite equipment factories manufactures 60,000 to 70,000 1.5-meter satellite dishes a year, the primary purpose of which is to make profits for the factory's survival (Kristof, 1993). Recently, the latest launch by the Chinese Defense Ministry's satellite unit was not a satellite, but a 31-flavor ice cream parlor in Beijing—the pink, purple and white, joint-venture Baskin-Robbins shop (Parker, 1993).

However, the major portion of funds generated at the international level is through selling satellite manufacturing and launching services to other countries. In 1985, China began a global campaign to commercialize its satellite launch services on the Long March boosters as well as other services, such as the manufacture of small-and medium-sized satellites and environmental-simulation testing. The startling chain of American and European rocket failures in 1986 enabled China to gain momentum in the race for the multi-billion-dollar launch service market. The successful launch of AsiaSat 1 with Long March 3 in 1990 formally marked China's entrance into the international market of commercial launch services (*China Academy of Launch Vehicle Technology*, 1991). So far, the country has launched five foreign satellites—one for Hong Kong, one for Sweden, one for Pakistan, and two for Australia (Kong & Su, 1992).

In the view of Zhang Tong—President of China Great Wall Industry Company, a manufacturer of space equipment and provider of launch services, commercialization of China's space program has not only promoted its own research, but also given a good supplement to the international market and provided new opportunities for satellite owners ("Foreign Firms," 1994). However, from a Western perspective, China's newly issued commercialization policy along with its reliable and cheaper services lured business away from more expensive systems operated by the Americans and Europeans ("China Knocks," 1994; "China Uses," 1994). For instance, China offered to send up payloads for US$20 million to US$30 million—less than half the price their American competitors charged (Kohler, 1989).

As Rhea (1986) pointed out, China's competitive edge lies in: (a) its low price, which is about at least 30% below the rates of NASA and Ariane; (b) the ability to custom fit the rocket to a client's payload and guaranteed availability of launch insurance; and (c) an impressive rate of successful launches. Although China also had failures, including an aborted attempt to send the Australian Optus 2 satellite into orbit in 1992 and the falling of the instrument cabin of a recoverable satellite to the earth in 1993, its launch services are still regarded as the most reliable ("French Experts," 1993).

ACHIEVEMENTS AND BENEFITS OF
THE SATELLITE POLICIES IN THE 1980S

The readjusted economic and social development oriented satellite policy has yielded many achievements, especially for the economy, cultural affairs, public education and scientific research.

TO THE NATIONAL ECONOMY

Satellites played a noticeable part in a growing number of economic sectors. Space technology brought about tremendous economic and social benefits in areas such as industry, agriculture, communications, finance, etc. With the assistance of satellite telecommunications transmitters, China now provides more than 2,000 long-distance telephone lines, 800-plus very small aperture terminals (VSATs) for digital transmission, and more than 200 VSATs for voice transmission ("China Speeds," 1993). According to the Ministry of Posts and Telecommunications, the country's telephone network now has a total of 40 million telephones, compared to 30 million just one year ago. Also, the first VAST earth receiving headquarters station in Shanghai opened for business to public, connecting any VAST station in China with the international networks (You & Liu, 1994; Zheng, 1994).

Between eight years from 1985 to 1992, China's telecommunications capabilities increased more than 20% annually, which not only exceeded the 15% growth rate of Hong Kong, Taiwan, Singapore and South Korea—the four "Asian Dragons," but also Japan's 15.4% during its "economic take-off" period. China's telecommunications industry was ranked as one of the world's ten most advanced. Some experts predicted that China, by using satellite technology, saved at least 10 to 20 years in its economic "take-off" to full development objective (Wang & Wang, 1993).

As a pioneer for economic development, the rapid expansion of telecommunications has greatly benefited China's modernization plans. For example, in 1993 telecommunications business in Shanghai, China's largest and most important industrial city—grew 50% percent, which has further enhanced the city's position as one of the centers for commerce and finance not only in China, but also in the world (Cao & Wang, 1994). In the newly-established province, Hainan, the telecommunications business in 1993 increased 88%, leading all other provinces in the country and making the province more attractive to foreign investors (Bao, 1994). In China's long economically stagnant northwestern areas—Shanxi, Gansu, Ningxia, Qinghai and Xinjiang— development of satellite telecommunications has increased economic cooperation among these provinces and foreign countries (Tian & Chen, 1993).

Moreover, in Tibet, the country's poorest region, thanks to a series of satellite programs, its telecommunications capabilities have reached the level of China's average provinces and major cities (Z.Yang, 1993). Recently, Tibet even opened its first stock-trading center. The center is linked by satellite communications to China's two stock exchanges in Shenzhen and Shanghai, taking this poorest region to a new level of modernization ("Stock Trading," 1994). Also, the connection of satellite receiving stations between Weihai in China's Shandong province and Seoul, South Korea, substantially promoted their economic relations (You, 1993).

Space technology was also used for offshore oil industry. For the first time, China's offshore oil industry had its own satellite communications network to facilitate communications between offshore oil and gas fields and onshore bases. Once operated by short-wave radio, microwave radio, and submarine cable, communication between offshore oil and gas fields and onshore bases remained a headache for decades. Now, the satellite communications network is capable of meeting the requirements for offshore oil fields: The transmission of digital signals produces high-quality communications, and the flexible combination can enable end-to-end calling and data transmission. The new technology can not only help improve safe operation and management, but can also serve in the tapping of offshore oil reserves ("China's Offshore," 1993; Gao, 1993).

TO CULTURAL AFFAIRS

For a country with a vast territory of which 80% is mountainous or desert, the effective and timely delivery of information via microwave has proved impractical. As a result of long-standing backwardness and geographical limitations, China's terrestrial broadcasting encountered almost insurmountable difficulties, thus holding up social development in many remote areas. For example, China Central Television (CCTV), the country's only national TV network, used to be transmitted via microwave to major cities. To reach remote areas, it had to record its programs and send videotapes by plane to local TV stations in regions such as Tibet where the audience watched the programs including news broadcasting 3 to 5 days later. In some areas with no civilian airports, programs were as much as 15 days later.

During the 1980s, five telecommunications and broadcasting satellites were launched, which made it possible to transmit television and radio programs from Beijing to all parts of the country. Now, 12 TV channels are transmitted via satellite. With more than 50,000 ground satellite TV receiving stations throughout the country, TV broadcasting coverage reaches 81.3% of the population, making it the world's largest TV audience—more than 800 million viewers ("China's Radio," 1993; "China Sat-5," 1993; Li, 1993).

Recently, China also imported a high capacity communication satellite to advance its broadcasting media. In 1993, ChinaSat 5, China's first-ever imported communication satellite, started relay broadcasting. The satellite carries 22 transmitters on different bands. Its footprint covers the nation's entire territory and some bordering countries and regions. In addition, the Central People's Broadcasting Station has opened 30 external language broadcast channels to the whole world through the satellite. ("China Sat-5," 1993; Min, 1992; Yan & Liu, 1993).

TO PUBLIC EDUCATION

Another of China's highest accomplishments using satellite technology for social development, especially in rural and remote areas, was the success of the television university. The country has been using satellite distribution to carry university courses in addition to educational programs broadcast by CCTV. The advent of TV universities aired via satellite not only provided the majority of the nation with a simultaneous broadcast of education and training programs, but more importantly, it also tremendously eased the critical shortage of secondary schools and vocational classes as well as colleges and universities for qualified students.

According to Min Guirong, (1992) Director of the China Space Technology Research Institute, in recent years educational TV programs beamed by satellite have become increasingly popular in the country. By 1991, more than 5,000 ground receiving terminals were installed, allowing more than one million college students to study at home. Five million people received continuing education through the satellite TV network. At least 20 million farmers learned practical farming techniques. Currently, some two million students get their education via satellite TV, including 1.2 million primary and middle school teachers. The transmission of TV training courses via satellite saves about RMB$ 5 billion a year (Li, 1991; Li, 1994; "Satellite TV," 1994; "Satellite Vital," 1993).

In some areas, satellite TV education plays a leading role in promoting economic development as well as cultural and social progress. For example, in Shandong province 1,200 educational TV receiving stations were constructed, ranking the province first in the country. It has 21 TV universities with 56 programs. Holding a current enrollment of 50,000 students, the universities have had 140,000 graduates, which is one third of the province's total college graduates. The cost for a TV college graduate is 60% less than a regular college graduate (X. Zhang, 1993). Even in Tibet— the "roof of the world,"—100 satellite TV ground stations were established with financial allocations from the State Education Commission. Educational TV programs in the Tibetan language are broadcast widely in the autonomous region ("Satellite TV," 1994).

TO SCIENTIFIC RESEARCH

A number of scientific satellites were launched for obtaining useful information on scientific experiments. Satellite technology has greatly helped the country to conduct many extensive programs studying space physics, space environment detectors, earth observation technology, rockets, balloons and microgravity experiment technology. Dozens of rockets and balloons were launched to gather data on solar x-rays, cosmic-ray high energy particles and space biology. Maps and marine charts were made based on reliable and high resolution photos taken by satellite. Remote sensing technology was also used to monitor forest fires. Recently, China's first microcaliber satellite communications test system was developed in Shanghai ("China's First," 1993; "China to launch experimental" 1993; "Satellite Vital," 1993).

Moreover, several meteorological satellites are in operation. The country thus can forecast weather 5 or 6 days ahead, compared to 3 or 4 days before. The operation of a numerical weather prediction system starting from 1993 made the increased forecast capacity possible. China also completed a new snow monitor for pasture areas. The satellite-monitoring system can forecast the possibility of disastrous snowstorms and estimate the damage that can result over a vast area of pasture from the Tibet-Qinghai plateau in the west to the greater Hinggan mountains in the east. By applying satellite remote sensing technology, local meteorological departments in the northwest area now can obtain satellite weather data. A total of 366 ground weather monitoring stations and 30 rain-monitoring radar systems were built in this underdeveloped area, forming a multi-functional weather monitoring system and providing a way to reduce and avoid losses caused by natural calamities like snowstorms, droughts, floods, forest fires and grassland fires, and enhance production conditions ("China Can," 1994; "China Develops," 1994; "Modern Technology," 1993).

The open door and market policies in the 1980s have put China's satellite technology into the fiercely competitive international arena, and made it an increasingly strong contender. The world's commercial satellite market is estimated at around 16 to 20 launches per year, with 60% secured by Europe's Ariane, and most of the rest won by U.S. companies, such as Titan, Delta and Atlas. However, this structure is being challenged. With a wealth of experience in space, Russia is also an eager contender in the satellite launch market. Perhaps more importantly, China has acted deci- sively and aggressively in the scramble for contracts to launch satellites. Although Ariane's share of the commercial launch cake was over half in 1994, its dominance is under threat. But the threat is not from U.S. compa- nies. Both the Atlas and Titan have an embarrassing tendency to blow up— they are based on ballistic missile technology of the 1950s and 1960s, and their critics argue that they are too unreliable and expensive to compete in an open market. Although there is some threat from Russia, that is not a major concern. Despite the fact that every year since the late 1960s more rockets have blasted off from the former Soviet Union than any other coun- try, the vast assembly lines which churn out Russian rockets were always excluded from the commercial launch market. Most experts agree that the greatest uncertainty lies in the potential of the Far Eastern space powers, and the majority favors China instead of Japan. Despite its technological advances, no one expects Japan to sweep other rivals—this is because Japan's position in the global competition is hampered by its very high launch costs ("China Knocks," 1994).

It is very likely that the threat will come from China. As early as the mid-1980s, China began to vigorously seek opportunities in the international market. Now, the country already has a foothold in the arena for launching satellites and gained considerable commercial achievements. China's com- mercial launching service has had a busy schedule:

- In mid-1994, it provided launching service for Hong Kong's Asia- Pacific Satellite 1.
- In late-1994, China launched an Australian telecommunications satellite Optus B3 built by the U.S. Hughes Aircraft Corporation.
- At the end of 1994, Hong Kong's Asia-Pacific Satellite 2 was placed in orbit.
- In early 1995, Hong Kong's AsiaSat 2 was launched.
- In 1995 and 1996, China will launch two satellites for the U.S. company Echostar Satellite, which will use the more than 100 channels to distribute sports, high-definition and cable television programs, pay-per-view movies, databases and educational ser- vices accessible anywhere in the United States with dish antennas as small as 18 inches.
- From 1995 to 1997, it will launch U.S. Space Systems/Loral's several commercial satellites, including InterSat VII/VIIA, Superbird, Tempo, and N-Star series satellites.
- From 1996 to 2002, it will launch 66 low-earth-orbit iridium satel- lites for the U.S. Motorola company, with two satellites for each launch, to build a global telecommunications network allowing portable phone users to communicate from anywhere in the world—on land, at sea or in the air.

- Beginning in 1997, the U.S. EchoStar's seven satellites will be launched by China; In addition, China and Hughes Aircraft Corporation signed a long-term agreement to launch 10 satellites for the U.S. company over the next 12 years, with at least three satellite launch deals set for the next two years (Sources: "Aerospace," 1994; "Asia-Pacific," 1994; "China Near," 1994; "China Prepares," 1994; "China Sets," 1994; "China Signs," 1994; "China Signs Contract," 1994; "China to Launch," 1994; "China to Launch Optus," 1994; "China to Launch First U.S.," 1994; "China to Launch Two," 1994; "China to Launch Regional," 1994; "French Experts," 1993; "Hughes Aircraft," 1993; "Loral Reserves," 1993; "Motorola Launches," 1993; "News Highlights," 1994; "Two Satellites," 1994; "U.S. Company," 1994; "U.S. Grants," 1994; Xu, 1993; L. Yang, 1993).

As one of the Chinese space program's goals, the country is also trying to expand into other satellite services such as satellite manufacturing and operating services. It has made successful progress:

- In 1993, Germany's biggest business conglomerate, Daimler-Benz AG, and China signed a contract to jointly produce and operate high-tech satellites. South Korea and China also signed an agreement in 1993 to jointly manufacture and launch a regional observation and communication satellite, which will be seven times the size of South Korea's second satellite.
- In 1993, Brazil and China announced a US$150 million project to jointly build two geographical research satellites to monitor atmospheric pollution, forest reserves, agricultural plagues and other earth resources, and in addition, Brazil will build a third satellite with China under a joint space program to be used for geographic, environmental and weather studies. Thailand is seeking the help of China for establishing a center offering education in satellite technology to train and produce Thai satellite experts, and in 1993 it agreed to buy three small Chinese satellites to relay telecommunications frequencies, provide scientific experiments and disaster mitigation systems, and do remote sensing.
- In early 1994, China won a contract worth an estimated US$200 million to operate the first communication satellite for the Philippines, after defeating at least 11 foreign firms including Hughes which even claimed during its presentation that it could help the Philippines tap a loan from the U.S. government if it could get the contract (See "Brazil-China," 1993; "Brazil strategic," 1993; "Brazil to Build," 1993; "Brazil to Meet," 1994; "China and Brazil," 1993; "China & Brazil Signs," 1993; "China, Brazil

sign," 1993; "China Hands," 1993; "Chinese President's," 1993; "China Signs Deal," 1993; "Daimler-Benz to Launch," 1993; "Foreign Firms," 1994; "Sino-Filipino," 1994; "South Korea," 1993; "Thai Agencies," 1993; "Thailand Seeks," 1993).

However, China is not able to achieve a full speed in international commercial service. In recent years, increasing international attention has been provoked, following China's decision to commercialize its satellite launching services. The world's major satellite launch providers, such as the European Ariane and the United States in particular, are afraid that China's quality launch services at a lower price may put the West out of business. Out of this concern in 1989 the United States signed a trade agreement with China providing U.S.-made communication satellite export licenses. In return, China agreed to launch no more than nine international communication satellites through 1994 and to maintain launch prices on a par with world markets (Gu, 1992). Without this agreement, there may have been more launches on China's schedule for international commercial services.

SATELLITE POLICIES IN THE 1990S

After entering the 1990s, China's satellite program took steps to move into a new level of space technology. Satellite policies during this period contain the basic characteristics of policies in the 1980s, but have two new features, which correspond to the country's general political and economic development plans for the 1990s. They may be described as faster paced and more advanced.

According to Qi Faren, President of China Academy of Space Technology, the satellite program in the 1990s should closely follow the course set by Deng Xiaoping, which requires that China's space program should focus on the development of urgently needed, applied satellites. Qi considers this the only right direction because it properly fits the nation's situation (He, 1993).

Under Deng's principles, the expansion and advancement of the space program in the 1990s should be implemented for three reasons.. First, it is to cater to the urgent need of rapid economic development and daily increases in people's material and cultural needs. Second, it is to serve national security. And third, when there is capacity left while pursuing the first two purposes, it is to provide commercial services for other countries as part of China's efforts to promote international exchanges and make contributions to mankind (Xu & Li, 1993).

China's third-generation leaders are paying great attention to the space program. Jiang Zeming, President of China as well as the nation's political and military leader, blueprinted three strategic goals for the satellite program to achieve by the year 2000: (a) should be close to the world's highest space technology; (b) should form a stable, operational system of applied satellite networks to serve the country's needs; and (c) it should become more competitive in the world and make more contributions to other countries and mankind (He, 1993).

Chinese Prime Minister Li Peng also emphasized that that there are three *strategic* objectives of China's space program to be accomplished by the year 2000: (a) to realize a remarkable development in applied satellites and application of applied satellites; (b) to industrialize the space program; and (c) to provide more and better services to cater to the needs of the international market (Li, 1994).

Corresponding to three strategic goals, three specific objectives were also established. First, China will increase the pace of developing more sophisticated satellite technology. A "Trans-Century Space Project" was proposed, which aims at improving China's space aeronautic technology by the year 2000. The Center for Space Science and Applied Research of the China Academy of Science, a leading institution for China's space technology, has recently recruited more than 100 outstanding space scientists to carry out research tasks covering space environments, ground stations, satellite equipment and microwave remote sensing techniques. By the year 2000, the nation will be able to manufacture spacecraft to launch to the moon and other planets. Moreover, plans to build a space station, to develop a heavy satellite launch vehicle, and to develop an earth-space transportation system, were all proposed (Chen, 1991; "China to Launch Experimental," 1993; He, 1993).

Second, China will pay more attention to developing applied satellites for both civilian and military purposes. The telecommunications manufacturing and service industry was designated as one of China's transcentury strategically key industries. It is estimated that the telecommunications industry will maintain a growth rate of 30% a year in the following few years. In the country's most important industrial cities such as Shanghai, the telecommunications industry has become the city's second largest industry only after automobile industry.

During the 1990s, a national communications network using fiber-optical cable, digital microwave and satellite communications will be established. At present, China is developing a new generation of multiuse applied satellites. Among them, a large-capacity 24-transponder communication and broadcasting satellite capable of covering all of China's land area and having a life expectancy of 8 years was completed and placed in orbit. The satellite can simultaneously transmit six color TV channels and 15,000 lines of telephone or telegraph, fax and data signals, thus greatly improving the communication links necessary for broadcasting, education and economic development. The national percentage of phone ownership will increase from the current 1 or 2% to 5 or 6% at the end of the decade. By 1995, the number of satellite transponders will increase to between 50 and 60 from 41—at present. The country will then open its third educational TV channel via satellite. By the year 2000, a fourth channel will begin transmission and the total broadcasting time for educational programming will extend to 70 hours per day.

In the meantime, China will continue to develop multiuse earth resource satellites and various meteorological satellites. These satellites will have 10 times greater payload capacity than those launched from 1985 to 1990. In addition to 14 earth receiving stations already in use, a number of earth stations have been under construction in Shanghai, Haikou, Harerbin and dozens of other cities. The scope of applications will thus be considerably expanded and the problems encountered in education, culture, communications, transportation services, environment, population and natural resources reduced ("China & South Korea Connect," 1994; "China to Launch Two Home-Built," 1993; Min, 1992; Ni & Su, 1993; Wang & Wang, 1993; You & Liu, 1994).

Third, China's space program will be more open and more actively involved in global competition. In order to be more competitive, the technological as well as functional capability of the space program will be advanced while maintaining its low cost advantage. According to contracts already signed, from 1994 to 2000 China will launch 25 to 30 satellites of different types for other countries—an average of four commercial satellite launches per year. As Agence France Presse (AFP) reported, ("China Knocks," 1994) the world's commercial satellite market is estimated at around 15 to 20 launches per year. China already has at least 20% of the share. However, China's share may well increase. Moreover, by the year 2000 the country's international commercial services will include not only satellite launching services, but satellite manufacturing as well. To fulfill this plan, as TASS reported, "the deadline had been set and the scheduled time will not be changed" ("China Ready," 1994; Xu & Li, 1993).

In Qi's view, both the three strategic goals and the three specific goals have not only increased the pressure on China's satellite program, but more importantly, presented opportunities and challenges as well. The president of the China Academy of Space Research is very confident in achieving these goals (Ping, 1993).

CONCLUSION

China's satellite technology is unique compared to either developed or other developing countries. In the 1970s, national security and political prestige were of primary importance. In the 1980s, significant changes in policy occurred, which were marked by efforts to open and commercialize the satellite program and to adopt applications in the civilian sector. In the

1990s, satellite policies featuring a much faster development pace and a more advanced technology were proposed. Although the political and economic climates in China often change dramatically, which seriously affects the country's development of many industries and technologies—the satellite program seems to continue unhindered. It always has maintained a high priority. For three decades, the space program has consistently been supported by the highest level of leadership to catch up with or surpass the advanced nations.

China's satellite policies during the 1970s, 1980s and 1990s have both advantages and disadvantages. Although all of these policies were derived from China's particular political, economic and social contexts and may not be exactly suitable to other nations, they are still worth studying because they may provide some useful lessons. At least, three advantages of China's satellite policies may be drawn.

First, the self-reliance policy made the country's satellite program an independent one. This independence enabled the leadership to freely use its satellite technology for different goals they set during different periods. For instance, one of the most prominent characteristics of China's satellite program was that, instead of relying on satellite technology from either the United States or the former Soviet Union, as did almost all other developing countries, China chose a tortuous path to develop its own capabilities from scratch. This not only allowed the country to avoid a dependency relationship, but also provided the nation with capability to do whatever it wished to do. The independence of technology resulted in an independence of politics, ideology, and even economy. Therefore, it is not difficult to understand that, despite China's willingness to join in cooperative satellite ventures with the world community and demonstrated openness and flexibility, its ultimate aim is still to be self-reliant. This is in keeping with China's overall strategic policy of technological autonomy, which is part of its general political policy. The country's satellite program was and still is predominantly an independent research and development effort, while cooperation with Western countries is now encouraged.

Second, the open and commercialization policy has dramatically increased the development speed of the country's satellite program—Not only in terms of the number of satellites it has manufactured and launched, but also in terms of the advancement and sophistication of its space technology. Within a short period of only 10 years, China has become an undeniable satellite giant and an increasingly strong and competitive contender in the global market. If the nation had not adopted the open and commercialization policy, its satellite program would not enjoy such status today. The combination of the self-reliance policy in the first phase and the open and commercialization policy in the second phase produced a unique position for the nation's satellite program to further develop and advance itself and enter the international market with high credibility and unique features.

Third, the shift of emphasis in the space program from political prestige and national defense to economic and social development substantially benefited China's modernization plans. If the 1970s was an exploratory and experimental period for China's satellite technology, the 1980s was a transition period from experimentation to application, and the 1990s a period of full application. Today, China has a total of more than a dozen satellites in service, which not only tops all other developing countries, but also exceeds many developed countries. All of the country's 31 provinces and autonomous regions are now covered by satellite transmission. Satellite technology thus makes great contributions to the nation's economic and social progress.

However, there are also some problems in China's satellite program; Three of them need to be noted. First, in general China's satellite policies were politically based. So the satellite program was often affected by changes in its domestic politics. For instance, following political policy during different periods, the development of the satellite program had different directions because the goals often changed. This inevitably hindered the development and advancement of China's space technology.

Second, for a long time the space program was a specially favored industry. It did not mean that the country had a strong, developed and advanced telecommunications infrastructure to take advantage of the space industry. In other words, China's industry as well as science and technology in general were not matched with the separately advanced space program. The satellite program was tightly bound to national security and political prestige, so the satellite program was one of the privileged industries. The success of satellite technology thus stood in sharp contrast with slow development in other fields. The satellite-related institutions and technologies enjoyed the latest modern technology, the support of a comprehensive industrial complex, a highly trained contingent of scientific and technical personnel and the first priority in funding (Hahn, 1986). Therefore, in studying these institutions and technologies, one should not ignore the Chinese leadership's unique way of interpreting development in terms of national power and international status, as opposed to GNP and the living standard.

Not surprisingly, despite great progress in satellite technology, the country's basic telecommunications facilities are still outdated. Nationwide telephone density is only about one per 100 people. In rural areas the figure falls drastically to .17 Both figures are well below the developing world's average density of three telephones for every 100 people (Zita, 1989). Also, the level of development in China's satellite technology is uneven with the launching system surpassing communication satellite technology and earth stations.

Third, although social application of satellites should undoubtedly be the first priority, in reality political, military and commercial considerations are often prior to social applications. The central role of the Chinese government is still apparent, and satellite technology is still viewed as an important part of the apparatus of governance. Social applications of satellite technology in terms of provision of health services and farming techniques for rural peasants, for example, are hardly seen. The lack of commitment in these areas seems to be common in Third World countries. This phenomenon led McAnany & Nettleton (1987) to conclude that a variety of internal, external, and structural reasons often prevent well-intentioned efforts to use a technology like satellites for social applications, even when there are obvious needs and real potential benefit. Only when there is a political advantage, backed by budgetary support, are social applications likely to succeed. In China, the military institutions still control fairly large elements of satellite technology and operate key facilities. It is still very likely that the direction in which military institutions orient satellite program development will be decisive. It might be very possible that a space station and space shuttle may be developed by the end of this century, but many social services via satellite probably will have to take a back seat. Although a major part of China's satellite capacity is devoted primarily to television transmission, the emphasis of television reflects the importance the Chinese leadership attaches to disseminating official information to individuals and organizations.

A considerable number of Third World countries have adopted satellite technology, but they have each used different methods to reach their goals. The interrelated elements, including ownership, financing, management, professional values, training, hardware, software, and beneficiaries, all seem different. Although China's experience and course have both pros and cons, they are based on the country's unique circumstances. As mentioned earlier in this chapter, communication technology does not exist in a vacuum. Rather, the adoption, production, dissemination, and utilization of a communication technology is inextricably linked with a particular society's political system, organizational institutions, hardware and software, and goals. In China, the central government assumed, and still does to a large extent, the sole responsibility for the satellite program. Unlike in other Third World countries such as India and Brazil where various political parties, interest groups, advertisers, foreign enterprises and local industrial lobbyists play important roles in shaping the policies governing the adoption, utilization and future development of satellite technology, in China such entities are more or less absent.

China's space program is expected to expand more rapidly during the transcentury period. Such trends as the country's further political opening, swift economic development, rapid advancement of science and technology, and steadily improving living standard will all provide good foundations for a much better space program. China has become both a big attraction and a big threat. Recently, the country is regarded both as a very powerful competitor in the global satellite arena and the last big untapped telecommunications market in the world. Therefore, its previous, present and future policies certainly deserve great attention.

REFERENCES

Aerospace. (1994, March 1). *Los Angeles Times*, p. A–3.

Asia-Pacific Sat-2 to be launched in China. (1994, January 18). *Xinhua General News Service [XGNS]*.

Bao, H. (1994, January 10). Hainan's telecommunications increases rapidly. *People's Daily*, p. 2.

Big China rocket launches two satellites. (1994, February 9). *The Orlando Sentinel*, p. A-6.

Brazil-China sign accord on satellites agency. (1993, September 15). *Reuters*.

Brazil strategic partner in LATAM—China minister. (1993, November 24). *Reuters*.

Brazil to build third satellite with China. (1993, November 11). *Agence France Presse* [AFP].

Brazil to meet standards on missile technology. (1994, February 11). *Reuters*.

Cao, Y., & Wang, L. (1994, January 20). Shanghai has reached the goal of a three-fold increase of telecommunications. *People's Daily*, p. 8. (In Chinese).

Central government hails new satellite launch. (1994, February 9). *XGNS*.

Chen, Y. (1991, May). China's space policy: a historical review. *Space Policy*, pp. 116-128. (In Chinese).

China Academy of Launch Vehicle Technology. (1991). Hong Kong: China Economy & Culture Publishing House. (In Chinese).

China and Brazil signed an agreement to launch two Brazilian satellites in 1996. (1993, November 24). *TASS*.

China and Brazil to launch satellites. (1993, November 9). *Reuters*.

China and South Korea connect satellite receiving stations. (1993, July 29). *People's Daily*, p. 1. (In Chinese).

China, Brazil sign 150 million dollar satellite deal. (1993, November 10). *AFP*.

China can now forecast weather five or six days ahead. (1994, January 13). *XGNS*.

China develops satellite snow-monitoring system. (1994, January 7). *XGNS*.

China hands Kohl $1.8 billion in agreement. (1993, November 16). *Reuters*.

China knocks on door of space club with double-satellite launch. (1994, February 8). *AFP*.

China launches its first satellite. (1970, April 28). *XGNS*.

China near satellite launch pact with Australia. (1994, February 18). *Reuters*.

China organizes first tour to see satellite launch. (1993, December 21). *AFP*.

China prepares to launch two satellites for US firm. (1994, February 24). *The New York Times*, p. C-1.

China ready for international space cooperation. (1994, February 20). *TASS.*

China Sat-5 operates well. (1993, October 20). *XGNS.*

China sets 1994 window for APSat-2 launch. (1994, January 19). *Reuters.*

China signs contract to launch two satellites for US firms. (1994, February 22). *AFP.*

China signs deal to launch joint satellite. (1993, September 28). *Reuters.*

China signs satellite accord with Hughes. (1994, February 28). *Reuters.*

China speeds up development of satellite telecommunications. (1993, October 20). *XGNS.*

China to aggressively market satellites. (1994, February 21). *Japan Economic Newswire.*

China to launch experimental satellite. (1993, December 3). *XGNS.*

China to launch first U.S. satellite since sanctions last year. (1994, January 19). *United Press International [UPI].*

China to launch Optus B-3 satellite. (1994, February 28). *AFP.*

China to launch regional satellite. (1994, January 18). *AFP.*

China to launch two home-built telecommunications satellites by 1995. (1993, October 21). *Japan Economic Newswire.*

China to launch two satellites for U.S. market. (1994, February 22). *Reuters.*

China to launch two US satellites. (1994, February 23). *Japan Economic Newswire.*

China to use U.S. space shuttle for research. (1993, December 4). *XGNS.*

China uses new rocket to launch satellite. (1994, February 8). *Reuters.*

China's first micro-caliber satellite communication test system has been developed in Shanghai. (1993, December 28). *XGNS.*

China's offshore oil industry begins satellite communications. (1993, October 13). *XGNS.*

China's radio and television thriving. (1993, October 20). *XGNS.*

China's space industry takes off. (1990, May 21). *Beijing Review*, pp. 17-21.

Chinese President's visit sparks optimism over trade. (1993, November 30). *AFP.*

Daimler-Benz to launch new business in China. (1993, November 9). *Japan Economic Newswire.*

Foreign firms vie for satellite sale to Philippines. (1994, January 24). *XGNS.*

French experts say China and U.S. both "right" about satellite. (1993, October 29). *AFP.*

Gao, X. (1993, October 14). Satellite communications network for off-shore oil industry established. *People's Daily*, p. 1. (In Chinese).

Grant, A. (1992). The umbrella model of communication technology. In A. Grant & K. Wilkinson (Eds.), *Communication technology update* (pp. 3-11). Austin, TX: Technology Futures Inc.

Gu, R. (1992). *Internal and external influences on China's satellite program.* M.A. thesis, Michigan State University.

Hahn, B. (1986, September/October). Space commerce. *The China Business Review*, p. 10.

He, P. (1993, December 14). Mao Zedong and China's satellites. *People's Daily*, p. 1. (In Chinese).

Hsieh, A. L. (1971). China's nuclear-missile program: Regional or intercontinental? *China Quarterly, 45*, 38-49.

Hughes aircraft seeks China boom despite politics. (1993, October 19). *Reuters.*

Hung, Y. (1970, June 5). Long live the great revolutionary aspirations of the Chinese people—Celebrating the successful launching of China's first man-made earth satellite. *Peking Review*, pp. 24-26.

IDB systems chosen to install satellite earth stations in Tianjin, China. (1994, February 23). PR *Newswire.*

Kohler, V. D. (1989, December). China's new long marches. *Analog Science Fiction Science Fact*, pp. 58-71.

Kong, X., & Su, K. (1992, October 7). One Chinese rocket successfully launches two satellites. *People's Daily*, p. 1. (In Chinese).

Kristof, N. (1993, April 14). China's satellite: A new era of information revolution. *The New York Times*, pp. 1-6.

Li, H. (1991, April 23). China to promote satellite technology. *China Daily*, p. 1.

Li, X. (February 23). Keeping the pace for space industry development and making new contributions to the nation and mankind. *People's Daily*, p. 1. (In Chinese).

Li, Z. (1993, August 30). China's TV industry develops rapidly. *People's Daily*, p. 1. (In Chinese).

Liu, L., & Huang, W. (1994, February 17). The launch of Long March 3A bears great significance. *People's Daily*, p. 3. (In Chinese).

Loral reserves launches on Chinese Long March rockets. (1993, September 24). *Business Wire.*

Ma, B. (1992, April 6). No change in satellite deal. *Beijing Review*, p. 11.

Mao, Zedong (1970, August). People of the world, unite and defeat the U.S. aggressors and all their running dogs. *China Reconstructs*, p. 4.

Mao, Zedong (1971). In commemoration of Dr. Sun Yat-sen. In *Selected works of Mao Zedong* (pp. 63-82). Peking: Foreign Language Press.

McAnany, E. G., & Nettleton, G. S. (1987, July/September). Brazil's domestic satellite system: changing goals and outcomes. *Revue Tiers Monde*, pp. 651-658.

Min, G. (1992, December 30). The development of China's satellite industry. *Beijing Review*, pp. 24-26.

Modern technology helps improve meteorological services in northwest China. (1993, September 29). *XGNS.*

Motorola launches major expansion in China. (1993, October 23). *AFP.*

News highlights. (1994, January 19). *Reuters.*

Ni, J., & Su, X. (1993, May 25). The future of China's telecommunication industry is promising. *People's Daily*, p. 2. (In Chinese).

Nie, R. (1984). *Memoirs of Nie Rongzen*. Beijing: Chinese People's Liberation
    Army Publishing House. (In Chinese).
Parker, J. (1993, October 18). China satellite industry launches ice cream
    shop. *Reuters*.
Ping, H. (1993, August 11). China's satellites face the world. *People's Daily*,
    p. 3. (In Chinese).
Qing, C. (1993, December 7). China and European space agency collabo-
    rate on cluster satellite program. *People's Daily*, p. 1. (In Chinese).
Rao, F. (1991). Facing the coming ten years. *China Today*, *40*(7), 103-115.
Rhea, J. (1986, October). Sinospace: China's new open door. *Space World*,
    pp. 16-17.
Satellite TV education developing rapidly in China. (1994, January 29).
    XGNS.
Satellite vital to national economic construction. (1993, November 12).
    XGNS.
Shanghai has become China's important base of high-tech telecommunica-
    tions industry. (1994, January 11). *People's Daily*. p. 1. (In Chinese).
Sino-Filipino joint venture on satellite formed. (1994, January 28). *XGNS*.
Software error caused crash of India's most powerful rocket. (1994, January
    3). *UPI*.
Song, Z. (1990). China communications towards modernization.
    Telecommunication World, *3*(4), 41-55.
South Korea, China might jointly develop regional satellite. (1993, October
    21). *AFP*.
Space in China. (1991). Beijing: China Great Wall Industry Corporation.
Stock trading center to open in Tibet. (1994, January 6). *Reuters*.
Thai agencies to join Chinese small satellite plan. (1993, November 26).
    XGNS.
Thailand seeks China's help in satellite technology. (1993, November 3).
    XGNS.
Tian, S., & Chen, J. (1993, April 22). Telecommunications in the northwest
    area develops rapidly. *People's Daily*, p. 1. (In Chinese).
Tu, S. (1988, May). A note on China's space technology. *Space Policy*, p.
    151.
Two satellites for China. (1994, February 24). *The Gazette*, p. A-10.
U.S. company news in brief. (1994, February 16). *Reuters*.
U.S. grants export license for second AsiaSat to be launched from China.
    (1994, January 12). *AFP*.
Wang, J. R., & Wang, J. L. (1993, September 22). The take-off of China's
    telecommunications. *People's Daily*, p. 1. (In Chinese).
Wu, G. (1988, February). China's space communication goals. *Space Policy*,
    pp. 41-45.
Xu, J. (1990, September 3). Progress in carrier rocket technology. *Beijing
    Review*, 27-30.

Xu, J., & Li, W. (1993, August 25). The rapid development of China's space program has made contributions to the mankind. *People's Daily*, p. 1. (In Chinese).

Xu, X. (1993, August 3). China will launch a number of satellites for Motorola. *People's Daily*, p. 1. (In Chinese).

Yan, B., & Liu, M. (1993, October 21). China Sat-5 works well. *People's Daily*, p. 1. (In Chinese).

Yang, L. (1993, June 1). China to launch Asia-Pacific Sat-1 next year. *People's Daily*, p. 1. (In Chinese).

Yang, Z. (1993, May 25). Telecommunications in Tibet reaches the level of average provinces and cities. *People's Daily*, p. 1. (In Chinese).

You, X. (1993, July 27). Weihai opens satellite receiving station. *People's Daily*, p. 1. (In Chinese).

You, X., & Liu, M. (1994, February 8). China has 40 million telephones. *People's Daily*, p. 1. (In Chinese).

Yu, Y. (1993, July 16). China to launch three overseas satellites. *People's Daily*, p. 1. (In Chinese).

Zhang, J. (1993, July 10). China opens satellite agency in Hong Kong. *People's Daily*, p. 3. (In Chinese).

Zhang, X. (1993, November 12). Shandong speeds up TV education through satellite. *People's Daily*, p. 3. (In Chinese).

Zheng, J. (1994, February 24). Shanghai VSAT earth station opens business to the society. *People's Daily*, p. 3. (In Chinese).

Zita, K. (1989, November/December). Telecommunications: China's uphill battle to modernize. *The China Business Review*, p. 18.

Zhou, Z., & Li, X. (1994, February 2). The launching by LM-3A is a great success. *People's Daily*, p. 1. (In Chinese).

CHAPTER 9

THE CHINA-HONG KONG RELATIONSHIP IN TELECOMMUNICATIONS

MICHAEL ZHAOXU YAN

INTRODUCTION

The interfacing of China and Hong Kong in telecommunications took place when the first telegraph services appeared in Mainland China and Hong Kong. Because the Qing Dynasty was reluctant to have anything to do with telecommunications and prohibited foreign marine cables to land, the first marine cable in Shanghai, introduced by Great Northern in 1871, could only link to the outside world. Hong Kong thus, from the very beginning, served as a transit point relaying telegraphs from China southward to Europe and further afield to the Americas and as a springboard for competitors vying for the main telegraph traffic market of China.

Prior to the Second World War, China was more advanced in telecommunications development[1] and more aggressive in building up a telecommunications relationship with Hong Kong.[2] The Japanese Invasion, however, heavily destroyed the telecommunications infrastructure in China and Hong Kong. Whereas Hong Kong recovered rapidly in the immediate postwar years, China was once again plunged into civil war. The efforts to

---

[1]Shanghai, at that time, was obviously the communications hub in the Far East region.

[2]As the history revealed, almost all the initiatives to link Hong Kong with China in telecommunications in its incipiency, be it telegraph, radio telegraph, telephone or radio telephone, came from China (Coates, 1990).

reestablish telecommunications links between China and Hong Kong were also impeded by the power shift in China with the establishment of the People's Republic of China in 1949.

There was little improvement in telecommunications cooperation between China and Hong Kong from the 1950s to 1970s, when China was politically closed and economically stagnate. During this period, Hong Kong's Cable & Wireless (C&W) improved its telecommunications services in Hong Kong and built up contacts with the rest of the world bypassing China and leaving it far behind.

It was only when China promulgated the open-door policy and promoted economic construction in the early 1980s that C&W looked northward to expand into China's telecommunications market. In 1983, C&W introduced a 740 channel microwave link to Guangdong province. A 247-kilometer fiber-optic cable link with the capacity of 7,680 circuits was set up in 1988 between the two places. China is now the biggest source of traffic volume and revenue for Hong Kong's international telephone service, and Hong Kong is the only transit center for China's international telecommunications.

Now a China-Hong Kong telecommunications market is steadily growing, with basic telephone services, roaming paging, mobile telephone, and value-added, as well as other telecommunications services, flourishing on both sides of the border. The relationship in their telecommunications is further strengthened by the increasing political and economic interdependence of China and Hong Kong resulting from China's open-door policy and Hong Kong's reversion to China in 1997.

This chapter is intended to examine the relationship between China and Hong Kong in their telecommunications development in the last decade against the backdrop of the new political and economic situations in both China and Hong Kong and the implications of the relationship for their future telecommunications developments.

ANALYTIC FRAMEWORK

A pluralistic approach is used to analyze the relationship between China and Hong Kong in their telecommunications developments during the last 10 plus years. This approach starts with the basic understanding of the concept of "telecommunications" as containing three dimensions of meaning; namely, technological, economic, and political. Technologically, telecommunications involves a technical network as the base of any telecommunications activity. Economically, telecommunications entails a vast market with many businesses. Politically, telecommunications, often regarded as public utility with many interested parties, pertains to public, strategic, or diplomatic policy making.

With this conceptualization, telecommunications development is seen as involving technological development, market fulfillment and public policy making. In this process, the rapid proliferation of innovative technology, combined with the resulting changes in market structures, generate forces pressing toward a certain telecommunications policy. Measures such as control of market access, regulation of service supply, and promotion of industrial policy, on the other hand, act as political forces to intervene in the telecommunications market. In other words, telecommunications development is a continuing process of interaction among the technological, economic, and political factors in pursuit of technological feasibility, economic profitability, and political desirability. As such, methodologically, technological determinism, market rationality imperatives, or political dominance cannot alone account for the course of telecommunications development. Rather, all the technological, economic, and political factors should be taken into consideration in explaining and predicting telecommunications changes. This is the essence of the pluralistic analytic method proposed here.

In international telecommunications, changes in national telecommunications reflect not only the complex interactions of a plurality of internal factors, but also the impact of a changing international telecommunications market. That is, national telecommunications developments have to take into account and react to the offerings and challenges, technologically, economically and politically, emerging from international telecommunications. As observed, transnational transfer of technology, flow of trade and investment as well as political dialogue in telecommunications have most characterized this interaction and interdependency in today's international telecommunications.

The theoretical and analytical framework of the China-Hong Kong relationship in telecommunications is shown in Figure 9.1. Interaction in telecommunications between China and Hong Kong is supposedly taking place at three general levels: technology transfer, trade and investment, and bilateral politics in telecommunications. Theoretically, the economic and political reforms in China, characterized by the decentralization of policymaking and the transfer of Hong Kong's administration, have given impetus to the strengthening of the China-Hong Kong relationship in telecommunications. This, in turn, has generated changes in China and Hong Kong's telecommunications environments, thus forming a continuing interactive process in telecommunications between China and Hong Kong. This chapter clarifies the influences China and Hong Kong exert on each other in this interactive process and ascertain the implications of these influences for their telecommunications development.

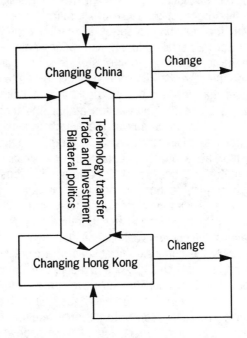

Figure 9.1. The analytical framework of the China-Hong Kong relationship in telecommunications

TRADE IN TELECOMMUNICATIONS
BETWEEN CHINA AND HONG KONG

The last decade saw the rapid growth of China's foreign trade in telecommunications equipment while China's telecommunications development gained momentum. China's active international trade in telecommunications gave Hong Kong manufacturers and traders good opportunities to play fully their roles as middlemen in the bilateral trades. As shown in Figure 9.2, over half of Hong Kong's locally produced telecommunications products were exported to China in 1991, and reexports to China accounted for about one fifth of Hong Kong's total entrepôt activity in telecommunications. Hong Kong has become the largest provider of telecommunications equipment to China (see Figure 9.3).

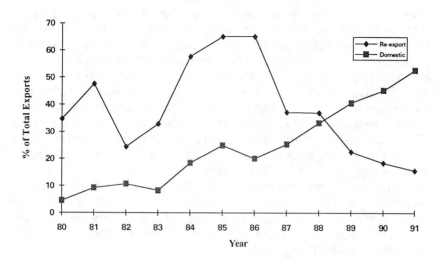

Figure 9.2. Hong Kong's exports to China as a percentage of its total exports in telecommunications equipment, 1980-1991. Note: Statistics taken from *Hong Kong External Trade Annual Review*, Census and Statistics Department, 1981-1992, Hong Kong: Government Printer.

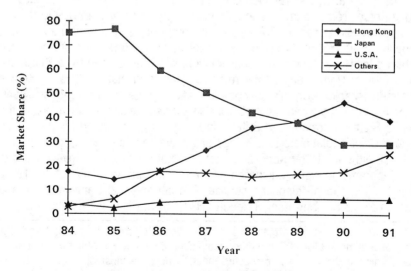

Figure 9.3. Hong Kong's comparative share in China's telecommunication equipment market. Note: Statistics taken from *Hong Kong External Trade Annual Review*, Census and Statistics Department, 1981-1992, Hong Kong: Government Printer.

In order to get access to key technology and protect domestic producers, China applies fewer controls over more sophisticated equipment such as Stored Program Control (SPC) switching, digital microwave, and fiber-optic transmission equipment, but puts up more import barriers to Customer Premise Equipment (CPE).[3] Obviously, sophisticated central office manufacturing is not the strength of Hong Kong. Its ability to supply competitive CPE also seems to be choked off by China's strategic emphasis on state-of-the-art technology. In fact, the decision making in procuring less sophisticated equipment in China is more decentralized and the market for CPE is growing faster with rising business demands for fax, key telephone systems (KTS), and small-scale Private Branch Exchange (PBX) equipment. This has given astute Hong Kong businessmen an avenue into China's market and served as a bridgehead for international suppliers to penetrate this fast growing and lucrative market (Sprafkin & O'Brien, 1989). As more and more medium- and small-sized corporations in China are released from central control, they will rely more on Hong Kong's comparative advantages in international trading (Sung, 1991).

Whereas Hong Kong has a significant interest in China's telecommunications equipment market, China does not involve itself deeply in Hong Kong's market. No consistent data are available that permit calculation of the comparative share of China's telecommunications equipment in Hong Kong's local market on a long-term basis. In 1990, China exported a total of HK$6,724 million of telecommunications equipment to Hong Kong, of which HK$973 million, 14.5% of the total, was retained in Hong Kong. In the same year, the value of Hong Kong's retained imports in this product segment was HK$7,990 million. That means China has a 12.2% share of Hong Kong's imports in 1990. Thus, roughly about 15% of China's telecommunications exports to Hong Kong were retained for Hong Kong's own consumption, which accounted for a little more than 10% of Hong Kong's total retained imports in that year. Hong Kong's intermediary role in China's telecommunications trade is thus very significant. From Figure 9.4, we can see that China's exports in telecommunications to the United States, Germany and Britain via Hong Kong accounted for more than 60% of China's total exports to Hong Kong in the past few years.

Although Hong Kong does not account for much of China's exports in telecommunications equipment, China is the biggest market for Hong Kong's international telephone service. The international traffic revenue and traffic volume of Hong Kong Telecom (HKT)[4] from China were 22% and 38%

---

[3]This is very different from the trend in international telecommunications trade. The international market for CPE and other equipment at the low end of the product spectrum, which in the past was protected most, is now the most open as a result of recent deregulation (Neu & Schnöring, 1989).

[4]In 1984, HKTC became HK Tel, a subsidiary of C&W (London). In 1988, HK Tel and C&W (HK), the franchised international public services provider in the territory, merged to form HKT, today's local and international common carrier.

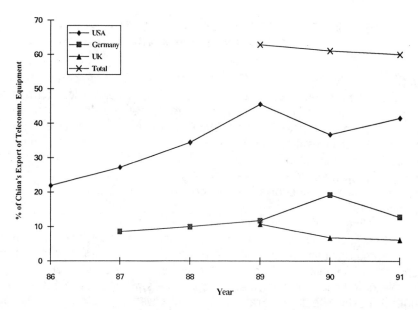

Figure 9.4. China's export of telecommunications equipment to the U.S., Germany, and the U.K. via Hong Kong, 1986-1992. Note: Statistics taken from *Hong Kong External Trade Annual Review*, Census and Statistics Department, 1981-1992, Hong Kong Government Printer.

respectively in 1990; and 20% and 25% in 1991.[5] As shown in Figure 9.5, during 1975-1984, Hong Kong Telephone Company Ltd.'s (HKTC) annual increase in traffic revenue of outgoing telephony to China grew much faster than that of all outgoing telephony.

Hong Kong's role as the transit point for China's telecommunications services is as important as its role in telecommunications equipment trade. Unlike other countries, which are restricted in their connections with China to satellite or submarine cable links through the Beijing and Shanghai gateways, Hong Kong has a number of choices to link up with China, including satellite, high-frequency radio, microwave, and terrestrial cable links. Hong Kong's advantage in accessing China and its extensive linkages to the rest of the world have made it the only transit point in extending China's telecommunications services to the rest of the world. China had direct circuit links with only 45 countries and regions by the end of 1990. With Hong Kong's transfers, however, people in China are able to dial 182 countries and regions by International Direct Dialing (IDD).

---

[5]Despite the declining percentage, international calls to China in absolute value in 1991 were 35% more than 1990.

DIRECT INVESTMENT IN TELECOMMUNICATIONS BETWEEN
CHINA AND HONG KONG

In China, Equity Joint Ventures (EJV), looked on as the most appropriate and rapid vehicle for both utilizing foreign funds and developing a long-term relationship with foreign high-tech sources, is more welcome than mere selling of products and services (Stewart, 1987). However, only a small portion of foreign direct investment (FDI) involving high-technology, capital-intensive projects has been established (Jacobs, 1986). In spite of this, or because of this, China aspires to encourage foreign vendors to invest in four sectors; namely, energy, transportation, telecommunications, and raw materials (Jones, 1990).

Hong Kong's investment in China is concentrated in construction, tourist facilities, and light manufacturing industries. Its investment in China's telecommunications manufacturing is mostly confined to CPE and other low-end parts. Actually, China has joint ventures in the production of more sophisticated equipment (such as central office switching, digital PBXs, fiber optics) mostly with Japan, France, Germany, Sweden, and other developed countries (Kaye, 1992; Sprafkin & O'Brien, 1989).

Though little room in equipment manufacturing is left for Hong Kong producers, many telecommunications companies in Hong Kong have found points of entry into China's telecommunications through network planning and installation, consultation, and transfer of management, as well as direct

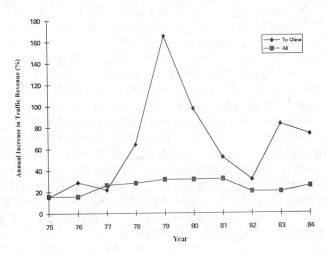

Figure 9.5. HKTC's annual increase in traffic revenue of outgoing telephony to China and that of all outgoing telephony, 1975-1984 Note: Statistics taken from *Hong Kong Telephone Company Limited Annual Report*, Hong Kong Telephone Company, 1975-1984. Hong Kong: Author.

service provision. Particularly, compared to other countries, Hong Kong's stake in China's telecommunications services is significant and enviable.

In paging services, Hing Tat Investment Ltd., which opened its first paging station in Canton in 1984, now owns 48 such stations nationwide with 350,000 customers, constituting more than 40% of China's paging market ("Main Show," 1992). In roaming paging communications, several companies have begun their services with the local PT departments and enterprises, especially those in Guangdong province. Whereas HKT CSL, ST Telecommunications Ltd. Hing Tat, and other companies are offering services mainly between Hong Kong and Guangdong province, Morning Star's business goes farther to Beijing ("Paging Craze," 1992).

In mobile communications, China Telecom Systems (HK) Ltd. has run mobile telephone service in Canton and Shenzhen since 1984. As for roaming service of mobile telephones, HKT's CSL is the "Big Brother," having 15,000 users, or over 20% of the market. It also shares a "mutual roaming agreement" with China's MPT, further strengthening its dominance in this market ("Five Chinese Provinces," 1992). Negotiations to open more roaming paging and mobile telephone services are underway between telecommunications companies and concerned governmental departments and companies in China.

China's social system requires that its telecommunications services, particularly long-distance and international service, be under the strict control of the State. Theoretically, foreign involvement in China's telecommunications service sector is far from reality. Practically, however, urgent demands for more telecommunications services generated by booming business activities, the big profits involved as well as the needs of local companies to look for a foreign partner to provide capital and technology, have facilitated the entry of foreign capital into China's telecommunications service market. It is conceivable that foreign investment in China's telecommunications sector can at most focus only on those marginal services (such as paging and mobile communications) or services that are not related to the core public services and national telecommunications infrastructure. Accordingly, the investments of Hong Kong companies, taking advantage of the existing market for transborder telecommunications services and Hong Kong's special status as a part of China in the near future, are largely limited to providing paging and mobile services in China and offering roaming services across the border.[6] Besides, due to the policy limitation on telecommunications ownership in China, generally, there should be no equity share between the Chinese and Hong Kong side. The joint provision of these services is often based on "cooperation."

---

[6]The only EJV providing local and long distance basic telephone services, Shenda Telephone Co, was set up by C&W and Shenzhen Telecommunications Development Co. in 1983. Initially the British side held 49% shares in the EJV but years ago, it returned its shares to the Chinese side.

China's presence in Hong Kong's telecommunications services is no less than Hong Kong's presence in China's telecommunications service market. As we know, China retained its economic presence in Hong Kong even in the era of its isolation from the rest of the world. Until 1977, however, China's principal investments in Hong Kong were limited to bilateral trade and other supporting activities such as financial and transportation services (Shih, 1989). Both the scale and the scope of the Chinese involvement in Hong Kong markets have been enhanced today. One eye catching development is China's increasing involvement in Hong Kong's telecommunications and other public utilities such as transport and communications, which are primarily conducted through the China International Trust and Investment Company (Citic).

Since it was founded in 1979 immediately after China opened its door, Citic has progressively become a major overseas investment arm of the Chinese government although its original purpose was to introduce foreign capital, modern technology and equipment into China from the outside (Friedland, 1990). Among the many interests of Citic abroad, developing natural resources and telecommunications are now its prime concentrations (Rafferty, 1991). In 1991, 60% of Citic's capital was in telecommunications, whereas 20% was in airlines and 10% in power (Zhuo, 1991).

Table 9.1 shows that Citic has claimed sizeable stakes in such sensitive utility industries as telecommunications and transportation in Hong Kong. In telecommunications, Citic bought 20% of HKT's capital shares in early 1990, valued at HK$10.3 billion, becoming the second biggest shareholder of HKT after C&W.[7] In addition, its new investment vehicle Citic-Pacific is now active in seeking telecommunications projects.[8]

Table 9.1. Citic's Holdings In Hong Kong's Utilities.

Utilities	Companies	Shares (%)
Telecommunication	AsiaSat	33.3
	HKT	20.0
Transportation	Cathay Pacific	12.5
	Dragonair	38
	Eastern Harbour Crossing Tunnel	24.5

[7]This was also the largest investment ever made by a Chinese-interest company in Hong Kong. In Macau, Citic acquired the same 20% of C&W's Companhia Telecommunicacoes de Macau in early 1989.

[8]Tylfull/Citic is the first Chinese-interest company to be listed on the Hong Kong stock exchange. It bid against nine other consortia for Hong Kong's fourth mobile telephone License in 1992, but failed. It also expressed interest in applying for the license of the second telecommunications network of Hong Kong, but in the end it did not bid for the second network.

Besides Citic, other Chinese-interest companies are also trying to enter into Hong Kong's telecommunications market. Earlier in 1989, several companies (including those of China's Ministry of Foreign Economic Relations and Trade, Ministry of Aeronautics and Aerospace, and Citic), jointly with other local and international consortia, expressed interest in Hong Kong's cable television (Lau & Baldwin, 1990). Among the 10 consortia bidding for Hong Kong's fourth mobile telephone license in 1992, 6 Chinese-interest companies participated in 4 consortia (see Table 9.2). The Smart Com Ltd., in which the Chinese MPTs subsidiary, Town Khan, has a share of 15%, won the bid.

TECHNOLOGY TRANSFER IN TELECOMMUNICATIONS BETWEEN CHINA AND HONG KONG

Because China's ultimate objective is to build up a high-tech telecommunications industry, technology transfer is highly emphasized in its business deals with foreigners. Nonetheless, whereas China's telecommunications technology is not advanced enough for Hong Kong, Hong Kong's technology innovation is also not strong enough to attract investment from Chinese enterprises. In Hong Kong, almost all the technology is imported (Ure, 1989), but high flexibility in technology usage and rapid response to market changes have allowed Hong Kong to survive its lack of aggressive innovation and made it rather well equipped with advanced technology (Kao & Young, 1991). Because of this, Hong Kong could contribute as a base from which China obtained access to sources of high technology in telecommunications.

For China, its poor technology deployment to some extent even drags the feet of Hong Kong in its infrastructure development. For example, the Hong Kong government has decided to substitute the current analog cellular system with a digital system by the year 2000. Companies operating roaming mobile phone services across both sides of the border however, are concerned that without China's following in digital technology and adopting the same GSM or USDC system, customers will have difficulty in cross border mobile telephone communications in the future.

BILATERAL POLITICS IN TELECOMMUNICATIONS BETWEEN CHINA AND HONG KONG

In Hong Kong's run-up to 1997, the opinions of the Chinese government are often heard directly. China has indicated its intention many times to be consulted on matters that would affect the post-1997 Hong Kong Special

Table 9.2. Chinese Interests in Bidding for Hong Kong's Digital Mobile Telephone License.

Consortium	Partner/Interest/Shares
Wharf-Nynex	Wharf (HK, 65%) Nynex (USA, 35%)
New World Telephone	New World Telephone (HK, 72%) Ameritech (USA, 28%)
Shun Tak	Shun Tak (HK, 51%) Detecom (Germany, NA) Siemens (Germany, NA) Ministry of Aerospace and Aeronautics (PRC, NA)
Smart Com Ltd.	Sun Hung Kai Properties (HK, 40%) ABC Ka Shin (HK, 15%) McMaw Cellular Communications, Inc. (USA, 30%) Town Khan (PRC, 15%)
Pacific Telecom Co.	Pacific Capital Ltd. (Taiwan, 51%) Wincall (PRC, 20%) Rogers Cantel (Canada, 19%) Fujian Enterprise (Holdings) Co. (PRC, 10%)
Bel Trade	BI Trade Holdings (HK, 70%) Bell Atlantic International, Inc. (USA, 20%) Innovative Group (HK, 10%)
Chevalier	Chevalier Group (HK, 50%) AOTC (Australia, 50%)
Kan Tel	Champion Group (HK, 50%) PACTEL (USA, 20%) LCC Inc. (USA, 10%) Standard and Charted Asia Ltd. (UK, 5%)
Iconese Ltd.	Citic-Pacific (PRC, 48%) China Resource Group (PRC, 26%) NTT (Japan, 26%)
Pacific Link	First Pacific Group (HK, 60%) Sun Hung Kai Industries (HK, 60%) VODAPHONE (UK, 3%)

Administrative Region (HKSAR).[9] In telecommunications, prominent issues, such as the introduction of a second telecommunications network, cable television and the liberalization of Hong Kong's public network, are within the scope of this claimed cooperative consultation.[10] For China, utilities such as power, transportation and telecommunications are strategic industries that should not remain solely in the hands of expatriates and private firms.[11] This is why China has sped up securing holdings in these industries in Hong Kong in the past few years.

Although there have been no open bilateral discussions on Hong Kong's telecommunications, China has used its political and economic muscle to influence Hong Kong's telecommunications, mainly through the commercial clout of Citic and also C&W's modus operandi in its global telecommunications strategy.

Essentially, the so-called C&W modus operandi is to enter into partnership with the host government by any means and use the government business partnership to secure long-term protection of a monopoly or from competition. This has been the pattern of C&W's global operation in telecommunications (Mueller, 1991). In Hong Kong, C&W in 1981 sold 20% of its shares to the Hong Kong government in exchange for an exclusive franchise for all international telecommunications. With 1997 approaching, however, C&W let Citic hold 20% of HKT's share, thus replacing in its government-business partnership the outgoing Hong Kong government with the incoming Chinese government.[12] Actually, before the Citic deal, C&W had already sold a small stake (about .1%) to Guangdong Posts and Telecommunications Administration (GDPTA) in June 1988. Both deals were at a discounted market price, underscoring their political nature.

Because of its political status as a state enterprise, Citic's strategic holdings in telecommunications and transportation have aroused much suspicion about the prospect of deregulation favored by local capitalists in Hong Kong in these areas. Actually, although Citic has two positions on the board of directors of HKT, neither participates in the company's everyday operations. So, though Citic has a large financial stake in HKT, its contribu-

---

[9]The negotiations and disputes over Hong Kong's new airport project and its political reform are good examples. On December 14, 1990, the Sino-British Joint Liaison Group announced that China had reached agreement with Britain that China should be kept informed of major franchises extending beyond 1997.

[10]For example, the Hong Kong government will have to report to the Chinese side about the licensing arrangement of pay television.

[11]The issue of Citic's acquisition of the share of HKT went to the State Council of the PRC at the very beginning. It was reported that it took one and a half days of debate before Premier Li Peng and his colleagues approved the deal (Rafferty, 1991).

[12]The British colonial government, in good cooperation, later publicly sold off its share in HKT. Half of these shares went back to C&W.

tion to HKT may not lie in the company's commercial activities. However, the liaison between Citic and HKT clearly strengthened the bargaining power of HKT in dealing with the government.[13]

On the other side, China's telecommunications development is not immune to international mercantilism. The Sino-American negotiations on Intellectual Property Rights (IPR), the debate over China's Most Favored Nation (MFN) status in the United States and, not the least, constraints of the Coordinating Committee for Multilateral Export Controls (COCOM) all imposed limitations on China's international trade and acquisition of technology and capital in telecommunications. Generally, however, Hong Kong can exert little direct political constraint on China's telecommunications development.

First of all, colonial Hong Kong depends on external forces to legitimize itself in the international political arena. Even in such vital matters as its future, Hong Kong seems to have no say, but is subject to the wills of China and the United Kingdom (King, 1986).

Second, to maintain a free economy the Hong Kong government has adopted a policy of "positive noninterventionism." It is very difficult to expect the government to practice interventionism and protectionism in international trade.

Third, from the Chinese perspective, what China needs most in telecommunications is mainly high technology and capital. However, Hong Kong is obviously not strong in telecommunications R&D. China has procured telecommunications equipment mainly from Japan, France, Sweden and other technologically advanced countries. Besides, as Table 9.3 shows, soft loans in telecommunications to China were offered by countries other than Hong Kong. Although Hong Kong is important for China's trade with the outside, it also cannot afford to lose its role as China's trade gateway. An example is China's MFN status, It was estimated by the Hong Kong government that if the United States were to revoke China's MFN status it would result in a 35-47% decline in reexports of China's products to the United States, not to mention the indirect consequences on trade and employment in Hong Kong. The decrease in entrepôt of telecommunications would be 30-40% ("Hong Kong Trade," 1992). In fact, every time the United States debated China's MFN status, the Hong Kong government and business groups stood with China in lobbying for the extension of China's MFN.

Further, with the competitive entry of foreign companies into China's market, China is using a supplier financing strategy to dictate technology choice, thus gaining more bargaining power. In the past several years, China has narrowed the field of central office switching suppliers to three foreign

---

[13]For example, in late June 1990, during HKT's negotiations with the government over increases in local telephone rates, Citic's Executive Director, Rong Zhi-jian, wrote a strongly worded letter to the Hong Kong Financial Secretary asking the Hong Kong government to give HKT permission to increase telephone rates (Mueller, 1991).

Table 9.3. Soft Loans to China in Post and Telecommunications (1982-1989).

Country	Loans (US$ million)
France	169.0
Japan	135.0
Canada	116.0
Sweden	85.7
Spain	35.0
Germany	30.0
Netherlands	29.7
Belgium	21.0
Italy	15.0
Norway	14.8
Total	645.5

companies; namely, Alcatel of France, NEC of Japan, and Siemens of Germany (Wang, 1991). It is interesting to note that the companies who have claimed important stakes in China's telecommunications market are coincidentally those whose governments are leaders in providing concessional loans to China.[14] China's increased bargaining power, because of the competition among foreign MNCs, makes it more difficult for Hong Kong, which can offer neither key technologies nor government soft loans to China, to exert any political influence on China's telecommunications.

CONCLUSION

Overall, the preceding analysis shows that on the one hand, Hong Kong's influence on China's telecommunications comes primarily from its economic strength, on the other, political force is China's primary method of influencing Hong Kong's telecommunications.

Specifically, this study reveals that:

1. Technologically, China and Hong Kong do not have much direct influence on each other. China is still very poor in telecommunications infrastructure and backward in equipment manufacturing, and Hong Kong is weak in technology innovation and buys almost

---

[14]It is also said that an attractive financing package could facilitate a decision by China to bend the rules of buying only from the said three companies (Wang, 1991).

all of its needed technology. However, Hong Kong serves as a base from which China can gain access to sources of high technology in telecommunications.

2. Economically, Hong Kong plays an important role via its equipment and service trade with China and participation in China's telecommunications construction. China's telecommunications equipment market accounts for about 1/2 of Hong Kong's domestic exports and the overwhelming majority of its entrepôt activity. Hong Kong is also the only transit point for China's international telecommunications services. In particular, Hong Kong has claimed sizeable and enviable stakes in China's telecommunications markets for marginal services. It has also cooperated with China in network construction, equipment installation and consultation, but Hong Kong has limited activity in China's telecommunications manufacturing involving few high technology items.

   As for China, its exports to Hong Kong are a small fraction of Hong Kong's domestic market for telecommunications equipment. Its investment in Hong Kong's telecommunications equipment production is also very limited, but its increasing involvement in Hong Kong's telecommunications service business has received much publicity. The new stakes in Hong Kong's digital mobile telephone network and Citic's holdings in HKT are the most notable examples.

3. Politically, the China-Hong Kong relationship is skewed by China's overwhelming power over Hong Kong. Although China can have a say in Hong Kong's major franchises and infrastructural projects extending beyond 1997, Hong Kong has little say in China's telecommunications policy making.

ASSESSING THE CHINA INFLUENCES

As stated earlier, the influence of China on Hong Kong's telecommunications stems from its political power. This, however, should not underestimate Citic and other Chinese-interest companies' economic influences. Undoubtedly, the presence of Chinese capital in Hong Kong's telecommunications is an important factor in influencing the future trend of Hong Kong's telecommunications because Chinese interest companies derive strength from their political background and reinforce it with Hong Kong's reversion to China.

   Hong Kong's return to China now sets the backdrop for any discussion of Hong Kong's domestic affairs. Hong Kong's telecommunications development is also contingent on the political and economic prospects of China and the implementation of the "one country, two systems" policy in the future HKSAR. However, the political influence from China on Hong Kong's telecommunications also depends on the behavior of the local telecommunications market and that of the Hong Kong government in making decisions regarding telecommunications policies.

As mentioned earlier, in June of 1990 Citic interviewed and exerted pressure on the Hong Kong government during its negotiations with HKT over increases in local telephone rates. For Hong Kong's international telecommunications, Citic has indicated clearly that "under no circumstances can a second network be allowed to cut into Hong Kong Telecom's international business before the expiry of the international franchise in 2006" (Crothall, 1990). In addition, the government's delayed decision on a second network and the end of the local telephone monopoly sparked speculation that getting consent from the Chinese side was one reason for the delay (Lee, 1992; Westlake, 1990).[15] Although the Hong Kong government has determined to introduce a second network and competition in the local telephone market after 1995 when the current franchise arrangement expires, it is doubtful whether the present Hong Kong government or the government of the HKSAR can use its authority to carry out the international telecommunications policy it once decided.[16]

The "positive nonintervention" policy adopted by the Hong Kong government, despite its merits in contributing to Hong Kong's earlier telecommunications takeoff, has been recently questioned (Lau, 1988). In the face of rapid changes in technology, markets, and political environments in Hong Kong, more governmental involvement is thought to be necessary to coordinate and set new rules for its telecommunications industry. With the emergence of dual authority in Hong Kong, however, the call for government intervention at this time only provides opportunities for the Chinese government to exert its influence. Besides, if the Hong Kong government intends to "internationalize" Hong Kong's local telecommunications market, as is widely believed, China, not yet politically united with Hong Kong, is one of the foreign interests the Hong Kong government has to bring in. These, taken together directly and indirectly, place limitations on the Hong Kong government's room to maneuver.

---

[15]The Hong Kong government instructed its consultancy team, Booz Allen and Hamilton, not to say anything about 1997 when the team was for the first time commissioned by the government to review Hong Kong's telecommunications (Mueller, 1991). After the first-round bid for cable television in Hong Kong was aborted in 1990, the team was again summoned by the government to do a consultative study. Twice the consultants recommended opening of the local telephone market. The latter study was completed in early 1991. Not until July 29, 1992, however, did the government announce its decision to open the local telephone market to competition.

[16]In Hong Kong, today's international telecommunications to a great extent means the Chinese market. Thus, without China's positive attitude toward its own or Hong Kong's international telecommunications policy, the Hong Kong government can do little to attract alternative network provider(s) and implement its procompetition policies.

In retrospect, the performance of local telecommunications providers reveals that local companies are making headway in courting China or roping in Chinese-interest enterprises to use as political chips. An example is the well-known cooperation between HKT, Hutchison Telecommunications (HT), and Citic in launching AsiaSat-I.[17] For China, nothing is better than good cooperation between HKT and HT and particularly, the larger relationship of HKT, HT and Citic.

After all, capitalists are realists. With such uncertainty surrounding Hong Kong's politics and economy, it is very difficult for them to make large investments in big telecommunications projects that generally have long term paybacks. Actually, many companies are diversifying their capital and business activities into overseas markets in view of 1997. HT's parent company, Hutchison Whampoa, is no exception. Its 10-year goal is to put 25% of its business overseas, compared with the current 10% (Caplen & Woronoff, 1988). In the run-up to 1997, only those who have both economic and political chips can afford to play games in Hong Kong's telecommunications. It remains unknown to what extent these companies can contribute to competition and the liberalization of Hong Kong's telecommunications market.

Therefore, theoretically, the political influence from China is partly contingent on local market forces and the Hong Kong government's decisions regarding telecommunications policies. Practically, signs have shown that the autonomy of the Hong Kong government is draining away and local capitalists are courting China and fostering ties with Chinese-interest concerns.

It is, however, doubtful that China will deliberately weaken Hong Kong's role as an international trade, financial, and telecommunications center. It has been reiterated by both the Chinese and Hong Kong governments that a strong Hong Kong means much to Hong Kong and China, economically and politically. Despite this, it seems unlikely that China will leave the post-1997 Hong Kong highly autonomous in terms of policy making, although this is stipulated in the Basic Law, given the increasing intervention in Hong Kong's recent major infrastructure decisions by China. What is more, local capitalists' self-restraint and concern for obtaining the good will of the Chinese leadership will further reduce the flexibility of Hong Kong.

Viewing China's influence from this perspective, it is the contention here that although the "97 factor" may not visibly hinder the telecommunications business and immediately lower service quality in Hong Kong, the possible gradual deterioration of Hong Kong's economic flexibility will slow its telecommunications development. The development of telecommunications depends on several variables; besides the policy framework, economic and technological infrastructure are also crucial. Any negative influence from unsound government policy could impede the advancement of Hong Kong's

---

[17]It is also worth noticing that HT's boss, Li Ka-shing also holds 4.99% stake in HKT through his Cheung Kong (Holdings) (Roy, 1988).

telecommunications and jeopardize Hong Kong's status as the regional communications hub.[18] These influences are more obvious if one takes into account the keen competition in telecommunications in the Asia-Pacific area and rapid development of information technology worldwide.[19]

ASSESSING THE HONG KONG INFLUENCE

Hong Kong's economic stakes in China's telecommunications, be they equipment trade, network construction, or service provision, are the result of China's open-door policy. They meet the needs arising in a changing telecommunications market in China that is characterized by, among other things, the tendency toward decentralization, the emergence of market forces and competition, and the growth of foreign interests (Yan, 1993). The economic influence of Hong Kong, along with these changes in China (sectoral fragmentation in the construction of the telecommunications infrastructure, decentralization in policy making and competition in some services), contributes to the strengthening of market forces vis-a-vis political controls in China's telecommunications. The strengthening of market forces in China's telecommunications will, in turn, further enhance the role of Hong Kong as an equipment and service trader and provider.

However, the Chinese government works on a double-track economic system (i.e., riding on the two tracks of a planned and market economy). This necessitates that the Government perform a delicate balancing act in striving for economic modernization without the so called "peaceful transformation" in its political system caused by economic reform. Thus, although on the one hand the Chinese leadership makes very friendly gestures to welcome the inflow of foreign capital and technology and push its telecommunications into the competitive world arena, thus increasingly integrating China's whole economy with the outside world, on the other, it keeps a close eye on the technology and market mechanisms in the telecommunications sector and is ready to intervene in the market to ensure it remains in the Government's hands.

Years ago, C&W (UK) had to withdraw from the Shenda Telephone Company, its EJV with the state-owned Shenzhen Telecommunications Development Company. In 1991, the Chinese government issued orders to nationalize all paging service stations co-owned with foreigners ("China

[18]There are concerns in Hong Kong that the HKSAR will be subject to the same constraints imposed by COCOM or its Western equivalent on China for getting access to high technologies.

[19]In this region, other teleports such as Tokyo, Singapore, and Sydney are powerful competitors for communications-hub status. There have been reports that some PTTs such as Singapore Telecom have signed on numerous customers from Hong Kong recently (Hammer, 1991).

Continues"1992). In signing the "mutual roaming agreement" on bilateral mobile phone communications with HKT, the Chinese MPT indicated that all Hong Kong companies should first reach agreement with the central MPT before providing mobile services with local PT administrations and enterprises ("Hitting Against," 1992). Clearly, the MPT is more concerned about the roaming services of mobile telephones than that of paging because the former involves an alternative technological network that can bypass the public international network more easily.

Although the presence of Hong Kong's market forces in China's telecommunications has special symbolic meaning because they are reforming the market structure of China's telecommunications and are changing people's conventional attitudes toward telecommunications ownership, under the double-track system these forces are counteracted and controlled by China's state mechanism.

IMPLICATIONS

The study of the China-Hong Kong relationship in telecommunications has special implications for the telecommunications development of both China and Hong Kong. Because the Chinese government has adopted the open door policy as a long-term strategy and Hong Kong will soon be an integrated part of China, the relationship between China and Hong Kong in telecommunications will certainly become closer. Besides, although the shift of China's telecommunications environment toward decentralization reserves a place in its telecommunications market for Hong Kong to play its economic role, and changes in Hong Kong's telecommunications toward greater government intervention encourage China's political presence in Hong Kong's telecommunications.

It is unknown, however to what extent China will reform its telecommunications and Hong Kong's economic strength will contribute to the development of market forces in China's telecommunications. Clearly, China only wants to open its door on its own terms. In its increasing interaction with the outside, gaining key foreign technology and utilizing foreign capital and, at the same time protecting the domestic market and achieving economic profits without yielding political control is a major headache for China's leaders. China is now performing a delicate balancing act to ensure the separation of economic and political interests. It remains uncertain whether this approach can work in the face of the vast market demand, a trend toward decentralization, potential competition, and, not least, increasing foreign involvement in China's telecommunications market

It is difficult, if not impossible, to predict the outcome of the tug of war between China's conservative political force and Hong Kong's liberating economic force. China might lift some limitations on the provision of such marginal services as paging and open it to local competitors and foreign interests given the vast demand for these services and the relatively few strategic interests involved. It is even possible that China would "arrange" for another telecommunications network provider (e.g., owner of the AsiaSat) to share in some of its international services in order to meet the demand for them and ease the burden of its public network. Meanwhile,it might also contract with one or two companies to provide roaming mobile phone service across the border. In China, however, because toll and inter-national telecommunications are highly valued in national political strategy, this would in no way mean openness to unregulated competition.

Similarly, it is not known how the Hong Kong government and local capitalists will align themselves to accommodate Hong Kong's politicized telecommunications environment, although signs of such adjustments are now discernible in some fronts. There are now grey areas with respect to whether decision making and supervisory bodies in Hong Kong have the autonomy to introduce more market competition and oversee exclusive fran-chise operations and whether local capitalists will play fairly and freely in a competitive and liberalized telecommunications market.

In face of the political power and activities of the Chinese-interest concerns in Hong Kong, many Hong Kong business concerns may have to court China in order to enter its market and gain political chips in the local market. The Hong Kong government, which used to have a good business-government relationship that was dictated by business giants in making poli-cies, may gradually accommodate itself to those capitalists favored by the Chinese side. The Chinese government, taking advantage of the self-restraint of business concerns and the weakness of the Hong Kong government may rearrange the telecommunications market of Hong Kong using its political-muscle and economic clout. However, given a strong market force in Hong Kong's telecommunications and China's need to maintain stability and pros-perity in Hong Kong's economy, China will increasingly use its commercial, rather than political, clout to affect Hong Kong's telecommunications.

Overall, the China-Hong Kong relationship in telecommunications is woven into the web of relationships among information technology develop-ment market operations and governmental politics on both sides. As we can see, all the variables are changing. The China-Hong Kong relationship in telecommunications is in a state of flux. Nevertheless, the present state of the relationship, in which Hong Kong is more influential economically where as China is politically more influential, will continue and become even more marked as China extends its market operations and Hong Kong approaches 1997.

REFERENCES

Caplen, B., & Woronoff, J. (1988, December). Trading places in Hong Kong. *Asia Business*, pp. 30-42.

Census & Statistics Department. (1981-1992). *Hong Kong external trade: Annual review*. Hong Kong: Government Printer.

China continues to take back paging operation. (1992, April 1). *Hong Kong Economic Journal*, p. 16. (In Chinese)

Coates, A. (1990). *Quick tidings of Hong Kong*. Hong Kong: Oxford University Press.

Crothall, G. (1990, September 27). Don't be unfair to Telecom—Citic. *South China Morning Post*, business section, p. 5.

Five Chinese provinces make arrangement with Hong Kong for cross-border mobile communication. (1992, June 2). *Ta Kung Pao*, p. 10. (In Chinese)

Friedland, J. (1990, January 11). The cadres' bargains. *Far Eastern Economic Review*, pp. 34-35.

Hammer, D. (1991, Summer). The "new" gateway alternatives. *Telecom Asia*, pp. 30-32.

Hitting against illegal cross-border mobile phones. (1992, May 8). *Hong Kong Economic Journal*, p. 6. (In Chinese)

Hong Kong Telephone Company. (1975-1984). *Hong Kong Telephone Company Limited Annual Report*. Hong Kong: Author.

Hong Kong trade loses $100 billion if China loses MFN status. (1992, March14). *Ming Pao*, p. 34. (In Chinese)

Jacobs, P. (1986). Hong Kong and the modernization of China. *Journal of International Affairs, 39*(2), 63-75.

Jones, K. M. (1990). The China syndrome: Westerners learn to read the tea leaves. *Management Review, 79*(4), 46-49.

Kao, C. K., & Young, K. (1991). *Technology road maps for Hong Kong: An in-depth study of four technology areas*. Hong Kong: The Chinese University Press.

Kaye, L. (1992, June 4). Long march from chaos. *Far Eastern Economic Review*, p. 54.

King, A. Y. C. (1986). The Hong Kong talks and Hong Kong politics Issues and Studies, 22(6), 52-75.

Lau, T. Y. (1988). Introducing cable television into Hong Kong: Political and economic implications. *Telecommunications Policy, 12*(12), 379-392

Lau, T. Y., & Baldwin, T. F. (1990). A public policy strategy for cable development: The experience of Hong Kong. *Telecommunications Policy, 14*(10), 412-424.

Lee, P. (1992). Regulatory issues in the communication policy of Hong Kong: Setting new rules of game for broadcasting and telecommunications. In M. D. Ofstrom & D.J. Wedemeyer (Eds.), *Pacific Telecommunications Council 14th Annual Conference: Proceedings* (pp. 696-704). Honolulu, HI: PTC.

Main show of China-Hong Kong paging competition. (1992, January 4). *Hong Kong Economic Journal*, p. 9. (In Chinese)

Mueller, M. (1991). *International telecommunications in Hong Kong: The case for liberation*. Hong Kong: The Chinese University Press.

Neu, W., & Schnoring, T. (1989). The telecommunications equipment industry in recent changes in its international trade pattern. *Telecommunications Policy, 13*(3), 25-39.

Ng, S. M. (1992, June 1). The prospects of Hong Kong's mobile telephone market. *Capital*, pp. 54-64. (In Chinese)

Paging craze in Mainland. (1992, March 14). *Hong Kong Economic Journal*, p. 14. (In Chinese)

Rafferty, K. (1991, June). China's enigmatic conglomerates. *Euromoney*, 24-32.

Roy, B. (1988, March 15). If you can't beat 'em, join 'em: Is Cable and Wireless wooing Hutchison to ward off bigger competitors? *Asian Finance*, pp. 48-50

Shih, T. L. (1989). The role of the People's Republic of China's Hong Kong-based conglomerates as development agents. In A. R. Negandhi (Ed.), *Multinationals and newly industrialized countries Strategies, environmental imperatives and practices* (pp. 215-230). Greenwich, CT: JAI Press.

Sprafkin, J., & O'Brien, R. (1989, November/December). Keeping telecommunications on hold. *The China Business Review*, pp. 24-28.

Stewart, S. (1987). The transfer of high technology to China: Problems and options *International Journal of Technology Management, 3*(1/2), 169-179.

Sun Hung Kay Properties, Wharf, Citic & Chevalier primarily selected for mobile phone licenses. (1992, June 19). *Hong Kong Economic Journal* p. 2. (In Chinese)

Sung, Y. W. (1991). Hong Kong's economic value to China. In Y. W. Sung & M. K. Lee (Eds.), *The Other Hong Kong Report 1991*. Hong Kong: The Chinese University Press.

Ure, J. (1989). The future of telecommunications in Hong Kong. *Telecommunications Policy, 13*(12), 371-378.

Wang, W. P. (1991). China: Adapting to new needs. *1992 Single Market Communications Review, 3*(2), 68.

Westlake, M. (1990, January 26). With strings attached. *Far Eastern Economic Review*, pp. 34-35.

Yan, Z. (1993). *Telecommunications development in China: Recent changes and policy implications*. Paper presented at the annual meeting of the Association for Education in Journalism and Mass Communication, Kansas City, MO.

Zhuo, Q. F. (1991, October). Citic diversifies like mercury spilling all over.*China-Hong Kong Economic Monthly, 3*, pp. 68-69. (In Chinese)

CHAPTER 10

THE BEGINNING OF A NEW ERA: PRIVATIZATION OF TELECOMMUNICATIONS IN TAIWAN

GEORGETTE WANG

FAN-TUNG TSENG

Taiwan, an island off the southeast coast of China, is a small political entity by any criterion. However, by the late 1980s it was ranked top among developing countries in the value of exported telecommunications equipment ahead of Singapore, Korea, and Hong Kong (*Handbook of International Trade and Development Statistics,* 1992).

Such a record is perhaps not surprising considering Taiwan's economic growth in the past few decades. From a per capita income no more than US$50 in the 1940s, today it has one of the world's largest foreign exchange reserves.[1] However, if telecommunications policy is in any way an indication of the welfare of the telecommunications industry, the aforementioned trade statistic is worthy of our close attention.

Since the early 1980s, evidence showing the importance of telecommunications to economic growth has attracted attention from policy makers and academics. In Egypt, for example, a study found a 1 to 40 cost-benefit ratio brought by investment in telecommunications (Pool & Steven, 1983). In Taiwan, the government has not overlooked the importance of telecommunications to economic growth. Telecommunications service has always been an important part of the nation's long-term planning—but with everything closely guarded by security authorities.

---

[1] As of December 1993, Taiwan's foreign exchange reserves stood at US$83.5 billion. It was the world's second largest after Japan.

Faced with the Communist threat from across the Taiwan Strait, political considerations often outweighed economic concerns in the early days of telecommunications development in Taiwan. As telecommunications facilities were viewed as a potential instrument for subversion and infiltration, close supervision and tight government controls were considered a necessity for the survival of the country. Under tight control, Taiwan's telecommunications industry not only missed the first wave of the island's industrialization in the 1970s, but was not given a chance to grow until the 1980s

In the 1990s, Taiwan's Directorate General of Telecommunications (DGT), the government agency that has enjoyed a monopoly over the telecommunications business for many decades, found itself unable to meet market demand and began to adopt the concept of privatization, following the successful examples of the United Kingdom, Japan, and other developed nations. With tensions gradually relaxing between China and Taiwan,[2] the telecommunications industry found new freedom to develop itself. However, the future of telecommunications reform is still very much dependent on the government's overall policy considerations.

Taiwan's experience is a unique example of how a nation's political and economic setting fosters telecommunications policy, and how telecommunications policy interacts with the development of the telecommunications industry.

With an in-depth analysis of Taiwan's critical change in telecommunications policy, this chapter examines reforms of the telecommunications infrastructure in Taiwan from both the policy and industry perspectives. It begins with a review of the background to policy change, followed by a description of the telecommunications infrastructure when the legislative body approves the revised telecommunications law,[3] and concludes with an analysis of the laws implications for the industry's future—including domestic services and international trade—and for society.

PATH TO REFORM

Records show that in 1950, telephone penetration in Taiwan was no more than .29 per 100 persons. Demand, however, picked up rapidly during the following decades as economic growth gathered momentum (see Table 10.1).

Due to the successful completion of several 4-year mid-term telecommunications construction plans, by January 1993 the number of telephone subscribers reached 7.45 million islandwide, with an average of 36 subscribers per 100 persons (see Table 10.2). The use of digital fiber systems reached over 106,000 core kilometer, covering 54% of local switching, 62% of interoffice trunks, 93% of toll switching, and 95% of toll trunks.

[2]By the mid-1990s, the relationship between Taiwan and China again deteriorated.
[3]The revised *Telecommunications Law* was passed in the Legislative Yuan in 1996.

    As for international network development, fiber and microwave backbone loops were linked to two satellite earth stations, two submarine cable landing stations, and two international switching gateways. Currently, Taiwan is pursuing a 6-year development plan that started in 1991 to further improve call completion, upgrade service performance, and rationalize tariff structures, with the goal of making Taiwan a telecommunications center in Asia (Directorate General of Telecommunication [DGT], 1993).

Table10.1. Per Capita Income and Common Carrier Penetration in Taiwan.

Year	Per Capita (in US$)	Phone (Per 100 Persons)
1950	137	.2
1960	143	.8
1970	360	2.6
1980	2,166	17.6
1990	7,285	30.0
1992	7,853	33.5

Note: Data compiled from Department of Statistics Ministry of Transportation and Communications (various years) and Tseng et al. (1987).

Table 10.2. Telecommunications Carriers in Taiwan.

	Total	% Growth 1992-1993
Telephone Subscriber	7,450,000	9.0
Telephone	*	*
Mobile Telephone	39,000	127.1
Radio Pagers	1,180,000	23.1
Local Switching Facilities	10,750,000	6.5
Toll Switching Facilities	6,647,000	17.7
Toll Lines	567,100	37.9

Note: Data compiled from Department of Statistics Ministry of Transportation and Communications.
*Difficult to estimate after privatization of CPE.

In addition to the expansion and modernization of telephone networks, other services, such as videotext, facsimile, cellular telephone, and packet switched data network communications, have been made available. In just a few years the penetration rate of cellular phones has reached 1.93 per 100 persons in 1993 (DGT, 1993), ranking Taiwan 10th in the world. Although me number of users for videotext and data communications has had a slower growth rate, the first integrated services digital network (ISDN) field trial began in 1989 in southern Taiwan, and several new types of customer premises equipment (CPE), including digital phones, voice data terminals, G4 facsimiles, picture phones, sketch phones, and videotext are being used experimentally on the system. Three more trial systems were installed in other parts of the island in 1991.

Despite such an achievement, the DGT has been faced with increasing difficulties in its operation. According to the Organization Statute of the Ministry of Transportation and Communications (MOTC) as amended in 1943, the DGT is a subsidiary office of the MOTC. Like telecommunications authorities in other nations, the DGT's responsibilities include licensing, frequency management, and drafting and enforcing laws and regulations.

Its responsibilities, however, are not limited to that of a regulator. As telecommunications was considered a public utility enterprise that should therefore be placed under state monopoly to guarantee universal service, the telecommunications business was made part of the Telecommunications Bureau's responsibilities at its birth in China during the Qing Dynasty. When the Republic of China was founded in 1911, the Telecommunications Bureau was reorganized into the DGT, which also inherited the Bureau's monopoly over the telephone and telegraph business.

In the early stage of Taiwan's development, the work of developing a modern telecommunications system might have been facilitated by such a structural arrangement because the government held a majority of the available resources. As market demand multiplied and services diversified, however, the DGT's structure became a major obstacle to continued growth.

Like all other government agencies, the DGT does not have full autonomy over either financial decisions or personnel management. By law the DGT's budget is subject to approval by the legislative body and its spending is under the supervision of the General Accounting Office. Such restraints often made the DGT vulnerable to political negotiations and compromises not to mention difficulties brought by rigid government accounting systems and time loss due to complicated procurement procedures. In addition, all but 2% of the DGT's staff were recruited through the national civil service examination system. The Personnel Administration Bureau determines the number and ranking of staff members the DGT is to employ in each division.

To meet growing demand, the DGT went through its first structural overhaul in 1969 when several major development projects were under way. Two institutions—the Telecommunications Laboratories (TL) which specializes in research and development, and the Telecommunications Training Institute (TTI), which is responsible for manpower development—were added to the DGT. A second structural overhaul came in 1981, leading to the inauguration of five subordinate telecommunications administrations (TAs), including three regional, one long-distance, and one international administration. These five TAs were charged with the responsibility for planning, construction, operation, and maintenance of telecommunications systems and services. In addition a Data Communications Institute (DCI) was created to provide public data communications services. Even with major structural changes, however, it was becoming clear to the MOTC that within its existing framework, the DGT would not be able to cope with growing demand for at least three reasons.

First, policy makers and corporate managers were alarmed by the development of an unbalanced telecommunications market structure and the slow growth of me telecommunications industry. In the 1980s, higher computer penetration rates triggered rapid growth in data communications in many industrialized nations. In the United States, for example, the market share of data communications was 30% of the total in 1986, and was expected to reach 50% in the 1990s. For Taiwan, however, the same service accounted for merely 1.5% of total telecommunications services in 1987 ("Telecommunications Liberalization," 1988). Despite modest growth, this rate remained at the same level throughout the 1980s (Huang, 1990). Value-added network services (VANs), another rapidly growing area in many industrialized nations, remained unseen in Taiwan at the time

This unbalanced telecommunications market structure paralleled sluggish growth in the telecommunications industry. In order to maintain economic growth in Taiwan, the information industry was listed by the government as a "strategic industry for development" in 1980 (*Information Industry Yearbook*, 1988). Under favorable investment policies, the computer industry recorded a growth of 170% in exports from 1982 to 1987. However, exports by the telecommunications industry, also an important part of the information industry, grew by only 30% over the same period. In terms of volume of trade, the value of telecommunications products exported in 1982 surpassed that of computer products by US$150 million, but in 1987 the value of information products exported not only overtook that of telecommunications products, but by an overwhelming margin of US$312 million. Because the two markets differed drastically in the extent to which they were regulated and controlled (for details see "Implications for the Telecommunications Industry," this chapter), the current telecommunications infrastructure and telecommunications laws were blamed for the industry's poor performance.

In addition to alarming signs from the industry, pressures were mounting on the DGT itself as demand for telecommunications services soared both in volume and in variety. The telephone installation fee, for example, was maintained at around US$450 in the 1960s and 1970s, a price only affordable to middle and upper social classes at the time. However, the situation turned around in 1980 when the DGT announced a 57.5% cut in the telephone installation fee.[4] With the economic boom entering its third decade and per capita income reaching US$5,000, this price reduction turned the telephone into an easily affordable household item. The dramatic increase in demand, however, resulted in a serious backlog in supply. At times consumers were kept waiting for over 6 months for telephones to be installed, a problem that became a target of criticism (Chen, 1989).

Another challenge came when technological development brought greater variety to services. As mentioned earlier, the DGT launched an array of new services in the 1980s to keep abreast of technological growth. In terms of business, most of these new services are faring well on the market, but they became added burdens for the DGT to an already over stretched infrastructure.

To rid the DGT of its government straightjacket, the MOTC proposed to corporatize telecommunications operations as early as 1977. Unfortunately, the bill failed to win support in the legislative body. Without autonomy over financial and personnel decisions, the DGT, soon after its second structural overhaul, found itself unable to deal with the challenges brought by technological development and market demand. In 1988, the DGT made its first move to open the telecommunications market by deregulating the CPE market, which includes trading in telephone sets, modems and other terminal equipment. Two years later, the VAN market was also opened to competition from the private sector.

Liberalization of the VAN market may have solved one problem, but it simultaneously served to underscore the DGT's confused role. As earlier mentioned, it is the highest government authority regulating telecommunications, but also holds a monopoly over the business it regulates—a situation often likened to a ball game in which the referee is also the player. As trade has been the pipeline for Taiwan's economic growth, private industry grew increasingly impatient over this strange role that the government played in telecommunications.

Encouraged by developments made in other nations, a series of actions were taken within the government. In 1986, the Council for Economic Planning and Development (CEPD) initiated a study of the telecommunications laws and recommended market liberalization In response to the study, task forces were formed within the DGT for further deliberation and planning. At the same time an ad-hoc group was organized by the MOTC to work on the legal framework of a liberalized and privatized telecommunications industry.

---

[4]This substantial cut in the telephone installation fee can be attributed to several reasons: the completion of building a subscriber loop, a government policy to encourage a second telephone in the family, and growing social pressures.

After a 2-year debate between various government departments and the private sector over issues such as the definition of Type-1 (basic services) and Type-2 (VAN) carriers—the extent to which foreign investment should be allowed and the nature of the corporatized DGT—the *Telecommunications Law* was revised and sent to the Legislative Yuan in the Spring of 1992. Another law related to the *Telecommunications Law,* the DGT *Organization Statute* for the regulatory body and the Statute of Chunghua Telecom Corporation (CTC) for the operating body have also been drafted.

However progress in promulgating the laws has since slowed down. As the MOTC was finalizing the DGT Organization Statute and the CTC Statute, changes in the international economic situation and cabinet shifts brought new debates in the strategy of reform. Under increasing pressure from the General Agreement on Tariffs and Trade (GATT) to open Taiwan's telecommunications market, some policy makers began to push for a one step privatization plan to replace the currently proposed two-step plan. Union members of the DGT, on the other hand, heavily lobbied against privatization for fear of losing job security

In the mid 1990s, telecommunications reform in Taiwan seems to be swaying between two extremes: one-step privatization or a complete halt of the process. Whereas liberalization without privatizing the DGT may be a meeting point of different interests, the importance of the revised Telecommunications Law now pending approval in the Legislative Yuan is not to be undermined. It has outlined an infrastructure that is basically acceptable to all parties, and will likely serve as a basis for additional changes.

TELECOMMUNICATIONS INFRASTRUCTURE UNDER THE NEW LAWS

According to the draft of the revised *Telecommunications Law,* the telecommunications industry is categorized into *Type-1* and *Type-2* carriers as shown in Figure 10.1. As stipulated in Article 11 of the revised *Telecommunications Law,* Type-1 telecommunications business refers to a business that installs telecommunications line facilities to provide telecommunications services. A Type-1 business therefore provides telecommunications services by installing circuit facilities including transmission line facilities connecting transmitting points with receiving points, switching facilities installed as an inseparable unit, and other accessory facilities. Type-2 operators, on the other hand, attach additional hardware and software to the telecommunications circuit facilities provided by Type 1 operators to provide VAN services

Under this new design, the existing DGT will be reorganized into two institutions: the new DGT, which will serve as the industry's regulatory body, and Chunghua Telecom, a state enterprise that will enjoy a monopoly over Type-1 business but will compete with private industry in the VAN market.

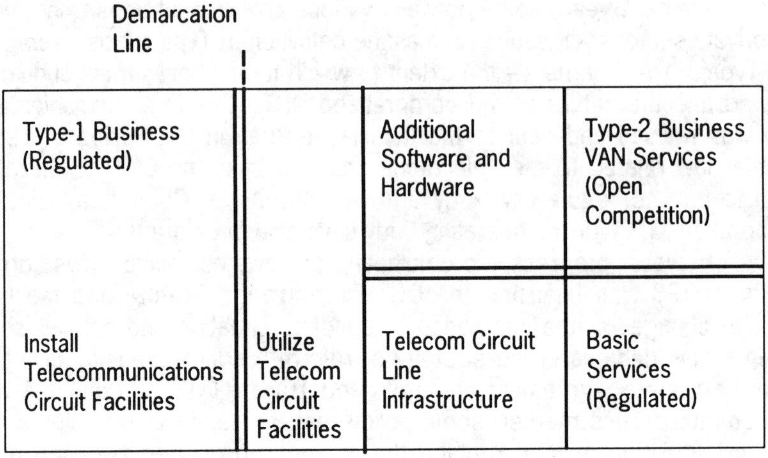

Demarcation Line			
Type-1 Business (Regulated)		Additional Software and Hardware	Type-2 Business VAN Services (Open Competition)
Install Telecommunications Circuit Facilities	Utilize Telecom Circuit Facilities	Telecom Circuit Line Infrastructure	Basic Services (Regulated)

Note. Type-1 business installs telecommunications circuit facilities; Type-2 business provides VAN

Figure 10.1. Telecommunications business categories

CHUNGHUA TELECOM

According to Article 12 of the revised *Telecommunications Law,* "Type-1 telecommunications business will be run by Chunghua Telecom only," thus providing the legal basis for its market monopoly privilege.

Because of its monopolistic nature, Chunghua Telecom is expected to provide quality universal service to the island's population of 21 million,, and at the same time devote itself to R&D. To ensure fair competition between Chunghua Telecom and private industry in the VAN market,, Chunghua Telecom is required to keep separate accounting books for its Type-1 and Type-2 businesses to prevent cross-subsidies between the two.

As a state enterprise, Chunghua Telecom will still be under the government's authority, but it is expected to enjoy a much higher degree of autonomy. In accordance with this greater autonomy, the company will also take the responsibility for its own survival and well-being. Unlike the DGT in the past, Chunghua Telecom's management will operate under market-oriented philosophies, emphasizing efficiency, competitiveness, and satisfaction of customer needs.

Under the draft Statute of Chunghua Telecom, the company will be organized into three service-oriented divisions: international communications, trunk line services, and telephone and data communications. The new company is expected to take on over 98% of the DGT's current employees and inherit almost all of its assets, but no decisions have been made as to its financial structure.

DGT

With its responsibilities for running telecommunications business taken over by Chunghua Telecom, the major functions of the new DGT will be limited to those of regulating the industry, monitoring growth in the field and promoting an integrated telecommunications development plan (see Figure 10.2). Although the DGT is to be scaled down both in size and function, the role it will play in the telecommunications industry will remain important.

Its Common Carrier Department, for example, is designed to act as a "referee" in supervising Type-1 and Type-2 business. It will be responsible for delineating the scope of Type-1 and Type-2 business, a topic of heated debate in the process of revising both the *Telecommunications Law* and the definition of the two types of businesses every six months according to technological development and market demand.

The same department will be responsible for authorizing the tariff structure. According to the new design, the tariff formula for Type-1 services will be prepared by the DGT and submitted to the Executive Yuan before its final approval from the legislative body. Major tariffs will then be calculated by the Type-1 carrier using the approved formula and submitted to the MOTC for authorization. The DGT, as a "referee," will no longer be the "player." Chunghua Telecom, the new "player," will be rid of its government straightjacket to become a market-oriented business, and VAN operators will be able to compete with Chunghua Telecom on equal terms. Other responsibilities of the Common Carrier Department will include licensing, stipulating technical standards, supervising telecommunications business operation, and determining the qualifications of telecommunications engineers and installation technicians, and so on.

The Telecommunications Policy Department, another division placed directly under the Directorate General, will be responsible for integrating national telecommunications plans and enhancing the development of an information society. Three Regional Telecommunications Bureaus will act as doorways to the public, whereas the Radio Management Department will be in charge of studying ways to effectively utilize radio frequencies, equipment type approval, socioeconomic research related to telecommunications, and other technical support.

One of the DGT's "traditional responsibilities"—that of regulating wire and wireless communications—will be divided between three different departments under the new design. The Private Carrier Department will be responsible for licensing and supervising private radio carriers and services including communications by police, private companies, government bodies, individuals (amateur short-wave radio operators), and mobile, marine, navigation and aeronautic communications. The Broadcast Technical Department will be responsible for the licensing and supervision of broadcasting sta-

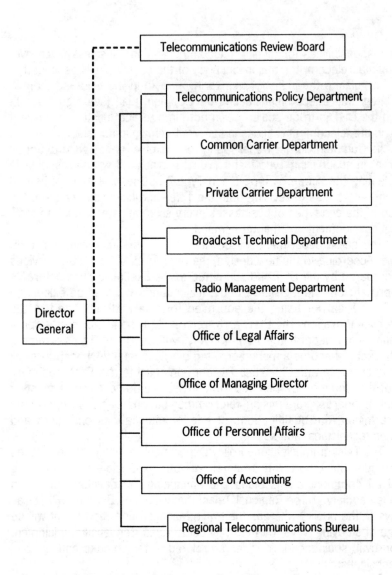

Figure 10.2. Proposed organization of the new DGT

tions, television networks, cable television systems, and satellite broadcasting. Finally, the Radio Management Department will be responsible for radio frequency allocation, assignment, registration and monitoring.

In addition to the aforementioned five departments, the DGT's role as a referee will be further underscored by its Telecommunications Review Board, to handle disputes among the telecommunications industry, private telecommunications operators, broadcasters, and radio frequencies, and to set up basic technical standards on telecommunications.

IMPLICATIONS FOR THE TELECOMMUNICATIONS INDUSTRY

According to the revised *Telecommunications Law* now awaiting approval in the legislative body, the emerging telecommunications infrastructure will differ from the existing one in several major respects. Although the current reform is but the first step towards a two-stage privatization plan currently under study at the MOTC, private industry and policy critics were quick to make known their responses to the first draft of the revised *Telecommunications Law* released in late 1991. The reception was, at best, mixed.

Generally, the government was credited for its initiative in reform. As noted by Huang (1990), liberalization of the telecommunications market in Taiwan was initiated within the government, rather than pressured by the legislative body as in Japan. In fact, the record shows that legislators have acted against reforms of such a nature more than once.[5] As mentioned earlier, the legislative body voted against the MOTC's first proposal to corporatize the DGT in 1977. In 1983, Chao Yao-tung, then-Minister of Economic Affairs, was again heavily attacked in the Legislative Yuan for his proposal to privatize state enterprises under his ministry's supervision. Although Chao's setback had little impact on the telecommunications industry per se, the conservative stance of Taiwan's legislative body continued to prevail until a greater number of locally elected representatives joined the Legislative Yuan in the late 1980s.

The pressure to change, therefore, may have come from different sources, including local private industry, transnational corporations applying pressure through bilateral trade talks, and interest groups. The prime movers for reform however, were ultimately policy makers who came to realize the importance for Taiwan to reach its development goals and catch up with industrialized nations. The reform, therefore, would not have been possible if not for the close cooperation and mutual support of key government agencies.

---

[5]Until 1991, the majority of Taiwan's legislators had been elected before the government was moved to the island in 1949. The conservative Legislative Yuan has more than once voted against liberal-minded policy proposals, including those on population control and privatization of state enterprises.

Despite the credit the government received for taking the first step in telecommunications reform, the scope of this reform was deemed by critics as too conservative to meet market demand. According to Chen (1992), if the major achievement of this round of reform was to separate the roles of the referee from that of the player, Taiwan would still fall behind the United States by half a century. Two issues of major concern were liberalization of the telecommunications industry and the interests of local versus foreign investors.

FURTHER LIBERALIZATION AND DEREGULATION

On completion of the reform package, key players in the telecommunications market in Taiwan will include Chunghua Telecom, private VAN carriers and CPE manufacturers. Under this system, private VAN carriers will no longer compete with the "referee and player." However, they and CPE manufacturers still thought there were too many restrictions under the revised *Telecommunications Law*. In a petition from associations of VAN operators and computer manufacturers (Liang & Huang, 1991), further liberalization and deregulation were called for in the following areas:

1. *The types of business VAN carriers are allowed to enter.* It was proposed that all business related to computer applications, such as digital video signal transmission, be open to the VAN market. Also called for were open competition in mobile communications, packet switched networks, direct broadcast satellite communications, and shared leased lines.
2. *The requirements to qualify for a VAN license.* Although the VAN market was already open to competition, according to the first draft of the revised *Telecommunications Law*, the DGT is still to hold the right to look into VAN operators' business plans, service charges, contract terms and even financial conditions. It was suggested that in an open market, the operators' ability to compete should be subject to market tests, not government supervision (Liang & Huang, 1991).
3. *Fair competition between Chunghua Telecom and private VAN carriers in the VAN market.* It was suggested that a clause ensuring equal treatment of VAN operators and average Type-1 service users be added to the revised *Telecommunications Law*.
4. *Supervision of the telecommunications industry for security reasons.* When the Nationalist Government moved to Taiwan in 1949, preventing Communist infiltration was a high priority of the government. Because telecommunications may be used as a means to achieve political purposes, the industry was put under close control for security reasons.

According to the *Provision for Regulating Electronics Component and Equipment*, all telecommunications equipment manufacturers and business owners have to have a special permit from the Taiwan Garrison Command in addition to the regular license prior to opening a business. The Taiwan Garrison Command, the nation's major security and intelligence authority, was therefore granted the power to oversee the telecommunications industry on the island.

In 1988, the government lifted the 40-year martial law that served as a basis for the *Provision for Regulating Electronics Component and Equipment*. As the Provision officially expired in July 1992, the Taiwan Garrison Command, itself a weakening institution, will no longer have a role to play in the telecommunications industry in Taiwan. To protect users' privacy, laws specifying government security control over telecommunications were called for.

Also of concern was the special permit required for running a telecommunications business in Taiwan. According to the revised *Telecommunications Law* now pending in the legislative body, following the expiry of the *Provision for Regulating Electronic Component and Equipment*, the new DGT will take over responsibility for granting permission to manufacture telecommunications equipment and operate maintenance and repair services. According to one critic, such control showed the lack of a real understanding of the VAN business (Chen, 1991).

TELECOMMUNICATIONS INDUSTRY

From the industry perspective, the desire to further liberate and deregulate telecommunications is not difficult to understand. As mentioned earlier, in terms of exports the performance of the telecommunications industry is far behind that of the computer industry. In fact, over the entire history of the telecommunications industry in Taiwan, there have been few impressive growth records as often observed in other industries.

In its early days of development, the DGT purchased all of its telecommunications equipment from abroad. In 1957, Far East Electrical Appliances, the first local company producing telecommunications equipment, came into existence. The next year, another, Taiwan Telecommunications Industries, appeared on the market. With technical assistance from Japan's NEC, the two began to produce common battery switching facilities and magnetic telephone sets, laying the foundations of a telecommunications industry (Taiwan Economics Research Institute, 1992).

The two companies continued to be the DGT's largest suppliers of telecommunications equipment in the 1960s. In 1973, however, the DGT decided to introduce electronic switching equipment. To ensure market supply, the DGT began to cooperate with transitional corporations such as GTE and ITT in local production.

The real turning point in Taiwan's telecommunications industry, how-ever, did not come until 1983 when the Industrial Technology Research Institute (ITRI) successfully developed integrated circuits for telephones and transferred the technology to private industries. This technological break-through not only opened the domestic market for digital phones, but came at the same time as the U.S. government decided to open its market for imported telephone sets. Stimulated by this rare market opportunity, the number of manufacturers producing telephone sets and other telecommuni-cations equipment soared to 300 within just a few years (Taiwan Economics Research Institute, 1992)

According to the Ministry of Economic Affairs (1991), the total value of Taiwan's telecommunications industry output grew four times from US$484 million in 1981 to US$1,974 million in 1990. Although the growth was significant, its share in the output value of the electrical appliance and electronics industries remained under 7%, and under 1.1% of Taiwan's total industrial output value (see Table 10.3)

A year-by-year examination of growth rates, however, shows the influence of policies on telecommunications industrial output. Aside from the record 91% growth in 1983, significant increases were observed in 1989 and 1990, the years following the deregulation of the domestic CPE market.

Table 10.3. Telecommunications Industry Output and DGT Revenue.

Year	Taiwan's Total Indust. Output	Telecom Industries	%	DGT Revenue
1981	2,756,349	12,117	.44	24,523
1982	2,726,055	12,436	.46	29,208
1983	3,022,073	23,833	.79	35,301
1984	3,463,575	24,033	.69	39,421
1985	3,448,057	22,017	.64	42,729
1986	3,752,765	29,125	.78	45,710
1987	4,075,384	29,804	.73	52,506
1988	4,275,589	32,350	.76	56,514
1989	4,500,286	38,031	.85	62,981
1990	4,486,630	49,374	1.10	75,005
1991	4,483,108	54,240	1.20	—

Note: Data compiled from Statistics Department, Ministry of Transportation and Communications (Various years) and Taiwan Economics Research Institute (1992).
*Except for percentages, all figures are in million NT dollars. In April 1992, exchange rate was US$1 for NT$25.5.

Policy reform, therefore, is expected to have a direct influence on industry performance. Although at this round of telecommunications reform the industry is only half way to a fully liberalized and deregulated market, a corporatized Chunghua Telecom is expected to bring more vigorous growth to business, which in turn will stimulate industrial output and enhance export capabilities. VAN business, on the other hand, is also expected to have a brighter future as both its scope and its relations with the Type-1 carrier are more clearly defined.

Caution, however, should be exercised in looking at the future. In the final stage of revising the *Telecommunications Law*, most of the afore-mentioned comments were incorporated in its design. Laws by themselves, however, do not guarantee growth and prosperity. Past records of state enterprises in Taiwan show that factors such as management style and policy control have also contributed to the success or failure of state enterprises. Therefore, to what extent Taiwan's telecommunications industry will benefit from the reform remains to be seen.

INTERESTS OF FOREIGN INVESTORS

According to the existing *Telecommunications Law*, no foreign investors are allowed to run telecommunications business in Taiwan. Such a restriction may be understandable as the telecommunications industry has traditionally been under heavy government control. As Taiwan's trade surplus against other nations widened, however, pressure to open the domestic market also mounted.

After numerous rounds of trade talks and pressures resulting from Taiwan's application to join GATT, the government recently decided to abolish former restrictions that kept foreign investors from entering Taiwan's VAN market. According to the current draft of the revised *Telecommunications Law*, a protection clause stipulates three conditions under which foreign investors are allowed to compete in Taiwan:

1. The service will bring in new technologies and technology transfer will be guaranteed;
2. Taiwan investors will be allowed to compete in the foreign investor's home country under equal terms;
3. Foreign investment will be allowed to enter the international VAN business two years after the revised *Telecommunications Law* comes into effect; for domestic VAN services, four years.

The revised law can be regarded as a compromise between fair trade and protection of local investors. Transnational corporations, with their financial resources and international networks unrivaled by local companies, are likely to play an important role in Taiwan's future VAN business. Like

Taiwan's automobile industry, without sound business plans, the protected VAN industries will sooner or later fail the market test. The pressure brought by foreign investors may serve as a stimulant to local businesses, but the government has to ensure the rules of fair competition.

As mentioned earlier, the forthcoming reform is meant to be the first step in a two stage MOTC plan that will eventually lead to privatization of the telecommunications industry in Taiwan. According to the original design, performance of the new DGT and Chunghua Telecom, development of the industry as a whole, and other nations' privatization experiences will serve as references to determine a timetable. Although the privatization agenda may undergo major changes due to economic considerations, the trend toward liberalization seems irreversible.

SOCIAL IMPLICATIONS

Many studies have attempted to delineate the contributions to economic growth. Although for Taiwan no evidence can yet prove a causal relationship between the two, the correlation has been rather consistent. This is perhaps why despite the arrival of a global recession in the early 1990s, upgrading the telecommunications infrastructure was listed as one of the priorities in Taiwan's development plan. From 1991 to 1996, a budget of NT$108.3 billion (about NT$26 to US$1 in 1994) was allocated for the development of telecommunications networks (DGT, 1993)

Like many other nations, Taiwan has taken its first step towards privatizing and liberalizing its telecommunications industry. Once fulfilled, it will have far-reaching effects on not only the telecommunications industry, but the nation's future social economic development. A state-of-the-art infrastructure that allows for vigorous market competition is expected to facilitate Taiwan's goals of maintaining its economic growth and also speeding up the transformation to an information society. Not to be overlooked in this important change in telecommunications policy direction are the political, social, and economic factors that were involved in bringing it about.

Although Taiwan's telecommunications service has yet to be fully privatized, it is clear that privatization or any major change in telecommunications policy, occurs only when necessary conditions are met. In Taiwan's case, national security and economic concerns were the two determining factors.

In different social settings and stages of development, different factors can be expected to have different weights for policy change and industrial development. In the past, blocking Communist infiltration was a sufficient reason for controlling the telecommunications industry. As Taiwan develops into a significant trade economy in the region, however, compliance with major international organization rules such as that of GATT has become a powerful factor in government policy considerations, including telecommunications policy.

For the future, the most important implication of this study is that telecommunications policy must be examined within its social, political, and economic context. After all telecommunications policy is but one element, although a critical one, in the operation of a society.

REFERENCES

Chen, B. S. (1991, December 16). Will the referee's son always be the champion? *Industry and Business Times*, p. 6. (In Chinese)

Chen, B. S. (1992, January 3). Myths in the liberalization of Taiwan's telecommunications, compared with the liberalization in the United States. *Industry and Business Times*, p. 6. (In Chinese)

Chen, M. H. (1989, December 24). The dilatory telecommunications construction the quality of postal service decried. *Independence Daily*, p. 5. (In Chinese)

Department of Statistics, Ministry of Transportation and Communications. (Various years). *Statistical abstracts of transportation and communications*. Taipei: Author. (In Chinese)

Directorate General of Telecommunications. (1993). *Telecommunications white paper*. Taipei: Author. (In Chinese)

Handbook of international trade and development statistics 1991. (1992). New York: United Nations.

Huang, H. N. (1990, January). Liberalization of our nation's telecommunications: A discussion of policy formulation, implementation and evaluation. *Economic Social and Legal System Research, 5,* 199-229. (In Chinese)

Information industry yearbook. (1988). Taipei: Institute for Information Industry. (In Chinese)

Liang, L. W., & Huang, H. J. (1991, November 25). Private sector should be allowed to develop telecommunications business. *Industry and Business Times*, p. 2. (In Chinese)

Pool, I. S., & P. M. Steven. (1983). Appropriate telecommunications for rural development. In I. B. Singh (Ed.), *Telecommunications in the year 2000* (pp. 150-157). Norwood, NJ: Ablex.

Taiwan Economics Research Institute. (1992). *Information and electronics industry yearbook 1991.* Taipei: Taiwan Economics Research Institute

Telecommunications liberalization is a must for modern information society (1988, May 27). *China Times*, p. 3. (In Chinese)

Tseng, F.T., Liao, Y.N., Cheng, J.C., Wang, J.T., Li, J.T., Wu, T.H., Chen, B.L., Huang, S.N., Chen, M.H., Chen, J.T., Hsu, Y.H., & Cheng, C.J. (1987). *A study of laws concerning telecommunications and information modernization.* Unpublished research report to the Council for Economic Planning and Development, Taipei, Taiwan. (In Chinese)

PART III

PROSPECTS

In this part, three chapters attempt to make some observations on the potentials of telecommunications and development in China. In "China's Telecommunications: Options and Opportunities," John Ure analyzes the shift from the supply-driven centrally determined telecommunications plans of the 1980s to more demand-driven market-oriented plans in the 1990s. He calculates that such a shift provides opportunities for foreign investment.

A common problem for LDCs is to secure capital to finance development projects. Apart from internal sources, LDCs have to rely on external means. Forging links with foreign capital is thus a common phenomenon in LDCs. Zixiang Tan addresses the issues of forging external links in developing telecommunications in "The Impact of Foreign Linkages on Telecommunications and Development in China." He discusses the pros and cons of foreign links in China's telecommunications development and analyzes the current cooperation with foreign investors and the negative effects of the Coordinating Committee on Multinational Export Control (COCOM). Although the COCOM was dissolved in early 1994, the Western industrial powers will probably continue to guard against exporting their most advanced technology.

In "Creating a Telecommunications Free Trade Zone in Greater China," Milton Mueller proposes a free trade zone of telecommunications services between of China, Taiwan, Hong Kong, and Macau. Under this design, all parties will enter into agreements to legalize the resale of international leased circuits among themselves. Mueller argues that resale will improve efficiency and eliminate price discrimination and that expanded geographical scope will increase the number of competitors in the market, intensifying service and price competition and fostering economies of scale in the industry. This will make Greater China a very attractive place for major users to utilize as a hub of telecommunications trade.

CHAPTER 11

CHINA'S TELECOMMUNICATIONS: OPTIONS AND OPPORTUNITIES

JOHN URE

By the end of 1992, according to the China Business Weekly February 21-27, 1993, the People's Republic of China's national telephone capacity was around 32 million circuits. Of these 13 million were in private or specialized usage by state bodies such as research establishments or ministries such as Aerospace, Defense, Energy, and Railways, and 19 million were part of the public switched telephone network (PSTN) operated by the Ministry of Posts and Telecommunications (MPT) and the provincial Posts & Telecommunications Bureaus (the PTTs) ("Telecom Expansion," 1993). According to the MPT, however, subscribers were only 11.5 million, or just 60% of capacity (Ministry of Posts and Telecommunications [MPT], 1993).

At that time, the number of telephones in public use was 18.9 million, or 1.6 telephones per main line, which compares with a ratio of 1.3 in Hong Kong. Until very recently most subscribers in China were ministries and other state organizations, which accounts for a high proportion of extension telephones. However this picture is changing very rapidly. In 1990 residents made up only 22% of subscribers, but by 1992 their numbers had soared to 45%. Subscribers classified as private or individual businesses are also rising, from 17% in 1990 to 21% in 1991. Most subscribers—about 80%—are in areas designated as urban, which is average for low-income developing countries in Asia (International Telecommunication Union [ITU]1993).

From these figures we can establish that the number of mainlines per 100 people for 1992, as defined by the number of subscribers, was a lowly .97 compared with the rate of telephones per 100 people for 1992 of 1.63.

Table 11.1. China's National Public Telephone Network.

	1990	1991	1992
Exchange Capacity PSTN (Millions)	12.321	14.921	19.151
Of Which:			
Urban (%)	67.000	69.200	70.800
Rural (%)	33.000	30.800	29.200
Main Access Lines Subscribers (Millions)	6.850	8.450	11.470
Of Which:			
Urban (%)	78.600	79.400	80.300
Rural (%)	21.400	20.600	19.700
Residential (%)	22.300	28.300	45.100
Business (%)	77.700	71.900	54.900
As Percentage of Capacity Subscribers (%)	55.600	56.600	59.900
Of Which:			
Urban (%)	65.200	64.900	67.900
Rural (%)	36.100	37.800	40.400
Number of Telephones (Millions)	12.735	14.900	18.888
Of Which:			
Urban (%)	80.600	81.100	81.800
Rural (%)	19.400	18.900	18.200
Teledensity			
Capacity/100	1.080	1.290	1.630
Subscriber/100	.600	.730	.970
Phones/100	1.100	1.290	1.610
Radio Telecommunications			
Pager (Million Subscribers)	.044	.088	2.220
Pager/100	.380	.750	1.890
Mobiles (Million Subscribers)	.019	.050	.180
Mobiles/100	.002	.040	.150

Note. Data compiled from Ministry of Posts and Telecommunication (various years) and State Statistical Bureau (various years).

In the summer of 1992 China's newly appointed Vice Premier Zhu Rongji endorsed the revised Eighth Five-Year Plan (1991-1995) and Ninth Five-Year Plan (1996-2000) targets for telecommunications ("The MPT to Further," 1992). These were subsequently revised again, upwards. By 1995 China was to have a switched circuit capacity of 50 million and 36 million telephones, and by the year 2000, 100 million switched circuit capacity and 78 million telephones. These are compound annual growth rates of 38% and 23% respectively from 1993 to the end of the century, or an additional 10 million lines a year between 1993 and 2000 The most recent Ninth Five-Year Plan targets 170 million switched circuit capacity by 2000.

It is difficult to make an accurate estimate of what this means in terms of capital expenditure, but we may note that China now manufactures switches at below US$80 per circuit. If we assume that the average cost of connection, including building and transmission costs, stands around US$800—as Ure (1995) makes clear, significantly below the ITU's benchmark of US$1,500 average total cost per main telephone line—we can estimate as follows: (a) telephone lines as 65% of planned exchange capacity—the Ninth Plan assumes 68%; (b) adding 14.3 million lines a year would cost around US$11.4 billion; (c) adding an additional 7.7 million exchange capacity a year will cost in the region of US$600 million; (d) capital expenditure to meet these targets could average US$12 billion annually to the year 2000.[1]

Long-distance circuits, which rose from 38,000 in 1985 to 152,000 in 1991 increased a further 535,000 to 687,000 by 1994—the original cumulative target for 1995 had been 520,000. The Ninth Five-Year Plan targets 2.4 million circuits of optical fiber cable, microwave, and satellite links in service, 1 million more than originally planned (Xiong, 1993), and a capacity potential of 6 million circuits.

At least a dozen additional satellite earth stations are planned by 2000 and launches of China's third-generation domestic satellite, Dongfanghong ("East is Red")—Series 3, should raise the number of satellite circuits to over 10,000. Qi Faren, President of the China Space Technology Institute was quoted in China Daily as saying that another 20 satellite launches are planned by the end of the century ("Twenty More," 1993). The Very Small Aperture Terminals (VSATs) market is already set to expand in parallel and China is participating directly in two Asia regional satellite ventures. China International Trust and Investment Company (CITIC), the State Council's overseas investment arm, is a one-third shareholder in AsiaSat, whereas the MPT's China Telecommunications and Broadcast Satellite Corporation is a partner in the Asia-Pacific Telecommunications Satellite (Apstar) launched in June 1994.

TELECOMMUNICATIONS AS A STRATEGIC NATIONAL OBJECTIVE

In the early to mid-1980s the State Council commissioned and endorsed proposals to give telecommunications development a key role in the national economy (Zita, 1987). The background of this decision was a combination

---

[1]The MPT has planned for a combined domestic and foreign investment of RMB 500 billion, or US$60 billion (at the exchange rate .83 RMB: 1US$) which accords to my estimates exactly. The current level of 1.7% foreign investment seems bound to increase.

of factors. From 1979 the Open Door policy was correctly seen as ushering China into a new era of exposure to the world economy. National economic efficiency would be put on trial, and without a modern telecommunications infrastructure China's newly formed Special Economic Zones (SEZs) would not succeed. Export-oriented foreign investment was to be encouraged and that required good international communications as well as domestic links to suppliers and officials of the local state bureaus.

National security was also involved. China is a vast country with many minorities from the northern plains of Inner Mongolia to the western high mountains of Tibet, and from the Moslem peoples of Xinjiang province in the Northwest to the Cantonese speakers of Guangdong province in the South, China has many different languages, including eight major dialects, ethnic groups, cultural traditions, and local loyalties to meld together. Long distance telecommunications are essential both for effective military maneuvering, and for national identification.

Figure 11.1, drawn from *China Statistical Yearbook* data and annual reports of the MPT, illustrates the strength of growth in China's telecommunications traffic since the Open Door policy (the vertical axis is in logarithmic scale). National long-distance telephone traffic growth is just as spectacular as international traffic growth. There is an important implication here:

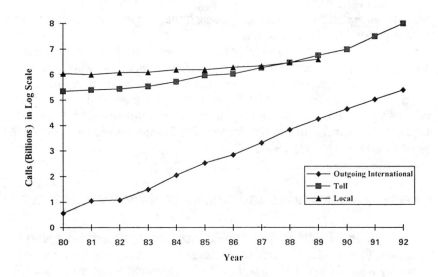

Figure 11.1. China's telephone traffic: Inland and outgoing International calls. Note: Data compiled from *Ministry of Posts & Telecommunications* (1993)

China's economic development is not confined to those areas open directly to the world market; for example, along the southern coast. An enormous commercial growth is taking place in transactions between provinces, and this underscores the scope of China's economic performance. It is more than a boom—it is genuine development. A word of caution, however, is advisable. During a boom the growth of what Marx would have called *fictitious capital;* that is, inflated market values that cannot be sustained by underlying productivity growth, is an ever-present danger. However, if the growth is so widespread, it also follows that the growing mobility of capital inside China will compensate for any sudden collapse of markets in one locality. The whole of Hong Kong may feel the effects of an almighty collapse in the Hang Seng index, but a similar event in Guangzhou would hardly cause a stir in Chengdu, Dalian, Shanghai, or Tianjin.

A third factor behind the State Council's concern with telecommunications was China's science and technology program (Conroy, 1992). Modernization has been a central theme of Deng Xiaoping's reforms, and the importance the Chinese attach to the promotion of high-technology industries cannot be overestimated. This affects telecommunications in two ways.

First, in the digital era telecommunications equipment has become a high tech industry in its own right. With its current encouragement of foreign direct investment (FDI), China places great stress on the importance of technology transfer. Foreign equipment manufacturers trying to enter the China market have to be prepared to enter into technology transfer agreements of one kind or another in order to establish joint ventures or foreign-owned enterprises

Second, telecommunications as infrastructure is an essential requirement for the effective deployment of information systems and the wider application of computer networks. China's lack of an effective national data network has not been a major bottleneck up to date because of the very low penetration of computer usage, even at the level of the PC, in most of China's industry and administration. That situation however, will change during the coming years. Besides the military, special research institutions and particular industrial sectors such as the Bank of China and the China International Travel Service (both of which use VSAT for long-distance information and data transfer), the demand for sophisticated data telecommunications has arisen from the still-small number of multinational enterprises operating from Beijing, Shanghai, Guangzhou, and Shenzhen.

DATA NETWORKS

To meet this demand China has undertaken two major initiatives. It has launched the second phase of its domestic data network operating from platforms that support X.25 packet switching, X.400 message handling, X.500 synchronous data transfer, and a potential for X.28 interface frame relay between LANS.[2] In 1989 gateways were open only to France, Japan, and the United States, but now X.75 direct connections service numerous destinations including Hong Kong, Germany, Italy, and the United Kingdom. Northern Telecom is supplying its DPN/100 equipment for this nationwide MPT network; however, local initiatives are also in train. For example, microwave is being used in Shenzhen to provide wide-area networking capability for computers, whereas Sprint has supplied e-mail systems to a number of provincial PTTs.

Second, in March 1991 an International Business Service (IBS) came into operation from Beijing and Shanghai in cooperation with KDD and AT&T and hubbing through Japan and the United States. International data speeds of up to 1.544Mbt/s are available. All told, about two-thirds of China's data traffic is international, having half of its registered users in Beijing where the market is dominated by American and Japanese multinationals and Embassies (Ure, 1991).

These are still early days, however, and the growing availability of domestic long-distance circuits by satellite, microwave, and landlines is likely to stimulate the demand for data networking during the 1990s. This will, in turn, put pressure on China's Ministry of Foreign Trade and Economic Cooperation (MOFTEC, now renamed Ministry of Foreign Economic Relations and Trade, MOFERT) to relax the foreign exchange restrictions on the import of computers. In this field, as in others, China's strategy must be to expand its own domestic production which means more joint ventures, technology transfers, licensing agreements, and wholly owned foreign companies being encouraged to set up in the mushrooming Technology Zones.

THE PSTN NETWORK

The most rapid growth areas in China's telecommunications markets, however, will remain for some time to come the demand for access to the basic network and for partial substitutes and business tools such as mobile telephones, Cordless Telephone Second Generation (CT2), and pagers. The MPTs estimate of China's 1992 national capital expenditure on public posts and telecommunications services was US$2.5 billion, a 70% increase over 1991, and representing over 70% of the total spent between 1986 and

---

[2]International technical standards are agreed by the CCITT (Consultative Committee for International Telegraph and Telecommunication, now renamed the Telecommunications Standardization Sector, or TSS) of the ITU (International Telecommunication Union), a United Nations organization based in Geneva, Switzerland.

1990—such is the acceleration now taking place. Prior to his retirement, *China Business Weekly* cited Minister Yang Taifang as forecasting expenditure during 1993 to rise to between US$4-5 billion ("Telecom Expansion," 1993).

This figure compares with the US$6.7 billion envisaged for the entire period of the Eighth Five-Year Plan (1991-1995), which was endorsed by the National People's Congress (NPC) in March 1992. Annual growth rates were subsequently revised upwards from 16% to over 20% for the 1990s following Deng Xiaoping's campaign for faster growth and a quicker pace of economic reform. The target of 3 telephones/100 persons was brought forward from the year 2000 to 1996, and a new target of over 5 telephones/100 persons was substituted. The new target now stands at 10 telephones/100 persons. Currently the MPT claims a figure of 2.5, a rise from 1.3 by the end of 1991. In the more prosperous cities such as Shenzhen and Guangzhou, Beijing, and Shanghai, how ever, penetration rates are much higher. According to *China Daily*, 11 cities have over 11 telephones/100 persons, led by Haikou, the capital of Hainan Province, with 25 telephones/100 persons ("Phone Galore," 1994).

Even this increased level of funding, when compared with my earlier rough estimates of required annual expenditures of over US$10 billion, leaves quite a shortfall to be made up. However, my "guestimate" (Ure, 1991) of the target for MPT revenues (including provincial PTTs) from telecommunications during 1993 falls not far short of US$3.5 billion, so telecommunications is clearly a very good investment.

Typically, for a phone-starved country experiencing very fast economic growth people are willing and able to find large sums of money to obtain a phone—officially if they can, under the counter if they cannot. Many casual observers are surprised at how high demand is when the cost of a telephone line can reach around US$900 in Beijing, although in Guangzhou it is closer to US$500. The surprise is compounded when it is known that, on average across China, residents make up 60% of the burgeoning waiting lists, and in many cities that figure is over 90%.[3] Recent suggestions by the International Monetary Fund (IMF) (1993) that China's annual purchasing power national per capita income is probably at least three times greater than the official estimate of US$350, however, throws a new and controversial perspective on the situation (for discussion, see Lardy, 1994).

Depending on how we interpret the income data, by comparison with other Asian low-income developing countries China has achieved at least the average teledensity (mainlines/100 persons) relative to its Gross National Income, which the World Bank officially estimates at US$370 for 1991. I do not put too much weight on the ITU's correlations between Gross National Product (GNP) per capita and teledensity, because although they

---

[3]Based on private interviews and research by the author. Also refer to the proportion of residential subscribers mentioned at the outset of this chapter.

tell you what the average between different comparable countries is, they do not explain the relationship between telecommunications and national economic growth. However for what they are worth, in looking at the ITU 1993 figures we may expect China to have a teledensity of around 0.8/100 per sons. In 1991 there were 0.73 mainlines/100 persons—in 1992, .97. However, if China has a per capita national income of over US$1,000, we might expect a teledensity of over 3; thus either China is already doing as well as can be expected or, more likely, has much catching up to do. The plans for expansion suggest a determination to do just that.

Part, although only part, of the income discrepancy may arise from the growing phenomenon of people holding down two or three jobs at the same time. The opportunities for money making in the towns and cities are expanding rapidly, ranging from taxi driving, petty commodity trading, television and car repair, and plumbing, to more speculative activities in equities, the property market, and black-market money dealing. Families with one member safely employed in a Ministry bureaucracy or a state enterprise will often have others risking the uncertainties of employment against the higher rewards of labor markets, a situation ironically known as "One Family, Two Systems." "Get-rich-quick" attitudes are now driving a scramble for material gain in many parts of China. As one Hong Kong businesswoman who does extensive business in China put it, Deng Xiaoping has told everybody "to be their own profit center."

NONPUBLIC NETWORKS

This message is being taken literally by many of the state's own bodies, such as ministries, including the People's Liberation Army (PLA) under the Ministry of Defense. Since the late 1980s, the State Council has made it clear to these organizations they must rely far less on central funding and far more on self-financing efforts. The resources under the command of numerous state bodies, which include skilled technical staff, research and development laboratories, manufacturing establishments, and maintenance and repair work shops, represent enormous business opportunities. In the field of telecommunications the main resources comprise of (a) private landline and microwave networks operated, for example, by the military, the Ministry of Railways, the Energy Ministry, among others; (b) skilled electronic engineers and research institutes; (c) factories and workshops; and (d) the right to use certain radio frequencies. As I pointed out at the beginning of this chapter, nonpublic networks account for around 40% of China's network capacity.

The State Council has decreed that national public telecommunications network design, development, and management is the responsibility of the Ministry of Posts and Telecommunications. It has also reserved the 900

MHz waveband for public cellular radio-mobile communications under the control of the MPT and its provincial bureaus. This is the European standard TACS or Total Access Communications System. The 800 MHz waveband, using the American standard AMPS or Advanced Mobile Phone System, is allocated for private network use only, although five of the poorest provinces in China's Northwest have been given permission to use second-hand AMPS equipment (supplied by AT&T) for public service. Nordic Mobile Telephone or NMT 450 is also in use in the western provinces.[4] Wavebands between 100 and 200 MHz are reserved for paging services, and again, in theory, public paging services were the responsibility of the MPT and its affiliates.

However, the picture is changing. China's push toward the communications age, if not exactly toward the information age as yet, is giving non-public network operators an argument to place their resources at the disposal of the public— a nice business proposition for them and a way to achieve a rapid expansion of public service at low capital cost. The major beneficiary has been the People's Liberation Army (PLA), which was given the green light to offer public services on the 800 MHz waveband.

PAGING

As in other countries, in China the road of entry into the public telecommunications network business lies in radio-based services because (a) although the capital cost of setting up the core of a microwave network may not be cheaper than a hardwired PSTN switch (base stations especially remain an expensive component of any system), the problems of constructing the local loop disappear; (b) spectrum use is usually regulated more flexibly than fixed-line network construction and operating licenses; (c) demand for the mobile functionality is high; and (d) radio-based services are usually helping to open up new markets and are therefore regarded as less of an immediate threat to PSTN operators, and, of course, they bring interconnect revenues to the PSTN operators.

Spectrum in China is regulated overall by the Radio Regulation Commission, which reports directly to the State Council. It also has offices

---

[4]As a general rule, the lower the frequency, the wider the coverage area but also the lower the system's circuit radio capacity. In thinly populated rural areas, low frequencies, such as 450MHz, can provide cheaper coverage. In densely populated urban areas, higher frequencies, such as 800MHz and 900MHz, cater to greater numbers of subscribers, but at the cost of more cells or base stations. As the system's capacity is reached, more subscribers can only be accommodated by adding more cells to the system, reducing the coverage area of each cell. Radio-compression techniques can squeeze on more subscribers, but at the risk of cross-talk interference, and yet higher frequencies such as 1.5 GHz and above, will be made available for digital and personal communications networks (PCNs).

at all provincial levels. Historically however, many state bodies have been using certain wavebands, including the bodies mentioned earlier. The first area of entry, the point of least resistance, was in paging. From 1984 China has been operating paging networks—originally through the provincial PTTs, but in recent years numerous organizations with spectrum at their disposal have entered the market. They have approached this cautiously because they are mostly dependent on the MPT and PTTs for leased circuits and there have been cases where the local PTT have simply cut their lines.

The largest, and most powerfully positioned, organization in this regard is the PLA, which can often secure spectrum from the local Radio Regulation Commission if it does not already control it. The PLA also has landlines and microwave circuits of its own to back up its paging networks. It also has many business units strung across its organization, some with a presence in every major city, others less ubiquitous. Each business unit can, and increasingly does, set up its own paging service.

But other bodies, like the Ministry of Railways, provincial Governments, and provincial Radio Commissions, are also setting up paging companies, however, some city Governments are very liberal in their licensing of paging companies, while others, such as Shanghai, are much more conservative. Often paging businesses come into operation as long as no one objects and licenses are then issued retrospectively. The rules tend to be written as the commercial opportunities arise, but the name of the game is to do it quietly, without drawing too much attention to one's self and with out aggressively challenging existing operators. As always in China, informal personal networking between the key players is necessary to establish trust and mutual interest. So long as no one is seen to lose out—and in a rapidly expanding market this condition is quite easily met—obstacles to a business venture can be removed. The result is that China today has more than 18 million pagers in use, up from 400,000 in 1991 (MPT, 1993), and waiting lists run into hundreds of thousands.

Because most mainland bodies do not have experience or expertise in setting up paging operations or managing them, many of them have turned to Hong Kong companies to provide turnkey operations with ongoing technical and managerial assistance. Joint ventures; that is, equity-sharing businesses, are not officially permitted in China's telecommunications networks yet, so another form of business cooperation is being used that involves revenue sharing.

The pager in China is both a complement and a quasi-substitute for access to the PSTN. Quasi in the sense that access to the PSTN is still desirable, but in the meantime numeric pagers can deliver simple messages with the help of code books. The Chinese alphanumeric pager can go further with word display, and also has the functionality of providing a mailbox service. The paging market, therefore, represents the first stage in the opening of China's telecommunications networks to international involvement.

MOBILE PHONES

The cellular mobile market promises to be the second broadening area. The demand for cellular telephones has rocketed in China, far outstripping the MPTs original forecasts for 1995 of 30,000 subscribers. The current total is nearly 3 million, about half of which are in use in Guangdong province just to the North of Hong Kong. The demand is such that even at official prices of handsets and registration fees of upwards of US$3,000 (using the exchange rate of RMB$8 = US$1) and the monthly service charge starting at US$18, there are long waiting lists and a flourishing black market. The areas most open to the world economy exhibit the strongest growth rates, but every city and large town across China is either building or has plans to build networks

Until recently only the PTTs could officially operate mobile telephone networks, using the 900 MHz waveband, but so profitable are these networks, and capital costs recovered so quickly from the sale of handsets at marked up prices, that other Chinese enterprises with spare cash are entering lease back arrangements with PTTs to take advantage of the revenues to be earned. The PTTs are setting up subsidiary companies to administer the growth of mobile communications, and in turn this creates a cohort of telecommunications engineers and managers who are experiencing and learning for the first time how to respond to a demand-led market. The earliest projections of the MPT arose in an era when supply was still organized in terms of centrally administered planning targets, very much as the national targets for the PSTN are still determined. Market-Driven realities have broken through the forecast, and the message from Deng Xiaoping has sanctioned the shift toward a totally commercial approach in the field of mobile telephones.

Up-to-date mobile networks have been built on a turnkey basis, with Ericsson, especially in the South, and Motorola, especially in the East, dominating the markets. Alternative digital cellular standards are currently being researched, and many companies are providing the MPT with demonstrations of their equipment The pan-European Groupe Speciale Mobile or GSM standard is the first to be adopted, and the Chinese are watching developments in Hong Kong and Western Europe with keen interest.

Two further issues, however, have arisen. One is the growing interest in the American technology known as Code Division Multiple Access (CDMA), as an alternative to the existing Time Division Multiple Access (TDMA) technology that is used to splice together many different voice channels to provide maximum efficiency in the usage of the available radio spectrum. CDMA promises to be more efficient and cheaper than TDMA. Should China postpone its decision to adopt a second digital standard? It is unlikely, because China also wishes to develop as soon as possible, through technology transfer, its own capacity to manufacture high quality digital equipment. On the other hand, China's neighbor, Korea, has opted to develop CDMA, so the question will remain open. The second issue is the decision by the State Council in September 1993 to affirm the right by the PLA to manage all radio spectrum set aside for military allocations. What this means in practice is that the PLA has increased its authority to manage for business purposes frequencies that it controls but may no longer need for purely military purposes. This includes allocations within the 800MHz frequencies, and there is speculation that eventually AMPS, and digital AMPS, networks may also be permitted as a standard in public cellular systems.

Now that the Chinese have decided to press ahead with GSM—Guangdong was the first province to adopt GSM in 1994—they will be insisting on a high degree of technology transfer. They see the development of a digital technological capability as being central to their national program of high technology development, which includes their military capability. Joint ventures and wholly owned semiconductor plants, microwave equipment manufacturing, and digital handset production will all figure high in the requirements they place on foreign companies wishing to sell equipment in China. Another factor will be their efforts to join the WTO. Freeing up imports will have a dangerous effect on the balance of trade, so insistence on local sourcing and manufacture is likely to increase.

The rapid fall in equipment, especially handset, prices may well extend the product life cycle of the analogue systems in China for a decade, but as the market-oriented economic reforms continue an accumulation of relative wealth among the new Chinese middle class is bound to create a demand for the latest, most up-to-date consumer goods and technologies. The messaging service available with GSM, for example, is a widely quoted advantage about which telecommunications engineers in China are enthusiastic.[5] In a country that still has very few residential phone lines, a messaging service adds considerable value to the product.

Entry into the public cellular telephone market was restricted to the PTAs, but the recent creation of a second telecommunications carrier—Lian-Tong or China Unicom (see below)—is now providing local competition in Beijing, Guangzhou, Shanghai, Tianjin, and several other cities in the GSM service. The PLA has also secured agreement from the MPT to interconnect its 800 MHz waveband systems to a public service, and if this were to become widespread, overnight it could greatly increase capacity.[6]

If this development happens, the opportunities for foreign companies with capital, equipment, systems expertise, operations experience, and managerial know-how will more than match those in the paging market. It also raises the possibility of a digital AMPS standard being introduced along

---

[5]Based on interviews conducted in China by the author.

[6]A comprehensive statement about the involvement of non-MPT bodies in China public networks, fixed-wire and mobile, was given by Vice-Minister Yang Xianzu (Yang, 1993).

side a GSM standard at some stage. Such a move would replicate the situation in Hong Kong would be logical.

I have hinted at the development of a form of competition emerging at the provincial level between operators of AMPS and TACS systems. Along the same lines, but more important, is the possible emergence of local competition between digital AMPS, CDMA, and GSM, and future competition within cities from personal communications systems technologies. This competition, already emerging, is not between private and public bodies but between a national ministry, its provincial administrations, and different sets of competing ministries and state enterprises. It is interesting to speculate how far this represents the emergence of a viable alternative model, one in which the national state maintains an interest in all the competing groups to safeguard what it sees as a national interest, while promoting consumer interests and offering a wider scope for foreign participation. Against this view is the argument that competition between state-controlled bodies will maximize duplication and bureaucratic inefficiencies, not consumer welfare.

Before leaving our discussion of mobile telephones, we should note that CT2 or "telepoint" technology, a transitional technology which in Hong Kong has already passed its peak, was a partial success in China. As Ingelbrecht (1993) reported, about 12 cities installed systems. Motorola led the way with the first network in Shenzhen in 1992, where capital costs were recouped within months through the sale of handsets which commanded premium prices. This underscored the popularity of mobile functionality and of the pent-up demand for access to the PSTN either directly through a mainline or indirectly through a mobile telephone of some sort. But Chinese telecommunications engineers were divided about the wisdom of investing too heavily in a transitionary technology, and the future rather belongs to cellular and future personal communications.

FIXED-WIRE TELEPHONE NETWORKS

Similar reforms are pressing at the national level where the MPT is responsible for all long-distance and international traffic. The first step toward a financially independent and customer-responsive telecommunications administration in China is the separation of the regulatory and operational functions of the MPT (Ure, 1992). This was formally approved by the State Council in 1994, and the Directorate-General of Telecommunications, or DGT, which was the operational arm of the MPT, has been given state enterprise status, the Chinese equivalent of corporatizing national telecommunications.

An equally dramatic development has been the State Council's approval for what, in effect, amounts to two second networks allowing other ministries to make their private networks available for pubic operations.These include the General Command of the PLA under the

Ministry of Defense, the Ministries of Aerospace, Energy and Railways, and the Ministry of Electronic Industries (MEI), which already competes through its hundreds of affiliate factories with the MPT to produce telecommunications equipment.

The State Council has sanctioned two new entrants. Ji-Tong, a corporation set up by the MEI and that includes shareholders ranging from provincial Governments in Guangdong and Jiangsu to CITIC, and to other Ministries, such as Energy, which will focus on equipment manufacturing and offering radio-based communications such as VSAT services and local trunked radio services by leasing capacity from private networks owned by other Ministries. In addition, Lian-Tong (also known as Unicom), which has been established with the Ministries of Electronics, Energy and Railways as share holders, will provide long-distance optical-fiber routes along railway tracks, offering voice and data services, and will build local loop voice networks and cellular mobile telephone systems. Lian-Tong launched its first GSM mobile networks during 1995.

The introduction of these complimentary networks, which of course threaten to develop into competing networks, has obvious advantages to a country so short on switching and transmission capacity. One advantage of separating the MPT as regulator from the MPT as operator is that the problems of coordinating the introduction of these second networks could be dealt with by a body that is seen to be impartial and can focus exclusively on the problems. Unfortunately, that seems unlikely for the foreseeable future as the MPT behaves like a traditional monopolist, defending its territory and putting up obstacles to market entry. For a developing country the key issue is the generation of revenues to fund basic telecommunications in remote and underserviced areas. Competition that lowers prices substantially may generate more funds if the demand for telecommunications services proves price to be elastic, but the subsequent distribution of those funds between networks and the allocation of them within networks is not guaranteed to meet national needs.

On a methodological note, I do not think that traditional economist's tools of price and income elasticity are adequate ways of measuring the responsiveness of the demand for telecommunications. First, the economies of scope associated with a modern telecommunications service make it increasingly difficult to separate out the demand for any one service. Second, the nature of demand itself is changing in various ways. Technically, there are structural changes in the relationship between the demand for, price, quality, accessibility, and so on of telecommunications services. Especially important is the changing role of telecommunications within modern economies. Telecommunications is no longer just an infrastructure providing a communications scaffolding around a building containing the economy; rather, it has become part of the building itself, literally in the case of so-called intelligent buildings (see Huber, 1987).

Telecommunications services are part of the productive input to the value-added process of business, and the demand for them cannot be measured simply by responses to changes in their price. Having said all that, an approximate answer could be offered: Overall demand in the richer regions is likely to be, or to become, price-inelastic, but between networks price could be very important. In remote regions, after the issue of access is solved, I suspect income to be a more important factor than price.

We now return to the issue of alternative networks: Lian-Tong may find it very difficult to break into the national long-distance market, but at the provincial level competing networks could emerge. This would dovetail into the possibility of town, city, and province-level alternative cellular mobile networks and would represent a very interesting experimental form of competition within the framework of overall state control. If the immediate aims are to increase capacity as fast as possible to meet planning targets, to improve the quality and range of services, and to encourage foreign network investment, then an experiment along these lines has much to recommend it. There is no doubt that the increase in China's telecommunications markets will be more than sufficient to sustain two interconnecting PSTN networks.

In principle, the same story as regards the opportunities such a development would open up for foreign companies supplying equipment, capital, and know-how holds true here as for paging and mobile communications. The additional twist in the PSTN network comes in the area of data and value-added service provision. Although this is one area the MPT has identified where it would welcome overseas expertise and investment, it is an area in which a market-led demand is less certain, and therefore the associated risks are higher.

CABLE TV

This is a related area of interest, and always a possible long-run vehicle for entry into telecommunications. Several agreements have already been reached, or are under negotiation, between Hong Kong companies and Chinese cities. China is acutely aware of the challenge from international satellite broadcasters, and has opted to vastly expand its own satellite broadcast and cable distribution systems (Zhou, 1992). China is also aware that its programming cannot compete for audience attention.

Although the Ministry of Radio, Film, and Television insists foreign direct investment is disallowed in China's burgeoning cable-TV networks, there would seem to be few clearly defined rules governing its development, even in terms of the division of responsibilities between the MPT and the broadcasting Ministry. Declarations by the State Council imposing bans and restrictions on satellite dishes to keep out uncensored foreign broadcasts seem to point toward a highly protectionist posture, but few observers inside China seem to believe that the ban is sustainable. Instead, China is following the Singapore model by building cable networks to control the inflow of broadcasts—at least that seems to be the top down logic coming from Beijing, but at the provincial and local levels the motivations are, as ever, less clear. Certainly this vast expansion of cable television will create an enormous demand for Chinese programming, and perhaps even more if these networks are of sufficient quality to provide online services, including telecommunications.

CONCLUSION

As Drucker (1993) observed:

> China is likely to be the first country where the balance of payments rather than the balance of trade is the key to economic relations. Indeed China may be the first country to be integrated into the world economy through services rather than through trade in goods. (p. 6)

His argument is that China will emerge as a strong manufacturer, but remain weak as a service provider and rely heavily on imports of tradable services, including educational services, health services, financial services, transportation services, and telecommunications and information services. Even allowing for overstatement, the point is made.

China has already responded to the need to import investment and know-how by greatly simplifying at provincial levels the red tape necessary to obtain licenses, permits, exemptions, and so forth. As an example, in Yunnan province "approval for small-to medium-scale enterprises can now be granted in a few weeks or even a few days" (Hong Kong Trade Development Council, 1992, p. 22). This story is now being repeated in many provinces.

Within telecommunications a considerable relaxation has taken place for foreign investors. Previously, overseas companies needed to contact the MPT first and then await permission to approach MPT-affiliated enterprises in provinces to which they were directed. Now, direct approaches are openly encouraged and sought after although the MPT remains the final arbiter. Both Ji-Tong and Lian-Tong now represent an alternative path to joint ventures, the one in data networking and systems integration, the other in carrier networks, although in neither case does China permit foreign direct investment in network ownership or service operations. MEI-affiliated factories are another alternative path to joint ventures and licensing agreements. The rules on wholly owned companies are also being relaxed, and the emerging picture is generally of growing competitiveness between provinces to attract overseas investment.

Finally, it has to be emphasized that doing business in China is a process of patience and commitment to a long-term arrangement of mutual benefit. There are no substitutes for the personal trust and confidence that comes from developing good relations between potential partners, or between overseas investors and state officials. There is little commercial law, and still less experience of working within it. China is a developing country with enormous achievements already to its credit, but with much to learn. Foreign companies, however, also have much to learn—and some ways are harder than others.

REFERENCES

Business briefing. (1994, February 17). *Far Eastern Economic Review*, p. 58.

Conroy, R. (1992). *Technological change in China*. Paris: OECD.

Drucker, P. (1993, March 4). China's growth area, the service sector. *Asian Wall Street Journal*, p. 6.

Hong Kong Trade Development Council. (1992, December). *Market report on Yunnan province*. Hong Kong: Author.

Huber, P. (1987). *The geodesic network: 1987 report on competition in the telephone industry*. Washington, DC: U.S. Department of Justice Antitrust Division.

Ingelbrecht, N. (1993, December). CT2 shows strong promise in China, Hong Kong. *Asia-Pacific Telecommunications*, p. 9.

International Monetary Fund. (1993). *World economic outlook*. Washington, DC: Author.

International Telecommunication Union. (1993). *Asia-Pacific telecommunication indicators*. Geneva: Author.

Lardy, N. (1994). *China in the world economy*. Washington, DC: International Institute of Economics.

Ministry of Posts & Telecommunications. (1993). *China posts and telecommunications*. Beijing: Author.

Phone galore in cities. (1994, February 8). *China Daily*, p. 3.

State Statistical Bureau. (1993). *China statistical yearbook 1993*. Beijing: China Statistical Press.

Telecom expansion unabated. (1993, February 21). *China Business Weekly*, p. 8.

The MPT to further speed up the communication construction to meet the reform and opening requirement. (1992). *China Telecommunications Construction*, 4(4), 3-5.

Twenty more satellites planned by 2000. (1993, February 15). *China Daily*, p. 1.

Ure, J. (1991). *China report*. New York: Northern Business Information.

Ure, J. (1992). The new era in telecommunications. *China Telecommunications Construction*, 4(6), 53-56.

Ure, J. (Ed.). (1995). *Telecommunications in Asia: Policy, planning and development.* Hong Kong: Hong Kong University Press.

Xiong, B. (1993). *The present and the future of telecommunications in China.* Paper presented to the 5th International Conference, Institute for Posts and Telecommunications Policy, Tokyo, Japan.

Yang, X. (1993, May). *The development and reforming of telecommunications in China.* Paper presented at the ITU Asia Telecom '93, Policy Symposium, Singapore.

Zhou, Z. (1992). A discussion of Chinese strategies and tactics for developing radio and television technology in the 1990s. *International Broadcast Information, 6*(12), 66-69.

Zita, K. (1987). *Modernizing China's telecommunications.* Hong Kong: The Economist Intelligence Unit/Business International.

CHAPTER 12

THE IMPACT OF FOREIGN LINKAGES ON TELECOMMUNICATIONS AND DEVELOPMENT IN CHINA

ZIXIANG (ALEX) TAN

INTRODUCTION

The Third Plenum of the 11th Congress of the Chinese Communist Party (CCP) in December 1978 was a milestone in contemporary Chinese history. It was at this conference that economic development replaced class struggle as the "Central Target" of the whole country. A large set of reform policies were designed to attack the stagnant Chinese economy. More importantly, "Openness to the Outside World" was proposed as part of the reform package.

As a result of the "open door" policy, China's economic ties with foreigners have been dramatically growing since 1978. Imports and exports, as well as direct foreign investment and various collaborations between China and its foreign partners, have all increased dramatically.

Telecommunications is one of the few sectors that enjoy priority attention from both the Chinese and foreigners. Since the 1980s, a large number of central office switching systems, Private Automatic Branch Exchanges (PABXs), and transmission systems and terminal equipment have been imported to modernize the out-of-date telephone networks in China. Generous collaboration arrangements, including technology transfers and joint ventures, have been made. One indication of China's importance to foreigners is their establishment of representative offices in China in the 1980s. AT&T, Motorola, Northern Telecom, NEC, Fujitsu, Alcatel, Ericsson, Phillips, and Siemens are among them. More importantly, they all have at least one type of collaboration with their Chinese partners, with the exception of direct selling—this situation has pushed China's telecommunications sector into an intensive linkage with foreigners.

As part of the country's strategic infrastructure, telecommunications plays a fundamental role in China's economic, sociocultural, and political development. Foreign linkages have helped to shape China's telecommunications infrastructure and have also had a profound influence on economic and social change in Chinese society. Little research has yet been done to examine the impact of foreign linkages on telecommunications in China. Based on the general theoretical framework and experience in other developing countries, this chapter first analyzes China's policy, the international environment, and current foreign linkages. Further discussion is devoted to the impact of these foreign linkages on the growth of the indigenous telecommunications industry and on the social and economic development in China.

THEORETICAL BACKGROUND

Foreign linkages can take many forms, including government agreements, information exchanges, and personal exchanges. This chapter concentrates on China's economic linkages with transnational and multinational corporations (referred to as "foreign companies'" or "foreigners" in this chapter). The linkages consist of direct selling, investment, and various other economic and technological collaborations.

China's adoption of an open-door policy created a significant role for foreigners in its economic and social life; however, the role of foreign linkages in the economic and social development of developing countries is controversial (United Nations 1974). Most economists in the Western world still claim that the role of foreign linkages is positive in terms of economic effects and that negative effects exist only in the political area. This is an oversimplification of the reality. Such a view needs a thorough reexamination in light of increased understanding of foreign linkages in developing countries (United Nations, 1978).

The reasoning behind the positive economic role of foreign linkages is straightforward. Economic development in developing countries creates a demand for finance, technology, management skills, and foreign market access. Many of these factors cannot be obtained domestically by developing countries. Linkages with foreigners can create a channel to meet these needs. In many cases, foreigners' contributions are of strategic importance because they help to overcome domestic scarcity and bottlenecks in crucial areas. What has happened in the Chinese telecommunications sector in recent years strongly supports this reasoning. Foreign financial and technical involvement has greatly helped in updating China's backward telephone networks in just 10 years—a task that would have definitely taken several decades if the Chinese had worked alone.

This view of a positive economic role has been questioned by some economists, however, especially those in developing countries. The financial contribution of foreigners to host countries has been debated for several reasons. In many cases, foreigners are blamed for taking more money out of the country than they bring in. Foreign finance, to some extent, contributes to unreasonable inflation in host countries. Furthermore, a huge foreign debt may bring the host country economic difficulties or even cause it to collapse. This chapter does not examine these issues in further detail; however, the negative effects of foreign financial involvement are supported by the experience of some Latin American countries (Areskoug, 1976).

The technological contribution of foreigners to host countries has also been questioned. The first question is whether technology has actually been transferred, as many foreigners are reluctant to give technology to others for profit and competitive reasons. Even in those cases where technology is transferred, its suitability is arguable. The technology may be ill-suited for host countries because it is designed for the original developed countries. The host countries may not possess the basic materials and technologies to effectively utilize the transferred technology. More importantly, the limited absorption capacity of host countries often prevents the successful transfer of technology. These questions cast heavy doubt on the technological contribution of foreign linkages.

Similar arguments can be applied to other economic contributions brought in by foreign linkages. The complete picture of foreign linkages, therefore, is not entirely positive as far as economic effects are concerned. It suggests that final results depend on many factors, including the policies of host countries and their negotiations with foreigners.

The political role of foreign linkages is usually taken as negative because of its historical relationship to the political subversion of host countries and the imperialism of foreign countries. At the present time, foreign companies tend to align with local groups that advocate policies that are favorable to foreigners. This alignment puts foreigners in direct conflict with other local groups that oppose those favorable policies. Foreign linkages may play a positive role when foreigners are aligned with local groups that represent the interests of the host country. Unfortunately, in many cases foreigners' interests are opposite to those of the host country.

In China, foreigners are sympathetic to economic reform. Most of them are aligned with reformers because they see economic reform and open-door policies creating opportunities and markets for them. Meanwhile, foreign companies are in favor of keeping a normal relationship between their home countries and China despite the political and ideological differences, because this is the precondition for them to remain in China. In one example, a group of U.S. companies with business in China fought with U.S. politicians for China's "most-favored-nation" status. This shows that China's foreign linkages can play a positive political role in its development.

Another important concern of host developing countries is the social and cultural influences brought in by foreign linkages. Foreigners tend to propagate, through language and behavior, the social and cultural values of the society from which they come. They are commonly blamed for contaminating local culture with egotism, acquisitiveness, aggressiveness, and economic corruption (Wang, 1984). The clash of foreign cultures with those host countries results in many negative effects in the social and cultural area in host developing countries. Local people may try to pursue unrealistic foreign living standards; their attitude toward society and family may thus be negatively affected, causing instability in host societies.

It cannot be denied that some positive social and cultural influences have been brought in by foreigners. Modernization in developing countries also includes social and cultural reform. In many developing countries, a change from lethargic and fatalistic to progressive and achievement-oriented attitudes may be credited to the global reach of transnational corporations (Wang, 1984). In China, this positive social and cultural role of foreign linkages has also been realized. Although the Chinese are trying to resist the negative effects of what they refer to as "spirit contamination," they are also encouraged to learn from foreign cultures in order to fight feudalism.

These arguments suggest both positive and negative roles of foreign linkages in economic, political, social, and cultural areas in host developing countries. This theoretical framework provides a basis for analyzing and understanding China's open-door policy and foreign linkages in depth.

CHINA'S POLICIES AND STRATEGIES REGARDING FOREIGN LINKAGES

China's achievements over its more than 2000-year history have instilled in the Chinese a sense of exaggerated self-confidence. A deep-rooted belief in the superiority of the Chinese over foreigners made the Chinese view themselves as the center of the world and as standard setters, preventing them from learning from foreigners. Meanwhile, the Chinese government never promoted foreign trade because of its pride in economic self-sufficiency. These two factors contributed to historically weak foreign linkages in China (Wang, 1984).

In the 18th and 19th centuries, the industrial revolution and the accompanying prosperity in the West coincided with decadence and stagnation in China. At this stage, the Chinese government lost the power to decide her own fate. The "open-door" policy initiated by the United States and accepted by other Great Powers forced China to accept unfavorable foreign linkages (Allen & Nonnithorne, 1954). The next 100 years, from 1840 to 1949, saw many foreign linkages imposed mainly by foreigners.

The establishment of the Communist regime in 1949 cut off most foreign linkages, except those with the Soviet Union, because of ideological beliefs and historical experience. Foreign linkages were considered imperialistic, exploitative, unfriendly, and unfair. Following Mao's famous slogan, 'We Chinese should build up our country by ourselves," foreign linkages were never allowed in China's economic and social developments until 1978.

Reform policies of 1978 brought both the adjustment of economic policies and some reexaminations of ideology. One of the most significant theoretical issues was the role of foreign linkages in China's modernization This was tackled primarily from two ideological angles. The first was the recognition of the strategic and fundamental role of foreign linkages in promoting China's modernization in the light of China's backward economy. As asserted by Ma Hong (1983), who was a senior academician and then Director General of the Research Center for Political, Economic, and Social Affairs of the State Council, "Economic reforms and the open door policy nurture each other" (pp. 33-39).

Another reinterpretation was the possibility that the positive role of foreign linkages might outweigh the negative role in China's modernization. According to this opinion, China's linkages with the outside world may bring in finance, technology, management skills, and foreign market access. These benefits may outweigh the negative effects that result from foreign linkages in the economic, political, and sociocultural areas. The point, then, is not whether foreign linkages play a positive or negative role in China's development, but whether they can be utilized to make a positive contribution through appropriate policies.

Following this theoretical change was the assignment of a new role to foreign linkages. 1979 saw many large turnkey projects and the import of finished products. Assembly lines with know-how were features of the early 1980s. Then, foreign linkages evolved to a higher level, focusing on technology transfers, joint ventures, and even joint R&D and marketing. It is very clear that China has been modifying its policy to maximize the positive role of foreign linkages while keeping its foreign partners happy.

Telecommunications has followed this pattern. Since the operation of the first F-150 (the trade name of Fujitsu's central office switching system) exchange from Fujitsu of Japan was inaugurated in Fuzhou city, Fujian province in 1982, numerous switches, transmission systems, and terminals have been imported into China. In the office exchange sector, eight kinds of systems from seven companies have been installed, including all the major exchange systems in the world (He, 1992). Obviously, direct importation is the easy and quick way to update out-of-date Chinese telephone networks. It did make the major contribution to China's 20% annual increase in telephone penetration in the late 1980s. However, direct importation of finished products is not the final way for China to maximize foreign linkages.

In the 1980s, China used procurement as leverage to bargain for technology transfers and joint ventures, referred to by the popular Chinese term "combination of purchasing with technology transfer." Because of the overcapacity of world telecommunications suppliers and fierce competition among them for the market in developing countries in the 1980s, China was in a good position to bargain for technology transfer. 1983 saw China's first success, bringing Alcatel's branch (then ITT's branch) in Belgium into a joint venture to manufacture its S-1240 digital exchange in Shanghai. In the following years, technology transfers and joint ventures were set up in PABXs, digital microwave systems, fiber-optical systems, components, and materials, to name just a few areas. More importantly, Motorola established its solely owned factory in Tianjin in 1992. In February 1993, AT&T signed a Memorandum of Understanding (MOU) with China's State Planning Commission establishing its long-term and large-scale cooperation with China; and Northern Telecom from Canada followed suit. These activities have moved China's foreign linkages to an even more impressive level.

Another movement involves Chinese engineers designing products and seeking foreign companies to manufacture the key components and parts. The products are then assembled in China. Researchers at Tsinghua University in Beijing have successfully cooperated with some Asian companies to manufacture digital multiplexers designed at the university. The products are greatly welcomed in China's market because the domestic designers understand China's market better than foreigners. This is a significant new dimension in foreign linkages that is encouraged by the Chinese government.

Until now, the foreign linkages in telecommunications have been limited to equipment supply and manufacturing—service operations have been strictly closed to foreigners. In reaction to some recent attempts by foreign companies, the Ministry of Posts and Telecommunications (MPT) reiterated its position that "it is necessary to stress that China will not allow any individuals, organizations or companies outside the mainland to manage its public and private networks wire or wireless communications services" (Xie, 1993 p. 1; also see chapter 3, 9, and 11, this volume).

INTERNATIONAL ENVIRONMENT

STRUCTURAL CHANGE IN THE INTERNATIONAL TELECOMMUNICATIONS INDUSTRY

The structure of the international telecommunications equipment and service industry has changed since the late 1970s, when a combination of techno-logical, economic, and regulatory changes occurred (Pisano, Russo, Teece, 1988). These changes have also affected China's foreign linkages with the major international players in telecommunications. Until recently, the world telecommunications industry was organized around domestic markets where there were usually national champions in the equipment sector and domestic monopolists in the service sector; in other words service industries were monopolized by government agencies or companies in almost all countries. These monopolists bought most of their equipment from one or several domestic suppliers. As a result, most manufacturers focused on their domestic markets. For example, AT&T (American Telephone and Telegraph) concentrated in the U.S. market through its manufacturing arm, Western Electric. The Japanese market was controlled by NEC, OKI, Fujitsu, and Hitachi. The German market was dominated by Siemens, the French by Thompson, and the British by GEC and Plessey. Only a few companies, including the former ITT, Ericsson, and Phillips, ventured beyond their domestic equipment markets.

The introduction of liberalization in telecommunications led to the opening of domestic markets to foreign suppliers. Technological advances in microelectronics and the convergence of computers and communications made it possible for other domestic or foreign suppliers to enter the market. The result was increased competition in domestic markets and encouraged internationalization among suppliers (Pisano et al., 1988). Suppliers viewed their penetration in other countries' markets both as the expansion of their business and a strategy for survival.

These changes put telecommunications markets in developing coun-tries on the agenda of most equipment suppliers. Meanwhile, successful economic development in some developing countries, such as Brazil, China, and oil-exporting countries, greatly stimulated their demand for telecommuni-cations equipment. As a result, the major international suppliers were eager to set up linkages with China, either for short- or long-term purposes.

ROLES OF FOREIGN GOVERNMENTS

Telecommunications is viewed as a strategic infrastructure in most devel-oped countries. In many countries telecommunications companies are among the largest enterprises; examples include AT&T in the United States,

Siemens in Germany, and NEC in Japan. Traditionally, such companies have a strong influence and lobbying power with their own governments.

Most governments provide huge subsidies for research and development to maintain the competitive edge of their domestic telecommunications suppliers. Grupp and Schnoering (1992) conducted a comprehensive study on R&D in telecommunications concluded that national governments accounted for a high percentage of the total R&D expenditure in civil telecommunications in 1987, ranging from 27% in Italy and 25% in Spain to 8% in the UK and 4% in Japan. In addition, governments also use their procurement power to protect the market share of domestic suppliers.

On the international level, the interests of governments are often combined with the goals of companies. As far as linkages with China are concerned, the diplomatic and political policies of foreign governments toward China obviously have a direct influence on their telecommunications companies because normal diplomatic relationships pave the way for business connections; however, trade policy is even more important. Most exporting countries, with the exception of the United States, have created special trade financing packages to promote telecommunications exports to China (Zita, 1987). The packages often take the form of grants or soft loans, and Ministries of Foreign Affairs usually work as administrators. Grants come directly from the development aid budget of foreign governments and soft loans are usually a mixture of development aid with credits from commercial banks. These packages are negotiated to partially finance exports or joint ventures.

The role of special financing packages cannot be overemphasized. Because China has limited internal finances to provide a desperately needed update to its telecommunications infrastructure, favorable financing aid packages give foreign companies critical power to obtain contracts. Huge Japanese credits from the Overseas Economic Cooperations Fund (OECF) greatly helped NEC and Fujitsu to expand their markets in China. The sale of switching equipment from Alcatel's Spanish branch, SESA, to four western provinces in 1992 strongly reflected the effect of special financial aid from the Spanish government, given SESA's traditionally weak competitive capacity in China. The active role of foreign governments can also been found in many other telecommunications projects in China.

THE OBSTACLE OF COCOM EXPORT CONTROL

It was not surprising to hear a junior engineer in a small telecommunications company in China talks about the Coordinating Committee for Multilateral Export Control (COCOM). The real impact of COCOM on China's economic and technological development was so pervasive that it was viewed as a ghost in China's linkages with foreigners

COCOM grew out of the Cold War. Rooted in NATO (the North Atlantic Treaty Organization), COCOM was initially formed by 14 of the 15 NATO countries, with Iceland being the exception. Japan joined COCOM in 1951, Spain in 1985, and Australia in 1989, giving COCOM a total of 17 members. Although COCOM was mainly controlled by the United States, its chairperson had always been an Italian civil servant.The COCOM dissolved in March 1994, and was replaced with a new organization that will have less power over its member countries over high-tech exports.

COCOM was formed to protect the West by preventing the export of technology to the East that might be put to military use. China, along with the former Soviet Bloc, was included in the East. COCOM's main task was to compile the prohibition lists of technology and equipment including telecommunications materials, that were not allowed to be exported to East. Its job also included evaluating individual applications, arranging agreements on strategic criteria for export controls, and coordinating enforcement efforts (MacDonald, 1990). Whether COCOM achieved its goal of preventing the export of potential military technology to the East is controversial. However, its role in China's linkages with foreigners, especially COCOM members, was profound in the telecommunications area.

First, COCOM's regulations, to some extent, discouraged China's linkages with COCOM members. Although most technology and equipment at the low end could be provided domestically, what China was searching for from abroad was usually on COCOM's prohibition list. Foreign companies either could not obtain export licenses or had to wait several years to get a license application—the outcome was either a direct cut off of the linkages or loss of patience on both sides.

Second, COCOM partially contributed to distorted foreign linkages in China. Because COCOM prevented China from acquiring the advanced technology and equipment from its member countries, China had to buy them from non-COCOM members. This often meant a sacrifice in quality for the Chinese, but it was better than nothing. In some situations, technology and equipment might be exported to China through a third country. In both cases, it was COCOM that forced China to shift its linkages from COCOM members to a third country. One example was a report that China imported high-speed optical communication terminals from an Israeli company instead of AT&T simply because AT&T could not acquire an export license.

Third, COCOM's control might have helped spur China's domestic efforts. Because COCOM's export controls had made foreign technology and equipment more difficult to acquire, China was encouraged to develop technology independently. COCOM's "total blocking" of China's access to advanced technology forced China to choose self-development and self-sufficiency as the only means to evolve into an economically and technologically advanced country. Meanwhile, independent development resulted in independent technical standards, which increased the difficulties of linking China with foreign countries. As a result of COCOM's dissolution, the above-mentioned distortion will be gradually corrected. However, it will take time.

CURRENT MAIN LINKAGES WITH WESTERN COUNTRIES

Since China opened its door to the outside world, telecommunications has been a priority for expansion. A variety of equipment was imported and many joint ventures and technology transfers were concluded.

CENTRAL OFFICE EXCHANGES AND PABXS

Central Office exchanges are the largest communications item imported into China. From the time that Fujitsu installed the first digital office exchange in Fuzhou in 1982 to the end of 1992, 5.5 million lines of imported digital office exchanges have been installed in China. These exchanges consisted of eight systems from seven companies, including all the major suppliers in the world. Their market shares are shown in Table 12.1.

China's office exchange market was dominated by the Japanese suppliers NEC and Fujitsu at first. Alcatel has caught up recently. This is partially because of its joint venture—Shanghai Bell Telephone Equipment Manufacturing Company (SBTEMC). Jointly owned by the China Postal and Telecommunications Industry Corporation (PTIC), Alcatel-Bell Telephone in Belgium, and the Belgian government, SBTEMC is the first large joint venture

Table 12.1. Market Share of Office Exchange by the End of 1992.

Company	Headquartered Country	System Type	Market Share (%)
Alcatel[a]	France	S-1240,E10	50.0
Ericsson	Sweden	AXE-10	16.7
NEC	Japan	Neax-61	12.0
Northern Telecom	Canada	DMS	8.3
Fujitsu	Japan	F-150	8.1
Siemens	Germany	EWSD	2.9
AT&T	USA	5ESS	2.0

Note. Data compiled from He (1992).
[a]Including products from the joint venture: Shanghai Bell Telephone Equipment Manufacturing Company.

in China's telecommunications industry (Mai, 1990). SBTEMC signed its contract in July 1983 and began to successfully install its products in 1985. It is now the largest domestic supplier of office exchanges in China.

In October 1988, a contract for another joint venture, the Beijing International Switching System Company Ltd. (BISSC), was signed in Beijing. The German side of this Sino-German joint venture is Siemens Company, which assumed 40% of the registered capital. The remaining 60% of capital came from the Beijing Wired Communications Factory, the Beijing Syndicated Investment Company, and the Beijing Telecommunications Administration of MPT. BISSC's products have also been recently installed in China.

Two joint ventures in office exchanges were the initial goals of the policy makers in China. However, the line was broken down first by NEC of Japan when it finalized a joint venture agreement with Tianjin 1990 to produce its NEAX-61 office switching system. The signing of a MOU in 1993 between AT&T and the State Planning Commission of China opened the possibility of jointly producing AT&T's 5ESS in Qingdao, Shandong province, and Northern Telecom has set up their joint venture in Guangdong province.

The establishment of five joint ventures raised the issue of excluding other foreign suppliers from the Chinese market or at least shrinking their market shares. Although the Chinese themselves believe that the large demand will be met both by direct imports, and by joint ventures and domestic suppliers in the near future, the role of joint ventures will definitely be strengthened as they mature.

The potentially large market in China for PABXs was recognized in the middle of the 1980s when many domestic suppliers were searching for ties with foreign partners. In order to maximize the impact of foreign linkages, government agencies coordinated negotiations. The outcome was nine collaboration arrangements in the form of either technology transfers or joint ventures, as shown in Table 12.2 (Marketing Department of World Telecommunications, 1991).

China's PABX market is dominated currently by those suppliers with foreign linkages; however, most products are still in the form of Semi-Knocked Down (SKD) or Completely Knocked Down (CKD) assembling. Local absorption capacity is seriously handicapped by China's underdeveloped Integrated Circuit (IC) industry.

TRANSMISSION SYSTEMS

Digital microwave systems are still a growing market in China—all of the high-performance systems are directly imported from foreign suppliers, including Siemens-GTE, Alcatel-TELETTRA, NEC, and Harris. NEC has transferred its 34Mb/s and 140Mb/s technology to the Beijing Radio Factory of MPT and the Guilin Radio Factory. In the satellite communication area, the

Table 12.2. Collaboration Agreements In China's PABXs Area.

Foreign partner	Chinese partner	Equipment Type	Cooperative form
Harris of USA	Guangzhou Telecom Factory	Harris 20-20	Technology Transfer
Siemens Germany	Beijing No. 239 Shanghai Xingquang	Hicom 300 Transfer	Technology
NEC of Japan	Benxi Telecom Equip. Company	HJC-SDS	Technology Transfer
GPT of the UK	Shanghai Telephone Equip. Ltd.	ISDX	Joint Venture
Ericsson of Sweden	Beijing Telecom Factory (No. 738)	MD110	Technology Transfer
Northern Telecom of Canada	China Tongquang Beidian Ltd.	MLS-1	Joint Venture
TAI of USA	Tianjin Tianzhi	MSX	Joint Venture
Phillips of Netherlands	Zhenhua Col Changde Telecom Suzhou Telecom	SOPHO-S	Technology Transfer
Alcatel Bell Tel. of Belgium	Shanghai Bell Tel Eqpt. Mfg. Co.	SSU-12	Joint Venture

joint venture between Canada's Spar and China's Nanjing Radio Factory has been very successful in producing a variety of earth-station equipment.

The hot area in transmission is fiber-optical systems. As China's local telephone capacity has grown, so has the need for the construction of long-distance trucking lines. By learning from the experience of developed countries, China has decided to use fiber-optical systems as the backbone of its long-distance networks. This is why most of the currently laid, or planned, East-West or North-South lines are using fiber optical systems.

Large-scale applications of fiber-optical systems coincide with foreign linking activities Furukawa Electric of Japan went into a joint venture with the Xian Electrical Cable Factory to manufacture optical fiber and cable in 1985. The Yangtze River Optical Fiber Communication Industry Group in Wuhan also set up China's largest fiber and cable joint venture with Phillips of the Netherlands in 1989. There is also a report that another major Japanese fiber and cable company, Sumitoma, is going to set up a joint venture in Shanxi province.

Optical terminal equipment is also a hot spot, and it is usually bound with general digital transmission equipment, such as Pulse Code Modulation (PCM) multiplex equipment. Alcatel-SEL in Germany started a joint venture with the Tianjin Optical Communication Company in the middle of the 1980s. The beginning of the 1990s saw a boom in joint ventures for optical terminal and general digital equipment. Italtel of Italy extended its cooperation with the Chongqin Telecom Equipment Factory of MPT into a joint venture. AT&T's subsidiary in the Netherlands set up their first joint venture with China in Shanghai, with the Shanghai Optical Communication Company. Fujitsu of Japan has set up a joint venture with the Nanjing Wired Communication Factory. NEC linked up with the Wuhan Yangtze River Optical Fiber Communication Industry Group to jointly produce and market NEC's transmission equipment. It seems as if all of the major transmission equipment suppliers in the world have joint ventures in China.

MOBILE COMMUNICATIONS

China's analog cellular mobile communication market is dominated by equipment imported from Motorola of the United States and Ericsson of Sweden. As part of their competitive strategies, both Motorola and Ericsson have set up further connections with Chinese partners. Except for its solely owned factory in Tianjin that produces integrated circuits (ICs) and mobile products, Motorola entered a joint venture in Hangzhou to produce mobile communication equipment. Ericsson set up a joint venture with the Nanjing Radio Factory to compete with Motorola.

As China adopts the European GSM as its digital cellular standard, many European suppliers such as Alcatel, Siemens, Nokia, and Italtel have entered China's mobile communication equipment market. More importantly, they have all established their joint ventures for GSM equipment in China.

OTHER AREAS

Joint ventures and technology transfers also occurred in areas such as fax machines, telephone sets, key systems, and ICs for telecommunications. More importantly, some foreign manufacturers have been asked to produce Chinese-designed products—this sets a new dimension for foreign linkages. This role will definitely expand as the Chinese and foreigners begin to understand each other more.

Service operation is the only area in China's telecommunications arena where foreign linkages are prohibited instead of promoted. Although recent developments may persuade the Chinese to adjust this policy, their scope will be limited (Tan, 1994).

IMPACTS ON SOCIAL AND ECONOMIC DEVELOPMENT

Increased foreign linkages in China's telecommunications have led to the importing of advanced equipment, transferring of technology, and setting up of joint ventures. These activities bring both positive and negative implications to China, although China has been trying to adjust its policies to maximize the positive side.

DIRECT CONTRIBUTION TO CHINA'S ECONOMIC AND SOCIAL DEVELOPMENT

Foreign linkages have greatly helped China modernize its out-of-date telephone networks. One indication of this is the growth of its annual telephone penetration rate, increased from 9.1% in 1978-1985 to 18.2% in 1986-1988, and to 22% after 1989 (Chen, 1990). Most equipment contributing to this growth was directly imported from foreign suppliers.

Developments in China's telecommunications industry have led to the expansion of related industries. Better telecommunications helped to decrease expenditures on business transactions and increase efficiency and information flow. They were used to replace transportation and save time and energy, which resulted in the improvement of the quality of life, and also helped to attract foreign investment and increase exports. In summary, past experience has led China to the conclusion that telecommunications is strategically important. Encouraging foreign linkages and investment in telecommunications should continue to be a priority in future policy (Chen, 1990).

IMPROVEMENT OF LOCAL MANUFACTURING CAPACITY

China's successful practice of combining direct imports with technology transfer has brought many collaboration agreements to its telecommunications industry. By securing long-term cooperation and complete technology transfer, most collaborations have been turned into joint ventures, mainly because of pressure from the Chinese side. The outcome has been five joint ventures in central office exchanges, nine collaborations in PABXs, five joint ventures in optical and general digital terminals, and a variety of other agreements.

One significant trend has been for joint ventures to share China's high-end market with foreign suppliers. For example, the market share of the joint venture SBTEMC (Shanghai Bell Telephone Equipment Manufacturing Corporation) has increased rapidly in recent years. Many newly constructed trunk lines using optical-fiber systems have employed products from joint ventures. Gradual growth of joint ventures' market share strongly suggests an improvement of local production capacity. Meanwhile, there are reports that Russia and Vietnam have purchased office exchanges from the joint venture SBTEMC. Benefits from foreign linkages will help China to both recapture the domestic market and export telecommunications equipment to its neighboring developing countries.

LOOSE EXPORT CONTROL AND TRANSFER OF MORE ADVANCED TECHNOLOGY

Although export controls, especially from COCOM, are commonly thought to be one of the major obstacles to China's foreign linkages, increased collaboration arrangements have led to looser export controls, the outcome being that more advanced technology may be transferred to Chinese partners. This process is driven mainly by domestic and international forces.

With regard to domestic forces, China has developed its own technology through internal efforts and/or through the indirect help of foreign linkages. COCOM had to update its prohibition list to catch up with the development. In one example, COCOM's list included a 140Mb/s optical system, whereas China could only provide a 34Mb/s system. After China moved to a 140Mb/s system, COCOM updated its list to a 565Mb/s system. This process is partially and indirectly, driven by foreign linkages.

With regard to international forces although some non COCOM member countries benefited from COCOM's export control for their market share in China, the competitive abilities of many member countries were seriously handicapped. Aware of the unfair competition, these concerned companies pushed their governments and COCOM for looser controls. AT&T's chief, Robert Allen, delivered a public speech on the subject when visiting Beijing ("AT&T's Chairman," 1993). "Communications technology is one of the most sharply restricted sectors of U.S. trade, [but] I believe the time has come to change that policy," Allen told a news conference in Beijing. He added that U.S. policy has "hindered" American companies in competing with rival nations' corporations whose governments sometimes place fewer restrictions on high-tech exports. "One way or another the Chinese or any other [nation] will obtain this technology," he said. Given AT&T's importance to American economic and political life, its attitude has definitely put pressure on the export policies of the United States and COCOM.

MORE TECHNOLOGICAL DEPENDENCE ON FOREIGN COUNTRIES

Because of China's poor industrial base and backward general manufacturing capacity, its absorption ability has been seriously weakened. Many products of joint ventures stay at the level of CKD or SKD assembly. It is argued that foreign linkages have created more dependence on foreign technology. Joint ventures are one of the marketing strategies used by foreign suppliers.

Many technologies and parts, such as software and advanced ICs used in office exchanges, will have to be provided by foreigners in the near future. China is trying to reduce its dependence on foreigners by setting up joint ventures for ICs and other basic industries. It will take some time for China to update its basic industries. Elsewhere in the world, some countries such as Korea and Taiwan have succeeded in developing their domestic industries with the help of foreign linkages—many developing countries have failed to achieve this goal. Whether foreign linkages will lead to more dependence or self-development in China remains to be seen; to a large extent, it depends on China's policies and internal efforts.

THE DEMISE OF DOMESTIC R&D AND THE POTENTIAL FOR FUTURE DEVELOPMENT

China used to have well-organized R&D facilities, although they were not highly efficient. Linkages with foreigners brought in a higher level of technology than what those R&D facilities were studying. In China, R&D institutes are separated from manufacturing factories. When foreign linkages turned advanced technologies over to the hands of manufacturing factories, R&D institutes lost their place in the system. Lack of funding and structural obstacles prevented R&D institutes from developing advanced, but expensive, technologies. Meanwhile, the manufacturing factories were reluctant to link up with domestic R&D institutes because buying foreign technology was cheaper and more competitive.

Based on the experiences of Korea and Taiwan, domestic R&D facilities appear to be crucial to long-term growth and development. They contribute to every country's absorptive capacity by providing technical and manpower supports and are also the engine that pushes domestic manufacturers to catch up with developed countries. Will foreign linkages lead to the crash of China's domestic R&D system? Does this create an opportunity that will force China to restructure its relationship between R&D facilities and industry? This is another issue China's policy has to address.

CONCLUSION

China's open-door policies have led to tremendous foreign linkages in its telecommunications industry. The recent economic success makes China the only country with double digit economic growth in the world; this achievement both stimulates China's demand for telecommunications and encourages more foreigners to seize the potential market through further links with their Chinese partners. Meanwhile it also creates a stage for Chinese governments, domestic players, and foreigners to play the cards of international links.

International linkages have made significant positive contributions to China's recent, impressive economic and social development; however, foreign linkages have also had some negative effects. China has been adjusting its policy to make the positive effects outweigh the negative ones. Whether China will realize its own goals—catching up to the advanced countries partially through links with foreigners—remains to be seen.

REFERENCES

Allen G. C., & Nonnithorne, A. G. (1954). *Western enterprise in far eastern economic development: China and Japan.* New York: MacMillan.

Areskoug, K. (1976). Private foreign investment and capital formation in developing countries. *Economic Development and Cultural Change, 24*(3), 539-547.

AT&T's Chairman, Robert Allen, holds its news conference in Beijing. (1993, August 12). *United Press International.*

Chen, Y. Q. (1990). Social economic benefits of telecommunications in People's Republic of China. *China Telecommunications Construction, 2*(3), 3 11.

Grupp, H., & Schnoering, T. (1992). Research and development in telecommunications: National systems under pressure. *Telecommunications Policy, 16*(1), 46-66.

He, Q. (1992). Construction and development of local telephone service in China. *China Telecommunications Construction, 5*(2), 39-41.

Ma, H. (1983). *New strategy for China's economy.* Beijing: New World Press.

MacDonald, S. (1990). *Strategic export controls: Hurting the East or weakening the West?* London: The Economist Publications.

Mai, Z. (1990). The developing Shanghai Bell. *China Telecommunications Construction, 2*(1), 12-18.

Marketing Department of World Telecommunications. (1991). SPC PBXs in China's market. *World Telecommunications, 4*(2), 23-38.

Pisano, G., Russo, M., & Teece, D. (1988). Joint ventures and collaborative arrangements in the telecommunications equipment industry. In D. Mowery, (Ed.), *International collaborative ventures* (pp. 23-69). Cambridge, MA: Ballinger.

Tan, Z. (1994). The challenges to MPT's monopoly. *Telecommunications Policy, 18*(3), 174-181.

United Nations. (1974). *The impact of multinational corporations on development and on international relations.* New York: Author.

United Nations. (1978). *Transnational corporations in world development: A reexamination.* New York: Author.

Wang, N. T. (1984). *China's modernization and transnational corporations.*
    Lexington, MA: Lexington Books.
Xie, L. (1993, May 11). Monopoly of telecom system is reaffirmed. *China
    Daily,* p. 1.
Zita, K. (1987). *Modernizing China's telecommunications: Implications for
    international firms.* London: The Economist Publications.

CHAPTER 13

CREATING A TELECOMMUNICATIONS
FREE TRADE ZONE IN GREATER CHINA

MILTON MUELLER

INTRODUCTION

This chapter addresses two of the broader trends affecting telecommunications and development in China. One is the rapid growth of inter-China trade—it is already commonplace to note that the economies of capitalist Hong Kong and Taiwan and the socialist People's Republic of China (PRC) are becoming increasingly interdependent. A concept of "greater China" has arisen to express the economic integration that has occurred despite the political boundaries which still separate the constituent parts of China. Taken together, greater China is one of the world's largest and most rapidly growing markets. The other trend is the political reunification of Hong Kong and China in 1997, of Macau and China in 1999, and the thawing of relations between Taiwan and the mainland. If this trend continues without disruption (a possibility that is by no means certain), it will represent the final healing of the scars of modernization and foreign encroachment experienced by China during the past century.

These two monumental changes—one essentially economic and the other essentially political—have profound implications for telecommunications policy. In this chapter, I argue that the most constructive way to respond to the challenge of integration is to forge a regional free-trade agreement in telecommunications services. This chapter advances a specific and fairly easy-to-implement policy to bring about the free-trade zone; namely, legalization of simple resale of international private leased circuits (IPLCs). Resale, as the following analysis demonstrates, clears the way for free trade in telecommunication services without requiring drastic legal and regulatory changes or a complete overhaul of the industry's market structure. Such a policy would accelerate development not only in the telecommunications sector, but in the many other economic sectors that rely on a transnational division of labor and information flows across the boundaries of greater China.

The chapter is divided into four parts. The first sketches the background of economic integration and the concomitant growth of telecommunications traffic flows between the entities of greater China. The second describes how international resale has become increasingly popular as a policy to rationalize prices and corrode monopoly power in the telecommunications sector, and sets forth a specific proposal focused on Hong Kong, China, and Taiwan. The third section analyzes the benefits of resale, and critically examines some of the arguments levied against the policy. The last section is an assessment of the political and economic obstacles to a liberalized resale policy, and notes that it is possible to hold both optimistic and pessimistic views about the future viability of free trade in telecommunication services in the region.

TELECOMMUNICATIONS AND ECONOMIC INTEGRATION

Economic theory analyses trade among nations as driven by the mutual gains from trade. A country relatively well-endowed with one factor of production (e.g., capital) will export that factor, and import those factors with which it is less well-endowed (e.g., labor). What Ricardo and other trade theorists did not point out is that these resource exchanges rely on an infrastructure of transport and communication, and must be coordinated by secure and regular information flows. Moreover, more recent analyses of trade note that in advanced economies, international trade in services, including transport and communication, has grown in importance (Drake & Nicolaidis, 1992; Feketekuty, 1988; Melvin, 1989; Riddle, 1986; Sampson & Snape, 1985). The service sector includes such things as banking, accounting, telecommunications, transport, and tourism. Services have different economic characteristics from commodities (Hill, 1977), but, like commodities, they can be subject to trade barriers and run surpluses or deficits (Cheong & Mullins, 1991). Thus, telecommunications is important not only as an input that supports other forms of trade, but as a tradable service itself (Aronson & Cowhey, 1988).

The case of greater China conforms admirably to the expectations of trade theory. Hong Kong and Taiwan have abundant capital resources and financial and managerial services, but labor is relatively scarce. China has abundant and cheap labor but, due to the legacy of a socialist-planned economy, managerial and financial services are primitive, infrastructure is undeveloped and investment capital is scarce. The reform and opening of China after 1978 thus touched off a predictable torrent of trade flows. Hong Kong and Taiwan firms are investing capital and moving labor-intensive production facilities into China. Their relatively developed economies are concentrating on the more skill-intensive processes of product design, testing, marketing, and technical support.

As Hong Kong and Taiwan export materials and components for assembly in China, the demand for telecommunication services between them and the mainland has increased astronomically. The growing number of affluent Chinese consumers import finished consumer goods from Hong Kong and Taiwan, just as the newly developing industries in China import technology and intermediate goods from the West. This has led to a progressive change in the balance of commodity trade, such that China now has a trade deficit with Hong Kong (Sung, 1991).

Indeed, during the first 9 months of 1993, China's overall trade deficit was US$7 billion. The movement of people from Hong Kong into China also has grown rapidly, to the point where statistically, each Hong Kong resident makes an average of three trips to mainland China each year (Sung, 1991). Also stimulating the movement of Chinese people across political boundaries is the greater openness in China and relaxed hostilities between Taiwan and China.

The movement of people, commodities, and capital is directly correlated with changes in telecommunications traffic (Kellerman, 1992; Staple & Mullins, 1989). As noted earlier, the first effect of increased trade is an enormous and sustained increase in the volume of traffic. Telecommunications traffic between Hong Kong and China has doubled every 2 years since 1986 (see Table 13.1). Hong Kong's minutes of outgoing voice telephone calls to China increased by a factor of nine from 1986 to 1991. Fax and data minutes to China increased by a factor of 1,000 during the same 6 years. Taiwan only authorized transit telecommunications traffic to mainland China via Hong Kong, the United States, and Japan in 1989—during the short period since that time, outgoing telephone traffic from Taiwan to the PRC jumped from 3 million minutes in 1989 to 50 million minutes in 1992.

In addition to the volume increase there is a significant change in the structure of the traffic patterns. To begin with, the entities of greater China are communicating with themselves proportionally more than with the rest of the world. As recently as 1986, the United States was Hong Kong's most frequent communication partner, with about 14% of its international volume. During the next 5 years mainland China became the largest single destination of international calls, and now accounts for nearly 40% of the total. Taiwan's percentage also grew relative to North America and Europe. By 1993, mainland China and Taiwan accounted for more than half of all outgoing calls from Hong Kong. In Taiwan, the PRC is already ranked as the fourth most common destination of international telephone calls, behind the United States, Hong Kong, and Japan. It won't be long before it ranks first.

The balance between incoming and outgoing traffic has also changed markedly, moving from a large outgoing surplus for China to a growing outgoing surplus for Hong Kong (see Table 13.2). China is receiving more commodities, and more telephone calls, from Hong Kong than it is returning. Put another way, Hong Kong's outgoing traffic to China has grown at a faster pace than incoming traffic from mainland China.

In sum, business and trade is responsible for a spectacular growth of telecommunications traffic in the area, and has restructured the balance of the trade and information flow as well. Economic integration is leading to a regional division of labor that must be coordinated through massive flows of information and people.

Table 13.1. Telecommunications Traffic Growth: From Hong Kong to China.

Year	Minutes of Outgoing Traffic (Voice + fax)
1986	29,137,000
1987	44,679,000
1988	78,523,000
1989	126,561,000
1990	181,252,000
1991	265,124,000

Table 13.2. Change in Traffic Balance, From Hong Kong to China.

Year	Traffic Balance (Outgoing MiTT/Incoming MiTT)
1986	.56
1987	.63
1988	.80
1989	.84
1990	.90
1991	1.07

Despite the impressive growth following on China's reform period, there are still significant obstacles created by trade barriers between the three Chinas, particularly in telecommunications markets. China's telecommunication infrastructure suffers from a persistent shortage of capacity. Its monopoly Ministry of Posts and Telecommunications must struggle to keep up with the torrid pace of growth. A large percentage of long-distance calls are blocked due to congestion (Cai, 1993), and businesses find it difficult to obtain advanced digital services in a timely fashion.

China's capacity shortage and higher prices have produced a growing imbalance of traffic with Hong Kong. Because Hong Kong Telecom must compensate China for each minute of imbalance, and the rate China charges for this compensation is high by world standards, the traffic imbalance means higher international telephone rates for Hong Kong businesses and residents.

A similar situation prevails with respect to Hong Kong and Taiwan. The monopoly position of the Taiwan's Directorate General of Telecommunications (DGT) has led to highly inflated prices for international service. An international private leased circuit between Taiwan and Hong Kong costs 72% more on the Taiwan end than on the Hong Kong end of the circuit. IDD charges are also practically double the Hong Kong rate in Taiwan. In both cases the facilities and services offered are the same. These rate disparities create significant traffic imbalances between Taiwan and Hong Kong.

Both China and Taiwan severely restrict competition in telecommunications service markets. Even "free-marker" Hong Kong limits international telephone service to one company due to an exclusive license given to Hong Kong Telecom in 1981 (Mueller, 1992). This prevents entrepreneurs in the region from developing innovative services on a regional basis, and keeps service prices inflated.

As Hong Kong and China move toward 1997, these trade barriers could prove costly. With 1997 on the horizon, both Taiwan and Singapore are positioning themselves to inherit Hong Kong's regional "hub" status for China trade generally, and telecommunications facilities specifically. Singapore's bid for preeminence is based on its modern and relatively efficient facilities, competitive tariffs, tax incentives, and relative political stability. It has been made explicit by the Taiwan DGT's Director General, as well as the executive branch's Council for Economic Planning and Development, that Taiwan is positioning itself as an alternative financial center to Hong Kong in the post-1997 world (Lee, 1992).

Becoming a financial hub requires competitive and efficient telecommunications, however. Taiwan's international leased circuit and switched IDD rates are not competitive with Hong Kong's, and its telecommunications authority is a state owned directorate not known for its efficiency and flexibility. It is also handicapped by its current inability to establish direct telecommunications or trade ties with mainland China. Unless Taiwan embarks on a comprehensive liberalization program, such as the one outlined later it has little chance of accomplishing these goals.

THE TELECOMMUNICATIONS FREE-TRADE ZONE PROPOSAL

If the greater China region is serious about seizing and advancing the opportunities for economic integration, it can take one simple but dramatic step in that direction. Hong Kong, Taiwan, China, and Macau should all enter into reciprocal agreements to legalize simple resale of international leased circuits among themselves. "Simple resale" means that a business can lease circuit capacity in bulk from the existing telephone company, and resell that capacity to third parties. Resellers can make money either by undercutting the "retail" rates of the existing telephone companies through arbitrage, or by creating new services and offering them to the public. I call this idea the "telecommunications free-trade zone." Such an agreement would establish significantly freer trade in virtually all telecommunications services by liberalizing and harmonizing the conditions governing the use of international dedicated circuits.

Under the "telecommunications free trade zone" proposal, resellers could provide any sort of service they wished. The freedom to resell would apply to basic as well as value-added services, and to voice as well as data and video. Resale would be legal for private circuits regardless of whether they are closed at both ends, interconnected to the public switched network at both ends, or closed at one end and open on the other. Of course, simple resale of this sort would only be allowed when the same rules were adopted by countries at both ends of the circuit. Like any customs union or common market, a telecommunications free-trade zone involves reciprocity among the countries involved.

The free-trade zone concept I am advancing is built entirely on simple resale at both ends of the circuit—it does not require pure free trade in all other areas of telecommunications service or equipment. Taiwan and the PRC, for example, currently restrict investment in telecommunications service by foreign companies. Whether or not this is a good idea, participation in a resale-based free-trade zone would not require elimination of these restrictions. The service providers who used resale to enter the market could be required to be PRC or Taiwan citizens if the governments involved so desired. Resale also does not interfere with or supersede monopoly licensing arrangements for underlying facilities-based carriers in the participating countries. It simply requires the monopoly to supply leased circuits to other businesses on a nondiscriminatory basis and to liberalize its economic and physical restrictions on the use of them.

Who should be part of this agreement? At the very least, the telecommunications free-trade zone should include Hong Kong, the Provincial Telecommunications Bureaus in mainland China's Guangdong, Fujian, Shanghai, and Hainan provinces, Macau, and Taiwan. This rapidly developing economic area would benefit most from such an initiative. Other than that, I would refrain from expressing an opinion about how much more inclusive the initiative should be. This depends on the motives of the parties particularly the extent to which they want to make greater China into a trade bloc—certainly Singapore would want to be and probably should be included. Japan and Australia would be interested. The United States, Canada, the United Kingdom, and New Zealand already permit simple resale to countries with reciprocal liberal arrangements, and thus would probably also be willing participants. The primary object of the proposal, however, is to promote free trade in telecommunications services among the entities of greater China itself.

THE BENEFITS OF INTERNATIONAL SIMPLE RESALE

Simple resale may seem like it is too small and technical a change to warrant a label as extravagant as a "telecommunications free-trade zone," but that is precisely the beauty of the proposal. Although it is a simple change to make, it could set in motion powerful economic forces resulting in substantial and immediate benefits for the users and economies involved. Let me explain in more detail some of the effects of international resale. Telecommunications has undergone a technological revolution since the end of World War II, and this revolution is still continuing. In most countries, however, the prices and service capabilities of the public network are more attuned to the 1940s than the 1990s. Prices have not adjusted rapidly to the new technologies because telephone companies are organized as national monopolies. The politicized nature of the industry has riddled it with cross-subsidies monopoly profits, and irrational rate structures. Long-distance services such as international telephone and data services are affected most.

A good example of distorted pricing occurs between Hong Kong and China. A call from Hong Kong to Beijing costs HK$9.50 per minute. On the other hand, a call from Hong Kong to Shenzhen costs only HK$2.40 per minute, and a call from Shenzhen to Beijing (the domestic long-distance rate) is only about HK$2.50. Thus, a call between the same two points can cost twice as much, depending on whether international or domestic rates apply. These rate disparities have nothing to do with the technical costs of providing service between the three points; rather, they are a product of political bargaining between monopolies at either end of the international circuit.

China imposes heavier charges, known as accounting rates, on the Hong Kong-Beijing traffic than it does on the Hong Kong-Shenzhen traffic. Of course, China does not permit international calls from Hong Kong to be switched through to Beijing at domestic rates. In this way it protects its ability to extract monopoly profits from international callers. The telecommunications free-trade zone would eliminate this power, by permitting businesses to arbitrage the rate disparity. They could base a private line from Hong Kong to Shenzhen, plug into the MPT's network there and connect to Beijing at domestic rates, thereby undercutting the official rate by a substantial margin

Resale has been used as an effective policy to rationalize prices via arbitrage for more than a decade, beginning in the United States in the 1980s. Few people outside the United States are aware of the extent to which long-distance competition in that country has been carried on by resellers and driven by resale competition. The vast majority of the more than 500 registered interexchange carriers in the United States are resellers who order circuit capacity from AT&T, MCI, Sprint, or Wiltel on a "wholesale" basis and then offer "retail" service to the public. Competition from Sprint and MCI in the late 1970s was not very successful until the FCC legalized resale of AT&T's wide-area telephone services (WATS) in 1981. WATS resale allowed them to complete telephone calls in every U.S. city by using AT&T facilities in areas where they had no facilities of their own. Competitors used market position gained through resale to build their own systems.

Building on this experience, regulators in a variety of countries have used resale to minimize monopoly power in the international arena (Federal Communications Commission, 1991; Carsberg, 1990). The United States, Canada, Sweden, the United Kingdom, Australia, and New Zealand all have legalized simple resale of international facilities, with the not insignificant proviso that reciprocal opportunities must be available at the foreign end of the circuit.

The following explains in more detail the benefits to the greater China region that would accrue from legalizing simple resale.

BENEFIT 1: PRICE RATIONALIZATION

Resale will rationalize telephone companies' prices, thereby improving efficiency and eliminating price discrimination. Resellers will be able to exploit large gaps between the per-minute charges for switched service and the flat monthly rate for private leased lines. If switched service is priced too high relative to the cost of a dedicated circuit, as is often the case, then a reseller will be able to offer customers significant discounts on switched traffic by connecting private leased circuits to the public network. On the other hand, if dedicated circuits are priced too low relative to switched service, the possibility of arbitrage will correct the pricing.

The effect of arbitrage is especially salient in greater China, where the gap between the rates for private and switched services appears to be growing. Telecommunications operators in Hong Kong, Australia, and Singapore have reduced some private leased circuit rates by as much as 50% in the past 3 years. No comparable reductions have been made in switched services. One reason for this disparity is that private lines bypass the accounting rate system (see Benefit 2) but another reason is site competition among the national telecommunications authorities. Some of the region's telecommunications authorities are actively recruiting the hub facilities of multinational business telecommunications users. They know that the multinational corporations have options, unlike the smaller users; they can relocate their facilities to take advantage of more favorable tariffs and features. Singapore, Hong Kong, Australia, and Japan are all actively engaged in site competition, and Taiwan eventually hopes to be a player, too. In short, there are already competitive forces affecting the prices of private leased circuits in open economies. No such competition exists in switched services in the greater China region.

The situation is roughly analogous to the early days of long-distance competition in the U.S. domestic market. Thirty years ago the FCC permitted competition in the private line market but protected AT&T's monopoly over public switched services. Large users acquired the right to build their own networks using microwave facilities. In reaction, AT&T introduced massive volume discounts for its private line services of up to 85% (Brock, 1981). While this was going on, the consumer's price of switched long-distance service gradually increased or remained the same. Clearly, AT&T responded to limited competition with preemptive price discrimination. The price reductions were designed to retain large users at the expense of smaller, captive users of switched services. Something very similar to this is going on in the international arena now. Resale introduces automatic correctives to prevent these distortions.

BENEFIT 2: ATTACKING ACCOUNTING RATE PROBLEM

Resale is the most effective way to attack the accounting rate problem. One reason international service prices have been slow to adjust to the efficiency of new technology is the accounting rate system. Accounting rates refer to the method used by a telephone company in one country to compensate the telephone company in another for completing its call. As has been pointed out by numerous analysts (Ergas & Paterson, 1991; FCC, 1991; Frieden, 1991) the accounting rate system rewards the telephone companies in countries that have more traffic coming in than going out. In this sense it can penalize telephone companies who reduce their international rates and thus generate more outgoing traffic. Many developing countries impose huge accounting rates on international traffic in order to exploit telecommunications traffic as a source of hard currency, and to generate monopoly profits for the domestic administration. The actual cost of providing international telecommunications service has plummeted in recent years, but rate reductions have been slow to follow in switched services, in part because of the rigidities of the accounting rate system. For example, in implementing its August 1993 international rate reductions, Hong Kong Telecom did not lower international rates to China and Taiwan, citing high accounting rates in those countries as an excuse.

Resale attacks the accounting rate problem head on by making it possible for more users to bypass the whole scheme. Dedicated circuits are not included in the accounting rate regime. Under a resale regime, a reseller offering telephone service between two countries will pay the cost of an international private line plus the domestic long-distance rate in the country of termination. If the terminating country's accounting rates are significantly higher than its domestic long-distance rates, the resale carrier will be able to profit from the difference. In order to avoid this kind of arbitrage, a carrier will have to rationalize the relationship between its accounting rate and its domestic long-distance tariffs.

Proof of the effectiveness of resale in lowering accounting rates comes from Canada. Within months of a regulatory decision permitting international resale competition on the United States-Canada route, Canada's accounting rates with the United States dropped by approximately one third (Cable & Wireless, 1991).

BENEFIT 3: EXTENDING BENEFITS TO THE WHOLE MARKET

Resale will extend the benefits of competitive forces to the whole market and not just large users. This point follows logically from the earlier analysis. Currently, large users who can afford dedicated facilities have more bargaining power and thus can get better rates and more options than smaller users. A resale environment allows entrepreneurs to aggregate the traffic of smaller users, allowing them to share in the benefits and options now restricted to users with large volumes.

As Tables 13.3 and 13.4 show, at the prices of international IDD service and IPLCs in 1992 a reseller serving Hong Kong, Taiwan, and Australia could undercut the price of the monopoly carriers by a substantial margin. For example, some calculations based on the monthly tariffs for 1.544 Mbps leased circuits show that a reseller of voice service between Taiwan and Hong Kong could undercut the rates of Taiwan's DGT by 40% and still clear a 20% per minute profit on all the traffic it carried. It could undercut Hong Kong Telecom's rate by 4.5% on traffic going in the other direction and still clear a 10% per minute profit. Applying the same assumptions to Australia-Hong Kong traffic, a reseller of IDD voice could undercut Hong Kong Telecom's rate by 37% and the Australian carrier's rate by 20%.

BENEFIT 4: ENCOURAGING INNOVATION AND ENTREPRENEURSHIP

Resale will encourage innovation and entrepreneurship in the telecommunications marketplace. In addition to its efficient pricing effects, resale provides a means of entering the telecommunications business that is less capital intensive than one which relies on constructing and operating facilities. By lowering the price of entry, resale helps to cultivate a new entrepreneurial class in telecommunications. New sources of business experience, technical expertise and service innovation outside of the dominant telephone company are thus cultivated.

Table 13.3. Arbitrage Opportunities: Taiwan-Hong Kong.

	per minute	
Circuit cost (HK$ 870,198/month	HK$	3.626
Administrative cost (HK$ 120,000/month		0.500
Switching cost		1.870
Termination		0.860
		———
RESELLERS'S TOTAL COST	HK$	6.854
Plus 10% profit		7.540
Plus 20% profit		8.225

RATE COMPARISON

RESELLER (+20%)	8.225	
DGT TAIWAN	13.830 (Reseller = 40% lower	
HONG KONG TELECOM	7.90 (Reseller = 5% lower)	
RESELLER (+10%)	7.54	

Assumptions:
1. 24 voice channels on a 1.544 Mbps leased circuit.
2. Switching costs = HK$1.87 per minute.
3. 10,000 conversation minutes per month per channel.

Note: Data compiled from Taiwan DGT tariffs, Hong Kong Telecom tariffs, and AT&T.

Table 13.4. Arbitrage Opportunities: Australia-Hong Kong.

	per minute	
Circuit cost (HK$ 733,448/month	HK$	3.056
Administrative cost (HK$ 120,000/month		0.500
Switching cost		1.870
Termination		1.020
		────
RESELLERS'S TOTAL COST	HK$	6.446
Plus 20% profit	7.735	

RATE COMPARISON

RESELLER:	7.735
OTC AUSTRALIA:	9.670 (Reseller= 20% lower)
HONG KONG TELECOM	12.300 (Reseller = 37% lower)

Assumptions:
1. 24 voice channels on a 1.544 Mbps leased circuit.
2. Switching costs = HK$ 1.87 per minute.
3. 10,000 conversation minutes per month per channel.

Note. Data compiled from Hong Kong Telecom tariffs, and AT&T.

BENEFIT 5:PROMOTING REGIONAL INTEGRATION

Reciprocal resale will promote regional integration of the telecommunications marketplace. In addition to the aforementioned effects, resale will have the far more important effect of integrating the regional market for telecommunications services. Arbitrage will lead to the homogenization of rates, and the opportunities for resale-based new entry will homogenize the market for services and features. Carriers and resellers will be able to more easily provide regional service offerings (because the demand for service clearly is becoming predominantly regional rather than local or global). The transactions costs of establishing international networks will decline significantly. Irrational price gaps across and within the participating countries will disappear through arbitrage. The geographic scope of the service market will broaden, increasing the number of players in the market, intensifying service and price competition promoting diversification and specialization, and fostering economies of scale in overall industry organization. For major users, this will make greater China a very attractive place to hub; for the trading economy as a whole, this will be a powerful boost.

One weakness of the resale approach is that a protected monopoly carrier may attempt to eliminate the price gaps that create arbitrage opportunities by raising rates which may already be too high. For example, in the case of voice resale between Hong Kong and Taiwan cited earlier, Taiwan's DGT could attempt to eliminate arbitrage opportunities by increasing its monthly rate for 1.544 Mbps lines, a rate that is already 72% higher than Hong Kong's. China, on the other hand, rather than lowering its accounting rate in response to bypass by resellers, might just increase domestic long distance rates. In a truly open market, such moves would be counter-productive, but as long as DGT and MPT are protected monopolies users would have no options. Although both scenarios are possible, they would most likely be so unpopular domestically and so obviously destructive of the country's telecommunications capabilities that such a development seems unlikely. Nevertheless, the possibility of such a development shows why resale is only a second-best alternative to full-fledged liberalization.

BENEFIT 6: FACILITATING LIBERALIZATION

Resale avoids many of the political and institutional problems associated with facilities-based competition—resale competition is an easier way to move toward liberalization and dodges or eliminates many of the political and institutional problems associated with facilities-based competition. Consider one by one the arguments against full-fledged liberalization that have been advanced in recent years.

RESPONSE TO ARGUMENTS AGAINST RESALE

LEGAL OBSTACLES

In Hong Kong, many people in government and industry are sympathetic to competitive liberalization of international telecommunications. However, Hong Kong Telecom was given an exclusive license for 25 years (it lasts until 2006), and they believe it is dangerously destabilizing for the territory to abrogate an exclusive license before it expires. Many other countries would likewise require major legal changes before facilities-based providers could enter the market. Resale, in contrast, does not require alteration of the terms of the HKTI license, nor does it alter Hong Kong Telecom's status as the exclusive provider—it is a purely regulatory matter.

ECONOMIES OF SCALE

Some critics of liberalization argue that competition will dissipate economies of scale in telecommunications service and lead to less economically efficient service. Resale, however, relies on the facilities of the established carrier. Economies of scale (assuming that they exist and are significant) would not be lost. The British Oftel regulatory agency reached the same conclusion in a 1990 study of international resale. It wrote, "[resale] is a form of competition that does not involve the loss of economies of scale to a significant extent on the public networks" (Carsberg, 1990, p. 3).

ACCOUNTING RATES

The accounting rate system has also been cited as an obstacle to full liberalization. The argument is that decreasing collection rates on the competitive side of the international circuit merely increases the traffic imbalance and rewards monopolistic carriers with high collection rates by increasing their settlement payments. This argument does not apply to reciprocal resale. Resale drives down accounting rates by allowing users to bypass the accounting rate system in cases where it exceeds domestic long-distance rates by unreasonable proportions.

DIVERSION OF REVENUES

Telecommunications authorities in developing countries fear that a competitive regime would divert traffic and revenue from the public network and thus prevent them from building infrastructure. Resale, of course, would not bypass public operators at all—it would merely exploit the arbitrage possibilities created by their rate structure. Once their rates were rationalized, resale would benefit them by increasing the demand for their services and network usage.

    In conclusion, all of the arguments against competition in the international arena do not apply to resale. A telecommunications free trade zone is an easy medicine to administer when compared to the drastic surgery of facilities-based competition. You don't have to break up your phone company; you don't have to reconfigure your network or negotiate hundreds of new operating agreements; you don't have to devise new interconnection arrangements or numbering plans; you don't have to worry about asymmetric regulation, cross subsidies, discriminatory pricing, and all of the other headaches that can occur when a dominant monopoly is beset by fledgling competitors.

    Although the resale prescription goes down easily, however, it really is a wonder drug. It would be a fertilizer for telecommunications entrepreneurs; a strong tonic for large and small users; a powerful stimulant for the telecommunications industry and trade in general. For the telephone companies, the immediate effects might seem unpleasant. It would nevertheless dramatically improve their long-term health by purging them of bloated IDD rates, unclogging the accounting rate system, and rationalizing their rate structures. (We might want to say that for telephone companies it would function rather like a laxative).

PROSPECTS FOR ADOPTION

Is the free-trade zone possible? Recent difficulties faced by the European Commission in economic integration and the rocky passage of the North American Free Trade Agreements (NAFTA) in the United States prove that bringing about a "common market" is no simple matter. The analysis discussed later shows that Hong Kong is ready for a free-trade zone, and that Taiwan, though conservative, could not help but go along if Hong Kong and China took steps in the direction of free trade. The ultimate fate of a telecommunications free-trade zone, therefore, hinges on the progress of telecommunications sector reform in mainland China.

Hong Kong has a direct interest in the implementation of a telecommunications free-trade zone. My analysis of the application of the "One Country, Two Systems" concept to telecommunications (Mueller, 1994) showed that there are four reasons why this is the case. First, integration of the Hong Kong and mainland telecommunications sectors would enhance Hong Kong's competitive advantage as a regional trade hub. Second, telecommunications infrastructure and usage growth on the Chinese side of the border is the major factor driving the growth of the telecommunications sector in Hong Kong. Third, unless accounting rates are reduced and/or prices drop and incomes rise on the China side of the border, Hong Kong's costly traffic imbalance with the mainland is likely to worsen. Finally, Hong Kong's attempt to promote competition and lower rates in its own telecommunications sector will be undermined unless China follows suit.

For these reasons the territory has already began to move toward various forms of resale. Hong Kong has explicitly legalized resale in the international value-added network service (IVANs) market, and it has tolerated a form of resale in the voice market. The process began in January 1991, when the Hong Kong government authorized competition in the supply of IVANs on the Hong Kong-United States route. IVANs are a form of resale, in that the service provider uses Hong Kong Telecom's underlying facilities, but "add value" in the form of some kind of information processing. Since then, Hong Kong has unilaterally legalized IVANs on all routes, forbearing the need for reciprocal agreements on the foreign end of the circuit.

Hong Kong's experience in the IVANs market has confirmed the ability of resale-based competition to serve as the foothold for new entrepreneurs. One year after the agreement was reached, 11 companies had taken out licenses to provide various IVAN services, and at least 5 of them were local enterprises.

An even more interesting case of resale based in Hong Kong is provided by the Canadian firm City Telecommunications International, Ltd. (CTI). Following the legalization of resale in Canada, CTI ordered international circuits to Hong Kong in bulk and resold them to the many Hong Kong emigres in Canada, undercutting Teleglobe Canada's rates by as much as 35%. In early 1993, the company claimed to control 25% of the Canada-to-Hong Kong traffic. CTI then decided to attempt to capture some of the Hong Kong-to-Canada traffic, and discovered an ingenious way to do so. CTI bought international toll-free service to Canada from Hong Kong Telecom, allowing customers in Hong Kong to call CTI's switching center in Toronto over the toll-free lines and then be routed to destinations in Canada, the United States, and Europe. On these routes, CTI can offer its customers savings of 17-25% under the normal IDD rate.

CTI occupied a legal grey area at first. Hong Kong's telecommunications regulatory authority had not specifically authorized resale, but on the other hand it did not feel as if it could prevent CTI or its customers from using a perfectly legal service offered publicity by Hong Kong Telecom (its international toll-free service). Hong Kong's Office of the Telecommunications Authority (OFTA) now appears to be predisposed toward encouraging as much resale and competition as it can without violating Hong Kong Telecom's exclusive license. It has, for example, decided to consider CTI-type services as a form of "voice value added service," and hence as legal. Late in 1993, Hong Kong's OFTA also licensed competing local network operators who will be able to enter the market when Hong Kong Telephone's exclusive license on local wireline voice services expires in 1995.

It is evident that Hong Kong, at least, is fully prepared to move toward a telecommunications free-trade zone. What about Taiwan and main land China? Here the outlook is not so optimistic

Taiwan must overcome major obstacles before it can join a telecommunications free-trade zone. Resale of dedicated circuits is currently prohibited. Moreover, Taiwan has a long history of discouraging the use of IPLCs, particularly high-capacity facilities. Taiwan's restrictive policy has been motivated more by security considerations than by trade and development motives. It is harder to monitor and control communications over privately managed, high-capacity circuits than the public switched network. Of course, it goes without saying that IPLCs between Taiwan and China would conflict with Taiwan's ban on direct contact with the PRC. It is possible to get leased circuits from Taiwan to Hong Kong, and from Hong Kong to the PRC, and it is likely that some customers order both and link them together, although this, too, is illegal. There is also a grey market in resale: Fax store and forward services are technically illegal, but several companies are offering them discreetly.

In many ways, Taiwan's telecommunications policy has proven to be as conservative as the PRC's, if not more so. Taiwan began to revise its telecommunications law in 1990, drawing up some impressive proposals for legal reform, including privatization of its telecommunications authority (see chapter 10, this volume). These liberalizing thrusts, however, were stalemated by the country's telecommunications monopoly, the Directorate General of Telecommunications (DGT) (Chen, 1994). Just as in mainland China, competition and new entry in Taiwan is confined to so-called value-added services. As in China, classification of services as "value-added" is performed on a case-by-case basis by the telecommunications ministry itself. As Chen has pointed out, such a framework creates a major conflict of interest, in that new entrants must seek licenses and approvals from their main competition , the DGT. A similar situation prevails in China, where regulatory and operational functions are still combined in the Ministry of Posts and Telecommunications. International telecommunications tariffs in Taiwan are abnormally high by regional standards, and represent a major source of monopoly profit for the DGT. Despite repeated assurances by Taiwanese officials that the country is planning to be a major financial hub and reform its telecommunications sector, very little has changed.

Taiwan is opening up foreign investment into its telecommunications industry gradually to give domestic providers a chance to acquire more substantial market share before it is opened to foreigners. In principle, then, it should be sympathetic to a resale policy structured in a way that would cultivate local entrepreneurs. More importantly, if Hong Kong and China entered into reciprocal resale agreements, Taiwan could not help but be included, because so much of the trade and communication between Taiwan and the mainland already passes through Hong Kong.

Telecommunications in the PRC are controlled by the Ministry of Posts and Telecommunications (MPT). MPT is publicly committed to retaining a monopoly on all basic services in China and does offer dedicated international data circuits and some private telephone circuits between China and Hong Kong. The number of leased circuits is very limited, and resale by both foreign and domestic companies is prohibited.

China's MPT can be expected to oppose the idea of a free-trade zone. MPT would probably view the heavy demand for dedicated circuits created by the free-trade zone as a burden on its already overburdened capacity, and would view resale as diminishing rather than enlarging its revenues. The real reason for its opposition, however, is that a free-trade zone would impose a rather harsh market discipline on the Ministry and seriously erode its monopoly control of the telecommunications sector. MPT would be forced to rationalize its rate structure and indeed be constantly engaged in a process of reading and responding to market forces. It would also lose its monopoly on numerous services, as resale competitors might prove more responsive to specialized forms of market demand.

There are, however, more liberal forces in the PRC. The Ministry of Electronics has openly proposed competing with MPT in telecommunications, and has won the right to enter some specialized markets (Ure, 1994). China is reforming its banking sector, eliminating its controlled currency rates, and has established stock markets in order to harness market forces in investment. In many ways these reforms are more far-reaching in nature than a telecommunications free-trade zone. It is possible, therefore, that conservative forces within the Ministry could be overcome by reformers at higher levels who wanted to improve the efficiency and service of the telecommunications sector. Add to this the political benefit of drawing Hong Kong and Taiwan closer into its economic orbit, and there are many reasons for China to pursue this policy.

Regardless of its political prospects, a telecommunications free trade zone would be a good policy for greater China.

REFERENCES

Aronson, J., & Cowhey, P. (1988). *When countries talk: International trade in telecommunications services*. Cambridge, MA. Ballinger AEI.

Brock, G. (1981). *The telecommunications industry: The dynamics of market structure*. Cambridge, MA: Harvard University Press.

Cable & Wireless Communications, Inc. (1991). *Comments in the matter of regulation of international accounting rates*. U.S. FCC CC, Docket No. 9-37, Phase II.

Cai, L. (1993, November). *China's telecommunications development and policy*. Paper presented at the China Telecommunications and Information Industry Forum, Beijing.

Carsberg, B. (1990). *International telephony: Simple resale and control of prices*. [Government Report to the Director General of Telecommunications to the Secretary of State]. London: Oftel.

Chen, B. (1994). Taiwan: Reform at a snail's pace. *Telecommunications Policy, 18*(3), 229-235.

Cheong, K., & Mullins, M. (1991). International telephone service imbalances: Accounting rates and regulatory policy. *Telecommunications Policy, 15*(2), 107-118.

Drake, W. J., & Nicolaidis, K. (1992). Ideas, interests, and institutionalization: "Trade in services" and the Uruguay Round. *International Organization, 64,* 37-100.

Ergas, H., & Paterson, P. (1991). International telecommunications settlements arrangements: An unsustainable inheritance? *Telecommunications Policy, 15*(1), 29-48

Federal Communications Commission. (1991). *In the matter of regulation of international accounting rates.* CC Docket 90-337 Further Notice of Proposed Rulemaking 6 FCC Rcd 3434, Phase II.

Feketekuty, G. (1988). *International trade in services: An overview and blueprint for negotiations.* Cambridge, MA: Ballinger-AEI.

Frieden, R. (1991). Accounting rates: The business of international telecommunications and the incentive to cheat. *Federal Communications Law Journal, 43,* 111-139

Hill, T.P. (1977). On goods and services. *Review of Income and Wealth, 23,* 315-338.

Hindley, B., & Smith, A. (1984). Comparative advantage and trade in services. *World Economy, 7,* 369-389.

Hong Kong Telecom. (Various years). *Annual Report.* Hong Kong: Author.

Kellerman, A. (1992). U.S. international telecommunications, 1961-1988: An international movement model. *Telecommunications Policy, 16*(5), 401-414.

Lee, P.Y. (1992). Telecommunications development and technology transfer in Taiwan, ROC. In M. D. Lofstrom & D. J. Wedemeyer (Eds.), *Proceedings of the 1992 Pacific Telecommunications Conference* (pp. 589-593). Honolulu, HI: Pacific Telecommunications Council.

Melvin, J. (1989). Trade in producer services: A Heckscher-Ohlin approach. *Journal of Political Economy, 79,* 1180-1196.

Mueller, M. (1991). *International telecommunications in Hong Kong* (2nd ed.). Hong Kong: The Chinese University Press.

Mueller, M. (1994). One country, two systems: What will 1997 mean in telecommunications? *Telecommunications Policy, 18*(3), 243-253.

Riddle, D. (1986). *Service-led growth: The role of the service sector in world development.* New York: Praeger.

Sampson, G., & Snape, R. (1985). Identifying the issues in trade in services. *World Economy, 8,* 171-181.

Staple, G., & Mullins, M. (1989). Telecom traffic statistics—MiTT matter. *Telecommunications Policy, 13*(2), 105-128.

Sung, Y. W. (1991). *The China-Hong Kong connection: The key to China's open door policy.* Cambridge: Cambridge University Press.

Ure, J. (1994). Telecommunications, with Chinese characteristics. *Telecommunications Policy, 18*(3), 182-194.

GLOSSARY

AHKUS The Association of Hong Kong Students in the United States. A discussion group interested in prodemocracy movements in China. To subscribe: send e-mail to REQUEST@AHKUS.ORG (192.55.187.25).

APSTAR Asia-Pacific Telecommunications Satellite.

Archie An INTERNET online union catalog that helps users to search for programs, data, or text files located in about 1,200 servers. Users ask it either to find filenames that contain a certain search string or suggest files with certain key words in their description. It returns the actual filenames that meet the search criteria, and the name of the servers containing those files.

ATTMAIL A commercial e-mail service provided by AT&T.

BBC British Broadcasting Corporation.

BBS Bulletin Board System. A computer system that functions as a centralizes information source and message switching system for a particular interest group. Users dial up the bulletin board, review and leave messages for other users, and communicated to other users on the system at the same time.

BIG5 This is the official Chinese language encoding system adopted by Taiwan, and it is an unofficial standard in places where traditional characters are used, such as Hong Kong. The system has codes for almost twice as many characters as GuoBiao.

BISSC Beijing International Switching Systems Company Limited.

bps Bit Per Second. It expresses the number of bytes that can be transmitted (or transferred) each second. It is used to measure the speed of data transfer in communications system.

CANET Chinese Academic Network. The name of the Beijing-Karlsruhe link between CNPAC and the Internet.

CASnet The campus network of the Computer Network Center of the Chinese Academy of Sciences.

CCITT Consultative Committee for International Telephony and Telegraphy, an international organization for communications standards. It is one of four organs of the International Telecommunications Union (ITU) founded in 1865, headquartered in Geneva, and compromised of over 150 member countries national post, telephone, and telegraph administrations.

CCNET The Chinese Computing Network. A computer network forum on technologies relating to the use of Chinese on computers To sub-scribe: "SUB CCNET-L <your name>" to server CCNET-L@UGA.BIT-NET, or CCNET-L@UGA.UGA.EDU.

CDMA Code Division Multiple Access. In communications, a multiple-access technique whereby groups of users may transmit simultaneously using the same frequency band. The signals are encoded so that information from a particular transmitter is only recovered by the appropriate receiving station.

CEPD The Council for Economic Planning and Development.

CHINA-NT A computer network serving the Independent Federation of Chinese Students and Scholars, a U.S.based association of Chinese expatriates. To subscribe: "SUB CHINA-NT <your name>" to server LISTSERV@UGA.BITNET.

CHINANET A network based at Texas A&M University with special interest in computer networking in China. To subscribe: "SUB CHINANET <your name>" to server LISTSERV@TAMVM1.BITNET.

ChiRK A Chinese reader on Tektronics compatible graphics terminals. It is a computer application that converts the computer codes into readable Chinese scripts.

CITIC The China International Trust and Investment Company. An investment arm of China in Hong Kong.

CKD Completely Knocked Down. Goods, especially machines, offered for sale or quoted CKD and supplied in separate parts that the buyer must put together at his or her own cost.

CMC Computer mediated communication.

CND China News Digest. A daily electronic news digest about what is happening in China. There are several versions—U.S., Canadian, European-Pacific, and global. To subscribe to the global version, which is compiled and distributed from Arizona State University: "SUB CHINA <your name>" to server LISTSERV@ASUACAD.BITNET.

CNPAC The China National Public Data Network. It is also referred to as CHI-NAPAC or China Pac. It is also the first public data network in China headquartered in Beijing. CNPAC's link to the Internet is by means of the Chinese Academic Network, or CANET.

COCOM The Coordinating Committee on Multilateral Export Control. An international trade organization of the western countries found to monitor trade flows between participating countries. The primary purpose is to prevent proliferation of weaponry, both conventional and nuclear, and other strategic commodities from the western countries to the communist bloc.

Cocoyoc Declaration In 1974, the participants at a seminar of United Nations Council on Trade and Development pointed out the need to include the satisfaction of basic needs as a development goal. Basic needs include nutrition, health, education, and shelter.

CPE Customer Premises Equipment. Communications equipment that resides on the customer's premises.

CSS Chinese students and scholars.

CT2 Cordless Telephone Second Generation. It is a UK-developed technology that uses Frequency Division Multiple Access/Time Division Duplex technology for one-way call-out wireless communications. The low-powered radio receiver/transmitter permitting communication with a local base unit within 200 meters. End products with CT2 technology is around one-third the price of digital cellular phone.

DBS Direct Broadcast Satellite. A one-way broadcast service direct from a satellite to a user's dish (antenna). DBS are used to deliver private information and TV services.

DCI Data Communication Institute. A Taiwanese government institution created by the Directorate General of Telecommunications in 1981 to provide public data communications services.

DGT Directorate General of Telecommunications. A Taiwanese government agency that has enjoyed monopoly over telecommunications business for many decades.

Download To transmit data from a central computer to a remote computer or from a file server to a workstation. It implies transmitting an entire file, rather that interacting back and forth in a conversational mode.

EEACT Eastern Extension Australasia and China Telegraph Company Limited. A British company operated in China during the 19th Century.

EJV Equity joint venture.

Fiber Optic Communications systems that use optical fibers for transmission. Optical fiber is a very thin glass wire designed for the transmission of light. It has enormous transmission capacities capable of carrying billions of bits per second.

FidoNet A store-and-forward e-mail network made up of 16,000 plus bulletin systems run by independent system operators in the United States. In 1991, Fidonet had 5,800 nodes on six continents and 800,000 users. It moves e-mail and e-news over the public telephone network using a unique protocol and data format.

FTP File Transfer Protocol. A communications protocol that can transmit files without loss of data. It implies that it can handle binary data as well as ASCII data.

Gateway A computer that acts as a host for two or more networks. It can function as a "protocol translator" between two networks with different protocols. See also "host," "local area network".

GNTC The Great Northern Telegraph Company, a 19th century Danish telegraph company with major holder from Britain and Russia, and operational interests in China.

GSM Groupe Speciale Mobile, a pan-European standard for mobile communications.

Guo Biao This is the official Chinese language encoding system adopted by mainland China, and it is an unofficial standard in Singapore and among many mainland Chinese living abroad. It is based on the simplified character set.

HDTV High-Definition Television. Televisions that double the resolution of the current 525-line NTSC standard.

Heliosphere The region in the ionosphere where helium ions are predominant. Ionosphere is the part of the earth's upper atmosphere that is sufficiently ionized by solar ultraviolet radiation so the concentration of free electrons affects the propagation of radio waves. Its base is about 70 or 80 kilometer above sea level.

HKNet Hong Kong Net. A U.S.based bulletin board service about Hong Kong. To subscribe, send mail to CST@HOBBES.CATT.NCSU.EDU or SO@CS.WISC.EDU. All postings should be sent to HKNET@ CS.WISC.EDU.

HKTDC Hong Kong Trade Development Council.

HXWZ Hua Xia Wen Zhai. A weekly electronic literary digest published in Chinese characters by China News Digest. To subscribe: "SUB CCMAN-L <your name>" to LISTSERV@UGA.BITNET.

IANA Internet Assigned Numbers Authority. An institution that acts as a central registration point for defining the character set and the location and syntax of file names used with e-mail messages. The primary objective is to foster e-mail connectivity standards.

ICC Interstate Commerce Commission, a U.S. Federal government agency.

IAMCRNET International Association of Mass Communication Research Network. An Internet discussion group devoted in part to social implications of new communication technologies.

IFCSS Independent Federation of Chinese Students and Scholars.

INTERNET The worldwide "network of networks" that are connected to each other, using the IP protocol and other similar protocols. It originated from a U.S. national research-oriented network comprised of over a thousand government and academic networks. INTERNET provides file transfer, remote login, e mail, news, and other services.

IP Internet Protocol. A layer of protocols between networks that was developed to allow "connectionless" interoperation of gateways and local area networks. See also "OSI/ISO," "TCP/IP."

IPLCs International Private Leased Circuits.

ISDN Integrated Services Digital Network. An international telecommunications standard for transmitting voice, video and data over a digital communications line. It uses out-of-the band signaling, which provides a separate channel for control information.

ISI Information Sciences Institute.

ITU International Telecommunications Union. A body that promotes international collaboration in telecommunications with a view to improving the efficiency of world services. It is a specialized agency of the United Nations. Its regulations have the status of formal treaties between participating countries and are binding on signatories who have acceded to them.

IVANs International Value-Added Network Services.

KTS Key Telephone Systems.

LANs Local-Area Networks. Communication network that serves several users within a confined geographic area.

Listserv Groups A listserv group gets its name from a computer dedicated as a list server, or a computer that channels e-mail communications to everyone on a "list." People join the list by e mailing a "subscribe" command to the list server.

Mail Exploder See "mail reflector".

Mail Reflector An electronic mailbox that resends a message to a list of other mailboxes, usually comprising a so called "interest group."

Mbps Megabyte Per Second. In computing, a megabyte unit of storage equal to 1,048,576 bytes. It is used for expressing the speed of data transmission.

MCI MCI Communications Corporation. One of the "big 3" U.S. telecommunications companies.

MCI Mail A commercial e-mail service provided by MCI Communications Corporation.

MEI Ministry of Electronic Industries.

MF Ministry of Finance.

MHS Message Handling Service/System. An electronic mail system. The term comes from the International Federation of Information Processing. MHS often refers to mail systems that conform to the OSI (Open System Interconnection) model, which are based on CCITT's X.400 international message protocol.

MOTC Ministry of Transportation and Communications.

MPT Ministry of Posts and Telecommunications.

MTV Music Television or Music TV.

Multiplexer In communications, a device that merges several low-speed transmissions into one high-speed transmission and reverse the operation at the other end.

MW/SW Relays, Transmitters Medium wave/short/wave relays, transmitters.

NAFTA North American Free Trade Agreement.

NCFC National Computing and Networking Facility of China. A metropolitan network in Beijing linking Tsinghua and Beijing Universities to several research institutes of the Chinese Academy of Sciences.

NIC Network Information Center. Generally refers to any organization that is responsible for supplying information about any network Specifically refers to the Defense Data Networks NIC, which plays an important role in overall INTERNET coordination.

NIEO New International Economic Order. The United Nations adopted a declaration in 1974 to establish a New International Economic Order that should correct inequalities, redress existing injustices, and eliminate the widening gap between the developed and the developing countries.

NPC National Telephone Congress.

NTC National Telephone Company. A British monopoly of public communication system evolved through consolidation of private telecommunications companies during 1884 and 1911.

OECD Organization of Economic Cooperation and Development.

OSI/ISO Open System Interconnection/International Standards Organization.A reference model that has been defined by ISO as a standard for worldwide communications. It defines a framework for implementing protocols in seven layers: application, presentation, session, transport, network, data link, and physical level. Most vendors have agreed to support the OSI model in one form or another. It is considered superior in may respects to TCP/IP. See also "protocol," "protocol suite,"and "TCP/IP."

PABX Private Automatic Branch Exchanges. An inhouse telephone switching system that electronically interconnects one telephone extension to another, as well as to the outside telephone network.

PAD Packet Assembly/Disassembly. The process of dividing a message into discrete components, or packets—usually a few kilobytes—and then routing them through a network by means of switching devices. The process is performed by a computer that links the end user's computer to a network. The message is reassembled near its destination.

PCM Pulse Code Modulation. A technique for digitizing analog information by sampling the signal and converting each sample into a fixed length binary number. PCM uses wave form coding that samples a 4 KHZ bandwidth 8,000 times a second. Each sample is an 8-bit number, resulting in 64 K bits of data per second.

PLA People's Liberation Army.

Protocol A procedure or set of rules that computers with different hardware and software use to communicate with one another.

Protocol Suite A set of protocols administered by a common body. See also "OSI" and "TCP/IP."

PSTN Public Switched Telephone Network.

PTB Posts and Telecommunications Bureaus. Local posts and telecommunication operations in PRC.

PTTs Post, Telephone, & Telegraph. Usually refers to state public communication monopolies of European countries that administer telecommunication services in their states.

RMB Renminbi. Also referred to as People's Currency.

SBTEMC Shanghai Bell Telephone Equipment Manufacturing Company.

SKD Semi-Knocked Down. Partially assembled goods, especially machines, offered for sale and quoted SKD with remaining parts shipped to the buyer separately. The buyer has to fit these parts back to the partially assembled machine at his or her cost.

SPA State Price Administration.

SPC Stored program control switching.

SRI Stanford Research Institute International.

SSB State Statistical Bureau.

Sysop System operator. A common title for the individual who manages a node, or computer acting as a file server in a network.

TACs Total Access Communications.

TCP/IP Transmission Control Protocol/Internet Protocol. A set of communications protocol developed for the Defense Advanced Research Projects Agency to internetwork dissimilar systems. TCP/IP includes the Simple Mail Transfer Protocol (SMTP), which most users employ when sending e-mail; the File Transfer Protocol (FTP), for accessing files on remote computers; the Domain Name System (DNS), which maps host names to network addresses; and TELNET, which provides virtual terminal emulation service.

TCS Lite A mobile satellite earth receiving station.

TDMA Time Division Multiple Access. Multiplexing technique that mixes several low speed signals into one high-speed transmission via a time-slot based interleaving method. At the receiving end, the different signals are divided out and merged back into single streams. The allocation of frequencies may be made on a fixed or on demand basis.

Unicode This is an international standard for character representation. It incorporates codes for simplified Chinese characters, traditional Chinese characters, Japanese characters, and Korean characters. It is reportedly flexible enough to encode any alphabet in the world.

USDC System United States Digital Cellular System. A U.S.-based digital mobile communications standard.

USENET Also known as news or netnews. It is a distributed bulletin board and discussion system that is international in scope. At present, there are 1,200 Usenet discussion groups on the Internet. The groups' communications are coordinated by an Internet service with the same name, Usenet. It started operation in late 1979.

VAN Value-Added Network.

VOA Voice of America.

VSAT Very Small Aperture Terminals. A VSAT network comprises a center, or hub, dish antenna of 5-8 meters, a geostationary communications satellite, and a number of small, remote earth stations with dish antennae of 1.2-2.4 meters in diameter.

WANs In communications, it refers to comprehensive multinode networks connecting large numbers of terminals and computers spread over a wide geographical area, even crossing geographic boundaries such as cities and states.

WATS Wide Area Telephone Services. A flat rate, or measured bulk rate, long distance telephone service provided on an outgoing- or incoming call basis.

X.25 A widely adopted set of CCITT-recommended standards for packet networks. Its principal function is to prevent congestion in a network by switching messages to underutilized channels. See also "CCITT."

XGNS Xinhua General News Service.

ZHONGWEN A discussion group based at the Royal Institute of Technology in Sweden that focuses on Chinese computing. It maintains an ftp archive of Chinese-related software. To subscribe: send e mail to server zhong-wen-request@nada.kth.se.

Author Index

SUBJECT INDEX

Common Carrier Department, 233
Communication
horizontal flow, 98
roles and functions, 91-94
Communist communication, 90
Companhia Telecommunicacoes de
Macau, 210n
Comparative advantage, 8
Competition
between competing technologies,
49
in U.K., 41
Completely knocked down (CKD),
273, 277
Compression technology, 8
Computer-mediated communication
(CMC), 152-153
Computer networking technology,
150
Computerization, 10
Consolidation, 35
Consumerism, 22
Control
Chinese government, 164
and communication, 22
directions of exertion, 28
drawbacks in China, 80
German government, 44
in Taiwan, 226
over VAN in Taiwan, 237
and telegraph, 28
Coordinating Committee for
Multilateral Export Controls
(COCOM), 214, 219n, 270-272,
277
Copen Family Fund, 156
Core, 6, 120
Correlational studies, 11, 135
Council for Economic Planning and
Development (CEPD), 230, 285
Cream-skimming, 34n, 35
Cross-subsidization
impact, 47
in Germany, 45

in Taiwan, 232
in rural areas, 14
and politicized nature, 287
and public utilities model, 13
removal, 50
and telephone penetration rates,
41
CSL, 209
CT2 (Cordless Telephone Generation
2), 79, 250, 257
Cultural autonomy, 7
Cultural Revolution, 72, 89-90, 98,
100-102, 173
Cultural values, 25
Customer premise equipment (CPE),
206, 208, 228, 230, 236, 238
Customer service orientation, 33
Cyclical effects, 139

D

Daimler-Benz AG, 188
Data Communications Institute (DCI),
229
Decentralization, 35, 43, 93, 144,
163, 203, 219
Delinkage, 6
Delta, 186
Demand elasticity, 47
Democracies, 5, 10, 14
Democratization, 28
Depoliticization, 104
Denationalization, 42
Deng Xiaoping, 74, 91, 106, 113,
179, 189, 249, 249-252, 255
Denmark, 61
Department of Tourism, Post and
Communications of Indonesia, 15
Dependency, 6
Dependency theories, 3
Deregulation
as ideology, 14
in Taiwan, 236
U.S.-style, 36-37